Corporate Law Anthology

FRANKLIN A. GEVURTZ
Professor of Law
McGeorge School of Law
University of the Pacific

LexisNexis™
Matthew Bender®

ISBN#: 0820570427

Editorial Offices
744 Broad Street, Newark, NJ 07102 (973) 820-2000
201 Mission St., San Francisco, CA 94105-1831 (415) 908-3200
701 East Water Street, Charlottesville, VA 22902-7587 (804) 972-7600
www.lexis.com

(Pub.3584)

Contents

Preface

This book seeks to aid the reader in understanding corporate law. Like other books in this series, or, indeed, most books of this nature, it operates on the assumption that reading scholarly articles as a supplement to primary source materials (cases and statutes) can enhance such understanding. The challenge for the editor is to determine what sort of articles will achieve this goal.

Essentially, I decided to look for articles, or, more precisely, excerpts from articles, that did one or more of three things. There are pieces which simply seek to explain what the law or legal doctrine is. After all, if the goal is to understand an area of law there is no sense ignoring the direct approach. Next, a fundamental tenet in our business is that one cannot really understand the legal doctrine without considering the policy issues which surround the rule. Accordingly, it will come as no surprise that the second type of piece is one which debates the policies for or against the various rules of corporate law. Finally—and here is where there may be the greatest potential for value added in a book such as this—I looked for empirical works which would serve as a "reality check" on the first two types of articles. For example, there are statistical surveys of large groups of decided cases to see if court decisions, in fact, correspond to stated doctrine. In addition, there are studies which look at the results of corporate litigation beyond simply what conclusion did a court reach and why. For example, what was the impact of corporate litigation upon the parties? How have the players in the corporate world, such as investors in the securities markets, reacted to milestone decisions in corporate law? Also, there are pieces which look at how the business world actually operates. For instance, what goes on in the board of directors of a public corporation and how does this compare with the assumptions underlying the duties the law imposes upon directors?

Having outlined the types of materials I looked for, some caveats are in order about what this book does not include. I make no claim that the selections here are the "best" articles in the field. Omitted are many "classic" articles—in the sense of being the most cited or considered to have advanced the field. I selected articles based upon their ability to communicate to the reader of this book rather than for their significance in developing the law or academic debate. I feel the works here cover the material in the most accessible and efficient manner I could find. This book tries to present a balance of viewpoints. This does not mean that there are two pieces on each issue subject to debate. To save time, this book might only include a piece written from one position if it fairly presented the other side. This book tries to cover the issues that arise in a basic corporations course, with the emphasis on those issues likely to be central to such a course. Issues likely to be peripheral to a basic course receive shorter treatment even when they have been the subject of copious literature.

A caveat is also in order about editing. It is no secret that law review writing tends toward the prolix. This may even be legitimate since the article writer must address a variety of audiences, including those ready to challenge every step of his or her discussion. Different imperatives—such as the need to present a large amount of material, respect for demands upon the reader's time, and recognition of the pedagogic principle that it is easy to lose the forest in the trees—drive this book. Hence, the editing is severe. Almost all footnotes are omitted. Case discussions are included only if vital to an understanding of the author's point—this book is not a substitute for reading court opinions.

Finally, a word of thanks to Pauline Rodriguez and the other secretaries who worked on this manuscript.

Chapter I

The Selection of Corporate Law: Private Choices and Public Policy

One or more individuals arrive at an attorney's office for help in starting a business. They must choose the form in which to conduct the business—proprietorship, partnership, limited partnership, limited liability company (recently), or a corporation. Traditionally, the primary reason they might select a corporation is to gain the advantage of limited liability in dealings with third parties. Assuming the parties decide to form a corporation, they must next choose the state in which to incorporate. The major significance of this choice, aside from added costs for a firm which does business solely in one state and incorporates in another, is that the laws of the state of incorporation generally govern the internal affairs—in other words, the relations among the owners and between the owners and managers—of the corporation. Finally, the parties must prepare various documents, such as articles of incorporation, bylaws, perhaps a shareholders' agreement, which will further dictate their relationship.

By virtue of each of these steps, private individuals are essentially choosing the legal rules to govern their business venture. This starting point for the attorney and his or her clients also provides a suitable point of departure for the student of corporate law. Why and to what extent should society facilitate choice of law by private parties engaged in business ventures? What public policies does such private choice achieve? What policies might it frustrate? We begin exploring these questions by asking why the law allows individuals, through the expediency of creating of a corporation, to enjoy the benefits of owning a business, while avoiding the burdens of personal liability for debts incurred by the enterprise.

A. Choosing the Corporate Form to Obtain Limited Liability

A sole proprietor bears personal responsibility for all the obligations of his or her business venture. Similarly, creditors can demand any partner in an ordinary partnership pay the entire debt of the firm out of the partner's personal assets—albeit, the partner might then call upon the firm or his or her fellow partners for indemnity (assuming, of course, they have any assets). By contrast, shareholders in a corporation normally are not liable for corporate debts beyond the amount of money they have paid for their stock. As the articles which follow illustrate, this rule of corporate law has historically been one the most controversial.

1. *Policy Perspectives*

Paul Halpern, Michael Trebilcock, Stuart Turnbull, *An Economic Analysis of Limited Liability in Corporation Law,* 30 U. Toronto L.J. 117 (1980)*

1 *Introduction*

The merits of the doctrine of limited liability in corporation law have been the subject of passionate disagreement amongst otherwise level-headed commentators ever since its general availability under English companies legislation enacted in the middle of the last century.

The Times of London in an editorial, 25 May 1824, declared: 'Nothing can be so unjust as for a few persons abounding in wealth to offer a portion of their excess for the information of a company, to play with that excess—to lend the importance of their whole name and credit to the society, and then should the funds prove insufficient to answer all demands, to retire into the security of their unhazarded fortune, and leave the bait to be devoured by the poor deceived fish.'

A different position was taken by the *Economist*, 1 July 1854:

> The question [of limited liability] has for a long time interested the public, and like many other questions much talked about but hung up for decision, its importance has been greatly diminished by the lapse of time. . . . The people, by quietly adapting their practices to the law, in general manage to wrest or work the law to their practices, and changes in the law, when made, are frequently more nominal than real. At present the law . . . is that every ostensible partner who shares the profits of a trading concern renders himself liable in the whole of his property to the whole of its debts; but in practice, as is the case with mutual assurance companies, all the partners contract with each other, and the company contracts with every person it deals with, that all claims shall be confined to the subscribed fund of the company. Every person with whom it deals entering voluntarily into the contract, the principle of limited liability is, by common consent, fully carried out, whatever the law may say to the contrary.

On the other hand, the *Economist* of 18 December 1926 emphatically espoused the economic virtues of limited liability:

> The economic historian of the future may assign to the nameless inventor of the principle of limited liability, as applied to trading corporations, a place of honour with Watt and Stephenson, and other pioneers of the Industrial Revolution. The genius of these men produced

> the means by which man's command of natural resources was multiplied many times over; the limited liability company the means by which huge aggregations of capital required to give effect to their discoveries were collected, organized and efficiently administered.

The arguments on each side of the limited liability issue, as articulated in the debates surrounding the enactment of the U.K. Limited Liability Act of 1855, can be fairly simply summarized. On the one hand, the defenders of the status quo hypothesized that under limited liability, if introduced, uncompensated transfers of the risk of business failure from shareholders to corporate creditors would occur on a substantial scale. Apart from any immediate equity or distributive considerations raised by this consequence, over time it would presumably curtail the availability of credit to limited liability corporations and reduce the level of economic activity accordingly. On the other hand, the proponents of limited liability hypothesized that its availability would facilitate investments of savings by the middle and working classes otherwise discouraged from investing by the large variance in possible investment outcomes under an unlimited liability regime. A twist on this hypothesis was a view advanced by John Stuart Mill that the rich would be more likely to invest money in business ventures involving members of the middle and working classes if the prospect of the former becoming the chief targets of creditors' attention in the event of a business failure was foreclosed by limited liability. According to either version of this hypothesis, limited liability would lead to a net increase in the aggregate level of economic activity. The argument espoused by the *Economist* in a column of 1 July 1854, that the issue was essentially trite, was based on the notion that affected parties would transact around either legal regime as mutual interests dictated (assuming this to be permitted), and at most all the law should attempt to do was provide maximum freedom to contract and presumably to minimize the transaction costs incurred by parties in achieving mutually desired allocations of risk.

* * *

Continuing attempts in the legal system to adjust the roles of limited and unlimited liability have been reflected in renewed academic debates about the implications of the two regimes. . . .

* * *

Explicit or implicit in the various older and more recent views as to the relative efficiencies of alternative liability regimes are two simple and contradictory assertions: on the one hand, it is claimed that a limited liability regime is inefficient because it enables shareholders to effect uncompensated transfers of business risks to creditors, thus creating incentives for excessive (inefficient) allocations of social resources to risky economic activities. On the other hand, it is claimed that an unlimited liability regime is inefficient because it would impair the efficient functioning of capital markets by discouraging investment by wealthier shareholders who would be especially vulnerable to the risk of personal liability for corporate debts; a related argument stresses the increased (and wasteful) transaction costs that shareholders would incur under such a regime in monitoring the actions of management to avoid unanticipated increases in the riskiness of their investments.

In this paper, we attempt to evaluate these two assertions by identifying as rigorously as we can what transaction, information, and related costs are likely to be generated for the various classes of actors by each of the two alternative liability regimes, and by identifying possible asymmetries in these costs depending on how the choice of liability regimes allocates particular risks. We develop the analysis by examining the effects of the choice of liability regime under a perfect capital market model, and then proceed to look at how various types of divergences from this model are likely to influence these effects. . . .

2 *Perfect capital markets*

* * *

A corporation can be conceived of as an entity which undertakes a set of production decisions that generate a probability distribution of future net operating income. The corporation, by choosing its optimal operating and financing strategies, issues claims which will result in the net operating income being divided among labour and trade creditors, equity, and debt holders. This division of the earnings stream determines how much of the total risk is borne by each group but does not influence the totality of risk. The form of the liability rule will determine the risk borne by each of these groups.

Consider the case where the firm is incorporated with unlimited liability. The owners of the firm are liable for the payment of any outstanding claims if the firm defaults on its obligations. . . . Since the owners are exposed to the default risk that has been removed from the creditors, they will require compensation in terms of the expected return on their equity investment in the company. However, the sum of the risks to all financial claimants and the overall cost of capital to the firm will reflect the overall risk of the net operating income of the firm. . . .

If the firm is incorporated with limited liability, the creditors have accepted a risk[ier] position, since there is the possibility that the firm will default on its obligations. Under a set of outcomes for net operating income, these creditors will receive payment in full on their claims, while for other outcomes the dollar value of their claims will be reduced or even become worthless. The voluntary creditor will consider the probabilities that these outcomes will occur and determine an expected yield at which funds will be lent to the corporation to compensate for the risk. For bond holders, this will be reflected in the promised (or stated) yield on debt, for labour the promised wage rate, and for trade creditors the terms at which their products are sold to the company. Since the owners are not liable for any claims in excess of the corporate assets, their risk and hence required compensation will be less than under the unlimited liability rule. Even though there has been a redistribution of the risk-bearing under limited liability compared with unlimited liability, the totality of risk has remained the same, ie, the probability distribution of net operating income of the firm is unaffected.

* * *

3 Imperfections in the capital market

Our analysis of perfect capital markets assumes that there are no transaction costs, broadly defined, and hence the liability rule makes no difference. Alternatively we could obtain the same conclusion if we assumed that any costs generated in the granting of credit were identical regardless of who bears them. This assumption is the point of departure for the analysis in this section. Given different forms of market imperfections, we investigate those conditions under which there are asymmetric costs. This will have implications for the type of liability rule that we would expect to evolve if parties were free to determine the liability rule. . . .

A BANKRUPTCY COSTS

. . . If payments to the creditors are delayed, the debtor is technically in default, and any resulting reorganization or bankruptcy imposes costs on the creditors. These costs can be in the form of opportunity costs and/or actual losses arising from payments to trustees and lawyers, as well as administrative costs. . . .

If there is limited liability and bankruptcy occurs, the creditors appoint a trustee. . . . [T]he trustee deals with a single entity, the corporation, and looks only to the assets of the corporation for payment of the claims.

If there is unlimited liability . . . then each owner is jointly and severally responsible for the creditors' claims. In this case, the trustee has the option of pursuing all of the owners. This must increase the bankruptcy costs, especially if the shares of the corporation are widely held. Only if there is one owner will the costs remain the same. In general, in order to reduce these bankruptcy costs, the trustee may decide to sue only the wealthiest owners of the firm. But there will still be costs associated with determining which of the owners has sufficient wealth to warrant suit.

* * *

From a consideration of bankruptcy costs, the cost-minimizing solution would be a limited liability rule . . . . However, since the difference in bankruptcy costs in a limited liability compared to a pure unlimited liability regime will be smallest for small or tightly held companies, it is possible that these companies could operate under a pure unlimited liability rule without imposing any allocative inefficiencies.

B COSTS OF INFORMATION

* * *

i / *Creditors' information requirements*

* * *

We cannot state a priori that the information costs will be higher under a pure unlimited liability rule than under a limited liability rule. The firm may already provide a substantial amount of information regardless of the liability rule. However, it is likely that a pure unlimited liability scenario would impose higher costs to the extent that creditors feel compelled to monitor the wealth of the owners and the assets and earning power of the firm; with limited liability the security of the creditors' investment depends upon the assets and earning power of the firm alone.

The differential in information costs between a limited and a pure unlimited liability regime will be smallest when firms are closely held or small. Therefore we would expect that unlimited liability might be an efficient rule for these companies. In fact, we observe that for small companies with limited liability creditors often require personal guarantees. This converts the limited liability company into one with unlimited liability.

* * *

ii / *Shareholders' information requirements*

Under a limited liability rule the owners must evaluate the earnings that will accrue to them under the various states of the world that can occur. However, with limited liability, they are not responsible for any deficiencies in payments to creditors in the event of a default. Thus, they will require information about the earnings outcomes given the existing set of assets and the impact of new investments on these earnings.

With a pure unlimited liability regime, the owners require the same set of information as owners under limited liability. However, they also require information about the possible magnitudes of their financial responsibility in the event of a default and the wealth of the other shareholders. Not only will they need to know the wealth levels at the point in time when they become owners but also at each moment in time in the future, since their financial responsibility in the event of a default may change as the composition of the owners changes.

* * *

Therefore, the information costs for owners will be lowest under a limited liability regime and highest under a pure unlimited liability regime.

iii / *Implications for the existence of an organized securities market*

The requirements for information by shareholders and creditors and the costs of obtaining this information have implications for the existence of a securities market under a pure unlimited liability world. . . .

Consider the wealthy shareholder who purchases one share of equity. His maximum potential loss depends on the wealth of the other shareholders but is independent of the number of shares he holds. Since control depends on the number of shares held, it is likely . . . that the wealthy shareholder will purchase a large number of shares so as to have some control over the operations of the company. This will permit the wealthy shareholder to protect his investment and limit his potential loss through a close scrutiny of the company's operations. . . .

Under this scenario it is very likely that there will be a concentration of the ownership of the equity securities in the hands of the wealthy shareholders. . . . [I]t is unlikely that there would be active trading in the market due to the concentration of ownership.

With the removal of the assumption of complete information on the wealth levels of the equity holders, then each individual must assume that he is responsible for the unsatisfied claims up to the limit of his personal wealth. Those potential shareholders with low levels of wealth will have a distribution of end-of-period wealth which has a substantial probability of a zero wealth level. Wealthy shareholders will have distributions of end-of-period wealth for which the probability of zero wealth is not as significant. In this case it is very likely that only wealthy shareholders will purchase the equity securities of corporations, and a capital market in which there is trading of outstanding securities is unlikely to exist.

Of course, in this world of unlimited liability other rules or contractual arrangements could evolve to facilitate the existence of a securities market. For example, an alternative scenario is a liability rule where each equity investor is liable for the amount of money invested in purchasing the equity plus a proportion of the unsatisfied claims arising from a default. The responsibility for these unsatisfied claims would be equal to the proportion of the total shares outstanding held by each investor. This can be called a pro rata liability rule. The investor would still choose his optimal portfolio based on maximizing his expected utility of end-of-period wealth, and the ability of the shareholder to diversify away firm specific risk will still exist. . . . In addition, each shareholder need not be as interested in monitoring the wealth composition of the shareholders of a company. . . .

One interesting implication of the pro rata liability rule is that the equilibrium price of a security may be negative. Consider a company which has a large expected loss due to bankruptcy. . . . Given the expected value of the earnings of the firm and the potential loss in bankruptcy, the equity investor may have to be paid to hold the shares of the company.

C INSURANCE

* * *

ii / *Moral hazard*

Whenever there is insurance, be it provided through market insurance or by creditors under a limited liability regime, there is the possibility of a moral hazard problem. . . . For example, once owners of a firm have default insurance . . . they may undertake new investment projects that result in an unanticipated increase in the risk to the insurer. . . .

* * *

The moral hazard problem is likely to be more severe for small, tightly held companies than for larger companies. [T]he owners of the former class of company have a direct interest in the operations of the firm and will obtain the full benefits of an alteration in the firm's operations. . . .

* * *

v / *Implications for investment decisions*

* * *

Under limited liability, the owners' probability distributions of end-of-period wealth are now truncated—they are not responsible for any unsatisfied claims in the event of default. It would thus be of benefit for the owners of the firm to undertake investment decisions with characteristics unanticipated by the creditors at the time credit was extended. These decisions would increase the risk of the assets and hence the variability of the probability distribution of the owners' terminal wealth. This unanticipated increased risk will result in an uncompensated increase in the risk to existing creditors and thus a reduction in the market value of their claims. The equity holders, however, have a lower limit on losses and, with a more variable distribution of terminal wealth, they have the potential for a large gain. The risky investment decision has increased the value of their equity equal to the loss in the value of the creditors' claims.

* * *

D INVOLUNTARY CREDITORS

When considering imperfections in markets, the involuntary creditor—paradigmatically a tort creditor like the pedestrian who was injured by the taxi in *Walkovsky v Carlton*—provides us with a polar case of transactions and information costs that may be prohibitively high. . . .

. . . In the case of the pedestrian, it must be assumed that the taxi cab corporation is the least-cost loss avoider, otherwise it is unlikely that there would be a finding of tortious liability for negligence. Limited liability here may undermine the deterrent objectives of the tort system . . . . In addition, there is no incentive for the owner to carry adequate insurance since, in the event of default, there is no cost to the owner.

Now assume that limited liability is removed in this case. The owner of the unlimited liability company will have the following major options: first, he can self-insure by having sufficient amounts of personal wealth to meet most tort claims; second, he can purchase insurance on his own account to meet most tort claims; third, he can have the corporation take out this insurance. Given the large size of the potential tort claims, it is unlikely that the first option would be taken. If either of the other two options are taken then the combination of unlimited liability and insurance results in a limited liability regime where the owner is no longer personally responsible in the event of default. Thus we are again faced with a moral hazard situation. However, there is an important difference between unlimited liability combined with insurance and limited liability. In the latter case the owners obtain insurance against third-party claims for which there is no cost. However, in the former case, the insurance premium has a market-determined price. Since the premium will depend upon the behaviour of the taxi owners, it will be in the best interests of the owners to undertake some cost-justified risk-reduction precautions (eg, hire safer drivers). Thus the incentive to efficient behaviour is increased. With respect to the compensation issue, either the second or third options will result in insurance being purchased which will cover most of the tort claims that the corporation would face.

Whether the corporation (or the owner) is the least-cost insurer in this context is an empirical question. However, several factors suggest that this may well be the case. Because the corporation (or the owner) is specialized in the taxi industry, it can probably more accurately assess the probability of negligent cab operation causing injury to pedestrians than can the pedestrians themselves. This access to superior information on accident risks makes it likely that market insurance will be more accurately priced than market insurance (eg, life or disability insurance) purchased by pedestrians. . . .

* * *

4 *Conclusions*

We now attempt to derive some implications from the foregoing analysis for the form of an efficient liability regime for corporations.

First, in the case of large, widely held companies, a limited liability regime, as a general rule, is the most efficient regime. By skewing the distribution of business risks amongst different shareholders, an unlimited liability regime would create a significant measure of uncertainty in the valuation of securities and threaten the existence of organized securities markets, thus inducing costly attempts by creditors and owners to transact around the regime. The case for a limited liability regime for this class of company is very compelling. The attenuated nature of the moral hazard factor in widely held companies does not create a strong countervailing consideration.

Second, in the case of small, tightly held companies, a limited liability regime will, in many cases, create incentives for owners to exploit a moral hazard and transfer uncompensated business risks to creditors, thus inducing costly attempts by creditors to reduce these risks. An unlimited liability regime for this class of enterprise . . . would seem to be the most efficient regime . . . .

A major effect of adopting an unlimited liability regime in [the] context [of small, tightly held companies] would be to shift to the corporation and its owners the onus of proposing contractual arrangements to creditors which limit the liability of the owners (where these are desired). Requiring explicit negotiation of such arrangements is likely to improve information flows to creditors about allocation of risks and sharpen the focus of creditors' incentives to monitor a corporation's activities. We acknowledge that the case for an unlimited liability regime for this class of company is not as compelling as the case for limited liability for large, widely held companies, given that in the former case, with fewer parties involved, most creditors and owners can contract around either regime at low cost, thus making the choice of liability regime relatively inconsequential. We also recognize that difficulties may be associated with attempting to distinguish by law small from large corporations for the purpose of applying different liability regimes, and that the distinction may induce some perverse and wasteful incentive effects as firms seek to manipulate internal structures to ensure compliance with the requirements of the preferred regime. However, our empirical intuition remains that, on balance, an unlimited liability regime is the most efficient regime for small, closely held companies.

* * *

Notes and Questions

1. Admittedly this piece was rather laden with economics jargon, no doubt because its authors are economists. On the other hand, think about that the next time one is tempted to fill one's writing with legal jargon. Let us see if we can translate some of the critical points.

2. Start with the 1854 editorial by the *Economist* quoted near the beginning of the piece. In 1854, English law did not provide limited liability for most companies. (We will return to this later in an article by Professor Blumberg.) The *Economist* editorial states that it does not matter because companies and their owners were able to obtain limited liability for themselves by contract with their creditors. Conversely, Professors Halpern, Trebilcock and Turnbull note that creditors of small corporations now often create unlimited liability for the owners by demanding the owners give personal guarantees for the firm's debts. In arguing that the law of limited liability is irrelevant because parties will contract for whatever liability rule they desire, the author of the *Economist* editorial anticipated by a century the work of Professor Ronald Coase. One of the foundations of the approach to legal analysis referred to as "law and economics" is the so-called Coase Theorem. This holds that, in the absence of transactions costs (in other words, the costs, such as attorneys fees, associated with making and enforcing contracts), parties in a transactional relationship will contract to an efficient result no matter what the legal rule. Coase, *The Problem of Social Cost*, 3 J.L. & ECON. 1 (1960). For an article developing the argument that the Coase Theorem applies to limited liability for corporate owners, making the law irrelevant, see Meiners, Mofsky & Tollinson, *Piercing the Veil of Limited Liability*, 4 DEL. J. CORP. L. 351 (1979). Do Professors Halpern, Trebelcock and Turnbull adequately answer the claim that the law does not matter because parties can contract for the liability rule they want? What about when dealing with tort victims, who cannot contract around limited liability?

3. Beyond the ability to contract around the liability rule, Professors Halpern, Trebelcock and Turnbull suggest that the rule would not matter in a world of perfect capital markets—in other words, perfectly informed parties and zero transactions costs—because any increase risk to owners from unlimited liability, or to creditors from limited liability, will be offset by an increase in returns demanded by the owners or by the creditors. In making this argument, Professors Halpern, Trebelcock and Turnbull employ a conception of the corporation whose significance goes beyond the issue of limited liability. They view the firm as an entity which mixes together various inputs—services, supplies, capital—to (hopefully) produce income, and issues claims to the suppliers of those inputs—employees, vendors, lenders, shareholders—entitling them to a share of the expected income. In other words, the corporation is a sort of "nexus of contracts" between various contributors to a business venture. For further reading developing this concept and its implications for corporate law, see Easterbrook & Fischel, THE ECONOMIC STRUCTURE OF CORPORATE LAW (1992). For a discussion of possible shortcomings with this approach to corporate law issues see Bratton, *The Economic Structure of the Post-Contractual Corporation*, 87 NW. U. L. REV. 180 (1992).

4. Professors Halpern, Trebelcock and Turnbull argue that, for a company with numerous owners, limited liability is efficient in the sense that what owners gain from having limited liability exceeds what creditors lose from not obtaining the right to go after the owners personally. Do you see why, if this is the case, both owners and creditors might be willing to agree to limited liability? The article's discussion of bankruptcy costs provides the easiest illustration of this point to understand. The costs of suing numerous owners in order to collect on a corporate debt might well chew up much of the expected recovery for the creditor. Hence, the creditor may be happy to give up the right to sue owners of a widely held corporation in exchange for a little extra interest, since what it will collect with unlimited liability is far less than what the owners will pay. For a more detailed development of this point, see Ribstein, *The Deregulation of Limited Liability and the Death of Partnership*, 70 WASH. U. L.Q. 417 (1992).

The more significant reason owners gain more from limited liability than creditors lose, however, may relate to the concerns Professors Halpern, Trebelcock and Turnbull raise about information costs and whether limited liability is necessary in order for owners to possess the advantage of being able to trade their stock in organized securities markets. For related arguments in favor of limited liability, see Easterbrook & Fischel, *Limited Liability and the Corporation*, 52 U. CHI. L. REV. 89 (1985). On the other hand, Professors Halpern, Trebelcock and Turnbull recognize that the concern with the advantages of securities trading may be less if each stockholder only has pro-rata personal liability (in other words, liability in proportion to his or her share in the company). For a detailed argument in favor of such pro-rata liability see Hansmann & Kraakman, *Toward Unlimited Liability for Corporate Torts*, 100 YALE L.J. 1879 (1991). For a rebuttal see Grundfest, *The Limited Future of Unlimited Liability: A Capital Markets Perspective*, 102 YALE L.J. 387 (1992).

5. The disadvantage of limited liability discussed by Professors Halpern, Trebelcock and Turnbull involves "moral hazard." An example may clarify the point. Suppose one could borrow money under an agreement wherein if the borrower makes money with the funds, he or she will repay the lender with fixed interest, but if the borrower loses all the funds, he or she will bear no personal responsibility. The borrower might invest the funds conservatively, say buying some commercial property to rent out. On the other hand, consider the incentives with such a loan to take the money and head to Las Vegas.

Of course, voluntary creditors might seek to protect themselves from such tactics. For example, they might demand some control over the use of the loaned funds or that the borrower also put some of his or her own money into the venture. Voluntary creditors may also charge an interest rate to compensate for the risk. What about tort creditors, however? Now, the hazard is not that the owners will recklessly gamble with borrowed funds, but rather that the firm will create risks of personal injury which would not be economically justified if the owners had to pay for their consequences. In this regard, recall the economic rationale for vicarious and products liability. It is from this rationale that Professors Halpern, Trebelcock and Turnbull draw when they use the concepts of "least cost loss avoider" and "least cost insurer." Notice it is only through the doctrines of vicarious and products liability that a corporation ever becomes liable for a tort. The effect of limited liability is to undercut these doctrines and frustrate their rationale. For a more detailed development of this concern and an attempt to weigh it against the advantages of limited liability, see Leebron, *Limited Liability, Tort Victims and Creditors*, 91 COLUM. L. REV. 1565 (1992).

6. The two bottom line conclusions of Professors Halpern, Trebelcock and Turnbull are that limited liability is efficient for widely held firms and inefficient for firms with few owners. The next two articles further examine these claims.

William A. Klein and Eric M. Zolt, *Business Form, Limited Liability, and Tax Regimes: Lurching Toward a Coherent Outcome?*, 65 U. COLO. L. REV. 1001 (1995)*

* * *

III. THE PROPER LIMITS OF LIMITED LIABILITY

"[T]o the early nineteenth-century legislators in states such as New York, who mandated limited liability for corporations' shareholders, the imposition of limited liability was perceived as a means of encouraging the small-scale entrepreneur, and of keeping the entry into business markets competitive and democratic."[85] This is not to say that the butcher, the baker, or the partners operating the general store should be entitled to limited liability. Something of a more substantial scale was no doubt contemplated—some activity that necessitated the use of the corporate form to raise capital, but not necessarily a large corporation or one that would, in the current era, have publicly traded shares.

---

85 . . . [Stephen B. Presser, *Thwarting the Killing of the Corporation: Limited Liability, Democracy, and Economics*, 87 NW. U. L. REV. 148, 155 (1992).]

This analysis seems to suggest that limited liability was enacted for the benefit not only of large but also of medium-sized ventures. It is almost impossible to imagine, then or now, that a state legislature would consciously provide that limited liability would be available to giant corporations but not to medium-sized ones. It is equally difficult to imagine, however, that in an earlier era a legislature would consciously provide for limited liability for small firms with one, or possibly several, owners who personally ran the business.

As incorporation became easily available, with no need to go to the legislature for a charter, corporate status, and along with it limited liability, did in fact become available to small firms. That result may have been accidental. . . .

Where does this leave us? Perhaps it supports the idea that in an era of free-and-easy incorporation limited liability should turn not on corporate status but rather on firm size. That idea is consistent with the arguments of economic efficiency offered in recent years by various commentators . . . who have defended limited liability on grounds that are relevant only to large-scale, publicly held firms. . . .

Suppose we take as given that large and mid-sized firms should, for better or worse, be entitled to limited liability. As for tort liability—or, more broadly, liability to involuntary creditors—is it plausible to suppose that a lawmaker would conclude that the same entitlement should be denied to smaller firms? Perhaps so. With smaller firms the shareholders are more likely to exercise control over the operation of the business than with larger firms. Consequently, with smaller firms the economic arguments supporting vicarious liability . . . are perhaps most plainly in conflict with the arguments for limited liability—though the conflict hardly disappears in the case of larger firms. Moreover, the problems of feasibility [of collecting a judgment] that arise when shareholders are numerous and geographically scattered largely disappear, and, the probability of conscious use of corporate form, with minimal capital investment, to shift the risk of dangerous activity to innocent victims, may be higher than with large firms. On balance, however, we think that a distinction based on firm size (or whether a firm is publicly owned or closely held) would, if addressed squarely, be considered unsound. Such a distinction is inconsistent with a commitment to competition and democratic values, as noted by Professor Presser.

As for obligations to voluntary creditors, Easterbrook and Fischel echo a familiar theme by stating, "[i]f limited liability were not the starting point in corporate law, firms would create it by contract—which is not hard to do." In other words, limited liability is irrelevant (unless, of course, one considers transaction costs). We are skeptical about the conclusion that acquiring limited liability by contract is "not hard to do," but we can lay that issue aside. What is presently relevant is that if one takes as given a decision to provide limited liability for publicly held firms, then, even if the arguments for that entitlement relate solely to large firms, there are strong reasons for extending the entitlement to smaller firms (even to the tiny ones). In other words, once one concludes that reasons of economic efficiency justify giving large firms limited liability, other considerations of efficiency and "democracy" (decentralization of power, etc.) argue persuasively for treating smaller firms in the same fashion.

* * *

Note

One example of a closely held corporation which Professors Klein and Zolt do not seem to consider is when the owner is another corporation, rather than individuals. The question of whether corporations, by creating subsidiaries, should be able to insulate some of their operations from liabilities created in other activities has provoked controversy. For a classic example of this debate, see Landers, *A Unified Approach to Parent, Subsidiary and Affiliate Questions in Bankruptcy*, 42 U. CHI. L. REV. 589 (1975); Posner, *The Rights of Creditors of Affiliated Corporations*, 43 U. CHI. L. REV. 499 (1976); Landers, *Another Word on Parents, Subsidiaries and Affiliates in Bankruptcy*, 43 U. CHI. L. REV. 527 (1976).

---

2. *Reality Check: The History of Limited Liability*

The economic argument that limited liability is important to the creation of securities markets and widely held companies mirrors the popular notion that limited liability was a necessary stimulus to the accumulation of capital for the industrial revolution. Does historical evidence support either of these notions? How did limited liability for corporations come about anyway?

Phillip I. Blumberg, *Limited Liability and Corporate Groups*, 11 J. CORP. L. 573 (1986)*

* * *

II. HISTORY OF LIMITED LIABILITY

The traditional view of the corporation in Anglo-American law, as well as in other Western legal systems, has firmly embraced entity law: the concept that a corporation is a separate legal person with its own rights and obligations, distinct from those of its shareholders. The concept of the corporation as a separate legal entity ultimately led to the acceptance of the very different doctrine of limited liability: the rule that shareholders are not liable for the obligations of the corporation beyond their capital investment.

Despite widespread confusion on the matter, it is clear that the entity view of the corporation rests essentially on philosophical notions and that this view was firmly established well before acceptance of the principle of limited liability. Limited liability emerged at a much later stage in the development of the corporation. It arose in the wake of the acceptance of the entity concept, but not as a necessary consequence.

* * *

A. The Emergence of Limited Liability in England (1855)

1. Early Development

At the time of the American Revolution, English corporation law, emerging from its misty historical origins in ecclesiastical and public corporations and reflecting concepts derived from medieval versions of Roman law, was still in the process of completing its slow evolution in the elimination of direct shareholder liability for corporate obligations.[10] Holdsworth and Gower conclude that direct liability, in the absence of charter provision, for shareholders of commercial corporations had ceased by the end of the sixteenth century. Other scholars place the date much later. DuBois, for example, concludes that, limited liability was of slight importance at this time, and that the relation between incorporation and limited liability was still equivocal. The Handlins concur, asserting that limited liability was still a fuzzy question at the end of the eighteenth century.

The evidence from the legal commentary of the time also provides support for the later date. Hobbes, writing in 1654, referred to the unlimited liability of members of "a body politic of merchants." Similarly, neither Sir Edward Coke, writing in 1612, nor Blackstone, writing in 1765, nor Kyd, writing in 1792, listed limited liability among the essential attributes of the corporation.

In the late eighteenth century, the Crown was still following an inconsistent course. It was issuing some charters that expressly provided for direct shareholder liability; other charters expressly provided that shareholders were not to be directly liable. Most charters simply were silent, and it had become accepted increasingly that in the absence of charter provision, shareholders were not directly liable. . . .

* * *

[C]orporation law on liability played only a minor role in the English commercial experience because commercial activity was handled increasingly by joint stock companies, not corporations. Corporate charters had been difficult and expensive to obtain. For example, during the entire eighteenth century, the English government had chartered only a half dozen corporations for manufacturing and "hardly more" for other businesses. . . .

2. The Predominance of Joint Stock Companies

Growing commercial enterprises increasingly turned to joint stock associations with transferable shares as an alternative to the corporate form. Such companies multiplied and became the predominant form for the conduct of business activity. By 1844, there were almost 1,000 joint stock associations including banks. Some associations had surprisingly widespread ownership of their shares. As early as 1808, the Birm-

---

10 Shareholder liability includes direct liability of shareholders for the obligations of the corporation and indirect liability through the liability of shareholders to the corporation for an assessment (or in the old English usage, a leviation) to provide the corporation with funds required for payment of the corporation's obligations.

ingham Flour and Bread Company had 8,000 shareholders. Originally conceived as a form of partnership, the joint stock association developed into an unincorporated association organized under a deed of settlement, with trustees owning the stock [(the property used by the business)] and holding it for the benefit of the members, who held transferable shares. In an effort to limit member liability arising from the partnership form of the organization, it became common for the deeds of settlement to include clauses limiting the power of the company to make calls on members and limiting members' liability to the amount of their stock interest. These clauses disposed of liability *inter se* and of indirect member liability through assessments although they could not terminate liability of members to third parties.[31]

Joint stock associations generally attempted to achieve limited liability of members for debts to third parties through such measures as inserting the term "limited" after the joint stock company name, including an appropriate legend on company stationery, and using limitation of liability clauses in their contracts. Beginning in the early nineteenth century, insurance policies issued by joint stock insurance companies began to contain clauses limiting liability to company capital. . . . Numerous trading companies followed suit, and similarly, inserted such clauses in their contracts. Although the validity of the contractual limitation as a question of law was not settled for some time,[35] the commercial practice was unmistakable. In this manner, joint stock associations under deeds of settlement attempted to achieve the advantages of incorporation, without a charter.

3. The Continuing Political Struggle Over Limited Liability

For three decades after the United States generally had accepted limited liability, limited liability continued to be a highly controversial political issue in England, vigorously debated against a rising tide of industrialization. . . .

In 1844, under Gladstone's leadership, the forces opposing limited liability temporarily gained the upper hand. The Joint Stock Companies Registration, Incorporation, and Regulation Act, 1844, which permitted general incorporation, imposed unlimited liability on members for unsatisfied corporate judgments. . . .

Although Hunt reports that from 1844 to 1856 almost 1,000 unlimited companies registered under the 1844 Act, it proved unworkable. It failed to solve the problem of evasion through transfer of shares. The 1844 Act was also perceived as having retarded investment by more wealthy investors because of their concern that creditors would first proceed against them in preference to less wealthy members.

The Depression of 1845-1848 and public acceptance of limited liability for railways helped tilt the balance toward limited liability. The railways were among the most

31 A number of commentators note that cumbersome procedural requirements for suits against members of joint stock companies in their capacity as partners provided de facto protection against member liability in widely held companies because of the difficulties of suing and levying execution on members of a fluctuating group. . . .

35 Eventually, a series of cases from 1849 to 1852 upheld as a matter of contract law, the enforceability of clauses in insurance policies that limited liability under the policy to the capital of the company.

successful of the growing English industries. . . . Their need for heavy capital investment led to an increasingly larger number of shareholders and widespread distribution of the shares. In turn, the distribution of shares led to the development of active security markets throughout England. The distribution of shares also inevitably resulted in less participation by members in the management of the enterprise and the separation of investors from managers. Finally, the railways' exposure to heavy tort liability could not be eliminated by contractual limitations and public notice. In light of these facts, few questioned the validity of limited liability for railways. Acceptance of limited liability for the railways foreshadowed the ultimate acceptance of limited liability generally.

Finally, Parliament enacted the Limited Liability Act, 1855 and the Joint Stock Companies Act, 1856. These statutes authorized general limited liability and thus ended the debate. They provided for registration of all existing unincorporated joint stock associations, registration of new companies, and limited liability for the members of all registering companies. . . .

* * *

4. Summary

* * *

Limited liability was not an essential component of the English legal system under which the first one hundred years of the Industrial Revolution flourished. Nor was it an inevitable component of the capitalist economic system. English industrial activity increased enormously under a legal rule imposing liability on shareholders.

* * *

B. The Emergence of Limited Liability in American Law (1830)

* * *

In England, Parliament's reluctance to grant corporate charters led to the emergence of the joint stock association as the common form for the conduct of business. The United States, however, followed a different route. Following the Revolution, the incorporating power moved to the thirteen states. The state legislatures did not share the English Parliamentary reluctance to grant corporate charters, and the special acts of incorporation were granted much more readily than in England. As a result, more than 300 American business corporations were formed between 1783 and 1801. Thus, in the new American nation, the corporation, not the joint stock association, became the predominant form.

In this early state, American corporate charters were granted readily, first for corporations with public functions such as bridges, canals, turnpikes, and subsequently, for financial institutions such as banks and insurance companies. Charters for manufacturing companies were another matter. Few manufacturing charters were granted in the first thirty years of the new nation. As relations with England deteriorated during the early nineteenth century, American readiness to depend on European manufactured goods disappeared, and manufacturing became an increasingly important political weapon, particularly in New England. The early reluctance to issue manufacturing charters changed; thus from 1808-1815, 128 manufacturing corporations were formed in Massachusetts alone.

1. Direct Shareholder Liability

As the corporate form became available more readily, businessmen used it increasingly, primarily to achieve perpetuity of existence and ready transferability of shares. Except for financial enterprises such as banks and insurance companies, limited liability was still of slight importance. . . .

By the start of the nineteenth century, direct shareholder liability was still common. In Massachusetts, about half of the early charters imposed full direct liability on shareholders for corporate debts; the others were silent. None provided for limited liability. . . . Similarly, New York charters for manufacturing businesses, with rare exceptions, provided for direct shareholder liability. . . .

* * *

4. The Shift to Limited Liability

a. Judicial Development

A cardinal legal question at the beginning of the nineteenth century was whether shareholders were directly liable for corporate debts if the charter was silent on shareholder liability. No answer is available. Professor Dodd states that eighteenth century thought in the United States on this question was "almost non-existent," . . . .

This fundamental issue was soon resolved in the first quarter of the nineteenth century. Both the Massachusetts courts and Justice Story sitting as a federal circuit court Judge in *Wood v. Dummer*[122] held that shareholders were not directly liable for corporate debts unless the statute or charter expressly so provided. The courts pointed to the numerous charters of the time that imposed direct liability as confirmation that, in the absence of such a provision, shareholders were not directly liable. . . .

At the same time, the Massachusetts courts, influenced by the wording of the Massachusetts statutes, concluded that in the absence of express charter provision, there was no indirect liability via assessments as well. . . .

b. Legislative Development

As industry continued its rapid growth, industrialists, whose political influence increased as their economic power grew, pressed for the extension to manufacturing companies of the limitations on shareholder liability that already had been accepted for companies with public function or financial objectives. These efforts gradually met with success, and states began to enact statutes that provided limited liability for manufacturing companies.

122 30 F. Cas. 435, 436 (C.C.D. Me. 1824) . . . .

New Hampshire in 1816, and Connecticut in 1818, adopted limited liability for manufacturing companies. Maine followed suit in 1823. The stage then moved to Massachusetts where businessmen and political figures argued that these other New England states were attracting capital investment as a result of their more liberal statutes. The depression of 1829 gave further impetus to the business campaign. In 1830, Massachusetts adopted a statute that provided limited liability. Although special incorporation was still required, it was freely granted.

New York in 1811, and New Jersey in 1816, adopted statutes for the incorporation of manufacturing companies that provided for double liability; ultimately, these statutes were replaced by limited liability statutes. Rhode Island, second only to Massachusetts with respect to industrialization, was the last New England state to yield. Limited liability for Rhode Island manufacturing companies was not enacted until 1847.

* * *

5. The Significance of Competing Legal Rules on Economic Development

Thus, for several decades, there was a remarkable juxtaposition of conflicting legal rules on limited liability in neighboring states. During the decade prior to 1830, Massachusetts and Rhode Island had unlimited liability while New Hampshire, Connecticut, and Maine had limited liability. Such a contrast could be expected to provide a fertile field for comparison of the impact of conflicting legal rules on liability upon the pace of economic development.

In fact, there is little sign that the different legal rules on shareholder liability adversely affected economic development in Massachusetts and Rhode Island during this period. Although activity in New Hampshire and Connecticut is reported to have been stimulated somewhat by the change to limited liability, these states, nevertheless, continued to lag behind Massachusetts and Rhode Island. Similarly, there was no discernable increase in incorporations when Massachusetts abandoned unlimited liability for limited liability in 1830. Nor was there any significant impact on Rhode Island during 1830 to 1847 when it was the only state in New England still operating under unlimited liability. Notwithstanding its less hospitable policy to business, Rhode Island retained its position as the second most active state in textiles. The change of liability rule in neighboring states did not have an impact that was important enough to offset other factors.

* * *

D. Later Survival of Shareholder Liability

In the United States, despite the acceptance of limited liability in the early nineteenth century, there were isolated survivals of shareholder liability for corporate obligations. . . .

1. Pro Rata Shareholder Liability in California (1849-1931)

One of the most important survivals of shareholder liability occurred in California from 1849 to 1931. The California experience is particularly interesting because it continued at an advanced stage of commercial and industrial development for more than three quarters of a century, well into comparatively recent times.

The California Constitutions of 1849 and 1879 and implementing statutes imposed on shareholders pro rata liability for all corporate debts and obligations incurred while they were shareholders. California law imposed liability on all shareholders both of corporations incorporated under California law, without regard to the law of the jurisdiction in which the debt was incurred, and foreign corporations doing business in California with respect to debts arising in California. . . .

* * *

In 1930, the constitutional provision was repealed, and the 1931 General Corporation Law repealed the provisions of article 322 of the Civil Code which had implemented the constitutional provision. Subsequent corporation laws were entirely silent on the issue of shareholder liability.

The most interesting questions with respect to this fascinating episode in American corporate history are unanswered. For example, did this unique legal rule have any signficiantly adverse impact on business activity as was asserted by the forces pressing for repeal? From California's rate of growth during the eighty years in which the constitutional and statutory provisions were in effect, it can be inferred that any such impact was limited; however, this inference remains to be demonstrated by economic historians.

2. Double or Triple Liability for Shareholders Generally

Double liability for shareholders (i.e. liability for corporate obligations in an amount equal to the par value of their shares) arose in American law during the early nineteenth century after unlimited liability had been discarded reluctantly in favor of general incorporation statutes. New York in its general incorporation act of 1811, and New Jersey in 1816, included provisions for double liability for shareholders generally. Professor Hurst reports that such explicit statutorily qualified liability for shareholders was common between 1810 to [sic] 1860. Writing as late as 1891, Beach described such liability as applicable in nearly all states. Although most of such statutes provided for double liability, some, as in Colorado, Maryland, and Pennsylvania, provided for triple liability.

* * *

3. Double Liability for Shareholders of Banks

While the double liability statutes of general application gradually disappeared, double liability for shareholders of bank corporations survived until well into the present century. Designed as a measure of protection for bank depositors, such statutes had been enacted widely and survived until after the Great Depression.

* * *

In the financial disasters of the Great Depression, double liability proved ineffective, and the country turned to deposit insurance as a more effective measure for the protection of depositors. . . .

* * *

4. Shareholder Liability for Wage Claims

Another area of surviving shareholder liability for corporate obligations involves obligations to employees. As late as the 1960's, there were as many as six states that by constitution or statute imposed some form of liability on shareholders (or insiders) for unpaid wages of corporate employees. . . .

* * *

F. Summary

For more than 150 years in the United States and Continental Europe, and for more than 100 years in England, limited liability for shareholders has been the firmly established legal principle underlying corporation law. This fundamental policy emerged after political and economic struggle. It was intended to stimulate economic activity by encouraging widespread investment in corporate shares. . . .

The triumph of limited liability flows from concerns of policy, not from any conceptual notion of the nature of the corporation. For many years, the acceptance of the principle was uneven. In a number of areas, pockets of shareholder liability survived, demonstrating that limited liability is not an essential condition for capitalist economic activity.

* * *

Notes and Questions

1. Professor Blumberg refers to corporations created by special charters and to general incorporation laws. A further explanation might be useful. Originally, individuals interested in forming a corporation, say to build and operate a tollroad, needed to go and convince the government—in England, the Crown or Parliament, in the United States, a state legislature—to grant a charter. In the early 1800s, various states in the United States began adopting general corporation acts. Such statutes allow anyone to establish a corporation by complying with the act without requiring special permission. General corporation acts are now the governing corporation statutes in every state. This raises an interesting question as to what precipitated the change from special chartering to general incorporation. In addition to the burden on the legislature to create special charters, consider the incentives created by a system in which private parties must plead for personal favors from a legislature (even in an era which pre-dated multimillion dollar election campaigns).

2. To what extent does the history of limited liability verify or undercut the economic analysis of Professors Halpern, Trebelcock and Turnbull? For example, what does the history of English joint stock companies say about the contention that unlimited liability will produce a concentration of ownership? For a more recent example of widely traded stock with pro-rata liability see Grossman, *The Market for Shares with Unlimited Liability: The Case of American Express*, 24 J. LEGAL STUDIES 63 (1995).

3. Notice footnote 31 suggesting that procedural problems provided de facto limited liability for members in widely held joint stock companies. For a modern consideration of some procedural problems facing any attempt to impose liability upon shareholders of a widely held corporation see Alexander, *Unlimited Shareholder Liability Through a Procedural Lens*, 106 HARV. L. REV. 387 (1992).

4. Consider the manner in which joint stock companies sought to create limited liability by contract. What contract law issues would this raise? How aware does one suppose the typical insured was of the policy provision limiting recovery to the insurance company's "capital?" How would the policy have defined "capital" and dealt with distributions of funds from the company to its owners? Is there anything to be said for creating an entity for which creditors will be aware that there is limited liability without reading the fineprint of a contract and for which there will be standard terms defining what property the creditors may assert a claim to?

5. Notice the argument made by proponents of limited liability in states like Massachusetts, once other states had adopted this rule. Does this suggest a danger that competition between states to make laws attractive to corporations can create a "race to the bottom?" What sort of policies might such competition frustrate? The concern with state competition in corporation law extends beyond the question of limited liability.

B. Choosing the Governing Law by Selecting the State of Incorporation

When a corporation conducts business in a state, it must observe the state's laws generally applicable to persons doing business there. These laws deal with such issues as worker safety, pollution, taxes and so on. The only way to avoid these sort of laws is for a corporation not to undertake business in that state (and, accordingly, forgo whatever profit the firm hoped to acheive through its operations there). By contrast, the laws of the state of incorporation traditionally have governed the so-called internal affairs of a corporation—in other words, the relations between shareholders and managers and among the shareholders. Individuals may choose to incorporate in any state, regardless of where the corporation will actually conduct its operations.

Presumably, one of the tasks of laws governing the internal affairs of a corporation is to protect minority shareholders from abuse by managers or majority shareholders. Yet, those anticipating the role of manager or majority shareholder are likely to be the parties choosing where to incorporate. The next two articles debate whether this is necessarily an undesirable state of affairs.

Ralph K. Winter, Jr., *State Law, Shareholder Protection, and the Theory of the Corporation*, 6 J. LEGAL STUDIES 271 (1977)*

. . . It is almost universally the opinion of academic commentators that state corporation codes do not impose sufficiently stringent controls on corporate management and are lax in protecting shareholders. Only federal intervention, it is said, can correct this sorry situation. . . .

Adoption of the proposals for federal intervention would drastically alter a number of elementary legal rules (or understandings about what the law is) which have accompanied the growth of the American economy for over a century. Elementary though they be, these rules bear repeating. First, most corporate charters are the creations of the laws of individual states. Second, incorporation laws are "general" rather than "special," which is to say only that the corporate form is readily available to all who would use it and not subject to the approval in each case of a bureaucrat or legislature. Third, the decision as to which state to incorporate in is in almost all cases a managerial decision, emanating from the (would-be) corporation itself, and not dictated by law or administrative decision. Fourth, state corporation law is almost exclusively concerned with the internal governance of the corporation and in particular with the relationship of the shareholders to management. Except for federal securities law, this relationship is largely subject only to state law. . . . Sixth, once incorporated in one state, a corporation may for the most part do business in any state and continue to be governed—whether because of constitutional command or judgments about comity between states—by the charter and corporation code of the state of incorporation.

* * *

The academic literature on the federal role in the shareholder-corporation relationship makes two claims. (1) Because state corporation codes do not require strict judicial scrutiny of many acts of corporate management, they leave shareholders in a vulnerable position. (2) The cause of this "tilt" in state corporation law lies in the operation of competitive legal systems. Because corporate chartering can generate substantial revenue for state treasuries, states compete for charters. Since the decision as

---

to where to incorporate is a management decision and management's interests are adverse to those of shareholders, competitive legal systems tend to permissiveness so far as management conduct is concerned and to inadequate protection for shareholders. . . .

II. DELAWARE'S "RACE FOR THE BOTTOM" AND THE CAPITAL MARKET

A. Competitive Legal Systems and the Capital Market

No one denies that Delaware's open bidding for corporate charters has led to a steady lessening of the restrictiveness of state corporation law. Restrictions on the longevity of a corporation, the businesses in which it may engage, the issuance of stock, the classes of stock issued, dividend policy, discretion as to the holding of shareholders' meetings, charter amendments, means of electing directors, sales of assets, mortgaging, and the indemnification of officers, among others, have all been eliminated or diminished in a series of amendments to state corporation codes. It would further appear that the ability of a corporation to work fundamental changes, such as mergers or the elimination of minority shareholders, has been increased, as has management's power to work its will in a variety of matters, including some in which it may have a conflict of interest, *e.g.*, management compensation.

The history of state corporation law is thus largely a history of drastic reduction of legal restrictions on management and of the legal rights of shareholders. This movement has not been at random but has rather occurred as corporations have sought charters in states with less restrictive codes. Other states have then adopted similar codes in response. As a result, the movement toward diminished restrictions have [sic] been national in scope and the Delaware Code is no longer significantly different from those of a number of other states.

An important mechanism generating change in American corporate law has thus been the competition among the states for charters. Both Delaware (40 per cent of the largest industrial corporations are chartered there) and its competitors candidly admit that the purpose of corporate code revisions has been the attraction of charters to their state in order to produce significant tax revenues. Delaware has benefitted in other ways. Not only is its corporation code an attraction to promoters and management but lawyers find it a hospitable jurisdiction in which to litigate issues of corporate law, with the result that the Wilmington Bar enjoys an unusually lucrative practice for a city of that size.

No one disputes these propositions. Rather, the controversy is over the effect on the governance of many of the nation's major economic units.

The most celebrated exposition of the conventional academic analysis, but avowedly not an original approach, is *Federalism and Corporate Law: Reflections Upon Delaware*, by Professor William Cary[15] of the Columbia University Law School, a former Chairman of the Securities and Exchange Commission. Characterizing Delaware as leading a "movement toward the least common denominator" and a

---

15 [83 YALE L.J. 663 (1974)] . . . .

"race for the bottom," Professor Carry argues that Delaware's lessening of the restrictiveness of its corporation code has left shareholders an easy prey to self-dealing management. . . .

The claim, it is absolutely critical to note, is not that an overriding social goal is sacrificed by state law, but simply that Delaware is preventing *private* parties from optimizing their *private* arrangements. With all due respect both to Professor Cary and to the almost universal academic support for his position, it is implausible on its face. The plausible argument runs in the opposite direction: (1) If Delaware permits corporate management to profit at the expense of shareholders and other states do not, then earnings of Delaware corporations must be less than earnings of comparable corporations chartered in other states and shares in the Delaware corporations must trade at lower prices. (2) Corporations with lower earnings will be at a disadvantage in raising debt or equity capital. (3) Corporations at a disadvantage in the capital market will be at a disadvantage in the product market and their share price will decline, thereby creating a threat of a takeover which may replace management. To avoid this result, corporations must seek out legal systems more attractive to capital. (4) States seeking corporate charters will thus try to provide legal systems which optimize the shareholder-corporation relationship.

The conclusion that Delaware shares sell for less is implicit in Professor Cary's analysis, for if a "higher" legal standard for management conduct will increase investor confidence, investor confidence in Delaware stock must have been less than in stocks of other states for more than a generation. This lack of confidence would have long been reflected in the price of Delaware shares. Moreover, a reduction in the earnings of a corporation will affect its ability to raise debt capital, as well as equity, since the risk of a lender is thereby increased and a higher interest rate will be charged. Delaware corporations, therefore, not only face a lower share price but also must pay higher interest rates.

This analysis is not crucially dependent upon the consumer of securities or lenders understanding the intricacies of corporate law or knowing of the general permissiveness of the Delaware Code. . . . The claim that Delaware is leading a "race for the bottom" has been made so frequently and by so many that it can hardly be described as a carefully guarded secret. Recent work on the stock market strongly suggests that relatively obscure—even confidential—information is transmitted extremely swiftly and almost automatically affects share price. That the impact of a legal system on investors would be known only to law professors . . . seems a rather tenuous proposition.

It is not in the interest of Delaware corporate management or the Delaware treasury for corporations chartered there to be at a disadvantage in raising debt or equity capital relative to corporations chartered in other states. Management must induce investors freely to choose their firm's stock instead of, among other things, stock in companies incorporated in other states or other countries, bonds, bank accounts, certificates of deposit, partnerships (general or limited), individual proprietorships, joint ventures, present consumption, etc. . . . If management is to secure initial capital and have continuous access to ready capital in the future, it must attract investors away from the almost infinite variety of competing opportunities. Moreover, to retain its position management has a powerful incentive to keep the price of stock high enough to prevent takeovers, a result obtained by making the corporation an attractive investment.

The Cary analysis thus seems implausible at an *a priori* level, because, when analyzed, it appears as little more than a claim that Delaware can facilitate the monopolization of the capital market, just as it can grant exclusive franchises for taxicabs in Wilmington. But the market for capital is international in scope and involves an undifferentiated product with no transportation costs. Delaware cannot create barriers which prevent it from flowing to the most attractive investments; any attempt at monopolization will only drive capital from that state.

The fact that other states have found it necessary to change their law in response to Delaware, therefore, strongly suggests that investors do not share Professor Cary's view and in fact believe that they do better under Delaware law than under the laws of the other states.

* * *

Lucian Arye Bebchuk, *Federalism and the Corporation: The Desirable Limits on State Competition in Corporate Law*, 105 Harv. L. Rev. 1435 (1992)*

* * *

II. State Competition and Managers' Opportunism

* * *

. . . The main constraint that is stressed by supporters of state competition, however, is the disciplinary force exerted by various markets. . . . Market discipline, it is argued, generally leads managers to prefer value-maximizing rules even when alternative rules seem to serve better the private interests of managers. . . .

The effectiveness of market discipline, however, varies greatly across issues. In particular, there are two types of issues with respect to which market discipline can hardly be relied on to induce managers to seek value-maximizing rules. These two types of issues are those that are "significantly redistributive" and those that directly affect the strength of market discipline. . . .

B. *Significantly Redistributive Issues*

With respect to redistributive issues, the effectiveness of market discipline in discouraging managers from seeking value-decreasing rules depends on the relationship between the size of the potential transfer involved (the distributive element) and the magnitude of the potential effect on overall value (the efficiency element). . . .

* * *

Consider, for example, a value-decreasing state law rule that reduces by \$1,000,000 the total value of a large company originally worth \$1,000,000,000. This 0.1% reduction in the company's total value is likely to increase only minimally the probability of a takeover bid or proxy contest. Therefore, if the corporate issue governed by this rule is significantly redistributive, and the value-decreasing rule produces a direct benefit to managers worth, for example, \$200,000, the very small increase in the probability of ouster resulting from incorporation in a state with this value-decreasing rule will be unlikely to discourage managers from incorporating in such a state.

* * *

Race for the top adherents also rely on the market for additional capital as a source of market discipline. When managers make incorporation decisions, they may contemplate the need to return to the equity markets to raise additional capital. To the extent that the company's state of incorporation has value-decreasing rules, so the argument goes, the corporation's effort to raise additional capital will be more difficult. Consequently, incorporation in a state with value-decreasing rules will be unattractive to managers.

Incorporation in a state that provides certain value-decreasing rules, however, would not generally prevent a company from raising additional equity. To be sure, fully informed investors would be willing to pay less for shares than they otherwise would. But managers would still be able to raise the same amount of capital simply by offering a larger number of shares (thus reducing the remaining stake of the existing shareholders).

Thus, reincorporation in a state with value-decreasing rules will not prevent the raising of additional capital to finance expansion; it will simply increase the cost to existing shareholders of such financing. . . .

Finally, the effect of future capital needs on managers' decisions is even weaker than the above discussion may indicate because extra capital can be obtained in the form of debt rather than equity. As long as the reincorporation in a state with value-decreasing rules does not change the likelihood that the company will default on its debt, which often would be the case, it will not change the cost of debt. Even if the cost of debt were to increase, this increase, again, would not hinder expansion but only reduce the value of the existing shareholders' stake.

* * *

C. Issues that Directly Affect the Strength of Market Discipline

* * *

With respect to all issues that directly implicate the strength of market discipline, managers making incorporation decisions may well seek rules that weaken this discipline even if these rules are value-decreasing. Consider, for example, whether managers would find attractive a state with a value-decreasing rule that impedes takeover bids and proxy contests. Even if managers recognized that this rule reduces share value, they may well prefer it. Recall that a major reason that managers care about share value is the market for corporate control; all other things being equal, any reduction in share value increases the probability of ouster in a takeover or proxy contest. But in the case of a rule that makes bids and contests more difficult, all other things are not equal. The direct effect of the rule in reducing the likelihood of ouster at any given stock price may be sufficiently significant so that, despite the accompanying reduction in share value, the probability of ouster with the rule will be substantially smaller than without it. To take an extreme case, consider a state law rule that completely insulates managers from tender offers and thereby reduces shareholder value. In considering the appeal of this rule, managers are unlikely to be deterred by the threat of a takeover. The rule will completely eliminate this very threat, and thus the likelihood of a takeover will be smaller with this value-decreasing rule than without it.

* * *

E. Companies with a Dominant Shareholder

* * *

Similarly, market forces can do very little to discourage the managers of a company with a controlling shareholder from seeking value-decreasing rules that transfer value to a controller. The market for corporate control exerts no disciplinary force because, with a dominant shareholder in place, takeover bids and proxy contests are not possible. . . .

* * *

2. A World with Both Initial Incorporations and Reincorporations

* * *

It remains to consider, however, the incentives of those states that do not presently serve as domicile for many public companies. . . . In particular, such a state, say Kansas, may seek to attract initial incorporations by adopting efficient rules with respect to the set of issues *X*. In this way, so the argument goes, Kansas would be able to attract a significant fraction of the initial incorporations taking place. Over time, Kansas would become home to many public companies, and these companies would be governed by efficient rules with respect to the set of issues *X*.

It should be pointed out at the outset that, for such a strategy to have a chance of succeeding, the price in initial public offerings of Kansas companies must reflect the value of the efficient rules offered by Kansas. Now note that the Kansas rules are likely to be "innovative" by virtue of their departure from the familiar rules that Delaware and other states with many in-state incorporations offer. And there are reasons to believe that the pricing of "innovative" rules is especially likely to be inaccurate.[140] But in any event, let us grant that buyers of stock would be perfectly informed about the rules offered by Kansas. As explained below, even under this strong assumption, it is far from clear that the considered strategy would work.

To start with, even if Kansas offers efficient rules with respect to the set of issues *X*, Delaware law may still, on the whole, be better for shareholders and thus more attractive to initial incorporators. . . . [E]ven if Kansas imitates all of the rules provided by Delaware with respect to issues that do not belong to the set *X*, Delaware still offers certain significant advantages such as a substantial body of precedents and an experienced judiciary.

More importantly, buyers of stock in the initial public offering of a Kansas company will not expect the company to be governed forever by the efficient rules that Kansas now offers with respect to the set of issues *X*. Accordingly, they will substantially discount the value that they attach to the fact that these efficient rules now govern the company. The buyers will have such expectations for two reasons. First, although the company is now incorporated in Kansas, it later may reincorporate in some other state, such as Delaware.[143] Second, Kansas may, at some later point in time, replace its current value-maximizing rules for the governance of *X* with the rules in force in Delaware. . . .

* * *

G. Conclusion: Managers' Opportunism and the Shortcomings of State Competition

This Part has identified several types of issues with respect to which state competition is likely to produce value-decreasing rules. First, state competition is likely to work poorly with respect to issues that are significantly redistributive, including self-dealing, taking of corporate opportunities, and insider trading. Second, state competition may well produce undesirable results with respect to issues that directly implicate the strength of market discipline, including the regulation of corporate takeovers and proxy contests. Third, state competition is likely to produce value-decreasing rules for the governance of issues that involve potential transfers between public shareholders and a dominant shareholder, including going-private freezeouts, parent-subsidiary mergers, and the allocation of opportunities between parent companies and subsidiaries.

140 . . . [Professor] Gordon argues that investors will view innovations with suspicion and therefore tend to draw negative inferences from departures from prevailing corporate law rules. Consequently, investors will pay less for the stock of companies governed by innovative arrangements. . . .

143 The fact that a reincorporation would require a vote of shareholder approval does not eliminate this possibility. Managers may be able to obtain the required approval even if the move to Delaware would be value-decreasing. This may result from the problem of uninformed voting, . . . or from the problem of distorted voting (as a result of the managers' coupling the reincorporation proposal with some other measure). . . .

With respect to all of these issues, state competition can be expected systematically to produce rules that favor managers and dominant shareholders more than would the value-maximizing rules. This conclusion in no way depends on a direct assessment of the merits of Delaware's or other states' law governing these issues. It simply follows from a recognition of the structural forces at work in the state charter competition.

* * *

III. State Competition and Externalities

* * *

. . . When a state designs consumer law, tort law, or employment law to govern operations conducted within the state, it will likely pay attention to the effects of the adopted rules on the state's consumers, potential tort victims, and employees. But the state in these cases can do so without fear that companies will be able to avoid the adopted rules while continuing their operations within the state. By contrast, companies can—simply by reincorporating elsewhere, without any change in their operations—completely avoid their state's corporate law rules.

* * *

2. *Protection of Creditors.*—Let us now turn to corporate law rules governing the relationship between a company and its creditors. Clearly, if a corporate law rule can be designed to transfer value from creditors to shareholders, then shareholders may well find the rule attractive even if it is inefficient (that is, produces a gain to the shareholders that is smaller than the creditors' loss). Therefore, to the extent that rules affecting creditors are left to state law, the concern arises that state competition will produce inefficient rules that diverge systematically from the socially desirable ones in ways that are unfavorable to creditors.

To be sure, it may be argued that state corporate law will not provide rules that are harmful to creditors—that is, rules that transfer value from creditors to shareholders—because creditors are able to protect themselves contractually. Lenders, so the argument goes, will anticipate the effects of state law rules and will charge an appropriate interest rate. . . .

Not all creditors, however, can protect themselves contractually against the adverse consequences of state law rules. For one thing, there are involuntary creditors such as tort victims. . . . In addition, there are some voluntary, contractual creditors that cannot protect themselves against the adverse consequences of corporate law rules. The transactions of these creditors with a company may be sufficiently small in value to make it difficult, given the informational and transactional costs involved, to adjust the terms of trade to counteract the state law rules governing the company. Because these two groups of creditors are unable to protect themselves contractually, it is possible to design corporate law rules that transfer value from these creditors to shareholders. And states would have an incentive to offer precisely such rules.

To illustrate this general point, consider the rules that govern the amount of dividends that companies may pay out to shareholders. When a company does not have "enough" capital, a payment of dividends may transfer to the shareholders some of the capital that would be otherwise used to pay debtholders. Regulation of corporate dividend policy is an important corporate law issue and traditionally has been accomplished by state law. As is well recognized, the limits on dividends established by state law are generally so weak and ineffectual as to have virtually no practical significance. To be sure, companies often agree to much stricter limitations on their dividend policy as part of their contracts with banks and bondholders. But why does state law not go somewhat in that direction and establish some basic meaningful limits on dividend payments? This Article suggests a simple answer: because companies are free to choose their states of incorporation (and thus the state corporate law that governs them), states have an incentive to offer shareholders rules that impose practically no significant restrictions on the payment of dividends.

* * *

Notes and Questions

1. In evaluating the ability of other states to compete with Delaware for incorporations, Professor Bebchuk notes Delaware's advantages beyond the specific rules of its corporation law. These include a substantial body of precedent interpreting its law, and courts with considerable experience in dealing with corporate litigation. While Professor Bebchuk uses this fact to rebut the defense of state competition put forward by Professor Winter, does this undercut as well the notion that Delaware must kowtow to managers in designing its corporate law? For a broader consideration of how Delaware seeks to create an attractive environment for incorporation see Romano, *The State Competition Debate in Corporate Law*, 8 CARDOZO L. REV. 709 (1987).

2. Professor Winter notes that not only the Delaware treasury benefits from encouraging incorporation in Delaware, but so do attorneys practicing in the state. On the other hand, do the attorneys in Delaware necessarily have an interest in rules which would minimize the exposure of corporate management to corporate litigation? For an exploration of this question see Macey & Miller, *Toward an Interest Group Theory of Delaware Corporate Law*, 65 TEX. L. REV. 469 (1987).

3. Even if one agrees with Professor Bebchuk about the failings of state competition, is there anything better? One possibility would be a federal corporations law. What incentives would the federal government have to create optimum rules of corporate law?

Alternately, who says the laws of the state of incorporation must govern the internal affairs of a company, no matter where it does business and most of its owners reside? Recall the discussion of California's pre-1931 law in Professor Blumberg's article. California purportedly made shareholders of non-California corporations personally liable for debts incurred in California. Notice how this would meet the concerns over externalities raised by Professor Bebchuk. What about protecting shareholders from pro-management rules? Again, California has attempted an aggressive approach. See Halloran & Hammer, *Application of California Corporation Law to Foreign Corporations—Section 2115 of the New General Corporation Law*, 23 UCLA L. REV. 1282 (1976). On the other hand, what problem results if more than one state attempts to dictate rules of governance?

C. The Purposes of Corporate Law

The material thus far leads one to a more fundamental question: What is corporations law trying to achieve? For example, both sides in the state competition debate recognize that such competition has produced more "permissive" corporations laws. The differing claims as to whether this is good or bad reflect an underlying difference in views as to what the law should do. Professor Winter writes from a "contractarian" perspective, which emphasizes private choice. Yet, this raises an obvious question: If the rules governing a corporation are whatever the participants agree, then why bother to have any corporations law at all? Professor Bebchuk writes from a perspective which presupposes the need for government regulation to protect shareholders and creditors. This raises the question of when and why shareholders and creditors cannot protect themselves. The two article excerpts in this section address these two issues.

Frank H. Easterbrook and Daniel R. Fischel, *The Corporate Contract*, 89 COLUM. L. REV. 1416 (1989)*

* * *

D. *Why Is There Corporate Law?*

One natural question after all this business of corporation-as-contract is: why law? Why not just abolish corporate law and let people negotiate whatever contracts they please? The short but not entirely satisfactory answer is that corporate law is a set of terms available off-the-rack so that participants in corporate ventures can save the cost of contracting. There are lots of terms, such as rules for voting, establishing quorums, and so on, that almost everyone will want to adopt. Corporate codes and existing judicial decisions supply these terms "for free" to every corporation, enabling the venturers to concentrate on matters that are specific to their undertaking. Even when they work through all the issues they expect will arise, they are apt to miss something. All sorts

---

* This article originally appeared at 89 Column. L. Rev. 1416 (1989). Reprinted by permission.

of complexities will arise later. Corporate law—and in particular the fiduciary principle enforced by courts—fills in the blanks and oversights with the terms that people would have bargained for had they anticipated the problems and been able to transact costlessly in advance. On this view corporate law supplements but never displaces actual bargains—save in situations of third-party effects or latecomer terms.

And there is a ready source of guidance for corporate codes and judicial decisions to draw on in filling in blanks (or establishing background terms): the deals people actually strike when they bargain over the subject. These actual bargains offer models for other firms too. It is possible that firms that have come to actual bargains on a subject are different from firms that remain silent; the very difference is the reason for the bargain. Possible, but unlikely; differences in transaction costs or perspicacity are more plausible, unless there is some identifiable difference that calls for different rules of governance. Larger firms will find it worthwhile to specify things others leave open, because the gains from resolution increase with the size of the firm. As amateur investors benefit from the work of professionals, so smaller firms and courts can benefit from the work of professional negotiators who solve problems for larger firms.

The story is not complete, however, because it still does not answer the question "why law?". Why don't law firms or corporate service bureaus or investment banks compile sets of terms on which corporations may be constructed? They can peddle these terms and recover the cost of working through all of the problems. Yet it is costly for the parties (or any private supplier of rules) to ponder unusual situations and dicker for the adoption of terms. Parties or their surrogates must identify problems and then transact in sufficient detail to solve them. This may all be wasted effort if the problem does not occur. Because change is the one constant of corporate life, waste is a certainty. Often the type of problem that the firm encounters does not occur to anyone until after the venture is under way. Court systems have a comparative advantage in supplying answers to questions that do not occur in time to be resolved ex ante. Common law systems need not answer questions unless they occur. This is an economizing device; it avoids working through problems that do not arise. The accumulation of cases dealing with unusual problems then supplies a level of detail that is costly to duplicate through private bargaining. To put it differently, "contractual" terms for many kinds of problems turn out to be public goods!

Even if law firms, investment banks, or other private suppliers of solutions could specify optimal solutions, they could not readily supply answers for all marginal cases. No one firm could capture all of the gains from working out all problems in advance, because other firms could copy the answers without paying the creator. If the value of new solutions is hard to appropriate, and if the gain from private bargaining is small, people will leave things to be worked out later. As we have emphasized repeatedly, what should be worked out and supplied by corporate law is the rule that, if uniformly applied, will maximize the value of corporate endeavor as a whole. The law completes open-ended contracts. There is no reason why it should be used to impose a term that defeats actual bargains or reduces the venturers' joint wealth.

* * *

Notes and Questions

1. Professors Easterbrook and Fischel provide a rationale for corporations law creating default rules—in other words, rules to govern issues the parties neglected to address in their agreement. While this goal is unexceptional, there is a difficulty in determining how courts and legislatures should go about arriving at such rules. The piece from Professors Easterbrook and Fischel provides two, not necessarily consistent, suggestions. One is empirical: Look at what other parties, whose agreements covered the issue, did. The other is more theoretical: Come up with a rule that, if uniformly applied, would maximize the value of the corporate endeavor as a whole. In evaluating these suggestions, one might ask what one is trying to achieve in selecting a default rule. For example, is the object to try and guess what the parties actually would have agreed to had they addressed the issue in their contract? If so, what basis do Professors Easterbrook and Fischel have for assuming that parties would have picked a rule that generally maximizes wealth for the corporate endeavor? Suppose that, while the total wealth of all involved in the corporation goes up by virtue of the rule, one participant's wealth goes down? Might there be other goals—such as achieving a "fair" distribution of the wealth generated by the corporation—that would be important to real world participants? Also, how are judges and legislatures supposed to figure out what is the wealth maximizing rule? Alternately, perhaps one might attempt to achieve different goals in the selection of default rules. For example, what sort of rule might be appropriate if the goal is to get parties to avoid leaving gaps in their agreements? See Ayres & Gertner, *Filling Gaps in Incomplete Contracts: An Economic Theory of Default Rules*, 99 YALE L.J. 87 (1989)(suggesting in some cases courts use default rules which penalize parties for leaving gaps in their contracts).

2. Professors Easterbrook and Fischel contend that the law should fill gaps, but not displace the parties' bargain. They make two possible exceptions: third party effects and "latecomer terms." We have seen reference to third party effects before—recall Professor Bebchuk's discussion of the effects which shareholder favored rules can have on creditors, such as tort victims, not in a position to protect themselves by contract. Latecomer terms refer to the ability of the majority in a corporation to amend the contract. Again, Professor Bebchuk provides an example when he notes the ability to change the state of incorporation—and hence the governing law—by virtue of a majority vote of the shareholders. Why might these two areas be appropriate subjects for mandatory rules?

As a key step in their rationale for government provided default rules, Professors Easterbrook and Fischel argue that judicial resolution of conflicts between corporate participants constitutes a "public good." A public good is one in which it is impractical to exclude other parties from gaining the benefit. A classic example is a streetlight. If government does not provide such goods, often private parties will not either—after all, each person might decide to wait for someone else to put up a streetlight and then enjoy the light for free. Might the public goods rationale create an argument for mandatory rather than just default rules? See Gordon, *The Mandatory Structure of Corporate Law*, 89 COLUM. L. REV. 1549 (1989) (arguing that allowing firms to deviate from standard terms will undermine the value of the standard terms by decreasing the frequency of judicial interpretation).

The following article takes a much broader view of the need for mandatory corporate law rules.

Melvin Aron Eisenberg, *The Structure of Corporation Law*, 89 COLUM. L. REV. 1461 (1989)*

* * *

This Article will consider the legal rules that directly concern the internal organization of the corporation and the conduct of corporate actors.[1] Viewed in terms of their form, these rules fall into three basic categories. *Enabling rules* give legal effect to rules that corporate actors adopt in a specified manner. *Suppletory* or *default rules* govern defined issues unless corporate actors adopt other rules in a specified manner. *Mandatory rules* govern defined issues in a manner that cannot be varied by corporate actors.

The major purpose of this Article is to develop the normative principles that determine which of the legal rules that concern the internal organization of the corporation and the conduct of corporate actors should be enabling or suppletory, and which should be mandatory. . . .

In practice, the application of these elements depends largely on the subject matter of the rule and the nature of the institutional setting. In terms of the nature of the institutional setting, I will distinguish between closely held corporations, publicly held corporations, and corporations that are about to go public. In terms of subject matter, I will distinguish between structural, distributional, and fiduciary rules. *Structural rules* govern the allocation of decisionmaking power among various corporate organs and agents and the conditions for the exercise of decisionmaking power; the allocation of control over corporate organs and agents; and the flow of information concerning the actions of corporate organs and agents. *Distributional rules* govern the distribution of assets (including earnings) to shareholders. *Fiduciary rules* govern the duties of managers and controlling shareholders. These three types of rules will be referred to collectively as *constitutive rules*, and that term will include both rules determined by law and rules determined by private action.

---

* Reprinted by permission.

1 These rules do not exhaust corporation law. For example, some rules of corporation law concern the relationship between the corporation and its organs on the one hand, and the outside world on the other. A leading example is the rule that shareholders have limited liability. Rules of this type often have an indirect effect on the internal organization of the corporation, but will not be considered in this Article.

* * *

I. Closely Held Corporations

I begin with closely held corporations—corporations that have a small number of shareholders, most of whom either participate in or directly monitor corporate management.

A. *Structural and Distributional Rules*

In closely held corporations, shareholders often will bargain out at least some structural and distributional rules. It is a general principle of law that a bargain should normally be enforced according to its terms, without regard to whether it is reasonable or fair. . . . The reasons for the bargain principle usually apply to bargains among the shareholders in a closely held corporation concerning the corporation's structural and distributional rules. Accordingly, at its core the law governing structural and distributional rules in closely held corporations should be enabling and suppletory, rather than mandatory.

This is essentially the position taken by modern corporate law. Modern case law has moved in the direction of enabling shareholders in closely held corporations to bargain out their own structural and distributional rules. Many of the modern statutes explicitly validate such rules for those closely held corporations that elect special statutory treatment.

At the periphery, however, a special type of mandatory legal rule should apply....

* * *

. . . It is almost impossible for contracting parties to assess adequately the future costs and benefits in a fluid long-term relationship, because the tree of events will branch far beyond the ideas of the future that will be conceived when the contract is made. Furthermore, corporations by their nature involve a form of activity in which uncertainty plays an essential role. Because of the difficulty of predicting and planning for future events and their impact on a business enterprise, an opportunistic shareholder who controls one or more aspects of a closely held corporation will often find ways to exploit bargained-out structural and distributional rules that seemed both fair and complete at the time of the bargain. It is almost impossible to deal adequately with this potential for ex post opportunism by ex ante contracting. Therefore, although the purpose of enforcing bargains is to protect expectations, the full enforcement of bargained-out structural and distributional rules in a closely held corporation may actually violate fair expectations. Accordingly, while the law governing the structural and distributional elements of closely held corporations should be largely enabling and suppletory, corporation law should also provide mandatory rules that empower the courts to override bargains concerning structural and distributional terms when necessary to prevent opportunism and protect probable fair expectations.

Modern corporation law has taken just this position. Both the courts and the legislatures have fashioned mandatory rules that limit the full force of bargains concerning structural and distributional rules in closely held corporations.

Some statutes simply limit the duration of such bargains. . . .

A more widespread approach, reflected in both cases and statutes, provides for judicial intervention when enforcement of bargained-out structural and distributional rules would defeat a shareholder's fair expectations. . . .

* * *

B. *Fiduciary Rules*

Structural and distributional legal rules for closely held corporations should be enabling and suppletory at the core but mandatory at the periphery. In contrast, fiduciary legal rules for closely held corporations should be mandatory at the core but enabling and suppletory at the periphery. The reasons behind these principles are straightforward. The bargain principle assumes that contracting parties are fully informed, or at least not systematically underinformed. Parties who bargain over structural and distributional rules are likely to understand the consequences of their bargain in most cases, at least over the short term, and mandatory rules are therefore needed only as a backstop. However, bargains to relax materially the fiduciary rules set by law would likely be systematically underinformed even over the short term. Even if the shareholders understood the content of the rules whose protection they attempted to waive—which is unlikely—they still could not begin to foresee the varying circumstances to which such a waiver would be applicable. Any such waiver would therefore inevitably permit unanticipated opportunistic behavior.

Some bargained-out fiduciary rules do not present the dangers of systematic error and exploitation. Bargains to change a legal rule that is not congruent with current concepts of fairness or that does not afford any real protection to shareholders, such as the old rules that interested transactions were voidable without regard to fairness or that interested directors could not be counted in determining a quorum, fall into this category. In some cases, a bargained-out fiduciary rule is specific, easily understood, and not easily susceptible to exploitation. A rule that clearly specifies a type of business venture that will not be considered a corporate opportunity may fall in this category. Similarly, shareholder approval of a specific conflict-of-interest transaction usually does not present the dangers of systematically underinformed consent and exploitation, because the approval relates to a specific event rather than to an unknowable future. In these peripheral cases, bargained-out fiduciary rules should be enforceable.

The law reflects these principles. . . .

II. Publicly Held Corporations

I turn now to publicly held corporations, by which I mean corporations that have a large number of shareholders, most of whom neither participate in the management of the corporation nor directly monitor corporate management. . . . Under these conditions, bargaining among the shareholders, or between managers and the shareholders as a body, is virtually impossible. Accordingly, most of the constitutive rules of such corporations are determined not by contract, but by law or by private bureaucratic rulemaking—for example, by managerial orders, by board or committee resolutions, by board-adopted by-laws, or by board determination of governance terms in preferred stock, stock rights, or debt instruments.

In such corporations, therefore, the principles that determine which legal rules should be enabling or suppletory and which should be mandatory depend on the force and limits of forms of private ordering other than bargain and contract. The force and limits of these forms of private ordering in publicly held corporations, in turn, depend very largely on the impact of the potential self-interest of top managers of such corporations and on the extent to which this impact is controlled by market forces other than bargain and contract.

A. *Divergencies of Interest*

The interests of the shareholders and managers in publicly held corporations converge in many respects: in general, if the shareholders do well, so will the managers. As in any principal-agent relationship, however, the interests of shareholders and managers also diverge. All agents have a potential interest in working at a slack pace and in avoiding the effort and discomfort involved in adapting to changed circumstances, such as the emergence of new technologies. This is the problem known as *shirking*. All agents have a potential interest in diverting the principal's assets to their own use through unfair self-dealing. This is the problem of *traditional conflicts of interest.*

. . . [T]op corporate managers have the power to give expression to still a third potential divergence of interest: an interest in maintaining and enhancing their positions even at the shareholders' expense. I will refer to instances of this type of divergence of interest as *positional conflicts.*

Positional conflicts may be expressed in a great variety of ways. For example, top managers may make it particularly difficult for anyone to objectively monitor their performance. They may impose high barriers to their own removal for inefficiency or other reasons. They may seek to increase corporate size as a way to maximize their power, prestige, and salary, even if an increase in corporate size does not increase shareholder wealth. They may seek to maximize the cash and other resources that they command, even when distributions to the shareholders would be more efficient. They may diversify the firm as a means to reduce the riskiness of their human-capital investments, even when diversification of the firm is not in the interest of shareholders because shareholders can diversify their own risks through portfolio management.

* * *

The divergencies of interest between corporate agents and shareholders, and the special problem of positional conflicts, explain why some constitutive rules that govern publicly held corporations should be enabling or suppletory while others should be mandatory. The legal rules that govern the internal organization of the corporation and the conduct of corporate actors *below the level of top managers* should by and large be enabling or suppletory. Top managers have both the self-interest and the power to install constitutive rules that will efficiently determine the roles, coordination, supervision, and monitoring of lower corporate agents and constrain those agents from giving expression to their own interests in preference to the interests of the shareholders.

In contrast, top managers of publicly held corporations have little incentive to adopt rules that put constraints on their own positions. . . . The core fiduciary and structural rules that govern material divergencies of interest of top managers in publicly held corporations, therefore, should be neither determined nor subject to material variation by the action of managers or managerial organs. The reason for this principle is not that legislatures or judges know more about such rules than top managers; they may or may not. Rather, the reason is that in this as in other areas of law, agents whose interests may materially diverge from the interests of their principals should not have the power to unilaterally determine or materially vary the rules that govern those divergencies of interest.

B. *The Limits of Shareholder Consent*

This first principle—that the core fiduciary and structural rules that govern material divergencies of interest of top managers in publicly held corporations should be neither determined nor subject to material variation by managers or managerial organs—spills into a second. Such rules should also normally not be subject to determination or material variation even with shareholder approval. Allowing such rules to be determined or materially varied on the basis of shareholder approval would effectively undercut the first principle, because, under current law and practice, shareholder consent to rules proposed by top managers in publicly held corporations may be either nominal, tainted by a conflict of interest, coerced or impoverished.

1. *Nominal consent.*—For many shareholders, the cost of reading and understanding each proposal in the proxy materials will exceed the likely economic effect of any given proposal. For such shareholders, it is rational not to read any proposals. Shareholders receive a number of management proposals in proxy statements. Because the interests of managers and shareholders converge to a significant extent, and because many proposals relate to housekeeping details (such as approval of auditors), shareholders have reason to believe that the typical management proposal will be value-increasing. . . .

* * *

2. *Consent that is tainted by a conflict of interest.*—Shareholder consent that is not nominal may nevertheless be tainted by a conflict of interest. Approximately fifty percent of the stock in publicly held corporations is owned by institutional investors. Many institutional investors have ties to management that inhibit voting against a management proposal. For example, if the trust department of a bank holds the stock of C Corporation in a pension portfolio, and C is also a client of the bank's commercial department, a trust officer will think long and hard before voting against a proposal made by C's management. . . .

. . . Managers often have significant holdings in their own corporations, and they are seldom if ever prohibited from voting their holdings in favor of a proposal that advances their own interests. Even more to the point, in many corporations a controlling block is held by one or more corporate or individual shareholders whose interests may diverge from those of the noncontrolling shareholders. . . .

3. *Coerced consent.*—Shareholder consent that is neither nominal nor tainted by a conflict of interest may nevertheless be coerced. For example, management may threaten to withhold approval of an action that is in the shareholders' best interests, such as an increase in dividends, unless the shareholders approve an unrelated management proposal. . . .

* * *

The many limits on the meaningfulness of shareholder consent do not compel the conclusion that shareholder voting is never meaningful. Some individual holders may read the proxy statement and vote their own stock. Some institutional holders have no conflicting ties to management. Many institutional holders that do have conflicts of interest will nevertheless vote in the interests of their beneficiaries, either because of a sense of moral duty or because of legal pressures or pressures to maximize their returns. As a result, management proposals that will have obvious and very large value-decreasing effects are unlikely to be adopted by shareholders, and even proposals that have smaller negative effects may not always be adopted. Furthermore, it is entirely conceivable that with further increases in institutional ownership, and changes in the moral, legal, and financial pressures that affect voting by institutional owners, the significance of shareholder voting will change in the future. Under prevailing conditions, however, the limits on the meaningfulness of shareholder consent are so substantial that allowing those rules to be determined or materially varied by top managers with shareholder approval often would be functionally equivalent to allowing those rules to be unilaterally determined or materially varied by top managers.

C. *The Structure of the Law Governing Publicly Held Corporations*

The general principle, then, is that in publicly held corporations, mandatory legal rules should govern those core fiduciary and structural areas in which the interests of shareholders and top managers may materially diverge. The content of these rules should reflect the basic types of potential divergence. To deal with traditional conflicts of interest, mandatory rules should impose a duty of fair dealing, should provide for disclosure of self-interested transactions, and should establish an effective enforcement mechanism. To deal with the problem of shirking, mandatory rules should impose a duty of care. As to these matters, the principle that governs publicly held corporations is the same as the principle that governs closely held corporations: fiduciary rules should be mandatory at the core.

In the case of publicly held corporations, however, an additional principle comes into play to deal with positional conflicts, which involve the most serious of the divergencies of interest between top managers and shareholders. In such corporations, core structural rules double as fiduciary rules, because it is structural rules that address positional conflicts. Accordingly, in publicly held corporations core structural rules as well as core fiduciary rules should be mandatory.

* * *

The core mandatory rules should operate to check positional conflicts without preventing advantageous corporate transactions. To this end, the core structural rules should require mechanisms for accountability and disclosure for top executives, shareholder approval of certain transactions, and appraisal rights for certain transactions, but they should not regulate the content of corporate transactions. Because mandatory rules generally should not regulate the content of transactions, distributional rules should generally be enabling, except as required to protect the interests of creditors.

The legal rules that actually govern publicly held corporations correspond reasonably well to the legal rules that should govern such corporations.

* * *

E. *The Effect of Markets and Other Forms of Private Ordering*

A second class of arguments that might be made against the principles developed so far is that market forces so adequately align the interests of top managers and shareholders and so adequately address the problem of managerial inefficiency that mandatory legal rules to address these issues are unnecessary and indeed undesirable.

* * *

1. *Product Markets.*—At the outset, it is occasionally argued that managers are severely inhibited from pursuing their own interests or acting inefficiently because product markets often will render insolvent any firm that does not minimize costs. This argument seriously overstates the power of product markets. . . . Most publicly held corporations have sufficient resources and market power to absorb substantial losses resulting from inefficiency, gross miscalculations, or unfair self-dealing.

2. *Management Compensation.*—A more weighty argument is that the interests of managers and shareholders are adequately aligned by executive compensation, because such compensation is closely tied to shareholder gain. It seems likely that compensation has some alignment effect. . . .

* * *

In short, the argument that the interests of managers and shareholders are adequately aligned by executive compensation is descriptively inaccurate because the dollar amounts involved are trivial or immaterial. Moreover, this argument is based on a fallacy. The fallacy, which runs through a great deal of the literature on the alignment effect of market forces, is that mandatory rules are unnecessary because *on average* the interests of managers and shareholders are adequately aligned by market forces. I shall call this the average-manager fallacy.

* * *

. . . [E]ven if a given market mechanism does align the interests of most top managers and shareholders in a statistically significant and material way, such a relationship does not in itself tell us that mandatory rules are unnecessary. For example, even if the correlation between executive compensation and shareholder gain was both very high and material (which it is not), that would provide only limited help in determining the shape of corporate law unless we also know the extent to which the relationship holds throughout the executive population.

3. *Inside Stock Ownership.*—Closely related to the argument that the interests of shareholders and managers are adequately aligned by executive compensation is the argument that those interests are adequately aligned by managers' inside stock ownership, that is ownership of stock in their own corporations. . . .

* * *

. . . [T]he argument that inside holdings have the effect of adequately aligning the interests of shareholders and managers, like the argument that executive compensation has that effect, reflects the average-manager fallacy. . . .

Moreover, even relatively significant inside holdings will have only a limited alignment effect in the three major areas in which the interests of top managers may diverge from those of shareholders. Take first the problem of unfair self-dealing. Assume that a manager who contemplates unfair self-dealing has a large inside holding. The manager's gain from the unfair self-dealing will nevertheless almost invariably swamp the resulting loss in the value in his stock, because the manager will normally realize the full value of the unfair self-dealing, but will lose only a fraction of the value of his stock. . . . Inside holdings also will have little or no effect on efficiency. Few if any inefficient managers are likely to believe themselves inefficient. . . .

Finally, inside holdings will have little or no effect on positional conflicts. Financial gain is only one incentive for top managers. Other and often far more important incentives include the sense of accomplishment, the self-esteem, and the power that accompany a top management position. The combined financial and nonfinancial value that a top manager places on his position is almost certain to swamp any possible loss in his inside holdings that results from actions he takes to maintain and enhance that position, even in the unlikely event that he believes those actions to be value-decreasing.

4. *The Market for Managers, the Prospect of Promotion, and the Risk of Discharge.*—Still another device that is said to adequately align the interests of managers and shareholders, and adequately address the problem of managerial inefficiency, is the market for managers. The idea here is that managers who perform poorly will find it difficult to market themselves.

There is in fact a market for middle and lower managers, although it is somewhat limited because of skill specificity and asymmetric information. However, it is top managers with whom corporation law should be and is concerned, and for these actors the market for managers, such as it is, is of limited relevance. That market is not relevant to the chief executive officer, because he is almost invariably in his final period as a manager. It is of limited relevance to top executives other than the chief executive officer, because their major concern is satisfying the chief executive. It is not relevant to outside directors, because outside directorships are normally sideline activities.

* * *

5. *The Market for Corporate Control.*—Another market mechanism that has been claimed adequately to align the interests of shareholders and managers, and adequately to address the problem of managerial inefficiency, is the market for corporate control—that is, the takeover market. The now-familiar idea is that if the managers of a corporation act in their own interests rather than the shareholders' interests, or are inefficient, a third party can make gains by bidding for the corporation's stock at a price that is above the market price, but below the value the stock would have if the corporation was properly managed.

* * *

To begin with, the takeover market has very little impact on traditional conflicts of interest. A hostile takeover bid cannot succeed unless it includes a premium that is significantly above the market price. . . . Because of the need to expend these large premiums and fees, a takeover bid will almost never be economically justified if the bidder's only strategy is to end unfair self-dealing by incumbent managers. . . .

The takeover market also has only a limited effect on positional conflicts. The threat of takeover will not cause managers to avoid taking actions to maintain and enhance their positions at the shareholders' expense. Indeed, just the reverse has occurred. . . .

* * *

6. *The Market for Capital.*—Another market-forces argument is that the market for capital will adequately constrain managers from adopting constitutive rules that are in the managers' interests but against the shareholders' interests. I shall refer to such rules as managerial rules. The idea of the argument is as follows: The adoption of a managerial rule would reduce the price of the corporation's stock. Reducing the price of the corporation's stock would increase the cost of the corporation's capital. Increasing the cost of the corporation's capital will lead either to bankruptcy of the corporation through the operation of the product market or ouster of management through the operation of the takeover market.

* * *

a. *Effect on the Product Market.*—To begin with, a corporation's ability to compete in the product market will not be impaired at all by the adoption of a managerial rule unless its out-of-pocket expenses are increased or its cash flow is reduced. However, many managerial rules are value-decreasing not because they increase present out-of-pocket expenses or decrease cash flow, but because they may lead to reduced profits at some point in the future or create the possibility of a future redistribution of corporate profits from shareholders to managers. . . .

* * *

Furthermore, a value-decreasing managerial rule may have little or no impact on out-of-pocket expenses even in the future. To begin with, few publicly held corporations raise capital by issuing new stock. A primary source of capital for most corporations is internally generated cash. . . .

* * *

In short, the adoption of a managerial rule would rarely lead to bankruptcy in the product market, because such a rule would rarely have any present impact on out-of-pocket costs and would often have no significant impact even on future out-of-pocket costs. Any impact that such a rule did have on out-of-pocket costs would normally be swamped by the slack in the product market.

b. *Effect on the Takeover Market.*—Although a managerial rule that has no impact on expenses or current cash flow may have no effect on the corporation's ability to compete in the product market, such a rule may cause the price of the corporation's stock to fall, which in turn could have an effect in the takeover market. But any decrease in the value of a corporation's stock that results from the adoption of a managerial rule will be typically either not measurable or relatively small and relatively small effects on the market price of a corporation's stock will not trigger a hostile takeover because they will be swamped by the huge premium and fees required. Therefore, the capital market, operating through either the product or takeover markets, will seldom if ever prevent managers from adopting managerial rules.

* * *

F. *The Pricing Argument*

There is a third type of argument that may be made against the principle that mandatory legal rules should govern areas in which the interests of shareholders and top managers may materially diverge. This argument proceeds as follows: Under the efficient-market hypothesis, the market accurately prices all constitutive rules. Therefore, if a corporation adopts a constitutive rule that unduly favors the interests of top managers at the expense of shareholder interests, the effect will be impounded in the price of the corporation's stock. Accordingly, a shareholder in a publicly held corporation cannot fairly complain that any given rule unduly favors management interests, because even if it does, the shareholder has gotten what he paid for.

* * *

The pricing argument has some force in the case of corporations that are about to go public, but it will not withstand scrutiny in the context of publicly held corporations. The argument is that a shareholder who buys stock cannot fairly complain that the corporation has a suboptimal managerial rule, because even if it does, the shareholder has gotten what he paid for. By its terms, therefore, the argument has no application in cases where there are shareholders who own stock in a corporation before a suboptimal managerial rule is adopted, and do not meaningfully consent to the new rule. That would nearly always be the case in corporations whose stock is already publicly held.

III. Corporations That Are About To Go Public

Assume now that a corporation adopts a constitutive rule just as it is about to go public. Two very different claims can then be made. First, it can be claimed that the pricing argument is now relevant, because all public shareholders will buy their stock after the rule has been adopted. Second, a market-forces claim can be made, along the following lines: Suppose an owner-manager holds all of the corporation's stock, and he intends to sell all his stock to the public and drop his managerial position. He then has every incentive to adopt constitutive rules that will maximize the value of the corporation's stock, and no incentive to adopt rules that will decrease that value.

Admittedly, this is not the typical case. Usually, an owner-manager intends to retain some stock and his managerial position. Even in that case, it can be argued, an owner-manager would not have a financial incentive to adopt managerial rules that would decrease the value of the corporation's stock. Although he would reap the benefit of such rules in his managerial capacity, he would suffer the impact of those rules in his ownership capacity, because the rules would decrease both the value of the stock he retained and the price of the stock he sold. By aggregating the pricing and market-force claims, the argument can be made that corporations that are about to go public should be permitted to vary core fiduciary or structural rules.

This line of reasoning, which I will call the initial-public-offering argument, does not prevail under current law. In general, the core fiduciary and structural rules that are mandatory for publicly held corporations are no less mandatory for corporations that might attempt to vary those rules before going public. An examination of the limits of the initial-public-offering argument shows why this should be so.

To begin with, the argument assumes that such variations, if permitted, would be accurately priced. In fact, however, there is no direct evidence that all such variations would be accurately priced, and some direct evidence that they would not. It must be borne in mind that the pricing and market for stock offered in an initial public offering ("IPO") may differ substantially from the pricing and market for stock that is already publicly traded. The price of stock that is already publicly traded is determined by the intersection of the valuations of a huge number of buyers and sellers, whose random biases may tend to cancel one another out. In contrast, the price of stock offered in an initial public offering is typically determined by negotiation between the corporation and an underwriter on the basis of general market conditions and preliminary expressions of interest by potential investors, many of whom would probably be unaware of the corporation's constitutive rules. . . .

* * *

Even assuming that despite all these problems variations in core fiduciary or structural rules would in fact be priced in an unbiased manner, that would not in itself be dispositive, because investors who purchased such stock without knowing about these variations would often be unfairly surprised. . . .

Under modern contract law, a contract term that is unfairly surprising is unenforceable even if the term is impounded in the contract price. For example, the courts routinely hold that unclear or inconspicuous terms in insurance contracts that violate the insured's fair expectations are unenforceable, without regard to whether the terms lowered the insured's premiums. . . .

* * *

It is no more likely that buyers in an initial public offering would know of variations in core fiduciary and structural rules than that buyers of insurance policies will know the fine print in their policies. Furthermore, even if the original buyers knew of the variations, subsequent buyers would not. . . .

* * *

Permitting owner-managers of publicly held corporations to vary core fiduciary and structural rules if they do so before their corporations go public could also lead to inefficiency in the capital markets. . . .

. . . [I]f core fiduciary or structural rules were subject to variation by certificate provisions adopted before an initial public offering, some publicly held corporations would be governed by core fiduciary and structural rules that are unduly favorable to top managers and some would not. Persons who proposed to buy stock in a publicly held corporation therefore would either have to expend resources to determine whether the corporation was subject to all the core rules that constrain unfair self-dealing, shirking, and positional conflicts by top managers, or assume that all corporations had adopted variations of those core rules. Either course of action would render capital markets less efficient, because investors would either put less of their money into corporate securities or demand a higher return from such securities, than would otherwise be the case.

* * *

Finally, permitting publicly held corporations to vary core fiduciary and structural rules if they did so before they went public might well lead to inefficiency in the national economy. . . . If . . . publicly held corporations could have governance structures determined by the decisions of owner-managers long gone from the scene who imposed rules that did not constrain positional conflicts, a significant portion of our national economy could eventually come to be vested in the hands of corporations in which inefficient managers were not effectively accountable and could not easily be removed. Such a regime could both jeopardize the efficiency of the economy and put the legitimacy of the corporate system into question.

* * *

Notes and Questions

1. Professor Eisenberg is critical of giving shareholders, even when directly contracting with each other in a closely held corporation, too much latitude to waive fiduciary duties. The same issue arises in the partnership context, witness the considerable controversy over whether to include provisions in the Revised Uniform Partnership Act which would allow partners to modify their fiduciary duties. See Vestal, *Fundamental Contractarian Error in the Revised Uniform Partnership Act of 1992*, 73 B.U. L. REV. 523 (1993); Ribstein, *The Revised Uniform Partnership Act: Not Ready for Prime Time*, 49 BUS. LAW. 45 (1993).

2. Professor Eisenberg's discussion of public corporations incorporates much of what has come to be known as the "Berle-Means Thesis." Berle & Means, THE MODERN CORPORATION AND PRIVATE PROPERTY (1932). This thesis starts with the observation that even the largest individual shareholders in a public corporation normally own only a very small fraction of the corporation's outstanding stock. Under this circumstance, shareholders are "rationally apathetic"; in other words, the rational shareholder will not find it worthwhile to spend much time or money worrying about control of the corporation. After all, it would be very costly to contact numerous scattered stockholders in order to obtain support for a change in management, and any given shareholder will only obtain a small fraction of the benefit of such change. Hence, if dissatisfied with current management, the best thing to do is to sell one's shares. As a result, the traditional model, that stockholders select managers to run the corporation on the stockholders' behalf, gives way to the reality that management, armed with the power to solicit proxies (votes) from the shareholders at corporate expense, perpetuates itself in office. Moreover, without the check of stockholder control, managers may act to benefit themselves at the shareholders' expense by shirking work, by engaging in unfair transactions which appropriate wealth from the corporation, or by acting to aggrandize themselves through decisions which are not profit maximizing. This, in turn, provides the rationale for mandatory corporate law which protects the shareholders and the economy generally.

As Professor Eisenberg implicitly recognizes, challenges to this thesis have come from a couple of directions. One is the argument that the various market forces discussed by Professor Eisenberg will constrain managers to act in the shareholders' interests despite the lack of effective direct stockholder control. For one of the leading articles expounding this view see Manne, *Our Two Corporation Systems: Law and Economics*, 53 VA. L. REV. 259 (1967). A more recent development is the growth of institutional shareholders (mutual funds, pension funds and the like) who may have the clout and incentives to discipline management. For differing views on the potential of such ownership to counteract the Berle-Means problem see Black, *Agents Watching Agents: The Promise of Institutional Investor Voice*, 39 UCLA L. REV. 811 (1992); Rock, *The Logic and (Uncertain) Significance of Institutional Shareholder Activism*, 79 GEO. L.J. 445 (1991).

3. The articles by Professors Easterbrook and Fischel and Professor Eisenberg are both part of an extensive symposium printed in the Columbia Law Review dealing with the question of whether and to what extent corporate law should be mandatory. This includes a response to Professor Eisenberg's article which argues that it contains a "nirvana fallacy." Specifically, even if one agrees with Professor Eisenberg that private rules in the corporate setting may be less than optimum in many cases, what guarantee does one have that the legislature or the courts are going to come up with better results?

D. Reality Check: Does Law Matter?

After all this discussion of efficiency and wealth maximizing rules, it might be worthwhile to look at some studies of the real world impact of legal rules.

Elliott J. Weiss and Lawrence J. White, *Of Econometrics and Indeterminacy: A Study Of Investors' Reactions To "Changes" In Corporate Law*, 75 CAL. L. REV. 551 (1987)*

INTRODUCTION

Is the market sensitive to changes in corporate law? . . .

* * *

I

STUDIES CONCERNING THE "MARKET FOR CORPORATE LAW"

* * *

B. Market Studies Concerning the Effects of Reincorporation in Delaware

Peter Dodd and Richard Leftwich were the first to evaluate the impact on stock prices of announcements that companies planned to reincorporate in Delaware.[30] Information about state corporation laws is publicly available, and Dodd and Leftwich assumed "that investors [will] weigh the costs and benefits of alternative state corporation codes when they consider investments in securities of firms incorporated in particular states." Thus, it seemed to follow that if Delaware law created more opportunities for exploitation of shareholders' interests than did the laws of other states, then the price of a company's stock would decline when the company announced that it planned to reincorporate in Delaware. Likewise, if Delaware law facilitated more efficient corporate operations, . . . then one would expect a reincorporation announcement to be followed by an increase in the price of that company's stock.

Dodd and Leftwich found no statistically significant abnormal positive or negative returns associated with firms' reincorporation announcements. . . .

---

30 Dodd & Leftwich, *The Market for Corporate Charters: "Unhealthy Competition" versus Federal Regulation*, 53 J. BUS. 259 (1980).

* * *

C. Our Research Effort: A Market Study Concerning the Effects of Changes in Delaware Corporate Law

Our study involved examination of market reactions to seven Delaware court decisions. We sought to test the hypothesis that the price of the stocks of Delaware companies will change when the market learns of substantial changes in Delaware's corporate governance rules.

Past tests of the [Efficient Capital Markets Hypothesis] demonstrate that securities prices rapidly incorporate new publicly-available information. In other contexts, new judicial decisions apparently have caused statistically significant changes in securities prices.[64] Thus, it seemed reasonable to expect investors to react to major corporate law decisions such as the seven Delaware court decisions we studied. Specifically, if any of the seven decisions affected shareholders' wealth adversely, investors would have reduced the prices they were prepared to pay (or accept) for the stock of Delaware companies. Conversely, if any of the seven decisions affected shareholders' wealth positively, investors would have increased the value they placed on the stock of Delaware companies. . . .

II
RESEARCH DESIGN, METHODOLOGY, AND RESULTS

* * *

A. Selection of Cases

* * *

One important conceptual problem in attempting to measure market reactions to judicial decisions involves the possibility that the market may have largely anticipated, and therefore impounded in securities prices, the result that a court announces. This possibility is substantial where a court's decision is consistent with well-established authority . . . . We believed this possibility would be much smaller where a decision appeared to depart from or reverse well-established authority. Thus, our first research task was to verify that all cases to be studied involved such departures or reversals.

* * *

---

64 . . .

Cipollone v. Liggett Group, Inc., 789 F.2d 181 (3d Cir. 1986), provides strong anecdotal evidence of the manner in which a judicial decision can influence securities prices. In *Cipollone*, the Third Circuit ruled that the health warnings required by federal law protect tobacco companies from claims that they failed to provide adequate notice of the dangers of smoking. . . . In the two days following announcement of that decision, the stock price of all three leading cigarette manufacturers rose by more than ten percent. . . .

B. Market Model Tests

1. Methodology

Since all of the decisions described above made substantial unanticipated changes in the rules of corporate governance established by Delaware law, it seemed reasonable to expect the share prices of Delaware companies either to rise or to fall significantly following the announcement of those decisions. . . .

The standard method of measuring changes in share prices that occur on or about a specific "event" day is to employ the "market model" for measuring the returns to holding a stock. The model assumes that individuals are interested solely in the risk and return of their investments. By holding a diversified portfolio, they are able to smooth out some of the idiosyncratic variance in the individual stocks (the "diversifiable risk"). The risk that cannot be diversified away is the covariance of a stock with the overall market—that is, the extent to which an individual stock's returns (its combination of percentage price changes and dividend returns) vary with the overall market's returns. Thus, to measure the unexpected changes in a stock's price, one first must know the usual pattern of that stock's movements relative to the market's movements.

Formally, then, we employ the following equation as our model:

$$R[jt] = a[j] + beta[j]\ R[mt] + e[jt] \qquad \text{(Equation 1)}$$

where:

R[jt] = the rate of return of stock j during day t

R[mt] = the rate of return of the market portfolio during day t

e[jt] = the error or disturbance term of stock j on day t

a[j], beta[j] = parameters of the relationship between approx. R[jt] and approx. R[mt]

Using ordinary least squares regression methods, one can estimate the relationship described in Equation 1 for a given stock for a time period prior to the event in question. In essence, the ordinary least squares estimates provide a baseline that indicates the normal expected behavior of that stock's daily returns given the market's daily returns. The actual behavior of the stock price at the time of the event and shortly thereafter can then be compared with its expected behavior, and standard statistical tests can be used to determine whether, based on the "noisiness" of the pattern of the stock's returns against the market's returns during the pre-event baseline period, the deviation of the actual returns from the expected returns is statistically significant.

2. Data and Specific Procedures

To test the effects of the Delaware court decisions, we used samples of approximately fifty companies incorporated in Delaware. Because the aggregate market might be heavily weighted with Delaware companies, making it difficult to distinguish the effects of the decisions on the Delaware companies from their effects on the market, we also collected roughly equal-sized samples of companies incorporated in other states (non-Delaware companies). Even if the overall market was heavily weighted with Delaware companies, we would still expect to find an opposite effect on the non-Delaware companies relative to the overall market if the described decisions had an effect on Delaware companies.

* * *

. . . For each announcement, we measured the "abnormal" daily returns of each stock in the sample for the announcement day and for twenty subsequent trading days by calculating the differences between the actual daily returns of the stock and the expected returns of that stock from the estimated baseline, given the daily market returns.

We then summed the daily abnormal returns for each stock into cumulative abnormal returns (CAR's) through each day t. The CAR's for each day were summed separately for each "portfolio" of Delaware and non-Delaware companies. . . .

3. Results

* * *

In no instance did we find statistically significant . . . negative CAR's for the Delaware portfolios; only for *Unocal* [*v. Mesa Petroleum Co.*] at t = 4 and t = 9 did we find statistically significant positive CAR's. Indeed, the pattern of positive and negative CAR's for the Delaware portfolios appears to be random.

As we noted above, much of "the market" that serves as the basis for computing the CAR's may be composed of Delaware companies. Consequently, an additional test focuses on the portfolios of non-Delaware companies and examines whether they showed significant CAR's relative to the market or relative to the Delaware portfolio CAR's. Only for *Unocal* at t = 2 and subsequent trading days do the non-Delaware portfolios show statistically significant CAR's. In this case, the non-Delaware CAR's show a positive return, but so do the Delaware CAR's, and the differences between them are not statistically significant. . . .

Overall, then, the results of the direct market model tests do not support the proposition that investors viewed any of the studied decisions as either favorable or adverse to shareholders' interests.

* * *

III
ANALYSIS OF THE RESULTS

The results of the standard market model tests . . . present a conundrum, given the beliefs that market judgments generally are unbiased and that the market for corporate equities, in particular, reacts both rapidly and rationally to all significant new information. That is, given those expectations, what explains the general absence of statistically significant market reactions . . . to any of the seven apparently unanticipated, apparently significant Delaware court decisions we studied?

A. Possible Explanations for the Results

We identified four possible explanations for our results:

(1) The market model event study approach may not be an appropriate technique for evaluating the consequences of the seven decisions.

(2) Investors may have believed that courts in other states would follow the decisions of the Delaware courts relatively quickly. If so, investors would have reacted to the decisions as if they affected both Delaware and non-Delaware companies equally, making it impossible to isolate the decisions' effects on either Delaware or non-Delaware companies.

(3) Investors may have concluded that even though all seven decisions involve substantial changes in corporate governance rules, those changes will affect the behavior of a very small number of corporations. If so, investors could have rationally concluded that the decisions should not significantly change their valuation of the shares of Delaware companies.

(4) Investors may have concluded that the nature of judicial decisionmaking in corporate governance cases makes it unlikely that the rule or rules a court applies in any given case will affect significantly the value of the stock of other companies ostensibly subject to those rules.

* * *

Notes and Questions

1. Professors Weiss and White's discussion of their methodology presupposes the reader's familiarity with certain concepts of corporate finance. In broad strokes, the "Efficient Capital Market Hypothesis" is a fancy way of saying that stock prices in active trading markets move very rapidly in response to information relevant to a stock and, thus, the stock's price will incorporate in very short order the information. One key question about this hypothesis is what type of information it covers. Here, the hypothesis breaks down into three flavors. The "weak" form states that the price incorporates all information one can glean from looking at past price movements. This, of course, is heresy to the many stock traders who spend countless hours poring over stock price charts looking for trendlines, resistance points and other such clues upon which to buy and sell. The "semi-strong" form holds that the price incorporates all publicly available information, while the "strong" form claims that the price impounds so-called inside information—in other words, information not supposed to be known outside the corporation—as well. One amusing aspect of the theory is that it will work only if, at least to some extent, stock traders do not believe it, since it is through the actions of traders gathering and acting on information that the price of stock impounds the data. If all traders assumed that the price of stocks already takes into account all information, they would not act and the market would not be efficient. For a discussion of the efficient capital market hypothesis, see Gilson & Kraakman, *The Mechanisms of Market Efficiency*, 70 VA. L. REV. 549 (1984).

It is worthwhile not to get too carried away with this notion of efficient markets. While one may accept the idea that the price of stocks incorporates available information, stock prices can incorporate much silliness as well, as witness the following newspaper account:

> As a case of mania, it pales beside what happened in the last week with the stock of Comparator Systems, a Newport Beach company that makes fingerprint identification equipment.
>
> For three days, beginning on May 3, [1996,] the tiny company of 29 employees, which lost $1.85 million last fiscal year on sales of $90,161, became the most actively traded stock in the country. An average of 150 million Comparator shares a day traded hands on the NASDAQ system. The company's stock price surged from 6.25 cents, where it had languished for months, to $1.88 before settling back to 50 cents. That 30-fold jump in price briefly gave the company, which has $4,000 in the bank, a market valuation in excess of $1 billion.
>
> The firm's own president has called the run-up "insane." The reason for the insanity is unclear. Part of it may have been due to rumors, since dispelled, that the company would contract with a major credit card firm. Part of the interest may have come from advance word that Comparator was about to announce a new product. NASDAQ is investigating to try to find out what triggered the unusual trading.
>
> But the mundane facts are that Comparator had been around for 20 years selling, not very successfully, fingerprint equipment to law enforcement agencies. For most of the last decade, it has been unable to meet its payroll or to pay vendors, defraying the expenses by issuing stock to them. Earlier this decade, when the undercapitalized company tried to expand with Malaysian capital, the effort came to a halt, Comparator reports, after its general manager misappropriated nearly $1 million. *The Sacramento Bee* (May 14, 1996).*

The existence of extraneous stock price moves—whether reflecting information other than the studied event or just "noise"—presents a difficulty for any study of the nature attempted by Professors Weiss and White. This study responds by employing a model of expected price movements, which it then compares to the actual price moves of the selected stocks around the event time. The model assumes a relationship, captured in the equation used by Professors Weiss and White, between the moves of an individual stock and that of the market as a whole. While a proof of this relationship depends upon portfolio theory, suffice it to say that this approach to event studies has been successfully used in a variety of circumstances. See Brown & Warner, *Using Daily Stock Returns: The Case of Event Studies*, 14 J. FIN. ECON. 3 (1985).

---

2. What conclusions can one draw from Professors Weiss and White's results (or non-results), as well as from the results of the Dodd and Leftwich reincorporation study described in Professors Weiss and White's article? Dodd and Leftwich concluded that the lack of abnormal negative returns upon reincorporation in Delaware contradicted Professor Cary's claim that Delaware was leading a race to the bottom in the protection of shareholders. How can one explain the lack of abnormal positive returns? Does it contradict the argument that Delaware is leading the way toward improved corporate laws? Might the lack of reaction either way be most consistent with Professor Bebchuk's suggestion that investors already have discounted the price they pay for the stock of non-Delaware corporations to reflect the likelihood that the company may reincorporate in Delaware (or that the present state's law will copy Delaware)?

Professors Weiss and White suggest four possible explanations for their own results. The most interesting are the notions that investors do not find the Delaware Supreme Court decisions involved in the study important—despite the sigificance of these decisions in the eyes of anyone involved in the study of corporate law—either because so few corporations will find themselves in a situation in which the rules announced will matter or because investors conclude that even when the rules become apropos they are not necessarily outcome determinative to corporate litigation (which typically involves mixed issues of fact and law and substantial judicial flexibility). Whatever the reasoning, perhaps the real moral is a counterpoint to the hubris of law professors who like to assume corporate law has a great impact upon shareholder wealth, or, even more self-satisfying, upon the well-being of the whole economy. For a consideration of the relationship between corporate goverance and economic performance see Gilson, *Corporate Governance and Economic Efficiency: When Do Institutions Matter?*, 74 WASH. U. L.Q. 327 (1996).

Joseph Bankman, *The Structure of Silicon Valley Start-Ups*, 41 UCLA L. REV. 1737 (1994)*

INTRODUCTION

Under current law, . . . partners in a partnership that conducts a new venture are able to deduct the costs of that venture against other sources of past or present income. A newly-formed corporation that undertakes a new venture is also able to deduct a large portion of the costs of that venture. However, such a company has no other sources of income and therefore gains no immediate tax savings from the deduction. In theory, the deduction may be carried forward to future years. In practice, new companies often lose some portion of the deduction due to the so-called "change of ownership" rules. Even if the deduction is not affected by those rules, its present value is reduced by the many years it may take the new venture to generate taxable income, and, more importantly, by the possibility that the venture may never generate taxable income.

The unfavorable tax treatment described above gives the newly-formed corporation an after-tax return on investment that is considerably less than that realized by the partnership. . . . Under plausible assumptions . . ., an expense that has an after-tax cost of $1 to a . . . partnership might cost a newly-formed corporation $1.40. A newly-formed company thus pays a premium of 40% on every single expense it incurs: Rent is 40% higher, salaries are 40% higher, and so on. In light of this decidedly adverse tax treatment, one might expect that speculative ventures would rarely, if ever, be carried out by a newly-formed corporation, but instead would . . . be organized as partnerships. In fact, in the biotechnology, electronics, and computing industries centered south of San Francisco and around Route 128 near Boston (collectively, "Silicon Valley"), new ventures are organized in a way that does not follow this tax logic. In Silicon Valley, notwithstanding the concomitant loss of tax benefits, a substantial number of new ventures are carried out by newly-formed corporations.

* * *

The organization of Silicon Valley ventures . . . raises questions for those interested in organizational structure. . . . The organization of Silicon Valley investment poses the following riddle: What advantages (if any) of the corporate structure justify the much higher after-tax costs for operating expenses which the use of that structure entails?

* * *

This paper explores the seemingly irrational structure of Silicon Valley investment. Information gleaned from interviews with Silicon Valley attorneys, investors, executives, and venture capitalists is pieced together in an attempt to offer plausible hypotheses to explain that structure.

* * *

III. Overview: Lack of Tax Awareness Among Executives and Venture Capitalists

The Silicon Valley executives and venture capitalists interviewed for this article were, by any measure, an impressive group. The chief executives generally had advanced technical degrees; many were accomplished scientists in their own right. The executives were also well informed of the legal rules they felt important—most particularly rules concerning technology transfer and Securities & Exchange Commission (S.E.C.) reporting standards. Venture capitalists most often had a technical background and a professional degree in law or business. In light of their education and intelligence, perhaps the most surprising aspect of both groups of interviewees was the relative lack of awareness of or interest in the tax consequences of the organization structure they had chosen.

* * *

The fact that highly educated and well-advised decision-makers are for the most part unaware of the tax disadvantages of the chosen industry structure may at first blush seem somewhat bizarre. . . . The relative ignorance of the effect of tax law is consistent with the hypothesis that the industry structure is suboptimal, and that the current structure is attributable in large part to a lack of knowledge.

On the other hand, the lack of interest in tax is also consistent with the hypothesis that the industry structure is optimal. A stand-alone corporation may offer significant advantages that outweigh the tax costs. In that event, there would be little payoff for a decision-maker to learn this aspect of the tax law. The unfavorable tax treatment would act as a background constraint that limited the supply of capital to the industry—a constraint that, from the perspective of the individual venture capitalist, was immutable and might therefore be ignored.

* * *

IV. Perceived Advantages of the Present Structure

A. *Minimization of Legal and Organizational Fees*

As noted above, the individuals interviewed took the organization of start-ups as freestanding corporations as a given. They were unaware of the tax costs of that form of organization and, perhaps for that reason, had not thought deeply about the offsetting advantages to the corporate form. When asked specifically to enumerate those advantages, many interviewees confessed that they had never focused on the issue. After a moment's reflection, however, virtually all of those interviewed came up with one of three or four responses. The most straightforward, though hardly the most significant, of those responses was that the formation of the start-up as a corporation minimized legal and organizational costs. As noted earlier, successful start-ups eventually issue equity interests to the public. Once an entity is publicly traded, it is treated as a corporation for tax purposes. There is, consequently, no tax advantage to retaining partnership status for state law purposes.

Moreover, there is a practical disadvantage to retaining partnership status for state law purposes. There are virtually no publicly traded partnerships. Venture capitalists felt that a venture organized as a partnership would be viewed suspiciously by the investment community and would thus command a lower valuation. A start-up originally formed as a partnership must therefore convert to the corporate form prior to the initial public offering. Conversion is unproblematic but legally and organizationally expensive. It may cost as much as $200,000 in legal fees to convert a partnership with a complicated ownership structure to corporate form. Conversion imposes additional costs in the form of accounting fees and expenditure of management's time. A company that is initially organized as a corporation to begin with avoids these costs. Adverting to these costs, one chief financial officer of a former start-up and now publicly traded semiconductor company stated, "It seems kind of silly to form as a partnership when you're sooner or later going to be a corporation."

While conversion costs are significant on an absolute level, avoidance of those costs cannot fully explain why start-ups are first organized as corporations. In almost all cases, conversion costs amount to only a small percentage of the value of tax deductions lost. The chief financial officer quoted above, for example, noted that his company had emerged from start-up status with "tens of millions" of dollars of unusable tax deductions.

B. *Use of Stock Options*

Another commonly offered explanation for the present organization structure of start-ups is built upon the perceived importance of compensating key employees primarily with stock and stock options, rather than cash. . . . [A] start-up that receives venture capital financing will issue a combination of stock and stock options to its founding employees; additional stock and stock options will be given to later-arriving employees. In exchange for this contingent compensation, employees sacrifice the higher cash salary and security of more established companies. . . .

One obvious objection to justifying the corporate structure on the basis of the contingent compensation made possible through the use of stock options and stock interests is that it would be possible to provide a near-identical form of contingent compensation if start-ups were organized as partnerships. . . .

When asked why it would not be possible to structure a start-up as a partnership and still provide contingent compensation to key employees, most of those interviewed stated that, in theory, the desired amount of risk sharing could be achieved through a partnership. In practice, however, most of those interviewed felt that explaining the equivalence of partnership and corporate contingent compensation would be a "hard sell" to employees. "Management gets spooked by partnership interests," according to one venture capitalist.

* * *

C. *The "Missing" Taxable Investors*

Another (partial) answer to the puzzle of organizational structure posed by this paper may lie in the identity of investors in start-ups. As discussed previously . . ., tax considerations suggest that freestanding start-ups would be organized as partnerships, rather than corporations. Losses from the partnership would flow through to the partners and could be used by those partners to offset other sources of income, while losses from the corporation remain "trapped" at the corporate level. This analysis, however, assumes that the investors in the partnerships would be entities such as corporations that have other sources of income that could be offset. With respect to some or all investors in some ventures, this assumption is true. In recent years, however, a majority of the investment in start-ups has come from tax-exempt institutional investors, such as pensions and university endowments. These investors generally have little or no taxable income with which to offset losses and would not benefit from the tax losses realized if the investment were structured as a partnership. Much of the remaining investment in start-ups is made by individual investors, who are subject to the so-called "passive loss" rules. In general, these rules limit the ability of individuals who invest in businesses that they do not actively manage, "passive activities," from using flow-through losses from such businesses to offset salary income, or investor-level income from portfolio investments such as stocks and bonds. . . .

The presence of institutional and tax-constrained individual investors may at first appear an adequate answer to the riddle of organizational structure; start-ups are not organized so as to provide taxable losses to their investors because, by and large, their investors cannot use taxable losses. In fact, the make-up of the present investor base merely pushes the mystery one level deeper. . . .

In a well-functioning market one would normally expect that venture capitalists would structure freestanding start-ups so as to maximize the expected after-tax return to potential marginal investors. In this case, assuming there are corporations or other potential marginal investors who can make any use of the flow-through losses, the optimal structure would be a partnership, since the before-tax rate of return the start-up must offer will be reduced by the amount of tax savings the start-up's early losses will generate. Once the start-up is structured as a partnership, one would expect (by normal clientele effect) that the interests will in fact be purchased by those who can use the flow-through losses, just as one expects municipal bonds to be purchased by those who value the tax-free nature of the return. Investors who cannot make use of the losses would disappear, or play only minor roles in financing start-ups. Eventually, the effect should be to push the entire industry of freestanding start-ups towards a partnership structure. The resulting savings from making optimal use of available tax benefits could be shared in some proportion by all parties, including, most notably, the venture capitalists responsible for the organizational innovation that produced that increase.

To put the matter somewhat differently, the presence of institutional and tax-constrained investors may be the result, rather than cause, of the present organizational structure. Given that under the present structure, tax losses are unusable by investors, it is not surprising that the majority of investors are exempt institutions for which such losses are of no value. The mystery is why the industry has settled upon that structure. . . .

* * *

D. *Gambler's Mentality of Investors and Venture Capitalists*

The preceding analysis has focused on those explanations for industry structure given by interviewees that seem most consistent with economic theory or . . . observable behavior. Absent from this analysis is the most common explanation for the industry structure: Attention to tax benefits from early losses runs counter to the expansive mind-set of investors and venture capitalists. "By their very nature," one lobbyist stated, "the kinds of people who are going into these things are very optimistic people—they don't think about tax benefits."

The belief that tax benefits are of little importance to venture capitalists because of the "big score" is held by some of the most sophisticated Silicon Valley decision-makers. . . .

* * *

CONCLUSION

* * *

Finally, the present structure is favored by tradition, or, to put the matter somewhat differently, by an inertial combination of present practice and collective-action problems. A venture capitalist who unilaterally adopts a new organizational structure must bear certain transition-related costs. The venture capitalist must reassure key employees, who receive equity interests in the enterprise, that the new structure does not diminish the value of those interests. The venture capitalist must also develop a new clientele of investors who can benefit from the new structure. The venture capitalist who incurs these costs must, in the long run, share the transition-related gains with other venture capitalists, who will "free ride" on his early efforts and compete for investments under the new structure. The gain to the venture capitalist who incurs these costs may not justify the expense and risk involved. Absent some sort of collective action, the industry may remain at an equilibrium that is not optimal but that cannot be easily or profitably changed through individual behavior.

Notes and Questions

Professor Bankman's study brings us back to the subject of choice of business form. He notes that selecting the corporate form can produce significant tax disadvantages. This flows from the fact that a corporation is a separate taxpaying entity, whereas a partnership is not. For a venture expected to generate tax deductible losses—like the high-tech start-ups discussed in Professor Bankman's article—this gives the partnership a tax advantage. Subject to some rather complex rules, partners can use such losses to offset (or "shelter") their other income, whereas the owners of a corporation generally cannot. While the corporation might eventually generate income against which to use its loss deductions, in many cases the firm will never realize much or all of the value of the deductions. What about for a firm presently generating taxable income rather than losses? Here, corporations sometimes claim an advantage because corporate income tax rates are typically lower than the tax rates on individuals. On the other hand, if and when the corporation pays out any of its after-tax earnings as a dividend to its shareholders, the shareholders must recognize the dividend as taxable income. Hence, corporate earnings face a "double tax," again a tax disadvantage relative to the partnership. There are some exceptions to this comparison of partnerships and corporations. Corporations with less than 75 shareholders may be able to elect partnership style tax treatment under subchapter S of the Internal Revenue Code. To be eligible for this election, however, the company can have only one class of stock—which is not the norm for Silicon Valley start-ups. Conversely, as Professor Bankman points up, the Internal Revenue Code treats a publicly traded partnership as a corporation for tax purposes. Hence, publicly traded firms may as well operate as a corporation. For a detailed exploration of the impact of tax rules on the choice of business form see GEVURTZ, BUSINESS PLANNING (2d ed. 1995).

Professor Bankman notes that Silicon Valley start-ups generally ignore these tax considerations in their choice of business form. Other industries, such as commercial real estate and motion picture production, have been much more tax sensitive. How can one explain this difference? Are commercial property developers and movie producers more sophisticated than technology types?

One obvious explanation for choice of the corporate form, which Professor Bankman and his interviewees appear to ignore, is limited liability. In fact, the desire to couple limited liability with partnership style tax treatment has become a common goal in more tax sensitive industries. As mentioned above, an S corporation might achieve this goal. Another common approach involves the use of limited partnerships, often with a corporation as general partner. Within the last few years, states have responded to this desire by enacting legislation creating a new entity, the limited liability company. Such companies can achieve partnership classification for federal tax purposes, yet the state statute blesses their owners with limited liability. From a policy standpoint, at first glance such statutes seem to bring us back to the question of the efficiency of limited liability. Yet, regardless of that issue, is there any sense imposing a federal tax penalty on limited liability?

Chapter II

The Limits of Limited Liability

We turn now from a broad theme to specific doctrines. This chapter looks at various exceptions to the general principle that participants in a corporation are not personally liable to the company's creditors. In reading the materials to follow, ask if the doctrines reflect the policies behind limited liability discussed in Chapter I.

A. Piercing the Corporate Veil

1. *The Doctrine Introduced*

Robert W. Hamilton, *The Corporate Entity,* 49 Tex. L. Rev. 979 (1971)*

* * *

The question of the status of a corporation often arises when a liability has been incurred in the name of a corporation, but the corporation has become insolvent. The creditor, seeking to find a solvent defendant, may sue some or all of the shareholders, arguing that for some reason they should be called upon to pay the corporation debts. . . .

Opinions by courts shed little light on the considerations that result in corporate obligations being imposed on the shareholders . . . .

. . . For example, despite . . . language [in some judicial opinions which suggest a court will impose liability upon individuals who form a corporation to avoid personal liability,] it is well established that shareholder liability will not result even when there is a single shareholder, and the corporation was formed for the specific purpose of limiting or escaping liability. Any other conclusion would make the whole process of incorporation a snare or a delusion. Other opinions decide the issue by pejorative. Courts solemnly refer to "piercing the corporate veil" as though that catch phrase

* Published originally in 49 Texas Law Review 979 (1971). Copyright © 1971 by The Texas Law Review Association. Reprinted with permission.

explains the result. Phrases such as "mere agent, representative, adjunct, device, stooge or dummy," "alter ego," "tool," or "corporate double" are used to describe the corporation whose existence is to be ignored. Fortunately, courts are increasingly aware that such name calling is unhelpful: at best the phrases state results rather than reasons, and at worst they obscure analysis.

Other commentary also sheds little light on recognition of shareholder responsibility. We are told that shareholder liability is an exceptional remedy and that this liability must be based on two factors: first, "a substantial identity of interest and ownership" between the corporation and the shareholder, and secondly, "the danger that the corporate form is being used or will be used to achieve an inequitable result." . . . The first proposition quoted above, however, appears to be satisfied by the relation between a closely held corporation and its shareholders. The reference in the second quoted proposition to "inequitable results" does not help to decide concrete cases. . . .

A somewhat more meaningful analysis of this problem may be undertaken. First, no conceptual problems emerge when liability is imposed upon shareholders under conventional theories of agency or tort law. To argue that the corporate veil is "pierced" in such cases is both unnecessary and confusing. If the shareholder is acting as a principal in his own name, he is clearly liable on the obligation. . . . Similarly, if the shareholder himself commits a tort while acting as agent for his corporation, it is the substantive law of agency that imposes liability for the act on the shareholder. . . .

Secondly, a major consideration in determining whether the shareholders or the third party should bear the loss is whether the third party dealt voluntarily with the corporation or whether he is an involuntary creditor, typically a tort claimant. In a contract case, the plaintiff has usually dealt in some way with the corporation and should be aware that the corporation lacks substance. In the absence of some sort of deception, the creditor more or less assumed the risk of loss when he dealt with a "shell"; if he was concerned, he should have insisted that some solvent third person guarantee the performance by the corporation. In tort cases, on the other hand, there is usually no element of voluntary dealing, and the question is whether it is reasonable for businessmen to transfer a risk of loss or injury to members of the general public through the device of conducting business in the name of a corporation that may be marginally financed. The issues of public policy raised by tort claims bear little relationship to the issues raised by a contract claim. It is astonishing to find that this fundamental distinction is only dimly perceived by many courts, which indiscriminately cite and purport to apply, tort precedents in contract cases and vice versa.

Thirdly, Professor Berle's notion of an enterprise entity continues to have vitality.[21] Though they seldom articulate this view, courts are suspicious of attempts to divide a single economic enterprise among several different corporations with the intention of minimizing the assets subject to claims of creditors of the enterprise. Perhaps this is because it is not "playing fair" with creditors who may believe that the entire enterprise

21 Berle, *The Theory of Enterprise Entity*, 47 COLUM. L. REV. 343 (1947).

is a single unit; in any event, courts may put the enterprise back together despite the shareholders' attempt to segregate it.[22]

The courts often stress two factors—inadequate capitalization and the commingling of shareholder and corporate affairs—when determining whether shareholders should be held responsible for claims against their corporation. . . .

A. Inadequate Capitalization

* * *

. . . "Inadequate capitalization" as used here means capitalization very small in relation to the nature of the business of the corporation and the risks the business necessarily entails. . . . Whether a corporation is undercapitalized obviously presents a question of fact that turns on the nature of the business of the particular corporation.

. . . . It may be argued that if the corporation is capitalized as required by the statute—that is, if the shares are fully paid in and the minimum capitalization requirement [under a statute which requires, for example, a corporation to have $1000 paid in capital before starting business] has been met—lack of additional capital should not result in shareholder liability. This argument, however, is inconsistent with statements in numerous court decisions.

In contract cases the separate existence of a minimally capitalized corporation should usually be recognized. As indicated above, if a person knowingly deals with an undercapitalized corporation he is, in effect, assuming the risk of loss if the transaction does not work out. . . .

There are some contract cases, however, in which inadequate capitalization may be relevant. If the shareholder misleads a third person regarding the financial status of the corporation so that he believes the corporation has more capital than it actually has, then the element of risk allocation disappears, and shareholder liability should perhaps be imposed. . . . It has been held, however, that mere silence about the financial position of the corporation is not grounds for imposing shareholder liability. Similarly, an oral promise by a shareholder to pay the corporation's debt, which itself is unenforceable under the Texas statute of frauds, is not ground for holding the shareholder on the theory he misled the plaintiff. . . .

In tort cases there is usually no element of prior dealing between the corporation and the plaintiff. As a result, inadequate capitalization should be an important factor in determining whether shareholders will be held liable for the tort liabilities of the corporation. . . .

* * *

22 In Walkovsky v. Carlton, 18 N.Y.2d 414, 223 N.E.2d 6, 276 N.Y.S.2d 585 (1966), for example, the court treated a business consisting of several taxicabs and a garage as a single unit even though several different corporations had been created. . . .

B. Confusion of Shareholder and Corporate Action

Anyone reading the Texas cases dealing with shareholder liability for corporate obligations will be struck by the emphasis of the courts on failure to follow the requisite corporation formalities as a ground for imposing shareholder liability. In most opinions, a failure to follow normal corporate routine appears a most significant consideration in deciding whether a corporation is the "alter ego" of the shareholder or whether the "corporate veil should be pierced." While a complete catalogue of dangerous acts is probably impossible to prepare, there appears to be a substantial risk that the separate corporate existence will be ignored when business is commenced without issuance of shares, when shareholder meetings or directors' meetings are not held, . . . when decisions are made by shareholders as though they were partners, when the shareholders do not sharply distinguish between corporate property and personal, when corporate funds are used to pay personal expenses, when personal funds are used for corporate expenses without proper accounting, or when complete corporate and financial records are not maintained. . . .

It is difficult to see, as a matter of logic, why corporate confusion and informality have been given the importance that they have. In most cases, the confusion and informality are not related to the claim advanced by either tort or contract plaintiffs. As a matter of fact, evidence of informality or commingling of affairs is first sought long after the transaction giving rise to the particular litigation took place. A judgment against shareholders based on these activities, which are unrelated to the plaintiff's claim, is a windfall. . . . One possible theory underlying these holdings is that the shareholder is liable because he should not be permitted first to ignore the rules of corporate behavior and then to claim the advantage of the corporate shield. In other words, the apparent theory is to punish an errant shareholder. The cases, however, do not articulate this theory, and there seems to be little reason to punish errant shareholders unless their actions are directed toward defrauding another party.

The use of confusion as an important part of the test for determining whether the corporation's separate existence will be recognized also tends to create a trap for the unwary shareholder in the closely held corporation. Shareholders in a small business often find managing the business a full-time occupation; formal corporate affairs are put off or ignored because there is full agreement in fact by all interested parties regarding what should be done and who should do it. Also, the play-acting aspects of corporate meetings, elections, and the like, may strike businessmen as rather silly. Insistence by an attorney that formal corporate procedures be followed may be dismissed as a subtle attempt at an additional fee. This attitude invites disaster.

When failure to follow appropriate corporate procedures tends to injure third persons, there can be little objection to holding the shareholder liable. Procedures within the corporation may be so undifferentiated that a person may believe he is dealing with a shareholder individually when he is dealing with the corporation. Similarly, intermingled personal and corporate assets may disappear into the personal coffers of the shareholder to the detriment of corporate creditors. . . .

Many cases in which shareholder liability has been found concern shareholders that are themselves corporations. In other words, a parent corporation is being held liable for the debts of a subsidiary. These cases have quite a different flavor than cases in which the shareholder is an individual. A similar type of case concerns corporate liability for the debts of a "brother-sister" corporation—one whose shares are owned by the same shareholders, individual or corporate. In the latter kind of case, technically a person other than the shareholder is being held liable for the corporate debt; but because of the single financial interest represented in the two corporations, the cases usually speak in terms of "piercing of the corporate veil" and the result is governed by the same principles that apply when the defendant is a parent corporation.

Some cases suggest that different tests should apply depending on whether the shareholder-defendant is an individual or a corporation. When a corporation is the defendant, only a larger corporate entity is being held responsible for the debt; but when an individual is the defendant, personal liability extending to non-business assets is being imposed. Whatever the merits of this suggestion as a basis for decision, courts are probably more willing to "pierce the corporate veil" when the defendant is a corporation rather than an individual. Courts are particularly likely to find the broader business entity liable under the following circumstances:

(a) when the business affairs of the two corporations are intertwined, and the separate corporate formalities of the subsidiary are not followed;
(b) when the subsidiary and parent are operating portions of a single business, and the subsidiary is undercapitalized; or
(c) when the subsidiary is being operated in an "unfair manner," e.g., by funneling profits to the parent.

* * *

Notes and Questions

1. Professor Hamilton refers to two elements which some courts list as required in order to pierce: (1) identity between the corporation and its shareholder, and (2) use of the corporate form to achieve an inequitable result. Other courts sometimes have referred to three elements: (1) domination of the corporation by a shareholder, (2) fraud or injustice in the use of the corporation, and (3) a causal connection between the misuse of the corporation and harm to the plaintiff. For a discussion of this three-part test see Krendl & Krendl, *Piercing the Corporate Veil: Focusing the Inquiry*, 55 DENVER L.J. 1 (1978). The second element in both formulations seems to refer to some abuse of operating in the corporate form. The notion that there ought to be some connection between that abuse and any harm to the plaintiff creditor might seem obvious enough to go without saying, so perhaps the two formulations are not dissimilar on that account. Professor Hamilton tosses off the first element as met simply by the relation between a closely held corporation and its shareholders. As this suggests, it is important not to give too much emphasis to the first element. Still, this element might have some significance. For one, it seems to rule out piercing against widely held corporations in which no shareholder owns enough stock to have control. In addition, it might answer the question of who will be responsible if the court decides to pierce. In other words, assuming some inequity or injustice in the use of the corporation—which is *why* the court pierces—the element of domination or identity tells the court *who* to pierce against: the shareholder who used his or her control to cause the injustice. This could be important in a closely held corporation when some shareholders are in control and others may be passive.

2. With respect to inequitable use of the corporate form, Professor Hamilton focuses on failure to follow formalities (where he is critical of the emphasis often accorded to this factor) and inadequate capitalization. The following excerpt attempts to answer some key questions regarding inadequate capital.

William P. Hackney and Tracey G. Benson, *Shareholder Liability for Inadequate Capital,* 43 U. Pitt. L. Rev. 837 (1982)*

* * *

15. *What is "Capital"?*

In virtually no cases have the courts clearly enunciated what they mean by inadequate capital when it is said to be a major factor in the imposition of shareholder liability. "Capital," when being assessed as to adequacy for the purposes under discussion, refers neither to total assets (which might be exceeded by liabilities), nor to stated or legal capital as such (which may be an arbitrary bookkeeping entry, nominal in many instances), nor to working capital (which may or may not signify solvency), but rather to the cushion of protection afforded to creditors—net assets, or the total contribution made by the shareholders. Assets so contributed are capital for this purpose, whether received in the form of cash or other property. Anything owned by the corporation which would contribute to its operating capabilities would qualify.

Where shareholders employ financing devices such as loans, mortgages, leases, guarantees and other extensions of credit to provide a newly-formed corporation with the use of assets required for the conduct of its business, the assets so provided may or may not be considered by the courts in determining the adequacy of risk capital, as to which see the next Section.

It would seem that courts should also look to other components of a cushion provided by the corporation for creditor protection, although not consisting of assets put at risk by the shareholders, such as liability insurance, performance bonds, bank loan commitments and the like. Because they are funds to which creditors can turn for satisfaction of corporate obligations, such form of protection should be included in any assessment of the adequacy of corporate capitalization.

---

16. *How Much Capital is Adequate?*

* * *

If the adequacy of capital is to be relied upon as justification for disregarding a corporate entity, then it is important that the law provide a workable standard that will allow shareholders, active in the affairs of a new corporation, to make a reasonably accurate judgment regarding the soundness of their shield of limited liability. Although it will not be possible to determine exactly how much capitalization will be adequate in a given situation, several controlling principles can be gleaned from the whole of the case law dealing with inadequacy of capital.

In a surprisingly large number of cases, the initial amount paid in by shareholders has been $2,000 or less; in many, no stock at all has been issued. The doctrine has often been stated in dicta to apply where the shareholder's capital is "trifling" or "purely nominal," or where the inadequacy is "obvious;" but when confronted with the issue, the courts have stated the requirement in terms of what is reasonably adequate to the anticipated needs of the business, considering the nature and magnitude of the enterprise and the likely risks to be incurred. Reasonableness from two distinct points of view would seem to be proper to consider: that of contract creditors and that of potential tort claimants. Thus one should consider the amount of beginning capital reasonably adequate to provide the enterprise with the prospect of being able to generate cash flow from revenues and other sources in sufficient amount to cover reasonably anticipated costs and expenses of doing business. In addition, if the nature of the business entails an anticipated risk of injury to customers, employees or the public at large, the ability (through insurance or otherwise) to provide compensation for such injuries should be a factor in determining the reasonableness of beginning capital.

* * *

The courts are sensitive to the financial risk involved when shareholders provide needed assets for the corporation's proposed activities by means other than direct equity contribution, such as leasing, loans, guarantees of corporate borrowing and other extensions of credit. Such financing methods will be approached with a "large measure of watchful care" by courts, which will readily require that extensions of credit by dominant shareholders be subordinated [(in other words, paid off only after outside creditors receive full payment)] where the corporation started life with nominal equity, the so-called "loans," leases or other credit providing virtually all the funds or assets required.

Of course loans by shareholders to their corporations are not per se invalid or subordinated. . . . It seems relevant to inquire whether the loans were on an arm's length basis and would have been made by an outside bank. . . .

In comparing subordination cases with cases denying limited liability, the question of inadequate capital involves a two-step analysis. If a shareholder has supplied a portion of what the court feels should have been the minimally adequate capital by way of loan, lease or other extension of credit, then the loan or credit will be treated as capital so as to require its subordination. . . . If the court is asked to deny to the shareholder his limited liability, however, the question then arises whether the loan which is treated as capital for subordination purposes will be treated as capital for purposes of testing the adequacy of initial capitalization. It would seem that where the advance was not intended to be repaid in the ordinary course of business, but rather was expected to remain outstanding so long as needed as a part of the corporation's financial structure (and particularly where this fact was made known to creditors), it would be proper to treat it as part of the capitalization for purposes of granting limited liability. Otherwise, where there is any hint of the shareholder draining away corporate assets by repayment of the loan, excessive interest, rental or management fees or the like, then the loan, lease or extension of credit would not be considered capital for purposes of determining whether limited liability will be denied.

* * *

Where the courts have spoken of capital solely in the sense of the dollar amount of balance sheet net worth, or in the sense of a projected cash flow in relation to the ability to pay obligations as they become due in the ordinary course of business, the end result in either case should hinge on whether the shareholders have created what has a reasonable chance of becoming an independent, viable enterprise.

* * *

17. *When to Measure Adequacy of Capital*

It seems clear that where a corporation has been provided with adequate capital, whether at formation or subsequently, the shield of limited liability which thereupon arises cannot be lost because of subsequent insolvency; otherwise the well-settled corporate attribute of limited liability would be meaningless. It is clear, therefore, that adequacy of capital must be measured at the beginning period of corporate existence. . . .

It also seems clear that limited shareholder liability should attach in situations where a corporation that was initially underfinanced subsequently becomes adequately capitalized either through additional shareholder contributions, or as a result of business success.

Conversely, where a corporation commences business with capital then adequate, and later substantially expands the size or nature of the business with an attendant substantial increase in business hazards, the corporation might be deemed inadequately capitalized unless there is an infusion of additional risk capital by shareholders.

* * *

Note

Shareholders may put money into their corporation in different ways. They may purchase stock—which without question contributes capital—or they may "loan" money to the company. As Hackney and Benson point out, such loans often create difficulties in determining whether the corporation is adequately capitalized. Shareholder loans also may lead to a different remedy than piercing. As Hackney and Benson discuss, courts may subordinate the shareholder loans so that they are paid only after outside creditors (assuming any money is left). Hackney and Benson also point out that courts may deny limited liability where there is any hint of the shareholder draining away corporate assets by repayment of shareholder loans, or payment of excessive interest, rental or management fees. As with subordination of shareholder loans, piercing is not the only remedy courts could impose for such payments. A court could treat the payment as a fraudulent conveyance and demand the shareholder put back the money. The following article explores the relationship between fraudulent conveyance law and the doctrine of piercing.

Robert Charles Clark, *The Duties of the Corporate Debtor to Its Creditors*, 90 HARV. L. REV. 505 (1977)*†

* * *

The law of fraudulent conveyances, of which the Uniform Fraudulent Conveyance Act (UFCA) is the principal but not exclusive embodiment, allows creditors to set aside certain transfers by debtors. . . .

* * *

IV. FRAUDULENT CONVEYANCES AND PIERCING THE CORPORATE VEIL

* * *

. . . [T]he courts [in piercing cases] have generally been struggling, not with the relatively academic issue of adequate initial capitalization, but with the widespread phenomenon of selfdealing [sic] on the eve of insolvency. This is often so even when courts mention inadequate capitalization as a basis for decision. As is often said, a fraudulent conveyance is but the reflex of an insolvent man. It strikes me as insuperably difficult to read and ponder a good sampling of the case law classified under the headings of equitable subordination and veil-piercing, and then to fail to concede that fraudulent transfers and obligations have been the focus of litigation and legal doctrine. . . .

* * *

---

† [Material moved from footnotes to text for clarity. Ed]

The ideals [behind fraudulent conveyance law] are clearly involved in piercing cases when the remedy is granted because of an unfair transfer. Usually, if the outside creditor had knowledge of specific unfair transfers, he would simply bring a fraudulent conveyance action instead of a piercing suit, or would add a fraudulent conveyance count to his complaint in the piercing suit. However, unfair transfers are occasionally involved in piercing suits without being explicitly analyzed as such or related to fraudulent conveyance law. The reason is similar to that which accounts for some of the equitable subordination cases. The number of unfair transactions with insiders may be large and indefinite, and proof of unfairness and the extent of lack of fair consideration in each instance of a transaction may be difficult or extremely costly.

* * *

The piercing cases appear to employ a shotgun remedy, that is, a remedy less precisely responsive than those invoked in fraudulent conveyance cases . . . . When not ignoring the question of the scope of the relief completely, courts in piercing cases often assume either [sic] that the proper remedy is simply the complete revocation of limited liability. One obvious alternative, where state decisional law recognizes the inadequate capitalization theory, is that the recovery be limited to the amount of the inadequacy of the capitalization. . . . [I]f the personal assets of the defendants exceed either the amount of funds improperly transferred to them from the corporation or the size of the inadequacy of the corporation's capitalization, piercing the veil and imposing liability to the full extent of their personal assets will overcompensate the creditors for the harm traceable to the defendants' provable or wrongful acts. This result has the effect of penalizing the defendants.

* * *

. . . The function of the [agency theory for piercing] in practice is that of loosening up the level of proof and the atomistic nature of the analyses required in a fraudulent conveyance action explicitly denominated as such. Instead of focusing sharply on each dealing of the defendant corporation with its controlling shareholders and confronting directly the doctrinal arguments for and against making inadequate capitalization per se a basis for calling off limited liability, the court may find that random instances of self-dealing and mismanagement, in the context of the shareholder's failure to keep corporate books and observe corporate formalities, his or its mingling of corporate and personal (or parent company) assets, and various other utterances and acts which suggest too weak a faith in the reality of the corporate fiction, is sufficient to make the shareholder unlimitedly liable. All of the latter kinds of "indicia" of agency—the inattention to formalities and the mingling of affairs and assets—are, upon analysis, singularly lacking in *direct* relevance to the question of the existence, and the amount, of harm caused the outside creditor by the misbehavior of the controlling shareholder. Yet these indicia do at least *suggest* that fraudulent transfers may have taken place, or that creditors justifiably relied on the creditworthiness of the dominant stockholder or an affiliated corporation, and when sufficiently suffused with intimations and evidence of some actual self-dealing, may create the appearance of a justification for going beyond the limits imposed by doctrine which would require atomistic analysis and a precise remedy.

. . . .[126]

* * *

Notes and Questions

Professor Clark asserts that the critical fact in many (most?) piercing cases is self-dealing (in other words, transactions between the corporation and its owner) on the eve of insolvency. Notice the two differences Professor Clark points to between attacking such transactions as a fraudulent conveyance and using such conduct as grounds to pierce. Proof that a specific transaction is a fraudulent conveyance would require, generally speaking, the creditor to show that the shareholder transferred property out of the corporation for the purpose of hindering the creditor's collection, or that the corporation made a transfer when the company was or would be insolvent and without receiving fair consideration in return. Does one see this sort of careful evaluation of the propriety of each transaction between the corporation and its shareholder in the typical piercing case? Upon finding a fraudulent conveyance, the remedy is to return the property. In contrast, piercing leaves the shareholder liable for the entire debt owed by the corporation to the plaintiff creditor, even if that is greater than what the shareholder improperly took from the company. What, if anything, justifies these differences? Would confining the creditor's claim to fraudulent conveyance law impose an unfair evidentiary burden when confronting shareholder self-dealing with a marginally solvent company? Would simply requiring return of property provide adequate deterrence? On the other hand, is this any different than dealing with non-corporate debtors,

126 It should also be mentioned that the technique of doctrinal suppression can be invoked not only to hurt but to help controlling shareholders, when the court feels for whatever reasons that the shareholders should be helped but might be unduly disadvantaged by an analysis in conventional fraudulent conveyance terms. A nice example is given by one of the major New York cases dealing with the attempt of contract creditors of a subsidiary corporation to pierce the corporate veils and obtain access to the assets of the parent corporation. In Bartle v. Home Owners Cooperative Inc., 309 N.Y. 103, 127 N.E. 2d 832 (1955) the creditors of the subsidiary corporation, a company in the business of building homes that were to be sold to the parent company's shareholders (who were mostly veterans), claimed that the parent corporation had dominated the subsidiary and had run it not in the best interest of the subsidiary itself but for the interest of the parent and its shareholders. In an opinion that is far from satisfactory in its explanation or motivations, the court rejected this claim which was a standard way of expressing the agency theory. Most interestingly, it completely brushed over the fact that plaintiffs had alleged that the subsidiary had sold its homes *at cost* to the veterans, 309 N.Y. at 107, 127 N.E. 2d at 834 (Van Voorhis, J., dissenting) and thus ignored the very real possibilities that a fraudulent convevance [sic] action could be brought to set aside these sales, or to recover the excess of market value, over cost from the veterans, or to recover the excess amount from the parent corporation on the theory that it, as controlling party, was the fraudulent transferor or at least an aider and abettor. Had the court recognized these possibilities, it might have been forced to acknowledge that the case before it was in substance one seeking to recover from the parent as a fraudulent transferor and, therefore, the fact that the homes were to be sold at cost to the veterans was crucial.

in which piercing would not be available as a substitute for a fraudulent conveyance action? Can you see a distinction in the role of the transferee when the fraudulent conveyance comes from a non-corporate debtor?

---

2. *Policy Critique*

Have you been able to form a judgment thus far as to whether piercing doctrine is consistent with the policies behind limited liability discussed in Chapter I? The next article excerpt attempts to do just that.

Frank H. Easterbrook and Daniel R. Fischel, *Limited Liability and the Corporation*, 52 U. CHI. L. REV. 89 (1985)*

* * *

We conclude . . . that the doctrine of piercing the corporate veil, and the distinctions drawn by courts, may make more sense than at first appears. The cases may be understood, at least roughly, as attempts to balance the benefits of limited liability against its costs. Courts are more likely to allow creditors to reach the assets of shareholders where limited liability provides minimal gains from improved liquidity and diversification, while creating a high probability that a firm will engage in a socially excessive level of risk taking. We discuss below the more important aspects of the doctrine.

A. Close Versus Public Corporations

Almost every case in which a court has allowed creditors to reach the assets of shareholders has involved a close corporation.[37] The distinction between close and public corporations is supported by economic logic. In close corporations, there is much less separation between management and risk bearing. This has profound implications for the role of limited liability. Because those who supply capital in close corporations typically are also involved in decisionmaking, limited liability does not reduce monitoring costs [by avoiding incentives for shareholders to engage in excessive monitoring of managers (as would exist if shareholders in a public corporation feared personal liability)]. Other benefits of limited liability in public corporations—facilitating efficient risk bearing and monitoring by the capital market—also are absent for close corporations.

Moreover, the incentive created by limited liability for managers to undertake overly risky projects is much more severe in close corporations. Whatever the liability rule, managers of publicly held corporations do not bear all of the costs of their

---

* Reprinted with permission.

37 We say "almost every" only because we have not examined them all. . . .

actions. There are many of them, and each owns but a small fraction of the firm's shares. This is not necessarily true in close corporations. Under a rule of unlimited liability, investor-managers bear all of the costs of their actions. Under a rule of absolutely limited liability, by contrast, investor-managers can limit their risk to the amount of capital in the corporate treasury and transfer more of the risk to third parties. Piercing the veil—especially in favor of trade and tort creditors who cannot negotiate with the firm—reduces the extent to which third parties bear these costs.

B. Corporate Versus Personal Shareholders

The other major category of piercing cases involves parent-subsidiary combinations, where creditors of the subsidiary attempt to reach assets of the parent. Courts' greater willingness to allow creditors to reach the assets of corporate as opposed to personal shareholders is again consistent with economic principles.

Allowing creditors to reach the assets of parent corporations does not create unlimited liability for any people. Thus the benefits of diversification, liquidity, and monitoring by the capital market are unaffected. Moreover, the moral-hazard problem is probably greater in parent-subsidiary situations because subsidiaries have less incentive to insure. In publicly held corporations, the inability of managers to diversify their firm-specific investments in human capital creates incentives to insure. The same is not true for managers of subsidiaries if, as often will be the case, these people are also managers of the parent. Bankruptcy of the subsidiary will not cause them to lose their positions in the parent or suffer any other loss of firm-specific human capital (though it might impose a reputational loss on them). If limited liability is absolute, a parent can form a subsidiary with minimal capitalization for the purpose of engaging in risky activities. If things go well, the parent captures the benefits. If things go poorly, the subsidiary declares bankruptcy, and the parent creates another with the same managers to engage in the same activities. This asymmetry between benefits and costs, if limited liability were absolute, would create incentives to engage in a socially excessive amount of risky activities.

It does not follow that parent and affiliate corporations always should be liable for the debts of those in which they hold stock. Far from it. Such general liability would give unaffiliated firms a competitive advantage. Think of the taxicab business. Taxi firms may incorporate each cab or put just a few cabs in a firm. If courts routinely pierced this arrangement and put the assets of the full venture at risk for the accidents of each cab, then "true" single-cab firms would have lower costs of operation because they alone could cut off liability. That would create a perverse incentive because, as we have emphasized, larger firms are apt to carry more insurance. Potential victims of torts would not gain from a legal rule that promoted corporate dis-integration. As a result, courts properly disregard the corporate form only when the corporate arrangement has increased risks over what they would be if firms generally were organized as separate ventures.

C. Contracts Versus Torts, and the Fraud or Misrepresentation Exception

Courts are more willing to disregard the corporate veil in tort than in contract cases. The rationale for this distinction follows directly from the economics of moral hazard—where corporations must pay for the risk faced by creditors as a result of limited liability, they are less likely to engage in activities with social costs that exceed their social benefits. Contract creditors, in other words, are compensated ex ante for the increased risk of default ex post. Tort creditors, by contrast, are not compensated.

This distinction between contract and tort creditors breaks down when the debtor engages in fraud or misrepresentation. For the costs of excessive risk taking to be fully internalized, creditors must be able to assess the risk of default accurately. If the creditor is misled into believing that the risk of default is lower than it actually is, the creditor will not demand adequate compensation. This will lead to an excessive amount of risk taking by firms, because some of the costs are now shifted to creditors.

Courts have responded to this problem by allowing creditors to go beyond the assets of the corporation in cases of fraud or misrepresentation. The problem can arise in a variety of ways. The most obvious occurs when a corporation misrepresents the nature of its activities, its ability to perform, or its financial condition. Less obvious situations crop up when a firm misleads a creditor into believing that it would have recourse to the assets of other corporations in the event of nonperformance. This could occur if managers make express statements that a parent corporation will stand behind the debts of a subsidiary or if the parent and the subsidiary have confusingly similar names, so that the creditor believes it is dealing with the parent. In all these situations, creditors are unable to assess the risk of default accurately and thus the probability that the firm will engage in excessively risky activities is increased.

D. Undercapitalization

A final factor commonly emphasized by courts in deciding whether to allow creditors to go beyond the corporation's assets is the extent of the firm's capitalization. Again the reason is clear: the lower the amount of the firm's capital, the greater the incentive to engage in excessively risky activities.

The extent of a firm's capitalization is most important in situations involving involuntary creditors, where high transactions costs preclude negotiation. But undercapitalization can also be relevant in situations involving voluntary creditors. Many credit transactions are too small to warrant a full investigation of the debtor's finances by the creditor. Someone who sells the firm a chair on thirty-days' credit is not going to engage in detailed negotiations about risk and security. In these situations, it is desirable that creditors be able to assume that the debtor is adequately capitalized. The firm should have a duty to notify the creditor of any unusual capitalization. It is cheaper for the firm (which has the best information about its capital structure) to notify creditors in the unusual case than for creditors to investigate in all cases. (By "adequately" capitalized we mean an amount of equity that is within the ordinary range for the business in question. . . .)

* * *

Notes and Questions

Professors Easterbrook and Fischel assert that assurances by a shareholder to stand behind a corporate debt can provide grounds to pierce. Recall that Professor Hamilton stated this was not the rule in Texas. Would piercing in this situation allow a creditor to circumvent the statute of frauds? On the other hand, if limited liability in a contract context ultimately exists by virtue of the creditor's willingness to do business on that basis, what do such personal assurances tell us about this willingness?

---

3. *Reality Check: What Courts Really Do*

The authors of the articles excerpted above based their conclusions as to what courts are doing in piercing cases upon reading a sampling of reported decisions (and, perhaps, a bit of the authors' own views of what the courts should be doing). What result would one get if one could survey virtually every reported decision involving piercing?

Robert B. Thompson, *Piercing the Corporate Veil: An Empirical Study,* 76 CORNELL L. REV. 1036 (1991)*

* * *

This empirical study evaluates . . . claims about piercing the veil cases by analyzing the nature of the corporations, the plaintiffs, the courts, and the reasons given by the courts for piercing or not piercing the corporate veil. The results suggest that the factors affecting the judicial outcome are not necessarily as suggested by previous commentary. . . .

* * *

This project includes all Westlaw cases through 1985 concerning the issue of piercing the corporate veil. Those cases that did not address corporate law were eliminated from the initial set of 2000, leaving a pool of about 1600 cases for which both factual and analytical data were collected. . . .

* * *

IV. EMPIRICAL RESULTS

A. The Frequency Distributions

1. *General Observations*

Some initial observations can be made based on review of the entire data set. Piercing of the corporate veil is limited to close corporations and corporate groups (parent/subsidiary or sibling corporations). In the entire data set, piercing did not occur in a publicly held corporation. . . .

* * *

Courts pierced the veil in about 40% of reported cases.

TABLE ONE

Category	All cases	Pierce	No Pierce	% Piercing
#	1583	636	947	40.18

The remainder of this article examines factors which lead to piercing percentages different from the overall percentage shown in Table 1. . . .

* * *

3. *Differences Based on the Number and Identity of the Shareholders*

The number of shareholders makes a difference in the propensity of courts to pierce the veil of corporations. Among close corporations, those with only one shareholder were pierced in almost 50% of the cases; for two or three shareholder corporations, the percentage dropped to just over 46%, and for close corporations with more than three shareholders, the percentage dropped to about 35%. . . .

* * *

The role that an individual plays within a corporation also has an effect on the outcome. Defendants who served only as shareholders were less likely to be successful targets of piercing suits than shareholders who also served as directors or officers. Further, in the few cases that characterized potential defendants as passive shareholders rather than active in the business as directors, officers, or otherwise, the courts almost always found no liability.

4. *Differences Based on Whether the Defendant is an Individual or a Corporation*

When potential defendants against whom liability is sought are grouped as either individuals or corporations, courts pierce the veil to get at individual defendants more often than they pierce to reach corporations. This result is contrary to what some commentators have suggested. . . .

* * *

6. *Differences Based on the Substantive Context in Which the Claim Arose*

When the cases are broken down based upon whether they arose in a contract situation or a tort situation, the results show that courts pierce more often in the contract context than in tort context. This difference is statistically significant.

TABLE NINE

Context	Total Cases	Pierce	No Pierce	% Piercing
Contract	779	327	452	41.98
Tort	226	70	156	30.97

* * *

These results, more than any other in the project, go against the conventional wisdom . . . .

* * *

B. Reasons Given by the Courts

. . . The next section presents the empirical results of the reasons given by the courts, focusing both on the relative frequency with which these reasons appear in piercing cases and the percentage of times that the appearance of these reasons coincides with a piercing result. . . .

2. *Undercapitalization*

Undercapitalization is a factor frequently cited by commentators as part of a normative standard in piercing cases. . . . The results of undercapitalization cases are surprising in light of this commentary . . . . Of 327 contract cases in which courts pierced the veil, undercapitalization is present only in sixty-one (about 19%); of seventy tort cases in which courts pierced the veil, undercapitalization is present in only nine (just under 13%). . . . In both contexts, courts refused to pierce in 25 to 30% of the cases even when undercapitalization was present, belying any automatic predictive value for that factor.

. . . The relative infrequency with which courts cite undercapitalization in tort-related piercing cases suggests it is an issue that appeals to commentators for reasons other than its predictive significance.

3. *Informalities*

. . . Other commentators note that courts nearly always cite disregard of formalities, and that failure to maintain formalities substantially increases the probability of piercing. Again the results do not provide confirmation for the commentary. Of 151 cases in which courts cited a corporation's failure to follow corporate formalities, courts pierced the veil in 101 (just under 67%). That percentage of piercing is a little less than the percentage for undercapitalization . . . .

Informalities are cited in 20% of the contract cases in which courts pierced, as compared to about 11% of the tort . . . cases in which courts pierced. . . .

* * *

Notes and Questions

One methodology question arises by virtue of Professor Thompson's use of reported decisions as his data base. Some statistical work suggests that reported decisions are not representative of the overall body of litigation. Clear-cut cases tend to settle, leaving the close cases to reach the stage of a judicial decision. Hence, one should expect to find the results of reported decisions evenly split between plaintiffs' and defendants' victories. See Priest & Klein, *The Selection of Disputes for Litigation*, 13 J. LEGAL STUD. 1 (1984). Still, while this might tend to explain the overall success rate for plaintiffs in reported piercing cases, it is unclear how this could account for the counterintuitive differences in success rates between tort and contract creditors or between individual or parent corporation defendants. Moreover, presumably settlement of a piercing case would involve some payment by the shareholder to the plaintiff creditor and thus some loss of limited liability. This fact, coupled with the large number of piercing cases and the substantial percentage of plaintiff victories, suggests loss of limited liability is not a rare occurrence, as often stated in traditional doctrine.

Another question about Professor Thompson's study is whether some of his conclusions fit his data. He suggests that the data undermine the significance of both inadequate capitalization and lack of formalities as grounds for piercing. Notice, however, when either of those factors were present, courts pierced in a large majority of cases. What Professor Thompson seems to be focusing on is the small percentage of decisions to pierce in which either of these two factors were present. Does this mean that these two factors are not grounds for piercing, or just that they are only two of a number of grounds? The latter possibility, however, raises the question of what other factors courts are looking at as a reason to pierce in the large majority of cases in which neither of these two factors were present. Unfortunately, Professor Thompson's study—either reflecting the lack of coherent explanation in judicial opinions or the difficulty of dealing with 1600 cases—is not particularly helpful in answering this question, since the more common "factors" picked up in the study as grounds for piercing consist of buzzwords like "alter ego." Moreover, once we recognize that courts usually pierce in cases where neither inadequate capitalization nor lack of formalities appear present, might this also suggest that even when those factors were present, they were not the cause of the decision to pierce and so Professor Thompson's conclusion is correct?

B. Defective Incorporation

In piercing, the court disregards the existence of the corporation to impose liability upon a shareholder for a corporate debt. We now turn to the situation in which, due to some gaffe, there was no corporation at the time the liability was incurred.

1. *The Doctrine Introduced*

Fred S. McChesney, *Doctrinal Analysis and Statistical Modeling in Law: The Case of Defective Incorporation*, 71 WASH. U. L.Q. 493 (1993)*

* * *

II. THE LAW OF DEFECTIVE INCORPORATION

A. Background

By statute, corporations come into existence upon the performance of certain formalities. These formalities have traditionally included filing the articles of incorporation with some state functionary (typically the Secretary of State), the owners' payment into the firm of a certain minimum capital, and so forth. Completion of the statutory requirements makes the firm a de jure corporation, with limited liability for its stockholders.

The problem of defective incorporation usually arises when the firm's incorporators have not completed one or more of the statutory conditions precedent to the formation of a de jure corporation, but owners or other parties—often unaware of any deficiency and believing a valid corporation to exist—undertake to act on behalf of the supposed corporation. When a plaintiff allegedly injured by the firm files suit and learns that the firm has insufficient assets to satisfy a judgment, the plaintiff then discovers that the firm in fact was not a valid corporation. The plaintiff then seeks to satisfy any judgment against the owners' personal assets as well.

Determining whether and under what circumstances to shield firm owners from personal liability in a defectively incorporated firm has vexed courts since general incorporation statues [sic] were first promulgated. The problems derive to a considerable extent from the conflicting overlaps among three related areas of law: contract, agency, and partnership. Under traditional contract law, the parties' intentions would decide the dispute. If both parties intended limited liability to apply to dealings between them, then no personal liability would come about in the event of subsequent breach of contract. Statutory compliance would be irrelevant. . . . The contract rules would not, of course, apply to torts committed in pursuit of the supposed corporation's business.

Traditional agency principles, however, would dictate a different set of results. A firm's agent who purported to contract with others on the basis that the firm was a corporation, when it was not, would effectively act as an agent for a nonexistent principal. The agent then would be personally liable. This would be true whether the agent was an owner or not. . . .

Under the law of partnership, a third set of rules would apply. If owners of a firm are not legally incorporated, they satisfy the common-law and statutory definitions of a partnership: co-owners of a business being operated for a profit. If so, the acts of any owner or even an agent in furtherance of the firm's business make all owners personally liable.

* * *

B. De Facto Incorporation and Corporation by Estoppel

. . . If individual owner-defendants can establish that the firm was nonetheless a "de facto corporation," they will be protected by limited liability just as if a true de jure corporation had been perfected by completion of the statutory requirements. . . .

Three requirements are typically cited for application of the de facto corporation doctrine. There must have been: (1) a statute in existence by which incorporation was legally possible; (2) a "colorable" attempt to comply with the statute; and (3) some actual use or exercise of corporate privileges. Because every state has a corporation statute and defendants ordinarily have been acting under the aegis of a supposed corporation, the three factors typically dissolve into one: whether defendants' attempts to incorporate had gone far enough to be deemed "colorable compliance." For example, an attempt to file the articles of incorporation, albeit unsuccessful, has frequently sufficed as the necessary attempt at statutory compliance. . . .

When the firm does not meet the requirements for a de facto corporation, limited liability may nonetheless be granted under the rules of corporation by estoppel. By that doctrine, a party who deals with the firm, believing a de jure corporation exists, will be estopped in subsequent litigation from denying a corporate existence. For example, a creditor who extends a loan to a firm, believing erroneously that it is a corporation, will be estopped to deny corporateness and seek satisfaction against owners personally in any legal action on the debt. The firm need not make an attempt to comply with the statute. In the typical case, for example, the firm owners have agreed privately as to the articles of incorporation, but the attorney handling the matter fails to file them.

The generally acknowledged formulae for the two doctrines have several implications. . . .

[D]e facto corporate status apparently depends on what defendants have done—whether a good faith attempt to comply with the statute was made—not on anything that plaintiffs have or have not done. This is in keeping with the fundamental reason offered for the de facto doctrine, that a defendant who has in good faith tried but failed by a mere technicality to complete the statutory requirements ought not suffer such harsh punishment as personal liability. However, in estoppel cases, a plaintiff's belief that he is dealing with a corporation, rather than what defendants have done or failed to do, is supposedly the controlling factor. . . .

* * *

Notes and Questions

Professor McChesney lists two theories of liability—agent for a non-existent principal, and partner—and two defenses to liability—de facto corporation, and estoppel—potentially applicable when there is a defective attempt to incorporate. The bulk of the cases raise issues concerning the two defenses. Is there any practical impact to the different theories of liability? Consider who would be liable under each of the theories.

2. *Reality Check: What Courts Really Do*

Once again, as with piercing, it is interesting to compare the stated doctrine to the results of the overall body of cases applying the law.

Alexander Hamilton Frey, *Legal Analysis and the "De Facto" Doctrine*, 100 U. PA. L. REV. 1153 (1952)*

* * *

. . . I have sought to gather and analyze all the reported American cases in which a "corporate" creditor[13] is seeking to obtain a judgment against one or more of the associates ("shareholders") personally, because of a non-compliance with some provision of a general incorporation act concerning the prescribed procedure for bringing a corporation into existence, and in which the outcome of the case is not controlled by an explicit statute.

* * *

CONCLUSION

* * *

. . . I have arrived at a few conclusions as to what the courts have been deciding concerning the personal liability of members of defectively incorporated associations for obligations of their associations.

* Reprinted with permission.

13 The expression "corporate" creditor refers to a creditor of an association resulting from a defective attempt to incorporate.

1. If the plaintiff did not accept the association as a corporation, as in the typical tort situation, or if the fact that the association claimed to be incorporated was unknown to him (*i.e.*, if the dealings were not on a corporate basis), and if he elects to sue the members of the association individually instead of the association as such, he is virtually certain to succeed, in so far as the issue of their personal liability is concerned, if he can show almost any kind of a failure to comply with the statutory provisions for incorporation or with statutory conditions precedent to the commencement of business in corporate form. I base this conclusion on the fact that in thirty out of thirty-two cases in which the dealings were not on a corporate basis, the plaintiff prevailed although the cases involved a considerable variety of different types of defects. And yet the emphasis in the "de facto" doctrine, as traditionally expressed, is entirely upon the character of the defect ("colorable" attempt) and not at all upon the nature of the dealings between the parties.

2. If the articles of incorporation had not been recorded at all, either with the secretary of state or locally in the designated county office, prior to the transaction with the plaintiff, and if the dealings with him were on a corporate basis, an action by the plaintiff to hold the members of the association personally liable to him has little more than an even chance of success. . . .

* * *

3. Where the plaintiff has dealt on a corporate basis with an association which, unbeknown to him, has made no attempt to incorporate, he is not precluded from suing the members of the association individually. In about half of the cases in which the plaintiff had dealt on a corporate basis with an association which had drafted articles of incorporation but had not recorded them with the secretary of state or at all, the defendant associates were held to be protected by the corporate nature of the dealings from personal liability. But where there have been no steps toward incorporation, the associates are afforded no such protection, and the fact that the transaction was on a corporate basis is not said to "estop" the plaintiff from pursuing the associates personally.

4. If the articles have been recorded with the secretary of state, although not recorded locally, and if the dealings were on a corporate basis, the associates are almost invariably accorded freedom from personal liability.

* * *

6. A summary of all the cases reveals that those active in the management of defectively incorporated associations have been subjected to personal liability to a somewhat greater extent than inactive shareholders. But when the cases involving any particular defect are separately examined, this factor does not stand out significantly, and one is not justified in concluding that participation in management is an important factor in predicting the probable impact of a defect in incorporation upon the liability of the members.

* * *

We come now to an inquiry into the "why" behind the decisions. Why do the courts almost invariably hold the associates personally liable if the dealings were not on a corporate basis, regardless of the nature of the defect? If the articles were recorded with the secretary of state but not locally, why do the courts with virtual unanimity exonerate the associates from personal liability if the dealings were on a corporate basis? If, on the other hand, the articles were recorded locally but not with the secretary of state, why do the courts almost half of the time impose personal liability on the associates even though the dealings were on a corporate basis?

Categorical answers to these questions cannot be extracted from the opinions. As indicated heretofore, if the decision is adverse to the defendants, the court is quite likely to assign as a reason that the association is not a "de facto" corporation; but, as observed above, this is not a reason but a mere reiteration of the ultimate judgment. If the decision is in favor of the defendants and the dealings were on a corporate basis, the court will frequently state that the plaintiff is "estopped" from imposing personal liability on the defendants. But why such plaintiffs are "estopped" when the articles have been recorded only with the secretary of state, and not when they have been recorded only locally, the opinions do not reveal.

* * *

Notes and Questions

Professor Frey seems at a loss to explain his results. Is the problem that the judges did not understand the relevant legal doctrine—specifically, that they are dealing with two separate defenses to liability, one, "de facto corporation," which focuses on how innocent or serious the defendant's error, and the other, estoppel, which focuses on the windfall to the creditor? Or is the answer—as Professor McChesney concludes in his article after reviewing the Frey data—that there is really only one rule and this rule involves a balancing of factors favoring the creditor and the defendant? If so, is this "rule" consistent with the policies behind limited liability considered in Chapter I?

---

3. *The Impact of Statutes*

Professor McChesney's discussion and Professor Frey's survey reflect decisions by courts without guidance from the state's corporations statute, except, of course, that the statute set out requirements to form a corporation which the defendants did not meet. Since Professor Frey's survey, many states have adopted provisions of the American Bar Association's Model Business Corporations Act which, as the following excerpt points out, address this area.

Wayne N. Bradley, Comment: *An Empirical Study of Defective Incorporation*, 39 Emory L.J. 523 (1990)*

* * *

B. *Defective Incorporation and the Model Act*

. . . By the time of the Model Act's inception many, including the writers of the Model Act, wanted to eliminate the de facto doctrine completely. Thus, section 50 of the 1950 Model Act provided that "[u]pon issuance of the certificate of incorporation, the corporate existence shall begin," and section 139 provided that "[a]ll persons who assume to act as a corporation without authority so to do shall be jointly and severally liable for all debts and liabilities incurred or arising as a result thereof." The Official Comment to section 50 stated somewhat equivocally that the de facto doctrine had been eliminated.

The 1969 revision of the Act did not change the language of either section 50 or 139, but the official comments were extensively reworded to make the intent of eliminating the de facto doctrine unmistakable. The official comment to section 56 (former section 50) stated that "a de facto corporation cannot exist under the Model Act" because "any steps short of securing a certificate of incorporation would not constitute apparent compliance." The Comment to section 146 (former section 139) stated:

> This section is designed to *prohibit* the application of any theory of de facto incorporation. The only authority to act as a corporation under the Model Act arises from completion of the [incorporation] procedures. . . . No other means being authorized, the effect of Section 146 is to negate the possibility of a de facto corporation.
>
> Abolition of the concept of de facto incorporation, which at best was fuzzy, is a sound result. No reason exists for its continuance under general corporate laws, where the process of acquiring de jure incorporation is both simple and clear. The vestigial appendage should be removed.

The elimination of the de facto doctrine had two very different effects, depending on the state. In some cases, these provisions were interpreted literally, and courts found that there could never be limited liability without the issuance of a certificate of incorporation. . . . In other states, courts simply ignored these provisions, despite their unequivocal intent, wherever the result would have been inequitable.

The 1984 Revised Act changed earlier versions of these provisions. The Revised Act provides that corporate existence begins with the filing of a certificate of incorporation, so the bright-line feature is preserved. The Committee, however, changed the wording of section 2.04 (former section 146) as follows:

> All persons purporting to act as or on behalf of a corporation, knowing there was no incorporation under this Act, are jointly and severally liable for all liabilities created while so acting.

The change was the result of "a review of the underlying policies represented in earlier versions of the Model Act" as well as a review of recent case law. The addition of the knowledge requirement was intended to allow for a more flexible standard. In other words, the new version of this section allows courts to take into account equitable considerations, in recognition of the fact that many courts were already doing this.

* * *

D. *The Effect of Statutes*

Another mode of analysis of the cases from 1970 to present analyzed the level of influence that statutes had on defective incorporation problems. Each of the 131 cases was classified into one of three categories. Either the case was treated as a common law problem, or it was decided based on a Model Act-type statute, or the decision was based on another type of statute, often a dissolution provision. . . . [C]ourts generally treat defective incorporation as a common law problem. Of 131 cases, 82 (62.6%) adopted a common law analysis of the defective corporation issue and few contained any reference to a statute. The remainder of the cases either discussed Model Act-type statutes (21.4%) or some other statute, often a dissolution provision (16.0%).

The [situation in which a creditor sues to hold would-be shareholders liable for debts of a defectively formed corporation] contained the highest percentage of cases which treated the problem as one controlled or heavily influenced by a statute. Of those cases, 35.8% referenced Model Act-type provisions and 13.4% mentioned other statutes. Even here, however, 50.7% of the cases treated the situation as a common law problem.

The effect of the Model Act on shareholder liability is apparent in the [situation in which a creditor sues to hold would-be shareholders liable for debts of a defectively formed corporation] . . . . The courts in 45.7% of the cases in which individual liability was imposed did so based on equivalents to RMBCA sections 2.03 and 2.04. On the other hand, in the cases where individual liability was not imposed, the courts considered these provisions in just 8 of 32 cases (25.0%). Of course, part of this disparity may be explained by the tendency of courts to cite the Model Act-type provisions when they are going to impose liability anyway and to ignore the provisions when they choose to find corporate attributes. However, at least some of the difference must be traced to the policy underlying the Model Act of attempting to eliminate the defective incorporation doctrines, as reflected in cases . . . where liability is imposed in situations in which limited liability would have been found before the introduction of the Model Act.

* * *

Notes and Questions

Notice how the drafters of the Model Act have gone from one extreme to the other when it comes to liability for innocent mistakes. Having set out in 1950 and 1969 to eliminate the de facto corporation defense, the 1984 version of the Act goes the defense one better by only imposing liability on those who know there was no corporation. Look again at the Frey survey. It contains no data on the defendants' knowledge, so we do not know how many cases the new Model Act would have changed. On the other hand, notice the large percentage of recent cases still decided under common law rules. Is it clear that Section 2.04 supplants, as opposed to supplements, the agency and partnership theories of liability? Do you see why this is a different issue than whether a provision creating a new statutory theory of liability is subject to common law defenses?

C. Promoters' Contracts

In the defective incorporation cases, the creditor, if not the defendant, believes at the time of contracting that a corporation exists. As the next piece describes, the analysis changes entirely when both parties are aware at the time of contracting that there is not yet a corporation.

Robert A. Kessler, *Promoters' Contracts: A Statutory Solution*, 15 RUT. L. REV. 566 (1961)*

A few years ago Sir Alec Guinness made a hilarious movie which is still playing the late late movie circuit. It was entitled "The Promoter" and humorously portrayed the crooked activities which are normally associated with people who bear that title. Despite his popular image, the corporate promoter is not always as despicable a figure as we might like to think. In fact when the term "promoter" is used in its broadest sense, it is clear that he plays an essential part in the formation of every corporation.

* * *

An example which most practitioners even with small corporate practices (in both senses) will recognize as typical will illustrate the corporate omnipresence of the promoter: A client enters the lawyer's office; he is a cook working on a salary, but he has heard that the diner down the street from the one at which he presently works is for sale. He and his brother together have enough cash to buy it; the place is a little run down, but his brother's wife will lend them what they need to fix it up; he has seen the

---

place—passes it every day on his way to work—and knows that it has a fair clientele, and since he knows "something about the business," he feels that he "can make a go of it"; he wants the protection of limited liability just in case, though, so he tells the lawyer to form a corporation and also to arrange the details of the purchase of the lunchwagon.

* * *

The typical promoter, who is, in reality, the typical small businessman, deserves greater protection from the dangers he faces. The major risk is that despite the fact that he has chosen the corporate form just to escape this personal liability, he will be held to be individually liable to the third parties with whom he has negotiated contracts for the corporation's necessaries. The corporation usually cannot be incorporated until it possesses all of its necessaries, yet *it* cannot get them until it has first been incorporated.

In our example with the diner, the client, sensibly, does not want to incorporate unless he knows the corporation will own the diner, yet the corporation cannot agree to buy the diner until after it has already been formed. If the purchase of the diner and the incorporation could be simultaneous events there would be no problem. Normally, of course, they cannot be. A commitment to purchase the corporation's necessaries must usually be made prior to the actual incorporation: The owner of the diner wants to sell now. He will sell to the corporation later *unless* a better offer comes along before the corporation comes into existence. The cook's lawyer may rush the process of incorporation, but if that better offer comes along before the receipt comes back from the Secretary of State, the client is left with a worthless charter, the lawyer without the client and perhaps with an uncollectible bill for legal services.

Because of these dangers, the usual alternative has been for the promoter to make a contract for the necessaries before waiting for the paperwork of incorporation to be completed. To return to our example, the cook would sign a contract of purchase for the diner. Perhaps his name is Charles Zilch, and he and his associates have agreed that the name of the corporation will be Charles Zilch, Incorporated. He may sign the contract simply "Charles Zilch," or he may sing it "Charles Zilch, for a corporation to be formed" or, perhaps, "Charles Zilch, Incorporated, by Charles Zilch."

Now he "has" the diner, and he can incorporate Charles Zilch, Incorporated to take it over, assured that the principal necessity for the corporation's successful birth has been "assembled." As is fortunately usually true, real legal problems will probably fail to materialize in this situation. If the corporation is formed, and it has sufficient assets to meet the obligations under the contract, and the contract still appears to be one which will be profitable for the corporation, there will generally be no trouble. The corporation will accept the liabilities and benefits under the contract, the third party contracting with the corporation will receive what he bargained for, and there will be no attempt made to hold the promoter to any personal liability.

But the law must deal with the "problem cases," and, unfortunately, they do arise: Perhaps one of the enterprisers decides to "drop out," and the corporation is never formed; or the other enterprisers feel that their associate agreed to pay more than the diner was worth, and they want to "get out" of the contract; or the business fails, and the seller decides that he would do better to try to make the individual pay than rely on the corporation's empty coffers.

What does the law say in these problem cases? The result would probably shock the poor cook and perhaps his lawyer. Obviously, where the promoter signs merely his own name, he, of course, is individually liable on the contract. But what if the promoter clearly indicates that he is signing not in his own behalf but for a corporation yet to be formed? Even where the promoter accepts an offer made to the "proposed" company or signs the contract "for a company to be organized and incorporated," the result surprisingly enough seems to be the same: the promoter is individually liable on the contract. This, despite the fact that disclosure is made through the form of the signature that the contract is to be a corporate one and presumably also, that the individual promoter does not intend to be bound personally.

* * *

How then can the promoter protect himself? The corporation can, of course, after incorporation attempt to take over liability on the contract. The most popular conceptualism for the corporation's undertaking to be bound on the contract is "adoption." The use of this term today is preferred to "ratification," the older expression, in order to preserve inviolate the agency law rule that ratification may only take place where the principal could have entered into the contract himself. Since the corporate principal was not in existence when the promoter's contract was made, it could not have entered into the contract. *Ergo*, it cannot "ratify" it.

* * *

. . . This, of course, is no help to the promoter where for some reason or other the corporation is never formed. Ironically, it is little help to the promoter even when such corporate liability does take place, for under the majority rule, in the absence of an actual novation, the promoter continues to be liable on the agreement, despite its ratification or adoption by the corporation.

Thus the effect of corporate adoption or ratification is merely to give the third party a choice of defendants. If the corporation fails to perform on the contract, he may still recover from the promoter. . . .

* * *

The parties may, of course, enter into an express agreement that upon formation of the corporation and acceptance of the contract by it, all liability of the promoter thereunder shall cease, and the corporation will be completely substituted in his place. In other words, the third party may give express advance assent to a novation. This is probably the most satisfactory way of protecting the promoter ordinarily available. It has, however, from his point of view, the disadvantage that it recognizes the initial personal liability of the promoter on the contract, something which is manifestly not in his interest.

The terms may proliferate: all liability of the promoter may automatically cease on a certain date whether or not the corporation is formed. But if such a term is inserted, the wise lawyer for the third party will require an additional term, an undertaking by the promoter guaranteeing formation of the corporation within a certain time. Basically, the promoter will want a contract never binding upon him as an individual, while the third party will want a contract which is definitely binding on at least someone, the promoter or the corporation, all along. . . .

* * *

Two other alternatives have been suggested . . . . The first alternative is to merely take an offer on behalf of the corporation which, upon its formation, the corporation itself may accept. Such an alternative would, of course, protect the promoter from any individual liability. However, as any first year law student knows, an ordinary offer may be withdrawn by the offeror any time before acceptance. The third party is not bound, and the corporation may find that it has incorporated for nothing: Its prime necessary may no longer be available once the process of incorporation has been completed. The promoter as such may be protected, but as a businessman assuring the success of his corporate enterprise he may well fail. The solution is thus unsatisfactory.

The final alternative suggested by some writers is the use of an option contract, *i.e.*, an offer which cannot be revoked at the whim of the third party. The promoter is not directly liable and hence safe, since there is no contract, except one to give an irrevocable offer. He must, however, put up consideration for the option. . . . Further, the drafting of the two most satisfactory arrangements, the contract with a novation provision and the option contract, both require the knowledge of an experienced corporate practitioner, services which the average small businessman is often unable to afford, and which his "3-simple-corporations-a year" lawyer is usually unable to offer.

From the point of view of the promoter, the "default law" treatment is inadequate. . . .

* * *

Notes and Questions

Professor Kessler finds the default rule making the promoter liable on pre-incorporation contracts to be unsatisfactory. Do you agree? The promoter, of course, would like to have the third party bound, but avoid any liability for him- or herself. In other words, the promoter wants to "have one's cake and eat it too." Do you see why making this the default rule would fly in the face of the basic principle that it takes two parties for a contract? Would a more reasonable interpretation of the parties' action be that there was no contract, but simply an offer which the corporation might accept after it came into existence? Professor Kessler notes that this is not in the promoter's interest, nor would it seem to be what the third party wants; which perhaps explains why this interpretation is not the default rule. An option contract takes some consideration and so does not seem to work as a default rule in a case when the contract does not identify any consideration independent of the future corporation's performance. A present contract between the third party and the promoter, subject to an advance agreement for a novation once the corporation is formed and accepts liability, is a possible interpretation. Is there any reason to think this is more likely to be what the parties had in mind? Does this interpretation impose any greater risks on the third party than the third party would have faced if the promoter had formed the corporation before negotiating the contract?

At any event, the basic policy here is to figure out what the parties intended. The best solution would be for the parties to be clear about their intent at the start. That may be too much for unsophisticated individuals without legal representation. Is it too much to expect, however, of Professor Kessler's "3-simple-corporations-a-year" lawyer? Should an attorney, even in a general practice, know that corporations cannot enter contracts if they do not yet exist and that it takes two parties to have a contract? Should such an attorney be aware of the possibilities of option contracts or a novation? If not, should the lawyer be forming any corporations a year?

D. Distribution Limits

We encountered the subject of distributions briefly in Chapter I, when Professor Bechuk used it has an example of creditor protection rules which state competition may have undermined. The following excerpt provides a discussion of the statutory limits on distributions.

Melvin Aron Eisenberg, *The Modernization of Corporate Law: An Essay for Bill Cary,* 37 U. Miami L. Rev. 187 (1983)*

* * *

C. *Corporate Distributions*

A Corporation normally distributes funds to its shareholders in one of two ways: by paying a dividend, or by repurchasing or redeeming a portion of its stock. Corporate law has traditionally set limits on such distributions through the use of various financial tests that center on the concept of preserving legal capital.

Most of the statutes adopt either a balance-sheet or an earned-surplus test. Under a balance-sheet test, distributions may be made only out of surplus, as opposed to legal capital. Broadly speaking, surplus falls into two basic categories: earned surplus, which is more or less equivalent to accumulated earnings; and capital surplus, which consists of a variety of sub-accounts, including paid-in, reduction, and revaluation surplus.

In apparent contrast, earned-surplus statutes begin by limiting distributions to that part of surplus that represents accumulated earnings. Typically, however, these statutes go on to permit distributions out of capital surplus under defined circumstances. In the final analysis, therefore, earned-surplus statutes, like balance-sheet statutes, turn on the preservation of legal capital.

What then is legal capital? Originally, it was the aggregate par value of issued stock. In a bygone era, all shares had a par value and most probably were issued at a price equal to par value. In that era, the concept of legal capital had a certain economic significance: legal capital was conventionally more or less equal to the economic capital created by the issue of stock. Modern statues, however, do not require that shares have a par value, and even shares that have a par value may carry a par value much lower than the price at which they are issued. Accordingly, the *economic capital* generated by the issue of stock may be much greater than the corporation's *legal capital*, which has become a mere legal construct determined in a wholly arbitrary manner. The excess of economic over legal capital that is created on the issuance of shares is designated as paid-in-surplus. Distributions can normally be made out of paid-in surplus without violating either a balance-sheet or an earned-surplus statute. Furthermore, legal capital itself can be reduced by a shareholder vote, and the resulting reduction surplus can also be used as a source of distributions under either type of statute. Thus the impoverished protection afforded creditors by prohibiting distributions out of legal capital is wholly bankrupted by the warrant to reduce capital and pay dividends out of the reduction.

A related lack of economic reality is found in the statutory treatment of a repurchase by a corporation of its own shares. From the perspective of creditors, a repurchase is economically indistinguishable from a dividend. Under most statutes, however, a repurchase of shares, unlike a dividend, may not irreversibly decrease surplus, because repurchased stock is conceived of as "treasury stock" and retains the status of issued stock until cancelled or reissued. The rationale of this treatment is that repurchased shares resemble an asset, because they can be resold. In modern corporations, however, authorized shares normally far outnumber issued shares, or easily can be made to do so by certificate amendment. Accordingly, a repurchase of shares normally enables a corporation to do nothing more than it could have done without the repurchase. Economically, therefore, repurchased shares are no more of an asset than are authorized but unissued shares.

In sum, the traditional statutory provisions concerning distributions bear virtually no relation to economic reality. Involuntary creditors, trade creditors, and short-term lenders must normally take this law as they find it. Institutional lenders and preferred-stock underwriters, however, have the power to impose contractual restrictions on distributions beyond those imposed by corporation law, and they normally do so. The contractual restrictions commonly employed in long-term and preferred-stock underwriting agreements tend to demonstrate what kinds of limits on distributions are economically significant and workable. Under the most common pattern found in long-term loan agreements, for example, the corporation promises not to make a distribution to shareholders unless the proposed distribution, plus all other distributions after a given date, would be less than earnings accumulated after that date plus the proceeds of new stock issues. The relevant date, known as the "peg date," is usually the beginning of the fiscal year in which the debt is issued. This requirement may be supplemented by a provision that working capital (current assets minus current liabilities) will not fall below a designated level, thereby helping to preserve the quality as well as the quantity of net worth.

In 1975, California modernized its statute along lines comparable to those of long-term loan agreements. To begin with, the California statute drops the concepts of "legal capital" and "surplus"; classifies dividends, repurchases, and redemptions as "distributions"; and treats all distributions under a common set of rules. To oversimplify slightly, a distribution to shareholders is permitted only if (1) retained earnings equal or exceed the proposed distribution, or (2) immediately after the distribution, the corporation's assets will be at least one-and-one-quarter times its liabilities, and current assets will equal or exceed current liabilities. In addition, the statute includes an equity insolvency test, and it prohibits any distribution to holders of a junior class if, following the distribution, the excess of assets over liabilities would be less than the aggregate liquidation preferences of senior classes. Finally, reacquired shares revert to the status of authorized but unissued stock. Thus the building blocks of the California statute are not empty legal concepts, like legal capital and treasury stock, but economic realities, like retained earnings, asset-liability ratios, and liquidation preferences.

In 1979, the Model Act was revised along similar lines. Prior to that time, the Model Act had become a wastebasket of dividend tests—allowing dividends out of earned surplus, out of current income without regard to earned surplus, out of amortization of wasting assets without regard to either earned surplus or current income, out of paid-in surplus, out of reduction surplus, and, according to an official comment, out of revaluation surplus. As revised, the Model Act, like the California statute, drops all references to par value, capital, and surplus; treats dividends and repurchases under the common heading of distributions; and provides that reacquired shares revert to the status of authorized but unissued stock. The commentary accompanying the adoption of these provisions states that "insolven[cy] in the equity sense . . . [is] the most important and fundamental test for the permissibility of distributions."

There are a number of important differences between the Model Act and California provisions. For example, as long as liquidation preferences are protected, the California statute permits a distribution if the corporation either has sufficient retained earnings or satisfies both a total and a current assets-to-liability ratio. The Model Act provides only a total assets-to-liabilities test, together with an equity insolvency test and protection of liquidation preferences. In calculating asset-liability ratios, the California statute excludes exotic items such as goodwill, capitalized research and development expenses, and deferred credits. The Model Act does not. The California assets-to-liability tests are based on values determined under generally accepted accounting principles. The Model Act requires only that determinations be based upon accounting principles and practices, or a fair valuation method, reasonable under the circumstances. For present purposes, however, the important point is not which statute is preferable, but that the new Model Act provisions, like those of California, are economically meaningful. This cannot be said of the vast majority of distribution provisions on the statute books.

Notes and Questions

1. Professor Eisenberg uses a number of terms which might be unfamiliar. Equitable insolvency is the inability to pay one's bills as they become due and so it is pretty obvious why the law would forbid the payment of dividends by a corporation in that condition. Figuring out all the different types of "surplus" mentioned by Professor Eisenberg is probably more trouble than it is worth, since in the end all of them can be the source of dividends. Hence, the bottom line question is what is surplus. Surplus is not some stash of money hidden in the corporate vault, but rather a number arrived at by subtracting from the total value of the corporation's assets, the total amount of the company's liabilities and its "capital." Now it becomes evident why Professor Eisenberg points out that the traditional statutes key on the preservation of legal capital. What policy might such an approach serve? Recall the discussion of moral hazard in Chapter I. If the shareholders could pull money out of a corporation until what was left equalled (or, worse, was less than) the amount of the firm's debts, what incentive would they thereafter have as far as risk taking by the company? The problem with the traditional statutes is that they allowed the shareholders to zero out capital through the mechanisms discussed by Professor Eisenberg, thereby creating precisely this hazard.

Now compare the two modern approaches discussed in the article. California attempts to preserve some cushion of owner equity in the company by use of the numerical tests Professor Eisenberg describes. By contrast, the revised Model Act reacted by making explicit what had evolved in the traditional statutes: Distributions generally are permissible so long as they leave assets at least equal to liabilities. Notice that this abandons any attempt to combat the moral hazard problem by forcing the shareholders to keep any of their own money in the corporation.

For a much more detailed comparison between the various approaches to distribution limits and an attempt to weigh their costs and benefits, see Kummert, *State Statutory Restrictions on Financial Distributions by Corporations to Shareholders*, 59 WASH. L. REV. 185 (1984). For an analysis of how closely California's statutory limits predict corporate bankruptcy—in other words, prevent distributions by corporations that within a few years went bankrupt, while at the same time not restricting corporations that did not later go bankrupt—see Yoav Ben-Dror, *An Empirical Study of Distribution Rules Under California Corporations Code § 500: Are Creditors Adequately Protected?*, 16 U. C. DAVIS L. REV. 375 (1983).

2. Interestingly enough, in enacting a limited liability company statute (where creditors face the same dangers from distributions as they do with corporations), the California legislature chose not to apply the restrictive tests found in California's corporations statute, but instead to follow the revised Model Act's permissive approach. For a discussion see Gevurtz, *California's New Limited Liability Company Act: A Look at the Good, the Bad and the Ambiguous*, 27 PAC. L.J. 261 (1996). Is California's action consistent with Professor Bebchuk's concerns about the effect of state competition?

Chapter III

Fiduciary Duties of Officers and Directors

We turn now from the claims of creditors against shareholders to the duties that officers and directors owe to the corporation and its shareholders. As you look at the specific doctrines to follow, reconsider the discussions in Chapter I. Are the fiduciary duties of officers and directors simply default rules whose only purpose is to save the parties the cost of contracting, or is there some other purpose? If the latter, then where did these duties come from and what further purpose do they serve?

A. The Duty of Care and the Business Judgment Rule

1. *The Doctrine Introduced and Critiqued*

Melvin A. Eisenberg, *The Duty of Care of Corporate Directors and Officers,* 51 U. Pitt. L. Rev. 945 (1990)*

* * *

Corporate directors and officers are under three general legal duties: the duty to act carefully, the duty to act loyally, and the duty to act lawfully. The subject of this Article is the first of those duties, generally known as the duty of care.

I. Background Principles

The duty of care of corporate directors and officers is a special case of the duty of care imposed throughout the law under the general heading of negligence. All law builds on moral, policy, and experiential propositions. The law of negligence is no exception. The moral proposition that underlies the law of negligence is that if a person assumes a role whose performance involves the risk of injury to others, he is under a moral duty to perform that role carefully. . . . So, for example, one who assumes the role of driver is under a moral duty to drive carefully; one who assumes the role of doctor is under a moral duty to practice medicine carefully; one who assumes the role of judge is under a moral duty to judge carefully. The moral duty to perform a role carefully does not require that one act so as not to create any risk of injury to others. Any action involves a risk of injury to others. Although a person who sets out to drive, practice medicine, or judge may cause an injury that would not have occurred if he stayed home, that alone is not enough to assign moral blame. To assign moral blame, it must be the case that the person has not merely caused an injury, but has acted in a manner that involved an unreasonably great risk of causing an injury, as he knew or in the reasonable exercise of his abilities should have known.

* * *

A moral obligation to exercise care in the performance of one's role is also imposed on corporate directors and officers. This moral obligation is an aggregate comprised of four relatively distinct duties, each of which requires separate analysis. These are:

(1) The duty of directors to reasonably monitor or oversee the conduct of the corporation's business, and, as a corollary, to take reasonable steps to keep abreast of the information that flows to the board as a result of monitoring procedures and techniques.
(2) The duty of inquiry—that is, the duty to follow up reasonably on information that has been acquired and should raise cause for concern.
(3) The duty to employ a reasonable decisionmaking process.
(4) The duty to make reasonable decisions.

The liability imposed on corporate directors and officers by law is congruent with, but not identical to, these four moral duties. The general legal principle, expressed in section 4.01(a) of the American Law Institute's Principles of Corporate Governance, is that a director or officer must act in a manner that he reasonably believes to be in the best interests of the corporation, and with the care that an ordinarily prudent person would reasonably be expected to exercise. A counterpart of this principle is to be found in most statutes. The translation of that general principle into specific legal rules involves a number of difficult issues. One source of these difficulties is that what constitutes reasonable care must always be colored by context, so that, for example, what constitutes reasonable care in the context of highly complex and inherently risky group decisionmaking will differ from what constitutes reasonable care in such paradigm contexts as automobile accidents. Another source of these difficulties is that special considerations of policy and fairness apply to decisionmaking by directors and officers. As I will show, broadly speaking the components of a director's or officer's liability resemble the components of the moral duty, except that for reasons of policy and fairness, in certain cases the law provides a partial immunity to directors and officers who have made decisions that could fairly be deemed unreasonable.

* * *

B. *Knowledge, Competence, and Skill*

What degree of knowledge, competence, and skill is expected of a director or officer in performing his functions?. . .

* * *

Unlike other professionals, directors, acting in that capacity, are usually generalists. That does not mean, however, that they need have no special knowledge, competence, or skill. In *Francis v. United Jersey Bank*, the court said:

> As a general rule, a director should acquire at least a rudimentary understanding of the business of the corporation. Accordingly, a director should become familiar with the fundamentals of the business in which the corporation is engaged. . . . If one "feels that he has not had sufficient business experience to qualify him to perform the duties of a director, he should either acquire the knowledge by inquiry, or refuse to act."[25]

In contrast to directors, officers usually are expected to have special competence and skill—the competence and skill of managers, and, if they hold a specialized position (such as a finance post), the competence and skill necessary for that position.

III. THE DUTY TO MONITOR

With this background, I shall now review the specific duties that comprise the legal duty of care. The first of these is the duty of directors to reasonably monitor or oversee the conduct of the corporation's business, and, as a corollary, to take reasonable steps to keep abreast of the information that flows to the board as a result of monitoring procedures and techniques. Typically, the duty to monitor is satisfied not, or not primarily, by direct observation, but by installing or reviewing the adequacy of procedures or techniques by which salient information concerning the conduct of a corporation's business will flow to the board, or to reliable executives or third-party professionals acting on the corporation's behalf and subject to the ultimate responsibility of the board. . . .

* * *

The duty to monitor does not require a director to acquire information on all aspects of a corporation's activities. As a practical matter, this would be infeasible. It would also be undesirable, because the benefits of acquiring information on some activities might not be worth the costs. Furthermore, the resulting overload might well inhibit the director's understanding of significant information. Accordingly, it is consistent with the monitoring obligation to give little or no attention to a given matter, depending on the status and scope of the matter, the reasonableness of delegations con-

25 87 N.J. 15, 432 A.2d 814, 821-822 (1981).

cerning the matter, and the director's judgment on such issues as the ripeness of the matter and its practical importance. . . .

. . . For example, the board may marshal relevant information, appraise the risks, and then make a deliberate decision not to install an antitrust-compliance program or a computer-security program. . . . [I]f a deliberate decision by the board on whether or how to monitor a given activity satisfies the conditions of the business-judgment rule, the board may be insulated from liability even though the decision was not a reasonable one.

* * *

IV. The Duty of Inquiry

A second basic duty of care, sometimes referred to as the duty of inquiry, is to follow up reasonably on information that has been acquired and should raise cause for concern.

* * *

The duty of inquiry may be triggered by information acquired through the duty to monitor, but it may also be triggered by information that reaches a director or officer in other ways—even adventitiously. . . .

* * *

V. Care in Making Decisions

The last two components of the duty of care involve care in performing the decisionmaking function. As in many other areas of law, the rules governing this area have a procedural and a substantive element. The procedural element concerns the process of decisionmaking, and more specifically, the manner in which a director or officer should inform himself before making a decision. The substantive element concerns the quality of the decision itself.

A. *The Procedural Element*

The procedural element of the law governing decisionmaking by directors and officers is based on the general principle that directors and officers must use reasonable care. Specifically, directors must use reasonable care in informing themselves, or to put it differently, must properly inform themselves, concerning a proposed action before making a decision. What is reasonable care in informing oneself in any given case depends on a great variety of considerations, such as the scale of the decision, the time available to make it, the cost involved, and the confidence the director or officer can reasonably have in analyses and recommendations by subordinates. The inquiry need not be exhaustive. Business decisions must sometimes be made with considerable haste. The inquiry that might reasonably be required if weeks were available might not be required if the risk of forgoing a profitable transaction compelled directors to act in a matter of hours. . . .

B. *The Substantive Element*

In contrast to the procedural element of the law governing decisionmaking by directors and officers, which is based on the general principle of reasonableness, the substantive element, which concerns the quality of decisions, is based on a special protective rule—the business-judgment rule. That rule has . . . conditions for its application.

First, the business-judgment rule is applicable only if a decision has been made. . . .

Second, the business-judgment rule is applicable only if the director or officer is not financially interested in the subject matter of a decision. So, for example, the rule is inapplicable to a decision by a director to approve a purchase by the corporation of his own property.

* * *

We come now to the heart of the business-judgment rule. If a director or officer makes a decision, and is disinterested and has reasonably informed himself, the quality of the decision will not be reviewed under the normal standard of reasonableness, but instead will be subject to only exceptionally limited review. The precise standard of review is stated in various ways. . . .

There is, it is true, a rule in negligence that sounds very much like the business-judgment rule. It is often said, especially in malpractice cases, that "honest errors of judgment" will not give rise to liability. . . .

* * *

. . . Although the malpractice cases usually do not explain precisely what is meant by the honest-error-of-judgment rule, it is clear that the purpose of the rule is to distinguish between bad decisions and decisions that turn out badly. . . .

The honest-error-of-judgment rule covers just this kind of decision—a decision that was reasonable when made, but turns out to be in "error" in the very restricted sense that if the decisionmaker had it to do all over again he would make a different decision. Indeed, if the courts are correct in their evaluations in these cases there is really no error at all. A decisionmaker faced with uncertainty knows that he must make a judgment concerning the relevant probability distribution, and must act on that judgment. If the decisionmaker makes a reasonable judgment about the shape of the distribution, and the outcome falls on the unlucky tail, the decisionmaker has not made any error in the normal sense of that term, because in any normal probability distribution some outcomes must inevitably fall on the unlucky tail.

* * *

The business-judgment rule applicable to directors and officers goes much further than the honest-error-of-judgment rule of general tort law. Under the business-judgment rule, there is no liability even though a decision is unreasonable. But why should a much lower standard of care be set for reviewing the quality of decisions by corporate directors and officers than for reviewing the quality of decisions by almost anyone else—even other professionals?

The answer to this question involves considerations of both fairness and policy.

* * *

Note

Professor Eisenberg served as Chief Reporter for the American Law Institute's project which drafted the *Principles of Corporate Governance: Analysis and Recommendations*. (It is too long a story to explain why the ALI did not just call this a restatement.) His description of the business judgment rule follows closely the ALI's formulation. Considerable controversy, however, surrounded the ALI's *Principles*, including its interpretation of the business judgment rule. *See, e.g.*, Phillips, *Principles of Corporate Governance: A Critique of Part IV*, 52 GEO. WASH. L. REV. 653 (1984)(this article is part of a symposium dealing with the ALI project, which includes a number of articles critical of the ALI's approach to the business judgment rule); Hanson, *The ALI Corporate Governance Project: Of the Duty of Care and the Business Judgment Rule, A Commentary*, 41 BUS. LAW. 1237 (1986). The drafters of the Model Business Corporation Act also attempted to define the business judgment rule, but ultimately decided they could not do it. For a discussion of the Model Act's duty of care provisions see Veasey & Manning, *Codified Standard—Safe Harbor or Uncharted Reef? An Analysis of the Model Act Standard of Care Compared With Delaware Law*, 35 BUS. LAW. 919 (1980); Arsht & Hinsey, *Codified Standard—Same Harbor but Charted Channel: A Response*, 35 BUS. LAW. ix (1980). The following article excerpt takes a more detailed look at the business judgment rule.

Franklin A. Gevurtz, *The Business Judgment Rule: Meaningless Verbiage or Misguided Notion?*, 67 S. CAL. L. REV. 287 (1994)*

* * *

I. WHAT IS THE BUSINESS JUDGMENT RULE?

* * *

Much of the difficulty with efforts to define the business judgment rule . . . stems from a faulty starting premise. This premise is that there is *a* business judgment rule. In fact, there is no single rule. Instead, the phrase "the business judgment rule" has a number of different meanings. To aid analysis, it is useful to group these meanings into two categories.

A. The Business Judgment Rule As a Tautological Statement

A widely used hornbook on corporate law[14] provides a good illustration of the first common usage of the phrase "the business judgment rule." In black letter, the book's authors state, "The 'business judgment' rule sustains corporate transactions and immunizes management from liability where the transaction is within the powers of the corporation (intra vires) and the authority of management, and involves the exercise of due care and compliance with applicable fiduciary duties." Numerous court decisions contain similar descriptions of the so-called rule. . . .

* * *

A moment's reflection establishes that these statements really do not say much of anything. Stating that directors will be immune from liability so long as they act with due care (or reasonable diligence) and comply with their fiduciary duties (that is, are disinterested and act in good faith) is simply saying that directors will not be liable for their decisions unless there is a reason for holding them liable. Specifically, directors will only be held liable if they breach their duties of care or loyalty. This is hardly an earth-shattering proposition. . . .

. . . Another common variation on this theme is to state the "rule" as containing a rebuttable presumption. The presumption is that the directors did not violate their duties—in other words, did not put themselves in a conflict of interest, act in bad faith or without due care, or the like—when they made their decision. Here, too, there is less substance then meets the eye. This "presumption" entails nothing more than saying that the plaintiff who challenges a decision of the board has the burden of proving that the directors breached one of their duties. Yet, the proposition that the plaintiff, in any context, has the burden of proving his or her prima facie case is a rule with which every first-year law student should be familiar.

Given the not-surprising conclusion that directors are only liable if the plaintiff proves that the directors breached their duties, the question then becomes whether the business judgment rule says anything significant about what it takes to prove a breach, particularly of the duty of care. For many courts and writers the answer is really no. These courts and writers apply concepts of ordinary negligence to identify conduct that breaches the directors' duty of care. For example, in one of the most often quoted reconciliations of the business judgment rule with the law of negligence, a New York trial court explained:

> The question is frequently asked, how does the operation of the so-called "business judgment rule" tie in with the concept of negligence? There is no conflict between the two. When courts say that they will not interfere in matters of business judgment, it is presupposed that judgment—reasonable diligence—has in fact been exercised.[26]

* * *

14 Harry G. Henn & John R. Alexander, Laws of Corporations (3d ed. 1983).

26 Casey [v. Woodruff], 49 N.Y.S.2d at 643.

This version of the business judgment rule continues the type of broad tautological statement quoted earlier to an unexceptional conclusion: Directors are not liable unless they breach their duties of loyalty or care, and the duty of care is that of reasonable skill and prudence—the same standard as is the norm throughout the law of torts. About the only thing the "rule" adds is a cautionary note that an error in judgment or a mistake—in the sense of a decision that does not turn out as one hoped—does not automatically equal negligence. This same caution could be sounded for doctors, lawyers, or automobile drivers sued for their mistakes.

* * *

B. The Business Judgment Rule As a Special Standard of Liability for Duty of Care Violations

An alternate interpretation of the business judgment rule is far more significant. Numerous courts and writers—now joined by the American Law Institute—view the business judgment rule as providing a special standard of culpability against which to assess whether directors breached their duty of care. Unfortunately, these courts and commentators disagree on what the standard is or should be. Worse still, several factors complicate any effort to delineate the respective views. For one thing, judicial opinions in this area are replete with imprecise and inconsistent use of language. . . . In addition, the different standards in this area range along a continuum, rather than representing discrete splits of authority. Nevertheless, it is possible to discern three major viewpoints which go far to define this spectrum. The viewpoints' common bond is that each holds that director liability under the business judgment rule requires greater fault than ordinary negligence.

1. *The Good Faith Standard*

At the opposite extreme from ordinary negligence are the courts and writers who view the business judgment rule as commanding a largely subjective approach. . . .

* * *

Under this approach, a court's review of a challenged decision focuses largely, if not exclusively, upon the subjective motivations for the action. While courts use a variety of terms to identify the pertinent inquiry—such as the presence or absence of good faith, honesty, or fraud—the heart of the matter is whether or not the directors believed that what they were doing was in the best interest of the corporation. Excluded from the courts' inquiry for the most part is any review of the objective reasonableness of such a belief.[48] Under the most extreme interpretation, the business judgment rule effectively abolishes the duty of care for any situation in which the plaintiff challenges an action by the board. Instead, all that remains of the duty under

48 As stated earlier, views of the business judgment rule as a standard for duty of care liability form a continuum rather than precisely defined positions. . . . The cases following a good faith approach illustrate this point. Few unequivocally rule out any review of objective reasonableness. Instead, after proclaiming that directors' decisions are unassailable in the absence of bad faith, dishonesty, or fraud, such opinions often soften such statements by backpaddling in varying degrees. Some opinions . . . supplement

this view is to avoid the sort of inattention and inactivity typified by cases such as *Francis v. United Jersey Bank*, in which the director ignored all corporate affairs while her sons looted the company.

2. *The Gross Negligence Standard*

One middle ground between ordinary negligence and the "good faith only" standard is found in Delaware. The Delaware Supreme Court has settled, at least since the mid-1980s, on the notion that the business judgment rule embodies a standard of gross negligence. Delaware's Supreme Court announced this position in *Aronson v. Lewis* by stating that "[w]hile the Delaware cases use a variety of terms to describe the applicable standard of care, our analysis satisfies us that under the business judgment rule director liability is predicated upon concepts of gross negligence."[51] The Delaware Supreme Court subsequently reaffirmed this standard in *Smith v. Van Gorkom*.[52] ... While Delaware thus provides the clearest and most important expression of this approach, the gross negligence standard extends well beyond the Delaware courts.

This leaves two related questions: First, what exactly does the gross negligence standard mean, and second, how is this standard different from ordinary negligence? One Delaware court has said that "in the corporate area, gross negligence would appear to mean, 'reckless indifference to or a deliberate disregard of the stockholders' ... or actions which are 'without the bounds of reason.'" The reader may be forgiven for finding such a definition less than entirely helpful. In fact, it is difficult to pin a precise meaning upon the term gross negligence. This has led some to suggest that the term has no significance or, put another way, gross negligence is the same thing as negligence "with the addition of a vituperative epithet." Reinforcing this skepticism is the fact that it is not easy to find cases applying the gross negligence standard to directors' actions in which use of this standard, rather than an ordinary negligence test, unquestionably made a critical difference to the outcome.

* * *

Still, one should not dismiss the term gross negligence too quickly. Even if not amenable to precise definition, most individuals would have no trouble understanding that gross negligence entails some worse level of dereliction than ordinary negligence.[63]...

---

holding claims limited to fraud or bad faith with a finding that the directors' decision was objectively reasonable (or, at least, finding the plaintiff had not shown the decision was unreasonable).... Shlensky v. Wrigley, 237 N.E.2d 776, 780-81 (Ill.App.Ct. 1968)(stating that baseball team director's failure to mirror practices of other team directors was not negligent). Other opinions adhering to a largely subjective approach expressly leave the door open to finding liability in a truly egregious case despite good motives....

51 473 A.2d 805, 812 (Del. 1984).

52 488 A.2d 858, 873 (Del. 1985).

63 ....

From a practical standpoint, the significance of a gross negligence test may be more a matter of altering statistical probabilities than of changing the results in any specific case. If enough fact finders in enough close cases are instructed they may find the defendants liable only if they find gross rather than ordinary negligence, there will be in all likelihood a greater number of defense verdicts.

3. *The Process-Versus-Substance Distinction*

The American Law Institute's *Principles of Corporate Governance* provides an example of a another approach to duty of care liability under the business judgment rule. This approach draws a distinction between the level of judicial scrutiny of the directors' decision itself, and review of the process the directors used to arrive at the decision. . . .

* * *

Essentially, the ALI proposes to focus the protective thrust of the business judgment rule on limiting judicial scrutiny of the substance of the directors' decision. The ALI formulates a standard of reasonable belief regarding the process the directors use to reach their decision, or, more specifically, whether directors gathered adequate information before acting. This would appear consistent with the norm of ordinary negligence. When it comes to the substance of the directors' decision, however, the ALI's proposed version of the business judgment rule lowers the standard of care to a rational belief. The ALI's comments suggest this rational belief standard may be similar to an absence of gross negligence.

There are a number of variations on this process-versus-substance theme. All have in common, however, the notion that the business judgment rule calls for less judicial scrutiny of the merits of the directors' decision than of the process the directors used in arriving at the determination. One obvious extreme is to conclude that the business judgment rule precludes any review at all of the substance of the decision. The opinion of the New York Court of Appeals in *Auerbach v. Bennett*[70] provides an example of this extreme.

* * *

II. Is the Business Judgment Rule a "Good" Rule?

* * *

A. Examining the Justifications for Insulating Directors from Liability for Ordinary Negligence

Over the years, numerous courts and writers have recited a variety of justifications for the business judgment rule insulating directors from liability for ordinary negligence. . . .

1. *Difficulties with After-the-Fact Review of Business Decisions*

The most traditional arguments for insulating directors from liability for ordinary negligence center upon the difficulties which can attend after-the-fact judicial review of business decisions. These arguments often begin with the observation that because business decisions involve taking risks, many decisions by directors end up producing

25 393 N.E.2d 994 (N.Y. 1979).

a loss for the company. Such an observation, however, hardly distinguishes business decisions from decisions in numerous other contexts, such as medicine or law, which often involve taking calculated risks and in which many decisions will also produce harm or loss. More fundamentally, this observation is not inconsistent with the premises underlying the negligence standard. Specifically, the mere fact that a decision involves taking risks or ultimately results in a loss does not make the decision negligent. Spinning off from Judge Hand's famous formula, if the magnitude of gain expected from a board decision, multiplied by the probability measured ex ante of achieving the gain, exceeds the magnitude of loss risked by the decision, multiplied by the probability of the loss, than [sic] the decision presumably is reasonable. Accordingly, a negligence standard should neither deter the taking of desirable risks nor punish simply bad results.

The problem, however, is that this sort of formula is easier to recite than actually to apply in an after-the-fact judicial proceeding. Such a proceeding is neither infallible nor cost-free. Rather, there is always the concern that a fact finder with the benefit of hindsight will confuse bad results with an unreasonable decision. Moreover, even if the defendant prevails, victory may come only after expensive litigation. Accordingly, the argument often goes, without protection from liability for ordinary negligence, directors have an incentive to avoid potentially more desirable higher-risk activities in favor of less profitable but more guaranteed undertakings.

Yet, in itself, this argument also does not distinguish business decisions from decisions in medicine, law, or a myriad of other undertakings to which the standard of ordinary negligence applies. Indeed, this line of reasoning is part of complaints by doctors and various other groups of prospective defendants who assert that the high cost of even a successful defense and the propensity of fact finders to confuse bad results with negligence have created a "malpractice crisis" and a need to reform the tort system. Hence, if one is to defend a business judgment rule that embodies a different standard of liability for directors, one must point to ways in which after-the-fact judicial review of business decisions poses greater difficulty than found in other areas. Specifically, the burden exists to show that there is a greater prospect for error in assessing the reasonableness of a business decision or that incentives to avoid risk pose some greater harm when dealing with business decisions. Those who defend a different standard for directors have made both claims.

Courts and writers have pointed to two factors which might make after-the-fact judicial review of business decisions more prone to erroneous factual conclusions than review of decisions in other areas. To begin with, judges and juries generally are not business experts. Yet, this perceived lack of competence has not prevented exacting judicial review under the intrinsic-fairness test of business decisions in which directors have a conflict of interest. More fundamentally, such lack of judicial expertise does not distinguish business decisions from medicine and innumerable other fields in which the negligence system holds sway.

If judicial expertise cannot justify different treatment, perhaps there is something about the nature of business decisions which renders review more speculative. A number of courts and writers have made the argument that each business decision is unique, heavily intuitive, and judgmental. These qualities, such courts and writers assert, both undermine the accuracy of after-the-fact review and are not true of other fields. For example, the principal reporter for the ALI Corporate Governance Project argued in a recent article that medical, unlike business, decisions involve established protocols which can guide both fact finders in accurately determining negligence and prospective defendants in avoiding the same.

There are a couple of difficulties with this argument. First and foremost, it is factually wrong. For one thing, the very existence of extensive formal business education would seem to contradict the notion that no norms guide the making of business decisions. . . .

If business decisions are not completely an unreviewable guesswork swamp, it is even more a myth to suppose medical or other professional decisions have been routinized down to the scientific application of accepted protocols. . . . In fact, law, medicine, business, and other professions may be largely alike in that they involve a substantial degree of what one author has labeled "knowing in action." In other words, the professional undertakes actions in unique situations based upon intuition and experience, without being able to articulate the exact reason for the course of action. To the extent this sort of intuitive "knowing in action" does not lend itself to an accurate after-the-fact judicial assessment of reasonableness, then perhaps there is a need to rethink the standards of malpractice generally. Such tort-law reform is well beyond the scope of this Article. The important point for present purposes is that business decisions do not represent a distinctly intuitive field in a way which renders them particularly inappropriate for judicial review; on the contrary, business decisions are very similar in this regard to decisions by other professionals.

* * *

If there is nothing about business decisions which makes an after-the-fact judicial review of reasonableness inherently less accurate than in other areas, one could still argue that deterrence of risk taking creates greater harm in the business context. Yet, there is little basis for such an argument. True, risk taking is important in business. But it is also important in medicine, law, and a host of other fields. For example, anyone who has been through the experience of discussing surgery in a doctor's office comes to realize that medical treatment inherently involves the taking of calculated risks. The same is true when deciding litigation and trial strategy and throughout much of the practice of law. Indeed, it is difficult to conceive of an area in which decisions do not involve a balancing of risks.

* * *

Overall, the concern that liability for ordinary negligence will deter directors from taking worthwhile risks sounds remarkably like the lament of doctors who complain that the threat of malpractice suits has forced them to engage in "defensive medicine" with the result of unnecessarily increased costs and the avoidance of worthwhile but more risky medical treatments. Similar laments can be heard coming from other professionals faced with liability for negligence. The concern about director liability and risk taking may well be valid. It is not, however, unique.

2. *Nature of the Damages*

A second group of arguments made in favor of a special standard of liability for directors focuses on the damages suffered by the corporation. Specifically, some writers have attempted to justify such a standard by noting that, unlike medical malpractice or many other torts which cause physical injuries, director gaffes cause only monetary loss. In addition, a number of writers have expressed concern about the potentially huge dollar losses which a director's decision could cause. . . .

It is difficult to find justification in such arguments for a different standard of liability for directors. Directors are hardly unique among prospective tort defendants in that their negligence is likely to cause economic loss rather than physical injury. To name one obvious group, the same could be said of attorneys.

Neither is the concern about the size of damage awards unique to directors. Doctors and other professionals have repeatedly expressed similar concerns about the size of awards against them. . . .

3. *Nature of the Plaintiff*

A third group of arguments in favor of less liability for directors centers on the nature of the plaintiff in a derivative suit. Several factors generally make the shareholder who brings such a suit a less than sympathetic victim. To begin with, normally the shareholder has voluntarily entered into the relationship with the directors. After all, no one forced the shareholder to buy stock, and the stockholders as a whole were the people who elected the board. Accordingly, if shareholders do not like the way the directors manage their company, they may either elect someone else or sell out. Further, according to currently popular financial theory, shareholders should protect themselves against the risks of mismanagement in any one company by holding a diversified portfolio of stock. Finally, the plaintiff in a derivative suit often is a fairly nominal shareholder who is serving primarily as a front for an attorney pursuing the action for the sake of fees. This fact, in turn, raises suspicions that plaintiffs may bring actions alleging a breach of the duty of care on only a slender basis and when the suit is not in the best interest of the corporation.

Each of these arguments, however, has a number of shortcomings. The fact that shareholders have entered into a voluntary relationship with the directors is not different from most situations involving malpractice claims. The same is generally true of patients with doctors, clients with attorneys, and a host of other situations out of which negligence actions may arise. . . .

The argument regarding diversification is more sophisticated, but ultimately is not more persuasive. . . . [T]he ability to protect oneself from director negligence by diversification is not entirely unique. . . . [M]edical and disability insurance cushion the financial risk from personal injury much as diversification cushions the loss from bad investments. . . .

Most fundamentally, however, the diversification argument proves too much. Holding diversified portfolios also dilutes the individual stockholder's risk from any given company becoming the victim of breaches of contract by those the company does business with, of illegal trade practices by the firm's competitors, of tortious activities by those outside the firm, or of other conduct which might harm and create a cause of action in favor of a corporation. Does anyone suggest the law abolish the ability of corporations to bring lawsuits, since their stockholders could always diversify to minimize such risks? The diversification argument—indeed, the whole cluster of arguments which focus on the plaintiff shareholder—ignores the fact that one of the original purposes for creating the legal fiction of corporate entities was to allow an entity to have rights and assert causes of action independent of its owners.

This fact is often obscured because shareholders suing derivatively on behalf of the corporation bring many, if not most, suits asserting director negligence. This makes it very tempting to attack perceived abuses in derivative suits by creating special liability rules, such as a business judgment rule, which insulates directors from liability for ordinary negligence. It is important to keep in mind, however, that liability rules will affect actions which are not shareholder derivative suits, such as when a trustee in bankruptcy or even the corporation's elected management decide to sue. Accordingly, if there is a problem with shareholder derivative suits, the answer lies in attacking the problem directly.

4. *Utility of Compensation or Deterrence*

* * *

A number of writers have argued that director liability for negligence poorly serves the goal of compensating corporations injured by such negligence. As a factual matter, recovery rarely comes from the negligent directors themselves. Rather, if there is a settlement, the corporation often will indemnify the directors. Alternately, liability insurance purchased by the corporation for its directors and officers commonly funds the payment. In the former instance, all that happens is that money makes a circuit as the corporation pays for its own recovery by indemnifying the defendants. Yet, it is not that simple or harmless since, as the money makes this circuit, much of it is lost to transaction costs such as attorneys fees, which the corporation also pays.

With liability insurance the loop is longer, but exists nevertheless as the insurance company uses premiums paid by corporations purchasing policies for their directors and officers to fund recovery. Of course, in this instance, it is not solely the recovering corporation which pays. Instead, all companies purchasing policies for their officers and directors have paid premiums. This is the risk-spreading function of insurance, the advantage of which is that unpredictable large losses typically produce a disproportionately greater harm than predictable small expenditures. Some writers have questioned whether this risk-spreading function is important in the corporate context given the ability of shareholders to limit risk by holding a diversified portfolio of stocks. This harkens back to the diversification argument discussed earlier. More fundamentally, however, risk spreading does not require courts to impose liability on directors. If enough corporations desire to insure against losses resulting from unreasonable director decisions, presumably they can voluntarily buy policies which do so.

In any event, even if recovery does not come from indemnity or insurance, it is open to debate just how desirable it is for directors to compensate their corporation. For one thing, corporations probably have more money than their directors and thus can better afford the loss. Moreover, directors may be poor at spreading the risk since they do not work for a large number of corporations.

One could, of course, quibble with portions of this sort of analysis. For example, statutes which allow a corporation to indemnify its directors for payments the directors agree to make to the corporation seem rather silly. Accordingly, maybe the problem lies with such statutes, rather than with director liability.

The fundamental problem with this whole line of reasoning, however, is not its invalidity, but rather its universality. Similar arguments provide the underpinnings for various no-fault proposals made to replace the negligence system in areas such as automobile accidents. The fact of the matter is that as a scheme solely for compensation (at least in the sense of avoiding financial hardship due to accidents), tort recovery is inefficient and probably makes little sense. The transaction costs to achieve compensation are high and compensation depends on fault rather than need. A more efficient way to achieve compensation is simply for individuals to purchase medical, disability and property-loss insurance, supplemented or supplanted if necessary by government-provided insurance. The fact that compensation may make little sense as a goal of negligent-director liability is simply a corollary of this broader phenomenon.

Given the above discussion, it is not surprising that many writers have sought to justify director liability for negligence primarily on deterrence rather than compensation grounds. Within the last decade or so, however, a number of writers principally associated with the law-and-economics movement have questioned the necessity of director liability to achieve deterrence. They argue that a number of economic incentives other than fear of liability exist for directors to make careful and reasonable decisions. These incentives include stock ownership by directors in their corporation, compensation schemes which tie financial rewards to corporate performance, the desire of officers and directors to develop and preserve their reputations for business acumen so as to advance their individual careers, and the fear that poor decisions will make the corporation a takeover target and result in the current directors losing their positions.

Other writers have questioned the efficacy of these incentives. . . .

The purpose of this Article is not to enter this debate. Rather, consistent with the general theme of this section, the larger flaw in the argument about other incentives is that it does not distinguish director liability from other contexts in which similar assertions could be made. For example, professionals often face market incentives for good performance. This may be most visible for trial attorneys whose reputations often hinge upon winning.

Another example may hit even closer to home for most readers. Consider the incentives automobile drivers have to drive carefully. While these lack the ring of "the market for corporate control," they would seem nevertheless powerful. Most significant could be simply the risk to the driver's personal safety of an accident. . . .

* * *

Note

For additional articles discussing the business judgment rule and various interpretations of the directors' duty of care see Dyson, *The Director's Liability for Negligence*, 40 IND. L.J. 341 (1964); Conard, *A Behavioral Analysis of Directors' Liability for Negligence*, 1972 DUKE L.J. 895; Cohn, *Demise of the Directors' Duty of Care: Judicial Avoidance of Standards and Sanctions Through the Business Judgment Rule*, 62 TEX. L. REV. 591 (1983); Soderquist, *The Proper Standard for Director's Negligence Liability*, 66 NOTRE DAME L. REV. 37 (1990).

---

2. *Reality Check: What Boards Do*

At this point, it is useful to compare the directors' duty of care with the actual manner in which boards of directors function. The article from which the following excerpt comes attempts to do precisely that.

Bayless Manning, *The Business Judgment Rule and the Director's Duty of Attention: Time for Reality,* 39 BUS. LAW. 1477 (1984)*

* * *

REAL-WORLD CONDUCT OF DIRECTORS

Practically all the current debate centers upon "outside" directors. In the real world, what do such directors—"good" directors—actually do in the discharge of their responsibilities? What is generally expected of them in the market place. [sic]

* * *

TIME DEVOTED

The outside directors of a corporation are part-time people with respect to the amount of working time that is allocated to the affairs of the company. The most recent survey (1982) shows that the average director of a publicly held company devotes a total of about 123 hours per year to his board and committee work, including travel. That averages less than 3 hours a week, or about 1.5 working days a month.

* * *

COMPLEXITY OF ENTERPRISE

Many of today's corporations are not only large, they have usually become highly diversified in their business operations—even those that are not conglomerates. . . .

No human being can stay on top of all this in a major company on a one-and-a-half-day-a-month basis.

PACE AND DELIBERATION

Much of the routine housekeeping work of a board of directors does not demand or warrant significant deliberation. Some important matters that come to the board can be and are dealt with in a deliberate manner over several meetings. A few matters, like the choice of a new CEO from among several in-house candidates, can often be pondered and observed carefully over a period of years, but most significant matters cannot be dealt with in that way by a board. The pace of commercial events often demands quick response or even, as in takeover situations, almost instant response. Even issues that are fully recognized to be vitally important can often not be considered extensively by a board because its agenda is at the time crammed with other exigent items or with matters which, though less significant, are mandated as compulsory agenda items under applicable laws or regulations.

UNCERTAINTY AND RISK-TAKING

. . . The businessman and the board of directors thrive or die in a sea of uncertainty. The chairman of a major bank recently made the point well when he said, "If I'm right three times out of ten, I am doing very well, and if I'm right four times out of ten, I'll do better than anybody else."

DIVERSITY OF DIRECTORS

CEOs understandably prefer other CEOs and corporate officers as directors because of their familiarity with the boardroom process and with the realities of business management, but today, increasing numbers of outside directors are persons who fall into other categories. Academics and persons with political backgrounds are often members of the modern board, while the percentage of lawyers and bankers has declined. A changing society has brought more women and persons of minority ethnic background into the boardroom. Moreover, it is increasingly common to include on boards some persons who have specialized skills that are invaluable to the work of the board, such as the musician on the board of the record company or the physicist board member of Silicon Valley, Inc. These increasingly diverse members can and do contribute significantly to the total work product of the board, but, at the same time, these members of diverse nonbusiness backgrounds are often not knowledgeable about many matters that come up on the board's agenda. . . .

DECISIONAL PROCESS

. . . The lawyer's professional experience in courts, legislatures, and semi-political bodies tends to lead him to assume that all decisional process is inevitably made up of a series of discrete, separate issues presented one at a time, debated by both or all sides, and voted on. In fact boards of directors typically do not operate that way at all, except, perhaps, in conditions of internal warfare or mortal crisis. Actions are usually by consensus. If a significant sentiment of disagreement is sensed by the chairman, the matter is usually put over for later action, and sources of compromise and persuasion are pursued in the interim. Advice from individual directors is most often volunteered to, or solicited by, the CEO informally on a one-on-one basis, rather than pursued in group debate at a board meeting.

CHARACTER OF THE AGENDA

A transcript of a typical board meeting will reflect four kinds of items on the agenda. Fully three quarters of the board's time will be devoted to reports by the management and board committees, routine housekeeping resolutions passed unanimously with little or no discussion, and information responding to specific questions that had earlier been put to the management by directors about a wide range of topics sometimes accompanied by suggestions from the board members, usually procedural in character. Perhaps the remaining one quarter of the meeting time will be addressed to a decision, typically unanimous, on one or two specific different business items, such as the sale of a subsidiary or the establishment of a compensation plan. If, as is the average, a board meets eight times a year, the arithmetic would indicate that a full year of the board's work would contain only ten or fifteen discrete transactional decisions of the type that are generally assumed to make up the main work of the board; and of those discrete transactional matters, many will be neither very important nor controversial, such as a decision to terminate a long-standing banking relationship in favor of a new one that provides better service.

* * *

AGENDA-SETTING—INITIATIVES BY THE BOARD

Agenda-setting and the scope of board initiative together comprise the single most important, and least understood, aspect of the board's work life.

. . . [T]he question of what the board will discuss and act on is typically determined by the management or by the corporation's automatic built-in secular equivalent of an ecclesiastical calendar, that is, shareholders' meeting date, fiscal year, cycle of audit committee meetings, and similar matters. The board can, and a good board will, from time to time suggest topics for exploration or discussion, or request the management to report in the near future on this or that matter of interest to the board. . . . But the board itself has little capacity to generate significant proposals, other than generalized suggestions looking toward the establishment of procedures or systems. Almost all of what a board does is made up of matters that are brought to it; matters generated by the board itself are very rare. Typically, boards cannot take, and are not expected to take, initiatives.

* * *

ACTIONS NOT TAKEN

All these realities of directional life add up to a deeper one. From among an infinite number of useful things that a board of directors *might* reasonably have done or looked into in a given time period, the number that will not have been done by the most qualified, best-run, and most diligent board in the world will always be far greater than the number that *were* done. . . .

* * *

RELIANCE

* * *

It is less widely understood, and not explicitly recognized in the law, that the dynamics of the boardroom are also deeply dependent upon a matrix of other reliances among individual officers and directors. Director X, at a meeting asks in respect of particular transaction A, "Will we have any trouble with our auditors if we do A?" Director Y, who is recognized by his colleagues to be the board's most knowledgeable member in matters of accounting (who may, or may not, be a member of the audit committee) says, "Don't worry, X, I don't think we'll have any problem there." Thereupon the conversation moves on to another topic, the group deferring in an informal way to the expertise and judgment of one of its members in whom it has confidence. . . .

* * *

JUDGMENT

Finally, we come to the matter of judgment itself. Assume, again, that a board is going through one of those episodes of discrete transactional decision which lawyer's discourse assumes to be normal but is in fact rare. Assume that questions have been asked and inquiry made to a satisfactory extent, whatever that may mean. Now, as perceived by the legal writing, the board weighs the matter and makes a judgment, and it is that judgment that is protected by the business judgment rule.

Boardroom reality is far different from this lawyer-oriented model, not only in the respects discussed earlier but usually in the character of "judgment" itself. The differences are fundamental and warrant comment.

* * *

[T]he work of corporate management and directors has the same general characteristics as that of the high political official or general. Actions are most often multiple. The company's course of conduct is a resultant of countless tradeoffs. . . . Occasionally one can discern a clean go or no-go issue that will be decided by a board of directors—whether to shut down all foreign operations and take a big current write-off, for example—but such instances are not frequent, and even when they appear to arise they are nearly always linked to other decisional implications, as when, for example, a board decides not to fire the chief executive today but at the same time takes other moves to pre-position possible successors for tomorrow. As a result, seeking in retrospect to revisit and evaluate a single "judgment on an issue" by a board of directors will almost always be a distortion of reality, because no such free-standing single judgment ever happened.

* * *

[J]udgments of boards of directors are mainly in the nature of decisions whether to hurl a veto.

A chief executive who generally enjoys the confidence of his board will usually be able to carry any proposal he makes if he does his homework, prepares his supporting arguments, is backed up by his other officers, and—of key importance—personally throws his full weight behind the proposal. Courts and the public must understand that quite commonly a director will go along with a business proposal that he does not really like. He may well think, and will sometimes say aloud in the board meeting, "I do not like this proposal. It seems risky and I believe other uses for the same resources would be more promising. But I may be wrong; I respect the contrary views of my colleagues; and I have to accord great weight to the CEO's strong support for this project. *After all, he is the one who will have the primary responsibility for seeing to it that it works out successfully.* So I will not vote no." When that happens, everyone in the corporate world knows the meaning of the italicized words. The director is saying that he will go along this time, but the CEO is on notice that if he proves to be wrong and the project fails, he may well have lost that director's confidence.

To cite another illustration. Even if a director is strongly opposed to a project, he may still go along because the CEO is determined to proceed and, in the director's best judgment, the disruption that would be caused by firing the CEO at this time would be more injurious to the interests of the company and its shareholders than the negative risks of the project proposed. In such a case, the real business judgment the director makes is not to throw his javelin today. . . .

* * *

Notes and Questions

1. Mr. Manning argues that the present formulations of the directors' duty of care are unrealistic in light of the way outside directors actually undertake their task. Do you agree? If there is a variance, should the legal standard here change to the director practices outlined in the piece or should these director practices change?

2. In addition to a possible dissonance between the legal doctrine and board practices, there might be a variance—a phenomenon we have seen before—between the statements of doctrine recited in judicial opinions and what, in fact, courts are actually doing in this area. According to a number of writers, there are only a handful of reported decisions in which courts found directors breached their duty of care in situations in which there was not also some element of self dealing. For the classic statement of this view see Bishop, *Sitting Ducks and Decoy Ducks: New Trends in Indemnification of Corporate Directors and Officers*, 77 YALE L.J. 1078 (1968). For a contrary view see Beveridge, *The Corporate Director's Duty of Care: Riddles Wisely Expounded*, 24 SUF. U.L. REV. 923 (1990). While perhaps surprising when contrasted with statements of the duty of care that sound like ordinary tort law—unless directors are a particularly careful lot—is this result inconsistent with the formulations of the business judgment rule which are highly protective of directors? Also, this sort of nose count ignores settlements.

3. Perhaps because of its rarity, when a court finds prominent directors in a public corporation breached their duty of care—as the Delaware Supreme Court did in *Smith v. Van Gorkom*—the result is to create quite a stir. This, in turn, may lead to legislative intervention.

3. *The Impact of Statutes*

James J. Hanks, Jr., *Evaluating Recent State Legislation on Director and Officer Liability Limitation and Indemnification,* 43 Bus. Law. 1207 (1988)*

* * *

Unfortunately, as the court in *Van Gorkom* noted: "It is, of course, a fact of corporate life that today when faced with difficult or sensitive issues, directors often are subject to suit, irrespective of the decisions they make." . . . These developments, combined with severely reduced capacity among [directors' and officers' liability insurance] carriers . . . , caused premiums to soar to record levels and coverages to decrease . . . . Almost immediately, outside directors of many major publicly-held corporations began to resign or not stand for reelection rather than continue to serve with inadequate or no insurance. . . .

The first state to respond to the developments of the mid-1980s was Indiana, in April 1986, followed by Delaware in June. Since then, forty other states have adopted some form of legislation designed to reduce the risk of directors' personal liability for money damages. These legislative initiatives have generally followed one or more of [the following] different approaches: . . .

CHARTER OPTION STATUTES

The most popular form of director liability statute has been the so-called "charter option" statute, first enacted by Delaware, effective July 1, 1986. Since then, charter option statutes have been adopted by thirty other states. In language typical of charter option statutes, the Delaware statute authorizes a corporation to adopt a "provision eliminating or limiting the personal liability of a director to the corporation or its stockholders for monetary damages for breach of fiduciary duty as a director," with certain exceptions. . . .

* * *

The principal difference among the charter option statutes is found in their exceptions, which in effect state the standard that a plaintiff must meet in order to impose personal liability for money damages upon a director. The Delaware statute and the statutes of fifteen other states . . . contain the same six exceptions:

(i) Breach of the director's duty of loyalty to the corporation or its stockholders;
(ii) Acts or omissions not in good faith;
(iii) Intentional misconduct;
(iv) Knowing violation of law;
(v) Unlawful distributions; and
(vi) Any transaction from which the director derived an improper personal benefit.

The potentially most troublesome of the Delaware exceptions is the one for breach of the duty of loyalty. The phrase "duty of loyalty" appears nowhere else in the Delaware General Corporation Law or, so far as is known, anywhere else in the corporation statute of any other state that has adopted this exception in a charter option statute. Even Delaware lawyers concede that the Delaware courts are unclear as to the parameters of the duty of loyalty. The Delaware Supreme Court itself has had difficulty in distinguishing the duty of care from the duty of loyalty. The fact that one of the other exceptions to the Delaware statute is for "improper personal benefit" suggests that breach of the duty of loyalty means something more than just self-dealing. . . .

It will not be surprising, therefore, if stockholders of Delaware corporations that have adopted exculpatory charter provisions begin alleging violations of the duty of loyalty for acts or omissions that until now would have supported a claim for breach of the duty of care. . . .

The improper personal benefit exception could also be exploited, especially because it is not limited to the actual receipt of money, property, or services and therefore might be interpreted to include less easily measurable considerations, such as business goodwill, personal friendship, or social ingratiation. In voting against a takeover proposal, for example, a director might be charged with having received an improper personal benefit in the form of continued tenure of the board.

* * *

SELF-EXECUTING STATUTES

The most radical legislative approach to director liability is direct alteration of the standard of liability necessary to recover money damages from directors. This self-executing approach was pioneered by Indiana. . . . Under the new Indiana Business Corporation Law, a director is liable only if he has breached or failed to perform his duties in compliance with the statutory standard of care and "the breach or failure to perform constitutes willful misconduct or recklessness." . . . Moreover, the statute does not provide for an Indiana corporation to opt out of this provision even if its stockholders so desire.

* * *

CAP ON MONEY DAMAGES

Virginia combines the charter option and self-executing approaches. It (i) limits the damages that may be assessed against an officer or director in a suit by or in the right of the corporation or by the stockholders directly to the greater of (a) $100,000 or (b) "the amount of cash compensation received by the officer or director from the corporation during the twelve months immediately preceding the act or omission for which liability was imposed" but (ii) permits the stockholders to reduce or eliminate (but not increase) this limit to the "monetary amount specified" in either a charter or by-law provision. . . .

* * *

EXPANDED INDEMNIFIABILITY IN DERIVATIVE SUITS

At least ten states . . . have enacted statutes expanding the right of corporations to indemnify their directors for expenses, settlements, and adverse judgments in derivative suits. The typical, unexpanded indemnification statute, as applied to derivative suits, requires the director or officer to be indemnified against expenses in the case of a successful defense but, in the case of an adverse judgment, permits indemnification for expenses only if ordered by a court and prohibits any indemnification for the amount of the judgment itself. Some states permit indemnification for amounts paid in settlement of derivative actions if ordered by a court. . . .

The most far-reaching statutory developments affecting derivative suits are provisions eliminating or substantially eliminating the distinction between third-party and derivative suits and permitting indemnification against judgments, settlements, and expenses for any director or officer who meets the general statutory standards for indemnification without a requirement of court approval.[51]

* * *

EXPANSION OF NONEXCLUSIVITY PROVISIONS

At least twenty-nine states have recently expanded the provisions of their indemnification statutes permitting corporations to provide rights other than indemnification by charter, by-law, board resolution, contract, or otherwise. Thus, if a state's indemnification statute is not sufficiently broad to provide the desired level of mandatory or permissive indemnification but permits additional nonindemnification protection, a corporation may achieve substantially the same economic result. The broad form of nonexclusivity provision has been typified by section 145(f) of the Delaware General

51 These standards typically require good faith conduct, reasonable belief that the individual's conduct was in or not opposed to the corporation's best interests, and in a criminal proceeding, no reason to believe the individual's conduct was unlawful. *E.g.*, Revised Model Business Corp. Act § 8.51(a) (1984). . . . These statutory standards for indemnification differ from the typical statutory standards of conduct for directors by omitting the requirement for the care of an ordinarily prudent person in similar circumstances and by modifying the reasonable belief requirement in the indemnification standards to require only a reasonable belief that the director's conduct "was at least not opposed to [the corporation's] best interests" in the case of conduct not in the director's official capacity.

Corporation Law, which provides that statutory indemnification "shall not be deemed exclusive of any other rights to which those seeking indemnification or advancement of expenses may be entitled under any by-law, agreement . . . or otherwise." . . .

* * *

ALTERNATIVE SOURCES OF REIMBURSEMENT

The typical indemnification statute permits the corporation to purchase insurance for directors and officers "whether or not the corporation would have the power to indemnify [the individual] against such liability" under the other provisions of the indemnification statute. However, as conventional insurance has become more expensive or even not available at any price, alternative sources of reimbursement have emerged. Examples include captive insurance subsidiaries, association captives formed by industry groups, trust funds, letters of credit, guaranties, and sureties. . . .

* * *

Legislation authorizing reimbursement from sources other than conventional third-party insurance generally results in the stockholders retaining the economic risk of the director's misconduct . . . since the funds for reimbursement are derived, either initially or ultimately, from the corporation.

POLICY ISSUES

RISK ALLOCATION

The principal public policy issue in director and officer liability legislation is the allocation of the economic cost of the directors' exculpated conduct. . . .

Charter option statutes simply permit the stockholders to decide for themselves whether to assume this risk or to leave it with the directors. By contrast, the other director liability statutes enacted to date are direct or indirect determinations by the legislatures to shift the risk from the directors to the stockholders. Self-executing statutes are a direct legislative determination that this risk should be borne by the stockholders. . . . Expanded indemnification statutes also leave the risk with the stockholders (with the added costs of the stockholders' and corporation's legal fees), unless insurance is available. . . .

* * *

It should be recognized, however, that if the statutory exculpation extends to third parties in addition to stockholders, that action is in effect a legislatively-ordained subsidy for the benefit of the corporations and, therefore, their stockholders. The cost of the subsidy will be borne by any third parties whose rights to sue directors are cut off. As to derivative suits, the cost of the subsidy will be borne by the corporation and the stockholders, who may well wonder why they should not be permitted to make their own arrangements inter se with the directors, whom they elect, rather than having a state-ordered resolution forced upon them. If the answer is that the stockholders will benefit in the long run by encouraging competent, experienced individuals to serve as directors, the stockholders may reply that they are the ones who should be permitted to make this decision. The only persuasive rationale is that society at large will benefit from having corporations managed by the best available directors. However, if this is the case, then there is no reason for the self-executing statutes to be limited to derivative and direct suits by stockholders . . .; instead, consistent application of this rationale would require that these benefits be extended to cover the directors in suits from third parties as well. . . .

In any event, when the stockholders decide whether to limit directors' liability under an enabling statute, they need no extensive public policy justification. Stockholders should be entitled to consider the matter on any basis they choose and to look at whatever factors they wish. It is only when the legislature itself makes this decision, in a self-executing or similar statute, that more searching analysis is necessary.

* * *

STANDARDS OF LIABILITY

The approach of the typical director liability statute is to limit liability (in the case of the self-executing statutes) or permit the limitation of liability (in the case of the charter option statutes) for everything other than certain specified types of conduct. . . .

All of these formulations recognize several important policy reasons for not permitting even the stockholders to eliminate completely all liability of the directors for money damages to the corporation or the stockholders. First, some conduct is so clearly without any benefit that the law should not appear to endorse it, even by permitting the stockholders to decide whether to waive any claim based upon it. Second, in the case of prospective limitation of liability, the stockholders will not be able to know in advance the exact nature or extent of any claims they are giving up. Third, the public has an interest in encouraging good corporate governance even if the limitation of liability does not extend to third parties. Finally, in many cases, there will be stockholders who vote against liability limitation or who do not vote. Those stockholders should have an irreducible core of protection, especially in view of the fact that in certain cases the votes of the directors themselves as stockholders may be sufficient to approve adoption of the provision.

* * *

RELATIONSHIP BETWEEN LIABILITY LIMITATION AND INDEMNIFICATION

Because liability limitation statutes and indemnification statutes are both directed at defining the area in which the economic risk of the director's conduct will be shifted from the directors to the stockholders, it is appropriate to examine the relationship between these two types of statutes. . . .

Clearly no policy justifies indemnification that is broader than either a self-executing or stockholder-approved limitation of liability. It would be inconsistent for a legislature to permit indemnification for conduct that the legislature had determined was so egregious that directors should not be protected from liability for money damages. No charter option or self-executing state is in this position.

* * *

In charter option states, . . . the indemnification must deal with both corporations that adopt liability-limitation charter provisions and those that do not. Most charter option states do not permit indemnification of directors to the same extent that stockholders are permitted to limit directors' liability. . . .

* * *

. . . [I]f the directors were authorized to indemnify to the same extent that the stockholders are authorized to limit liability, they would have no incentive to let the stockholders decide the issue. In other words, the stockholders should have a broader authority to shift the economic cost of the directors' misconduct than the directors themselves. For this reason, the stockholders should be able to approve charter or bylaw provisions authorizing indemnification to the same extent that they are permitted to limit liability. In self-executing states, however, where there is no role for the stockholders in the resolution of the issue, it is difficult to understand why the standards for liability limitation and indemnification should not be coextensive. . . .

* * *

EXCLUDED CLAIMS

Most director liability statutes, including those of California, Delaware, Maryland, New York, and Virginia, apply only to claims by the corporation or by the stockholders suing either derivatively on behalf of the corporation or directly for themselves. Some statutes, like those of Indiana and Ohio, apply to all suits, including suits by third parties. . . .

. . . If the purpose of limiting director liability is to permit directors to act in the best interests of the corporation without the overhanging specter of personal liability, then exculpation should include suits by the corporation, the stockholders, and third parties. On the other hand, if one of the justifications for limiting liability is that the stockholders should be permitted to decide for themselves the standard to which they want to hold their directors, then any exculpation should be limited to claims by the corporation or the stockholders.

INCLUDED PERSONS

The impetus for liability limitation statutes originating in the *Van Gorkom* and other cases focused on the liability of directors. It is not surprising, therefore, that most of the statutes enacted in response to these cases covered only directors. . . . There are several important policy reasons for also including officers in liability limitation statutes.

First, in states with charter option statutes, there is no logical policy reason for permitting stockholders to limit the liability of directors but not officers. . . .

* * *

Notes and Questions

1. Mr. Hanks defends charter option statutes as simply allowing shareholder choice. Recall the concerns about such choice raised by Professor Eisenberg in his article excerpted in Chapter I. To put this debate in a broader context, note that the question as to whether waivers of negligence claims are valid arises in a variety of areas besides corporate law. For example, you may have seen such attempted waivers on the back of parking lot tickets you received, and, in a classic case, a hospital had incoming patients sign such waivers. Compare the concerns Professor Eisenberg raises about shareholder voting to the concerns courts have about waivers in these other contexts. Do shareholders face coercion (as the emergency room patient)? Are they ignorant of (and, hence, not really agreeing to) the waiver (as perhaps the recipient of the parking lot ticket)?

2. Statutes that place a cap on damages are one way to address the concern about the size of potential liability facing directors. Recall that doctors and other prospective malpractice defendants have raised similar concerns about large damage awards. Indeed, legislative damage caps appeared for doctors before they did for directors. This, in turn, raises a broader comment about the legislative process. Do you see a pattern here in which various categories of prospective defendants go before the legislature and ask for relief from liability? If their arguments are valid, but not unique, does this suggest a problem in the current tort system and a need for an answer that is not confined by defendant group? Do you see any disadvantage in a group-by-group approach? What will happen when an unpopular group (lawyers?) asks for relief?

3. Mr. Hanks notes that, in addition to directly protecting board members by eliminating liability for negligence, statutes and charter provisions might indirectly protect board members by authorizing indemnity or insurance. From the standpoint of the directors, these techniques may provide equivalent financial protection; from a policy standpoint, however, do they raise equivalent issues? Begin with indemnity. If a court finds a director liable to the corporation, but then the corporation reimburses the director for everything the director paid to the corporation (plus the director's litigation expenses), what has one accomplished? On the other hand, if the judgment vindicates the director, what can one say about the desirability of indemnity? Suppose, however, the director settles the suit? Alternately, consider a suit against a director by an outsider to the corporation. Now what are the policy questions concerning indemnity if a court holds the director liable to the third party? Should it matter whether the director had to pay a fine imposed to deter misconduct or damages awarded to compensate the third party? Next consider liability insurance. Is there any objection to doctors purchasing such insurance? Note that it is the patients who ultimately pay for the insurance. Is there any difference when the corporation buys insurance for its directors?

What is the difference, however, with the various insurance alternatives discussed by Mr Hanks? For an attempt to reconcile the policies behind indemnity, insurance, and liability standards see Oesterle, *Limits on a Corporation's Protection of its Directors and Officers from Personal Liability*, 1983 WIS. L. REV. 513.

4. Mr. Hanks raises issues about whether these statutes cover corporate officers and claims by third parties. Should directors have greater protection from liability than lower level corporate employees? Suppose the directors make a decision (say with respect to a particularly important product recall) that results in injury to a third party. Should the law insulate directors from the injured party's claim for negligence? Note that corporate employees remain liable for their own torts even though committed in the scope of their employment (thereby making the corporation vicariously liable as well).

5. Recall from Chapter I the effort by Professors Weiss and White to assess stock reactions to a number of Delaware Supreme Court decisions. For a study using similar methodology, which found a negative market reaction to the Delaware legislature's enactment of the charter option statute described by Mr. Hanks, see Bradley & Schipani, *The Relevance of the Duty of Care Standard in Corporate Governance*, 75 IOWA L. REV. 1 (1989).

B. The Duty of Loyalty: Conflict of Interest Transactions

1. *The Doctrine Introduced and Critiqued*

Harold Marsh, Jr., *Are Directors Trustees? Conflict of Interest and Corporate Morality*, 22 BUS. LAW. 35 (1966)*

* * *

I. Types of Legal Regulations.

a. *Prohibition.*

In 1880 it could have been stated with confidence that in the United States the general rule was that any contract between a director and his corporation was voidable at the instance of the corporation or its shareholders, without regard to the fairness or unfairness of the transaction. This rule was stated in powerful terms by a number of highly regarded courts and judges in cases which arose generally out of the railroad frauds of the 1860's and 1870's.

* * *

Under this rule it mattered not the slightest that there was a majority of so-called disinterested directors who approved the contract. The courts stated that the corporation was entitled to the unprejudiced judgment and advice of all of its directors and therefore it did no good to say that the interested director did not participate in the making of the contract on behalf of the corporation. . . . Furthermore, the courts said that it was impossible to measure the influence which one director might have over his associates, even though ostensibly abstaining from participation in the discussion or vote. . . .

* * *

This rule applied not only to individual contracts with directors, but also to the situation of interlocking directorates where even a minority of the boards were common to the two contracting corporations. Not only that, it was also applied to the situation where one corporation owned a majority of the stock of another and appointed its directors, even though they might not be the same men as sat on the board of the parent corporation.

* * *

This principle, absolutely inhibiting contracts between a corporation and its directors or any of them, appeared to be impregnable in 1880. . . .

* * *

Thirty years later this principle was dead.

b. *Approval by a disinterested majority of the board.*

It could have been stated with reasonable confidence in 1910 that the general rule was that a contract between a director and his corporation was valid if it was approved by a disinterested majority of his fellow directors and was not found to be unfair or fraudulent by the court if challenged; but that a contract in which a majority of the board was interested was voidable at the instance of the corporation or its shareholders without regard to any question of fairness.

One searches in vain in the decided cases for a reasoned defense of this change in legal philosophy, or for the slightest attempt to refute the powerful arguments which had been made in support of the previous rule. Did the courts discover in the last quarter of the Nineteenth Century that greed was no longer a factor in human conduct? . . .

The only explanation which seems to have been given for this change in position was the technical one that a trustee, while forbidden to deal with himself in connection with the trust property, could deal directly with the cestui que trust if he made full disclosure and took no unfair advantage; and that the case of a director who abstained from representing the corporation but dealt in his personal capacity with a majority of disinterested directors was properly analogized to a trustee dealing with the cestui que trust. . . .

* * *

But in no case is there any discussion or attempted refutation of the reasons previously given by the courts as to why it is impossible, in such a situation, for any director to be disinterested. Some courts seem simply to admit that the practice has grown too widespread for them to cope with. . . .

* * *

Under the rule that a disinterested majority of the directors must approve a transaction with one of their number, the question arose whether this meant a disinterested quorum (i.e., normally a majority of the whole board) or merely a disinterested majority of a quorum, so that the interested director or directors could be counted to make up the quorum. Virtually all of the cases held that the interested director could not be counted for quorum purposes. . . .

* * *

c. *Judicial review of the fairness of the transaction.*

By 1960 it could be said with some assurance that the general rule was that no transaction of a corporation with any or all of its directors was automatically voidable at the suit of a shareholder, whether there was a disinterested majority of the board or not; but that the courts would review such a contract and subject it to rigid and careful scrutiny, and would invalidate the contract if it was found to be unfair to the corporation.

It is difficult in most States to determine with exactness the point of time at which the rule changed again, or indeed to prove beyond a reasonable doubt that it has in fact changed in a particular State. There are a large number of cases which deal with situations where a majority of the board were interested and which discuss them solely in terms of a review of the fairness of the transactions, without bothering to cite or discuss any of the previous decisions, perhaps in the same State, enunciating the rule that there must be approval by a disinterested majority of the board. . . .

* * *

Statutory sanction. Even if . . . the decisions in the particular State have not clearly adopted the modern rule, there still may be a statute which authorizes all such transactions involving conflict of interest, subject only to a fairness test. Most of these statutes have been copied from or modelled upon [former] California Corporations Code § 820. . . . These statutes purport to validate any transaction by a corporation with a director or another corporation in which the director is interested if (a) it is approved by a disinterested majority of the board, with the interested director eligible to be counted as a part of the quorum; *or* (b) it is approved by a majority of the shareholders; *or* (c) it is "just and reasonable" as to the corporation. While literally under such a statute a transaction which was unjust and unreasonable would be immune from attack if it had been approved by a disinterested majority of the directors or by the shareholders, there is a California decision[41] which indicates that the courts will in any event review the transaction for fairness (whatever the statute says). So the entire statute could just as well have been compressed into the final clause.

* * *

The final conclusion is that under statute, judicial decision or charter provision, it would be a rarity today to find a transaction involving interested directors which was not permitted by the law, subject only to possible invalidation for unfairness.

d. *Effect of shareholder approval.*

One factor which we have not yet mentioned is the effect under any of the rules discussed above of shareholder ratification of the transaction, after full disclosure, even though it might otherwise have been automatically voidable because it did not meet the standards required for director action. All of the cases seem to hold that such ratification will suffice to validate the transaction with an interested director, at least in the absence of fraud or unfairness. Furthermore, the stock of the interested director or directors may be voted on the question of ratification, and *as shareholders* they may cast the deciding votes. . . .

* * *

Under the modern rule, that there is no need for a disinterested majority of the directors to approve such a transaction, the question of shareholder ratification becomes less significant, since in most States shareholder ratification will not serve to validate a fraud and it is not needed if the transaction is found to be fair by the court. However, such shareholder action may still be significant in that it may shift the burden of proof on the issue of fairness from the interested directors to the one attacking the transaction.

* * *

III. Analysis of Conflicts of Interest.

We have been discussing conflict of interest as though it were a unitary problem, with all such conflicts raising the same issues and being subject perhaps to the same legal treatment. No legal problem is quite that simple . . . .

* * *

a. *Salaries.*

One type of conflict of interest arises of necessity from the fact that the director occupies the position which he does with the corporation. The most obvious illustra-

41 Remillard Brick Co. v. Remillard-Dandini Co., 109 Cal. App. 2d 405, 241 P.2d 66 (1952). . . .

tion of this problem is the question of fixing the salaries of those directors who are also full-time officers of the corporation. As directors they have the duty to negotiate for the best officer talent at the lowest cost to the corporation; as the officers receiving the salaries it is in their self-interest to bargain for the highest compensation obtainable.

There seems to be no way in which to avoid such a conflict of interest except by insisting that no full-time salaried officer of the corporation may sit on the board of directors. . . .

It would be highly undesirable for the law to insist that every corporation have an entirely outside board. . . .

Probably most of the reported cases hold that, if a majority of the directors participate in fixing their own salaries as officers, the agreement is voidable without regard to its fairness. This rule applies even though the device is used of each director abstaining from voting on his own salary. However, even under this rule, the agreement for the salary may be ratified by a majority of the shareholders, including if necessary the vote of the interested director as a shareholder. More recent cases take the position that such an agreement for the payment of salaries is not automatically voidable even if the majority of the directors are interested, but the burden is upon the directors to sustain the fairness of the compensation. Shareholder ratification may shift this burden to the person objecting to the salaries.

However, this review of the decided cases would be highly misleading if it were presented as an accurate statement of the current law. In the first place, it does not take account of the effect of a charter or by-law provision expressly authorizing the directors to fix their own compensation as officers, which normally would be effective to eliminate any automatic voidability of the arrangement. Also, the statutes previously discussed authorizing contracts with interested directors despite the lack of a disinterested quorum would be applicable to this problem. In addition, a number of States, recognizing that this problem presents a special case, have enacted statutes permitting the directors to fix their own compensation, even though such States may not have a general statute on contracts with interested directors. . . . Most of them . . . merely state that the board "shall have authority to fix the compensation for directors." While these latter statutes do not expressly say that there need not be a disinterested quorum nor expressly cover compensation as officers, they would have very little purpose unless the intent is to cover both of these points. Certainly they were not enacted simply to permit the directors to fix their meeting fees.

b. *Defense of control.*

Another aspect of the position of a director which may inescapably involve him in a conflict of interest is the fact that the directors of a publicly-held corporation are in a position of control. The desire to retain this control, when challenged by an insurgent group, may involve the board's self-interest in the compensation and perquisites attached thereto, or may be entirely motivated by a belief in the unwisdom of the policies advocated by the insurgents. It is impossible to command the directors in this situation to avoid any conflict of interest, since it has been unavoidably thrust upon them.

. . .

However, another factor is injected into the problem when the directors use corporate funds to defend their control. The use of such funds for the expenses of an incumbent board in a proxy fight has been generally approved by the courts, despite the inconclusive nature of the leading New York case of *Rosenfeld v. Fairchild Engine and Airline Corp.*,[89] although the courts say that this can only be done if the dispute is over policy rather than personality. I do not recall any case in which the incumbent management has admitted that it was fighting merely to preserve its position for its own benefit.

While this result may be unfair to some extent, the contrary rule would be even more regrettable. That would mean that any incumbent board which was unwilling to spend vast sums, perhaps millions, out of their own pockets would simply have to surrender to any insurgent shareholder with a long enough purse and a strong enough desire to gain control of the corporation. It is highly unlikely that this would lead to the most disinterested and most competent management for corporations generally.

* * *

An even more serious question is presented if the incumbent management, when faced with the buying up of a large block of shares by an outsider and perhaps a threatened proxy fight, uses corporate funds either to purchase shares in the market in competition with the outsider or to buy out the outsider. A series of cases in Delaware have upheld such action of the management. . . .

* * *

c. *Dividend policy.*

Some situations in which the directors of a corporation may inescapably become involved in a conflict of interest arise, paradoxically enough, from their positions as shareholders in the corporation. It might seem that a director's interest as a shareholder would always coincide with the interests of other shareholders, but this is not necessarily true. A common example is the situation where a controlling shareholder owns a large block of stock and, because of his tax bracket and the fact that he is receiving a handsome salary, does not want to receive any dividends. . . .

d. *Recapitalizations.*

Another case in which the interest of the management as shareholders may conflict with the interests of the whole body of shareholders arises whenever there are more than one class of shares outstanding and the management owns a much larger proportion of one class than another. Perhaps the most common instance of this occurs when a reclassification or merger is proposed to [wipe out] . . . accrued preferred dividends, and the directors own large amounts of the common stock but none of the preferred. Obviously, their personal interest as common shareholders is opposed to their fiduciary duty to the whole body of shareholders, preferred and common alike. . . .

89 309 N.Y. 168, 128 N.E.2d 291 (1955). . . .

e. *Business dealings with a director or an organization in which he is interested.*

The classic situation in which a conflict of interest arises, and the one which is the subject of almost all of the cases discussed in Part I of this paper, involves business dealings of a corporation with its director or officer or an organization in which he is interested. Nothing further need be said concerning contracts with directors individually, but where a director is interested in another corporation or organization doing business with the corporation the question arises as to how substantial this interest must be in order for any serious conflict to be present. Obviously, the ownership of 100 or 200 shares of General Motors by a director of a corporation which is purchasing trucks from that manufacturer should not give anyone a moment's concern. His share of the profit that may be made on this contract by General Motors is so infinitesimal that it could not conceivably influence his vote on whether to buy from General Motors or Ford.

* * *

f. *Loans to the corporation.*

One type of business transaction between the corporation and a director or an organization in which he is interested deserves separate treatment. This is a loan by the director to the corporation. Some of the earliest cases repudiating the strict rule prohibiting all contracts with directors dealt with such a loan . . . .

* * *

However, the picture painted by some of the cases espousing the modern rule, of altruistic directors rushing to lend money to a distressed corporation at the prime rate, is one which I have not observed too often in practice. . . .

g. *Loans from the corporation.*

Just as loans to the corporation by a director involve a situation where there is perhaps little danger of overreaching, so loans *by* the corporation to a director have been considered to present an extremely dangerous practice which has been expressly prohibited by a number of statutes. . . .

On the other hand, four States expressly *authorize* any loan by a corporation to its directors or officers. . . .

h. *Business dealings with relatives of a director.*

Where the business dealings are not with the director himself, but with one of his relatives, the question arises whether this should be treated as a situation creating a conflict of interest to be dealt with in the same way as a contract with the director; and, if so, to what degree of consanguinity or affinity such anti-nepotism regulation should be carried.

Surprisingly enough, in view of their generally lenient attitude in this field, the courts have held that a contract with a son, wife, brother, or even grandchildren of a director is to be treated as a case involving an interested director.

* * *

i. *Common directors.*

A business transaction by a corporation with another corporation where they have one or more of the members of their boards in common, but such directors do not own any stock (or only an insignificant amount of stock) in the other corporation, presents a different problem than such a transaction with a corporation wholly or partially owned by a director. . . .

* * *

Notes and Questions

1. Mr. Marsh asserts that the general rule in 1880 was that transactions between a corporation and any of its directors were voidable regardless of approval by other disinterested directors or whether the deal was fair to the company. For a different view as to the prevailing rule at that time see Beveridge, *The Corporate Director's Fiduciary Duty of Loyalty: Understanding the Self-Interested Director Transaction*, 41 DEPAUL L. REV. 655 (1992). Putting aside this historical debate, do you see any problem with a rule of absolute voidability, which may explain why it is no longer (if it ever was) the law? Is it possible to avoid all conflict of interest transactions between a corporation and members of its board? For all his criticism of the change, does Mr. Marsh expect directors, particularly those who are also full time officers of the company, to work for nothing? If it is desirable for directors to hold stock in the company—which generally aligns their interests with the shareholders—should the directors be unable to buy stock from the corporation itself? Once one allows some types of transactions because they are sufficiently worthwhile to the corporation, is it not just a short step to approving any conflict of interest transaction so long as it is fair (which presumably includes the notion that the corporation expected some benefit from the deal)? For a more recent attack, however, on allowing conflict of interest transactions if fair see Mitchell, *Fairness and Trust in Corporate Law*, 1993 DUKE L.J. 425.

2. Among the conflict of interest situations discussed by Mr. Marsh are actions taken by the directors to continue their control of the company. For consideration of the appropriate standard for reviewing board actions which chill proxy challenges see Klein, *The Case for Heightened Scrutiny of the Shareholders' Franchise Right*, 44 STAN. L. REV. 129 (1991). For a discussion of when the corporation should cover the expenses of soliciting proxies in a contested election for membership on the board see Bebchuk & Kahan, *A Framework for Analyzing Legal Policy Towards Proxy Contests*, 78 CAL. L. REV. 1071 (1990). We will return to the subject of board actions to fend off hostile takeovers in Chapter VI.

3. Mr. Marsh concludes that the validity of a conflict of interest transaction under current law comes down to a test of fairness. What does this mean? How does it compare to the review of disinterested transactions under the business judgment rule? The next article provides an interesting answer.

Charles M. Yablon, *On the Allocation of Burdens of Proof in Corporate Law: An Essay on Fairness and Fuzzy Sets*, 13 CARDOZO L. REV. 497 (1991)*

I. A DEFINITION OF THE PROBLEM

The legal rules governing liability of corporate officers and directors for breach of fiduciary duty contain few, if any, categorical prohibitions on the kinds of transactions that may be conducted by corporate management. Rather, the rules operate (and are generally believed to deter a certain amount of managerial misconduct) by describing the effect of undertaking certain types of transactions *on the allocation of the burden of proof* in a subsequent lawsuit against such officers or directors for breach of fiduciary duty. Burdens of proof are described as "shifting" back and forth between plaintiffs and defendants, bouncing between them like a tennis ball.

Thus we are told that:

> [A] plaintiff attacking a corporate payment has the heavy burden of demonstrating that no reasonable businessman could find that adequate consideration had been supplied for the payment. However, where the directors have a personal interest in the application of the corporate payments, such as where they are fixing their own compensation, the business judgment rule no longer applies and the burden shifts to the directors to demonstrate affirmatively that the transactions were engaged in with good faith and were fair, i.e., that adequate consideration had been supplied.[1]

However, if there has been a ratification of the transaction by a majority of the disinterested directors or shareholders, the burden shifts yet again and, "the objecting stockholder has the burden of showing that no person of ordinary sound business judgment would say that the consideration received for the options was a fair exchange for the options granted."[2]

Given all this discussion of shifting burdens of proof, some students get the mistaken impression that proof standards change *during* the course of a trial for breach of fiduciary duty. . . .

In fact, these burden-shifting rules have nothing to do with trial procedure or the presentation of evidence. In fiduciary duty trials, as in most other trials, attorneys for

---

1 Cohen v. Ayers, 596 F.2d 733, 739-40 (7th Cir. 1979). . . .

2 Michelson v. Duncan, 407 A.2d 211, 224 (Del. 1979).

plaintiffs present their case first and put forth all evidence they have on self-dealing, fairness, and any other relevant issues. Defendants follow and do the same. The parties may not even know who has been allocated the burden of persuasion on the fairness issue until they read in the judge's opinion whether or not the appropriate evidentiary standard has been met.

In short, the rules governing allocations of burdens of proof in corporate law are not designed to affect the presentation of evidence at trial; rather they are a way of structuring the decision-making process of the finder of fact, who, in these kinds of cases, is usually the same judge who will be deciding such legal issues as the appropriate allocation of the burden of proof. Once we recognize this, however, another problem arises, and that is the one which this paper seeks to address.

Simply put, the question is, Why is it so important *which side* has the burden of proof to establish fairness and similar issues in fiduciary duty litigation? That it does matter seems to be a very basic assumption of this area of corporate law. Courts spend much time and effort in their opinions discussing and clarifying exactly who has the burden of persuasion on each aspect of the claim. Statutes and even American Law Institute ("ALI") restatements are explicit in allocating such burdens. Certainly, the common assumption among corporate law practitioners is that if your client has the burden of proof in these matters, you are very, very likely to lose the case.

As a former corporate lawyer, I share those assumptions, yet I find them at odds with the theoretical literature involving burdens of proof in civil actions. That work implies that the allocation of the burden of proof should be relatively unimportant in all but a small number of civil cases, and rarely significant on the issue of fairness. After all, the basic standard of proof in almost all corporate actions, including breach of fiduciary duty cases, is the preponderance of the evidence. Most of the theoretical work involving the civil burden of proof assumes that a preponderance standard requires no more than a showing that the disputed fact is "more likely than not" to be the case, or that the probability of its occurrence is greater than fifty percent. . . .

Under a preponderance-of-the-evidence standard of proof, *allocation* of the burden of persuasion should rarely be important. If *some* evidence on the issue is available, enough that the court can form some rational (albeit subjective) assessment of the likelihood of the disputed fact, allocation of the burden of persuasion should only matter where that assessment is *exactly* fifty percent. If the judge believes it is even slightly more probable than not that the terms of the transaction are fair, if she finds, for example, that the testimony of plaintiff's expert is just a bit more credible than that of the defendant concerning the appropriate valuation of the stock at issue, allocation of the burden of proof should become unimportant. . . .

Allocation issues will admittedly still be important in those cases in which the issue is one on which neither side is able to adduce any evidence (e.g., whether defendant manufactured the defective product purchased by plaintiff many years ago). It seems unlikely, however, that the dispositive issue in a breach of fiduciary duty case, particularly the issue of fairness, is likely to be one on which little or no evidence is available. Quite the contrary, the fairness of a given transaction is an issue on which experts can almost always be found to testify for both sides, creating the kind of "battle of the experts" also found in medical malpractice cases, condemnation proceedings and certain other kinds of litigation. It seems unlikely that an experienced finder of fact, hearing all the expert testimony subjected to competent cross examination, would not find herself at least somewhat persuaded that one or the other side had the stronger position. . . .

* * *

Most careful corporate lawyers would rightly note that the legal standards applicable to transactions subject to the business judgment rule (or applicable to transactions ratified by shareholders or disinterested directors), and those legal standards applicable to self-dealing or interested-director transactions, involve more than just a shift in the burden of proof. Interested-director transactions constitute a breach of fiduciary duty unless they are "intrinsically fair" to the corporation. Transactions subject to the business judgment rule, in contrast, or those ratified by the appropriate disinterested groups, only breach management's fiduciary duty if they involve "waste" or a "gift" of corporate assets.

The difference between the "intrinsic fairness" and "waste" standards is more than a difference in the allocation of the burden of proof. It seems to involve a substantive difference in the kind of thing that must be proven to establish liability, like the difference between negligence and recklessness in tort law, or the difference between a complaint which merely fails to state a claim under Rule 12(b)(6) of the Federal Rules of Civil Procedure and one which is "frivolous" and triggers sanctions under rule 11.

But even after one acknowledges, as I think one must, that there is this substantive difference in relevant standards, the fact remains that corporate law judges are quite insistent that their rules involve not only substantive differences in standards, but also shifts in allocations of the burden of proof. . . . The question remains, therefore, in light of the preponderance of the evidence standard, why shifting the allocation of the burden of proof is believed to have this significant impact on the outcome of cases.

Furthermore, while waste and intrinsic fairness do seem to be different substantive standards, they do not appear to measure entirely different things. Quite the contrary, waste is usually defined in terms of particularly egregious or extreme forms of unfairness. If so, the analysis of fairness as a fuzzy variable admitting of various degrees may not only shed some light on the allocation of burdens of proof, but may also help define the relationship between the fairness and waste standards.

* * *

II. Fairness as a Fuzzy Property

In order to answer the question posed in the preceding section, we should take a closer look at what it means to describe a given transaction as fair or unfair. *Fairness*, as that term is understood and used in fiduciary-duty litigation, is a property which may characterize transactions in various degrees. Like the properties of being *tall* or *pretty* or *old* or *hot*, a deal may be *fair* to various degrees: that is, it is plausible and sensible to speak of deals that are *very fair* to shareholders, *somewhat fair, almost fair,* and *egregiously unfair*, just as it is intelligible to speak of things as *very tall, somewhat pretty,* or *extremely hot.*

* * *

. . . The value of most corporations and other profit-making enterprises, as well as the stock which represents claims on the control and future profits of such enterprises, is generally thought to be most accurately determined by computing the present value of the likely future income or cash flows anticipated from the enterprise. Such an analysis necessarily involves making speculative and imperfectly informed predictions about the future business and financial prospects of the enterprise. It is not surprising that valuations based on such speculative and uncertain data can yield no more than a range of potentially fair prices.

Viewing fairness in corporate law as a property involving a range of values is not only justified by economic theory, but is reflected in practice as well. When investment bankers are asked to elucidate the meaning of the formal "opinions" they issue in connection with tender offers or other corporate combinations, in which they state that the price being offered to shareholders is fair, they are careful to point out that they are not defining that price as *the* single fair price. Rather they are simply giving an opinion that the price is within the fair range, again implicitly recognizing a certain fuzziness in the parameters of fairness.

* * *

Consider then the issue of fairness as it is likely to be presented to the judge in a fiduciary-duty litigation. There will rarely be any dispute about the amount actually being offered in the transaction. Say, for purposes of the following hypothetical, that it is $25 per share, offered by the majority shareholder to purchase all the remaining minority shares of the company. If the market price for the stock in the preceding year has averaged $20 per share, everyone might agree that a price below $20 would be very unfair, and by the same token, it might generally be agreed that a fifty percent premium over that market price, or $30 per share, was undeniably within the range of fairness to the plaintiff. But the judge must decide whether $25 per share, a price which, on our hypothetical, is neither clearly fair nor clearly unfair, is fair for purposes of the lawsuit.

Note, moreover, that it is probably no accident that the price being considered by the judge falls right in the middle of the fuzzy range. The majority shareholder has an obvious economic interest in paying as little for the stock as possible, and has presumably asked its lawyers and financial advisors, in originally structuring this transaction, what was likely to be the lowest amount that it could pay and still have a good chance of winning the subsequent lawsuit. While natural or professional caution and uncertainty might cause such advisors to err on the side of generosity to shareholders, it seems far more likely that the dominant motive will be economic, and will incline lawyers and financial advisors to approve prices that will present hard cases to the judge—prices that might be described in the vocabulary of fuzziness as just barely fair or minimally fair or not quite fair.

If this analysis is correct, determining whether a price in fiduciary duty litigation is fair is a difficult question in much the same way that it is a difficult question whether a man whose height is 5 feet 10 inches is tall or a temperature of seventy-eight degrees Fahrenheit in June is hot. In all of these cases, the problem is not a lack of information about the thing to be evaluated (we know exactly what the price, height or temperature is). Rather, it is the nature of the criteria we are using to evaluate the thing which leads to uncertainty in the evaluation. Since those criteria are not crisply defined, but fuzzy, we may find it difficult to give a simple yes or no answer to the question presented.

* * *

III. Fuzzy Set Theory and Allocations of the Burden of Proof

Standard logic, which utilizes *the law of the excluded middle*, holds that every variable *x* either has the property *P* or the property *not P*. Put slightly more colloquially, everything is either *red* or *not red, divisible by two* or *not divisible by two, President of the United States* or *not President of the United States*. From the perspective of set theory, everything is either a member of the set of red things or it is not. . . .

Fuzzy set theory relaxes the law of the excluded middle to the extent of recognizing that some variables may be neither fully members of a set nor fully excluded from it. . . .

* * *

What does this have to do with determinations of fairness in fiduciary duty litigation? Consider . . . the question, Is that coffee hot? It is an ambiguous question in that we do not know whether, in asking about the fuzzy predicate hot, the questioner meant *piping hot* or just not ice cold. . . .

The question, Is the transaction price fair? is also, as we have seen, an ambiguous question in that it does not tell the judge the degree of fairness that must characterize the transaction to satisfy the criteria. But the judicial opinions themselves, in seeking to answer that question, may provide their own subtle indication of the criteria they are actually applying. The case law often states that the criteria for approval of these transactions is not just fairness, but "full fairness," "entire fairness," "intrinsic fairness," or "the most scrupulous inherent fairness."

Little attention has been paid to these extra adjectives, and indeed, it is difficult to define, in any abstract sense, what the difference between fairness and entire fairness or intrinsic fairness might be. Yet in the context of fairness as a fuzzy property, there seems little doubt that all these adjectives function as intensifiers to the property "fairness" and as such, send a subtle message to the judge concerning the substantive criteria to be used in determining fairness. In our hypothetical, the judge may be quite uncertain whether $25 is a fair price for the stock, but as she peruses the case law, and is instructed to rule against any prices not fully or entirely or inherently fair, she will view these adjectives as setting a higher standard than mere fairness—something akin to a very fair standard.

. . . If we envision a cardinally ranked scale of fairness/unfairness, where the egregiously unfair or wasteful transaction is ranked as 0 and the intrinsically fair transaction is ranked as 1, we can see that any rule that shifts from a standard of waste to a standard of intrinsic fairness involves a major substantive change in the criteria applied to the transactions at issue. Many transactions that would easily pass muster under the former standard will be struck down under the latter.

* * *

Our aim is to understand the allocation rules from the perspective of the judicial finder of fact. To do that, we must further consider the effects of judicial uncertainty. . . .

Consider again the corporate freeze-out of $25 per share. This time, however, plaintiff, in an effort to show the price is unfair, puts on an expert who testifies that, based on certain assumptions and projections about the future earnings of the company, the company should generate cash and earnings which imply that a fair price for the stock at the present is $30 per share. You, as judge, are not particularly persuaded by the presentation, and assign it a .4 subjective probability. Defendants, on the other hand, put forward their own view of the future earnings and cash flow potential of the business, which implies that the stock has a present fair value of only $24. You find this the more persuasive view, and assign it a .6 subjective probability.

Two possible decision-making procedures are now available to you as judge. One is to conclude that since a preponderance of the evidence favors defendants, (i.e., you assigned a .6 probability that the transaction price is fair) you should rule for defendant. If the disputed issue involved the occurrence or nonoccurrence of some past event (e.g., did defendant manufacture the faulty tire) this would seem to be the only decision-making procedure available.

However, when dealing with questions of fairness in valuation, the fact that such valuations depend on probability assessments of future events, and the fact that intermediate valuations between plaintiff's and defendant's assessments are available, means that you as judge might approach the decision-making process in another way. You might conclude that since there is a .6 likelihood of future events which will lead to a present valuation of $24 per share, and a .4 likelihood of future events which will lead to a present valuation of $30, a weighted average reflecting the relative likelihood of the occurrence of either set of events ((.6 x 24) + (.4 x 30)) yields a present value for the stock of $26.40 per share. Since $26.40 is more than the $25 per share offered by defendant, the judge applying this method might well conclude that defendant had not met its burden of persuasion, even if defendant's presentation of evidence was more persuasive than the plaintiff's presentation.

* * *

While the numbers lend these cases a spurious exactitude that would not be found in the context of actual litigation, they illustrate why it is perfectly possible that a judge, knowing that defendants have the burden of proving fairness, and uncertain as between evidence put forth by plaintiff and defendant (i.e., she finds both valuations plausible, even if one is somewhat more plausible than the other), might hold that defendant had failed to meet their [sic] burden of proof on the issue of fairness, even if she thought defendant's presentation was somewhat more persuasive. . . .

This analysis, then, provides a potential answer to the question posed in the first section. It describes a decision-making mechanism in which the allocation of the burden of proof, as well as the substantive legal standard, can have a major impact on the outcome of the case. The analysis implies that the party without the burden may be able to prevail by making no more than a plausible case that the transaction was unfair (or, where the plaintiff has the burden, that the transaction does not constitute waste).

Two basic questions have to be asked about this analysis: first, Is there any indication that judges actually decide cases in this manner? . . .

* * *

. . . [C]onsider the following quotation from *Beard v. Elster*,[38] a widely cited case in which the Delaware Supreme Court was asked to determine whether a stock option plan, approved by disinterested directors, constituted a "waste" of corporate assets. The court stated:

> We have before us a plan which, in the judgment of a disinterested Board, is adequately designed to further the corporate purpose of securing the retention of key employees' services. It is theoretically possible, we suppose, that some businessmen could be found who would hold the opinion that options exercisable at once were improvidently granted, but, on the other hand, there are businessmen who would hold a favorable view, as this Board of independent businessmen in fact did. *At most, therefore, we find ourselves in the twilight zone where reasonable businessmen, fully informed, might differ.* We think, therefore, we are precluded from substituting our uninformed opinion for that of experienced business managers of a corporation who have no personal interest in the outcome, and whose sole interest is the furtherance of the corporate enterprise.

The substantive standard for waste, as set forth in *Beard v. Elster*, was that there be a "reasonable assurance" that the option plan would provide a benefit to the corporation. In the paragraph just quoted, however, the court is unable to make a finding of reasonable assurance, but locates the case in a "twilight zone" where reasonable businessmen might differ on that issue. One might expect, under a preponderance-of-the-evidence standard, that the court would ask which side had made the stronger showing. Instead, the court indicates that the fact that the issue is uncertain and that the plan possibly provides benefits is determinative of the issue.

It is as if the plaintiff had to prove that the plan was "definitely unfair," or totally excluded from the set of fair plans, or had a zero degree of participation in the set of fair plans. By showing that there was at least a possibility that the plan was fair (even if only barely fair), defendants had shown by a subjective probability greater than zero that the plan was fair to a degree greater than zero. If the mere possibility that the plan

38 39 Del. Ch. 153, 160 A.2d 731 (1960).

is fair (even if a preponderance of the evidence shows otherwise) can be considered, then any plan about which such a showing can be made will, on a weighted average, have a value greater than zero and will not constitute waste. That, in effect, seems to be what *Beard v. Elster* holds.

In short, there seems to be some indication that, in considering issues of fairness, courts do not really apply a preponderance of the evidence standard, but a sliding scale in which the degree of credibility they ascribe to the evidence is directly related to the degree of fairness that the court finds. In such cases, the prime considerations will be allocation of the burden of proof and the substantive degree of fairness that must be proved. A plaintiff who must prove that the deal is very unfair (i.e., waste) may be defeated by a moderate showing that the deal is barely fair. A defendant who must prove that the deal is very fair (intrinsically fair) may also be defeated by a moderate showing that the deal is barely fair. . . .

* * *

Notes and Questions

1. Professor Yablon's article explains how the decision whether to apply the fairness or the business judgment test is often outcome determinative in litigation challenging a board action. Application of the fairness rather than the business judgment test, in turn, depends upon finding the directors are in a conflict of interest. Recall the discussion of various possible conflicts in the article by Mr. Marsh. Do they lend themselves to clear-cut boundaries? For example, most would agree that a transaction with the spouse of a director presents a conflict. Suppose a transaction (say a loan from a bank) is with a party (say a real estate developer) who has employed the son of a bank director; is this a conflict of interest situation? Alternately, suppose the chief executive officer and chairman of the board of a corporation has reached retirement age and would like to sell out his stock holdings in the corporation. He negotiates to sell the company in a deal in which all the shareholders, including himself, will get cash. Is this a conflict of interest? Or, say directors of a magazine publishing company negotiate an agreement with directors of a company which produces movies. Part of the merger agreement specifies what roles the managing directors of the two merging firms will have in running the combined entity. Is this a conflict? Professor Yablon explains that fairness is a "fuzzy" property. Can the same be said about conflicts of interest? If so, should the law take such a bipolar approach in determining how to review a board decision? For a suggested intermediate standard of review see Palmiter, *Reshaping the Corporate Fiduciary Model: A Director's Duty of Independence*, 67 TEX. L. REV. 1351 (1989).

2. Professor Yablon uses throughout his article an example which involves the fairness of a price paid for stock. Moreover, in explaining why fairness is a fuzzy property, he discusses the uncertainties involved in valuing corporations and stock. In fact, disputes over fairness very often involve the valuation of businesses and interests in businesses. How does one go about determining whether the price offered for a corporation or stock in a corporation is fair? As Professor Yablon states, this may be a matter for expert testimony; but what do the experts base their opinions on?

It is often said that a fair price is one which a willing buyer would pay and a willing seller would accept. In that case, can one determine the fair price of a constantly traded stock simply by looking at the most recent selling price? Of course, this would not work in a closely held or other corporation in which there was little trading. Moreover, does multiplying the market price of a small block of shares tell one the market price of the entire corporation or even of a majority of the stock in the company? For a discussion of this question see Stout, *Are Takeover Premiums Really Premiums? Market Price, Fair Value, and Corporate Law*, an excerpt from which appears in Chapter VI of this book.

Alternately, could one simply add up the total of the company's assets, subtract the total of its debts, and the difference would be the worth of the corporation? In fact, this is the way a corporation's balance represents the net worth of the company. On the other hand, how does one determine the worth of the individual assets? The balance sheet generally looks at their cost to the company (less a formula for depreciation). Is this typically what the assets are now worth? Suppose one was dealing with a software company; is the value of its software simply what the company paid on research and development? Also, does a going business have some worth beyond simply the sum of its individual properties?

Professor Yablon asserts that valuation generally involves predicting the future income of a business (or from owning an interest in a business) and then determining what the present value of that future income is. This follows from the fact that one normally purchases an investment for the income it generates. Professor Yablon notes that predicting future income is speculative; but how does one even begin to go about such speculation? If the corporation has an established track record of income to this point, might this record give some basis for a future prediction? The concept of discounting future income to present value reflects the fact that a dollar of income tomorrow is not worth a dollar right now. Rather, the future income is worth less than its expected total because one must delay one's enjoyment, inflation could decrease the purchasing power of future dollars, and there is always the risk that one will not receive the future income. There are formulas and tables one can use—given a determination of the appropriate rate of return to compensate for these three factors—to calculate the present value of future income. The problem is that the rate of return, since it depends upon an estimate of risk, is a matter of judgment.

There is extensive literature on business valuation. For some of the more accessible discussions see Haynsworth, *Valuation of Business Interests*, 33 MERCER L. REV. 457 (1982); Bauman & Komarynsky, *Security Analysis in* HANDBOOK OF MODERN FINANCE (Logue ed., 2d ed. 1990); Klein & Coffee, BUSINESS ORGANIZATION AND FINANCE: LEGAL AND ECONOMIC PRINCIPLES (6th ed. 1996).

3. As pointed out before, compensation for corporate management is an inherent area of conflict of interest. How can one assess the fairness of salaries and other forms of compensation? For consideration of this area see Vagts, *Challenges to Executive Compensation: For the Market or the Courts?*, 8 J. CORP. L. 231 (1983).

---

2. *The Impact of Statutes*

Mr. Marsh mentioned statutes that authorize conflict of interest transactions. He asserts that such statutes, like the modern common law, come down to a fairness test. In fact, as the next article excerpt describes, the workings of these statutes are more complex.

Kenneth B. Davis, Jr., *Approval by Disinterested Directors*, 20 J. CORP. L. 215 (1995)*

I. INTRODUCTION

Almost every state's corporation law now includes a section governing transactions in which one or more of the corporation's directors have a personal stake. The typical statute provides that the director's resulting conflict of interest will not suffice to render the transaction voidable so long as the transaction is either approved by the corporation's disinterested directors, approved by the shareholders, or found to be fair and reasonable to the corporation.

The second and third of these statutory prongs cause little stir today. Despite the common law's early intolerance of self-dealing by directors, courts in most jurisdictions came to uphold such transactions, if proven to be fair, well before the widespread adoption of the interested-director statutes. . . . Likewise, long before the statutes, courts upheld the shareholders' power to affirm transactions rendered voidable by defects in the board's process of approval, including the presence or participation of an interested director. Shareholder ratification therefore served to shift the burden to the person challenging the transaction to prove forms of misconduct that were beyond the power of a shareholder majority to cure—fraud, illegality, waste, and the like.

In contrast, the effect of approval by disinterested directors pursuant to the statutes has been an ongoing source of controversy. From the earliest cases to the modern discussion of "structural bias" in the boardroom, many courts and commentators have voiced skepticism over the capacity of board members to be totally objective when called upon to pass judgment on transactions involving their peers. . . .

Little evidence suggests that the original state interested-director statutes—either when first enacted by California in 1931 or when widely adopted on a national basis during the 1960s—were intended to foreclose judicial inquiry into the fairness of an

---

interested-director transaction simply because the corporation's disinterested directors approved the transaction. Rather, the limited legislative history generally suggests that the purpose of the statutes was merely to confirm that an interested director's participation did not render the transaction strictly voidable, as had been the case in some jurisdictions under the common law. In the same vein, the initial cases, while typically involving approval by interested or disinterested shareholders rather than by disinterested directors, regularly rejected arguments that literal compliance with the statutory approval provisions served to validate an interested-director transaction without regard to its underlying fairness. But more recent events suggest a different perspective on these issues. The corporate governance debate that began in the mid-1970s saw independent directors as the solution to a variety of business ills and called for their increased presence and more active participation on boards and key board committees. What was sauce for the goose then became sauce for the gander. Courts increasingly came to defer to the decisions of independent directors on matters such as the dismissal of derivative suits, parent-subsidiary mergers, and takeover defenses.

Not surprisingly, therefore, the two principal corporate lawmaking projects of the 1980s chose specifically to address the effect that should be accorded approval by disinterested directors; and they reached opposite results. The American Law Institute's *Principles of Corporate Governance* sought to ensure the opportunity for limited judicial fairness review even though disinterested directors approved the interested-director transaction. As ultimately adopted, the test requires that the disinterested directors "could reasonably have concluded that the transaction was fair." At roughly the same time, the drafters of the Revised Model Business Corporation Act opted for a "bright line" approach to interested-director transactions. This approach features an exclusive definition of what constitutes a "director's conflicting interest transaction" coupled with the prescription that no such transaction may "be enjoined, set aside or give rise to an award of damages or other sanctions" by virtue of the director's conflict if qualified directors or shareholders approve the transaction pursuant to the statute. The individual state statutes are comparably split. To date, seven states have adopted the 1988 Revised Model Act amendments. About the same number of jurisdictions have statutes specifically applying a fairness requirement, notwithstanding approval by the disinterested directors, with both California and Illinois falling into this category. Therefore, the issue necessarily is left to case law in the overwhelming majority of jurisdictions, with no square holdings as of yet. However, the Supreme Court of Delaware has gone out of its way on four separate occasions to indicate in dicta that approval by the corporation's disinterested directors brings an interested-director transaction within the protection of the business judgment rule.

The purpose of this Article is not to plunge four-square into the controversy over the legal consequences of approval by disinterested directors. . . . Instead, this Article focuses on a set of issues that bears importantly on that debate but has received comparatively little attention: What is required for approval by disinterested directors and how does it relate to the general requirements for valid corporate action? If disinterested-director approval is going to suffice to trigger the business judgment rule—as appears to be the emerging rule in at least some jurisdictions—the procedural elements of perfecting that approval take on a heightened significance. . . .

* * *

It will be useful throughout the analysis that follows to think in terms of the following hypothetical fact situation. Suppose that the bylaws of HiLo Tech Corp. provide for a board of seven directors. At a meeting called to consider a transaction involving some of the board members, only four directors attend, two of whom are parties to the transaction. As typically required by the various state statutes, the two interested directors disclose both the existence of their conflict and the material facts in their possession that bear on the transaction. The board then votes 4-0 to approve the transaction. Does this constitute valid board action? And if so, does it satisfy the statutory requirements for approval by the disinterested directors?

II. Disqualification of Interested Directors

A. Common Law Background

* * *

. . . [B]y the beginning of the 1900s the rule was relaxed to uphold an interested director transaction upon proof that it was fair, so long as the other directors adequately represented the corporation's interests. In other words, the participation and votes of interested directors no longer rendered a transaction strictly voidable, but could not be counted in determining whether the transaction had been validly approved by the board. . . .

. . . Two distinct rules followed from this position. First, the interested director's vote could not be counted in making up a majority of the board. Second, with the interested director thus disqualified from voting, his or her presence at the meeting could not be counted for purposes of satisfying quorum requirements. . . .

* * *

B. The Current Statutes

* * *

[H]ere one can use the former Model Act language as an illustration:

> No contract or other transaction . . . shall be either void or voidable . . . because such interested director or directors are present at the meeting of the board of directors or a committee thereof which authorizes, approves or ratifies such contract or transaction or because *his or their votes are counted for such purpose*. . . .

For this board or committee authorization, approval, or ratification also to satisfy the disinterested-director prong of the statute, it must be sufficient "without counting the votes or consents of such interested directors." The obvious implication is that those votes or consents would count for all other purposes.

Applied to the HiLo Tech hypothetical, these provisions allow the 4-0 vote of directors to satisfy the two general requirements for valid board action: (1) the presence of a quorum, ordinarily a majority of the total number of directors, and (2) the affirmative vote of a majority of those directors present. Even if the board's 4-0 vote does not satisfy the disinterested-director-approval prong of the statute—a separate issue this Article discusses below—this vote serves the purpose of supplying the requisite corporate authority, so that the transaction may then be upheld on the basis of either shareholder ratification or fairness. Under this type of statute, therefore, the proper exercise of corporate authority and the rebuttal of the common law rule of voidability function as separate and independent requirements.

* * *

III. Requirements for Disinterested-Director Approval

Assuming that the 4-0 vote of the HiLo Tech board satisfies the requirements for valid corporate action (as it does under most of the state statutes), the next question is whether the votes of the two disinterested directors also satisfy the separate statutory conditions for disinterested-director approval. Again, the answer varies with the particular state statute, with substantial room for interpretation along the way. Embedded in these questions of statutory interpretation are important policy issues about the level of participation by disinterested directors that should be required if we are to use their approval as a justification for limiting or foreclosing judicial scrutiny of the transaction.

A. The "Sufficient for Such Purpose" Test

To specify the level of disinterested board approval required, the 1931 California statute employed the phrase "by a vote sufficient for such purpose without counting the vote or votes of [the interested] director or directors." That formulation—like the other elements of the California statute—was to become a mainstay of the various state statutes enacted beginning in the 1960s, and it remains the linchpin test today in California, New York, and eleven other jurisdictions.

Case law and commentary to date suggest three alternative interpretations of the phrase, with differing consequences for HiLo Tech. The most rigorous of these alternatives interprets "sufficient for such purpose" to require that the number of disinterested directors voting to approve the transaction (or at least the number present) be sufficient to constitute a quorum: four directors in the HiLo Tech example. . . .

At the other extreme, the test is read as requiring only a majority of those disinterested directors present and voting, an interpretation that would be satisfied by the 2-0 disinterested vote in HiLo Tech. . . .

Instead, the most plausible construction of "sufficient for such purpose" is one that takes the middle ground. The disinterested votes must be sufficient in number to satisfy the applicable requirements for board approval—ordinarily the affirmative vote of a majority of the directors present at a meeting at which a quorum is present. For HiLo Tech, therefore, the board's vote fails to satisfy the requirement. Once the presence of the two interested directors is taken into account not only for quorum purposes but also in determining the number of votes necessary for a majority, the votes of the two disinterested directors, taken alone, fall short of a majority of those present.

. . . As a matter of policy, [the third interpretation] effectively responds to the pressures faced by directors in judging transactions involving their peers by assuring, in conjunction with the quorum requirements, that a "critical mass" of disinterested directors vote in favor of the transaction. This works in two ways. First, the number of disinterested directors required to approve an interested-director transaction may in no case be less than a majority of the applicable quorum requirement—in other words, a minimum of three disinterested directors in the HiLo Tech example. Second, as the number of interested directors present at the meeting (and therefore the likely peer pressure) increases, the number of disinterested directors' votes necessary to constitute a majority of those present likewise increases.

* * *

C. The Delaware Statute

When originally enacted in 1967, the Delaware statute contained the traditional "sufficient for such purpose" language. It was amended to its present form in 1969 to clarify that the disinterested directors need not constitute a quorum and now requires "the affirmative votes of a majority of the disinterested directors, even though the disinterested directors be less than a quorum." To date, the statutes of eleven other states employ this wording as well. [T]he inevitable question is whether the statute refers to [a majority of] all of the disinterested directors or simply [a majority of the disinterested directors present]. The phrase "a majority of the disinterested directors," without a qualifying reference to any particular meeting, seems more consistent with the first alternative, but the Delaware corporations statute taken as a whole reveals no standardized usage.

Policy considerations also favor reading the statute to require a majority of all disinterested directors. Again, consider the vote in the HiLo Tech example. Proponents of a more liberal construction of the statute might argue that, if anything, the votes of the two disinterested directors in favor of the transaction demonstrate a lack of opposition and serve as the best evidence of how their three absent colleagues might have voted had they been there. While this may often be the case, it is easy to think of exceptions. Anticipating opposition by these three disinterested directors, for example, the interested directors may have noticed the board meeting for a time when attendance by the three is difficult. Alternatively, the three may have reservations about the transaction, but choose to avoid the issue by avoiding the meeting. The task of statutory interpretation therefore comes down to determining the appropriate level of assurance that the transaction does, in fact, have the approval of the disinterested directors as a body. It is one thing if that approval merely serves to rebut the common law result of strict voidability. But if its effect is to limit or foreclose judicial inquiry into the transaction's fairness, the statutes should not be read to err on the side of finding approval that is in truth lacking.

* * *

E. The 1984 Revised Model Act

The 1984 version of the Revised Model Act, adopted by thirteen states to date, eliminates the ambiguities inherent in the "sufficient for such purpose" and the "majority of the disinterested directors" phrasings. It requires the "affirmative vote of a majority of the directors on the board of directors (or on the committee) who have no direct or indirect interest in the transaction."...

The other concept introduced by the 1984 statute is the limitation that approval by a single disinterested director will not suffice, even if he or she is the only member of the board who is disinterested. This limitation was also incorporated into the *ALI Principles of Corporate Governance* in the same year. Why two directors as an absolute minimum? . . . [C]oncerns over a lone, disinterested director's capacity for independent decision making draw support from both research in social psychology and gut-level instinct. At the same time, however, the minimum of two disinterested directors may prove unrealistic for smaller corporations. . . .

F. The 1988 Revised Model Act Amendments

Ambiguity reenters the picture with the comprehensive revision of the Revised Model Act interested-director provisions approved in 1988. As rewritten, the requirements for disinterested-director approval call for:

> [T]he affirmative vote of a majority (but no fewer than two) of those qualified directors *on the board of directors* or on a duly empowered committee of the board *who voted on the transaction* after either required disclosure to them (to the extent the information was not known by them) or compliance with subsection (b). . . .

* * *

The ambiguity centers on the function of the italicized "who voted on the transaction" clause. A cold reading of the statutory text, and in particular the absence of a comma to precede the italicized clause, suggests that it should be read as a restrictive clause defining which of the qualified directors are the subject of the majority requirement. In other words, the statute requires a majority of those directors who in fact voted. . . .

The alternative interpretation of the "who voted" language—preferable from a policy standpoint—is as a nonrestrictive clause whose sole function is to embody the disclosure requirement. That is, the transaction must be approved by a majority of the qualified directors "on the board of directors," and those directors must receive the required disclosure prior to their vote. The wording of the Official Comment to the section supports this interpretation. . . .

* * *

IV. Tensions Between the Requirements for Board Action and the Role of Disinterested Directors

. . . Earlier we noted . . . that an interested-director transaction may be upheld if proven to be fair, even though the presence of the interested directors was necessary for a quorum or their votes necessary for passage. The converse, which we now take up, is that action meeting the statutory requirements for approval by the corporation's disinterested directors may nonetheless fail to qualify as a valid exercise of the board's authority. . . .

To examine these issues, consider a final variation on the HiLo Tech hypothetical. Suppose that the two interested directors properly disclose their interest in the transaction and then, in order to assure an independent board evaluation (or at least its appearance), either abstain from voting or leave the meeting. The two disinterested directors vote their approval. In effect, the interested directors have chosen to impose upon themselves the same disqualification earlier demanded by the common law but since reversed by statute in almost all jurisdictions. The problem is that unless the interested-director statutes are read to preempt the otherwise applicable requirements for valid board action, the HiLo Tech board's purported approval may be invalid.

A. Continuing Applicability of the General Requirements for Approval by the Full Board

The important threshold question is, therefore, whether approval by the corporation's disinterested directors should be deemed to have this preemptive effect. The orthodox view is that the statutory requirements for board approval continue to govern and that the sole function of disinterested-director approval pursuant to the statute—or for that matter, satisfaction of the statute's shareholder-approval or fairness prongs—is to rebut the common law result of strict voidability. But courts haves [sic] sometimes reasoned to the contrary. . . .

* * *

B. Abstention by the Interested Directors

What then are the implications if the two interested HiLo Tech directors abstain from voting on their transaction with the corporation? In the absence of preemption by the interested-director statutes, attention must be turned to the general requirements for valid board approval, which commonly are framed in terms of a majority of the directors present, not a majority of the votes cast. The effect, . . . is to treat a director who is present but abstains as a "nay" vote, so that the HiLo Tech vote fails.

* * *

C. Recusal of the Interested Directors

These procedural problems aside, the interested directors' abstention, by itself, seems a rather paltry means of promoting the independent judgment of their disinterested colleagues. The better course would be for the interested directors to recuse themselves from the meeting when their transaction comes up for discussion. But this action risks breaking the quorum. The traditional statutory formulation requires board approval to be by a majority of those present "at a meeting at which a quorum is present." Does this mean that the quorum need to be present only at the outset of the meeting or also at the time of each particular vote? Under general principles of parliamentary procedure, no business may be transacted in the absence of a quorum. . . .

Taken at face value, the traditional prerequisites for valid board action therefore seem to impede disinterested directors in their efforts to carry out an independent evaluation of transactions involving their fellow directors, especially when those disinterested directors represent only a minority of the full board. But so long as the full board is truly committed to fostering an atmosphere of independent decision making, these problems are more formal than real. [T]he board can establish a committee consisting of the disinterested directors and delegate to it the board's full authority concerning the transaction. Even in the absence of a prior grant of authority, the disinterested directors may meet on their own to evaluate the transaction and then take their decision to the full board for ratification. Thus, even though the departure of HiLo Tech's two interested directors would likely foreclose valid board action in most states, their return to the meeting would restore the quorum and permit the board to ratify whatever decision their disinterested colleagues reached in their absence. If they should neglect a formal vote of ratification, case law doctrines such as implied ratification and acquiescence potentially are available to validate the transaction nonetheless, at least in the absence of opposition from the three absent directors.

* * *

Notes and Questions

1. Heretofore, we have explored corporate law primarily as a matter of broad economic and other theory and judicially developed legal doctrine. As this piece illustrates, however, much of the practice of corporate law involves precise analysis of statutory provisions and using those provisions to structure transactions.

2. The basic pattern of the conflict of interest statutes is to validate such transactions based upon (1) disinterested director approval, (2) shareholder approval, "or" (3) fairness. Professor Davis begins his article by noting the controversy over the relationship between the first and third prongs of these statutes: To what extent is the "or" really an "and"?

Start with the situation in which there is no approval by disinterested directors sufficient to meet the first prong of the statute. One reason for this failure, that focused upon in this article, is insufficient votes cast by the disinterested directors—either because there are not enough disinterested directors on the board (as would occur, for example, if every member of the board had an interest in the transaction), not enough disinterested directors show up at the meeting, or a number of the disinterested directors vote against the deal. As Professor Davis explains, assuming a majority of the quorum voted for the transaction, even if this took the votes of interested directors, the transaction can still be valid if fair to the corporation. In this context, the first and third prongs stand as disjunctive tests.

There is, however, another way in which a transaction may flunk the disinterested director approval element. The statutes refer to approval after disclosure of the conflict of interest. In other words, if the disinterested directors approved the transaction without knowing that some of their colleagues had a personal interest in the deal, this approval would not meet the first prong. Many of the statutes also state that the interested directors must disclose not only their personal interest, but any other material (in other words important) facts they know about the deal. Suppose the interested directors fail to make such disclosure: Can they still argue that the transaction was fair and so valid under the third prong? Consider the following answer:

> But why isn't fairness of price enough without full disclosure? There are several answers to this question. To begin with, in all areas of the law full disclosure must be made by persons who are in a relation of trust and confidence with those with whom they deal. This requirement reflects the expectations one has when he deals with those with whom he has such a relationship.
>
> Moreover, a rule that fairness of price was enough without full disclosure would in effect remove decisionmaking from the corporation's hands and place in it the hands of the court. . . . [I]f by a "fair price" we mean the price that would have been arrived at by a buyer and a seller dealing at arm's length, in the case of a self-interested transaction involving a differentiated commodity, a court attempting to determine whether the price was fair can do no more than to say that the price was or was not within the range at which parties dealing at arm's length would have concluded a deal. For example, a given office building might be fairly priced, in this sense, at anywhere from $40 million to $44 million, because any price within that range might have been arrived at by parties dealing at arm's length. Suppose that C Corporation purchases the office building for $42 million from a director or senior executive who has failed to disclose a material fact. The price may have been fair in the sense that third parties dealing at arm's length might have transacted at that price, but there is no way to know whether C would have paid $42 million if it had known the material fact. If there had been full disclosure, C might have agreed to purchase only at some price lower than $42 million.
>
> Indeed, there is no way to know whether C would have purchased the building at all if the material fact had been disclosed. . . .

* * *

> The argument is sometimes made that a distinction should be drawn between a failure to disclosure a conflict of interest and a failure to disclose a material fact concerning the transaction itself. Under this argument, a failure to disclose a conflict of interest may be fatal, but a failure to disclose a material fact concerning the transaction should not be. The premise of the argument is that once the director or senior executive had disclosed his conflict of interest, the corporation is as much on guard as if it were dealing with a third party, and there is no need to require the director or senior executive to disclose more than a third party would have to. This premise is wrong. Knowing that a director or senior executive has an interest in an exchange transaction doesn't necessarily put the corporation on guard. When persons are in a relation of trust and confidence, they do not go on guard simply because they are dealing in an exchange context. If *A* sells his used car to his sister, she assumes that he will be forthcoming about the car in a way a stranger would not, even though she knows he has an interest in the transaction. The same is true of dealings between a director or senior executive and his colleagues.
>
> Furthermore, even if the corporation was put on guard as a result of the disclosure of the conflict of interest, there would be an unfair informational disequilibrium between the parties unless the director or senior executive disclosed all material facts concerning the transaction. The director or senior executive knows, or at least is in a position to know, every material fact the corporation knows about the transaction. In order to level the playing field, the corporation should know every material fact the director or senior executive knows. Eisenberg, *Self-Interested Transactions in Corporate Law*, 13 J. CORP. L. 997 (1988).*

Still, it does not necessarily contradict the "or" term in the statute to say that the failure to disclose to the disinterested directors invalidates the transaction despite fair terms. Rather, one could explain that fairness has a procedural as well as a substantive element and that the failure to disclose renders the transaction procedurally unfair. Hence, non-disclosure ruins both the first and third methods of validating a conflict transaction under the statute.

The main controversy lies in the flip situation. Suppose the transaction receives sufficient disinterested director approval after full disclosure: Can the court still review the transaction under a fairness test? Mr. Marsh cites a California court decision that said this, which is why he concludes that even under the statutes the whole issue comes down to fairness. The 1976 revision of California's corporation code codified this result by adding a fairness requirement to the disinterested director approval prong. Professor Davis notes that other jurisdictions—either by statute or judicial opinion—are in disagreement on this question (with Delaware most notably taking a position contrary to California). Keep in mind that refusing to apply a fairness test does not mean the transaction is beyond any judicial review. Even a transaction in which no directors have an interest is subject to review. The significance is that the review will be under the deferential business judgment standard.

One obvious problem with this early California court decision is that it appears to contradict the statute's use of the word "or." Notice Professor Davis' attempt to deal with this difficulty by reference to the legislative history. Is this persuasive? California's current statute avoids this problem, but introduces a new one. What is the point of including a disinterested director approval prong if one ends up applying the same fairness review as the court would go through had there been no disinterested director approval? Compare the American Law Institute's approach outlined by Professor Davis. It contains an intermediate test for a conflict transaction approved by disinterested directors: Not the business judgment rule, but also not a requirement that the court find the deal was fair; Rather, the court must find that the directors could reasonably have thought the transaction was fair. For a criticism of the ALI approach and an argument in favor of the business judgment standard see Johnston & Alexander, *The Effect of Disinterested Director Approval of Conflict Transactions Under the ALI Corporate Governance Project—A Practitioner's Perspective*, 48 BUS. LAW. 1393 (1993). For a response see Small, *Conflicts of Interest and the ALI Corporate Governance Project—A Reporter's Perspective*, 48 BUS. LAW. 1377 (1993).

From a policy standpoint, the question comes down to the costs of fairness review versus how much one trusts disinterested directors to look out for the corporation when a transaction involves their colleagues. The latter factor suggests an empirical study could be useful.

---

3. *Reality Check: The Effectiveness of Disinterested Director Review*

Victor Brudney, *The Independent Director—Heavenly City or Potemkin Village?*, 95 HARV. L. REV. 597 (1982)*

* * *

... In the context of self-dealing, independence implies an adversarial role for the independent director. He is, in theory, a proxy for the market and presumably presses for results comparable to those that would have been produced by arms-length bargaining. But practical considerations soften his adversarial role. The independent director has rarely been appointed without at least the prior approval of management. ... But quite apart from that connection, inquiry into the propriety of self-dealing transactions requires the board to confront management on issues that tend to cut more deeply than relatively impersonal differences about corporate operations. . . . [H]is zeal as a monitor will be tempered by the need to relate constructively to inside directors in all other corporate matters.

The institutionally generated disinclination to hold colleagues at arm's length is furthered by other psychological and social considerations. Besides pressure to follow the leader in the boardroom along lines described in the learning on small group dynamics, other factors make independent directors particularly apt to view management's demands congenially. If they are not themselves corporate executives, independent directors tend nevertheless to share common business and professional backgrounds with, and to live in the same social and economic milieu as does, management—although there may be occasional exceptions from the educational or non-profit world. . . .

* * *

Shifting the focus from a priori speculation about whether the independent director will adequately enforce such standards as can be found with respect to managerial over-reaching to an examination of the experience that independent directors have had in this role does not produce an encouraging view.[53] . . . Much work remains to be done to collect evidence on how effectively the independent director curbs over-reaching and to compare the costs and benefits of independent directors with those of a categorical prohibition or other public regulation to restrain overreaching in self-dealing. Until that evidence is collected, we are left to such inference as can be drawn from the slim bits of relevant observed behavior.

(a) A more than casual but less than exhaustive examination of the litigated cases involving charges of self-dealing or misappropriation of corporate assets by management of public corporations either that were decided for the plaintiff or in which there were substantial settlements, does not disclose many instances of outside directors' having dissented from the subsequently challenged managerial appropriations. Nor does the behavior of the independent directors of investment companies, as revealed in litigated cases, suggest any greater diligence where self-dealing conflicts of interest were involved. . . . [A] search of reported court and Securities and Exchange Commission (SEC) cases under the Investment Company Act does not reveal any successful or partially successful challenge claiming improper diversion to management of corporate assets in which independent directors were recorded as dissenting from the challenged behavior. . . .

* * *

(b) To be sure, this record [of reviewed court and SEC cases] does not prove that independent directors of investment companies or other corporations did not press for compliance with standards limiting the returns from self-dealing. Nor does it show that

53 There is evidence that overt executive emoluments are somewhat higher in firms in which inside directors dominate numerically than in firms dominated by outsiders, but there is conflict over its import. . . .

they have not had some success in the matter or that their presence alone did not inhibit insiders. . . . But it remains relevant that rarely in cases of adjudged insider misbehavior, or of challenged behavior that produced substantial settlements, does there seem to be any evidence of objections by independent directors. . . .

* * *

Notes and Questions

1. Is there a problem of selection bias in the sample Professor Brudney examines—this being cases in which we already know disinterested director review did not work? Must disinterested directors in every corporation have opposed all unfair self-dealing before one concludes they are sufficiently trustworthy overall to merit the business judgment standard? For a survey of various attempts to study the effectiveness of outside directors in dealing with management conflicts of interest see Lin, *The Effectiveness of Outside Directors as a Corporate Governance Mechanism*, 90 NW. U. L. REV. 898 (1996).

On the other hand, what is the downside to requiring fairness review of conflict of interest transactions despite disinterested director approval? Will the uncertainty of judicial reaction cause directors to forgo interested transactions which might be worthwhile for the corporation, or might it cause them to make sure the company is getting a good deal? Are conflict of interest transactions so frequent that a more intrusive review will result in excessive litigation costs?

2. Shareholder approval is the third manner of validating conflict of interest transactions. Mr. Marsh spends little time on this subject and Professor Davis states that it causes little controversy today. Still, despite the lack of attention in law review articles, shareholder approval does raise questions:

(i) Will the shares voted by the directors in a conflict of interest count? Mr. Marsh gave an affirmative answer, although the Model Business Corporations Act, the current California statute and many other state statutes now are explicitly to the contrary. Older provisions, like Delaware's, however, may fail to specify an answer. A rule that only disinterested shareholder votes count can, in turn, raise issues concerning the number of disinterested votes needed along the lines discussed by Professor Davis in connection with disinterested director approval.

(ii) What is the impact of a favorable shareholder vote? Both Mr. Marsh and Professor Yablon suggest that it may shift the burden of proof by placing it on those opposed to the transaction. What standard of review, however, will apply: Fairness? Business judgment rule? Something else? Mr. Marsh throws in the term "fraud." If, by that, he means the directors lied to the shareholders to get their votes—or even failed to disclose material facts to the shareholders—this should vitiate the effectiveness of shareholder approval and may even constitute unfairness (as discussed earlier) so as to preclude reliance on that prong as well. Mr. Marsh, however, seems to use the term fraud in a different way. Sometimes, one will find judicial opinions use the term fraud as a label for substantively unfair self-dealing. This explains why even here Mr.

Marsh concludes the whole test for conflict of interest transactions comes down to a review of fairness. Professor Yablon quotes a Delaware court opinion which also refers to fairness even after shareholder ratification. On the other hand, does this quoted test—whether "no person of ordinary sound business judgment would say that the consideration received was a fair exchange"—sound like an exacting fairness review? Or, does this sound something like the deferential approach identified with the business judgment rule? Courts often refer to this standard as an examination to see if the transaction amounts to "waste."

C. The Duty of Loyalty: Corporate Opportunities

Victor Brudney and Robert Charles Clark, *A New Look at Corporate Opportunities*, 94 HARV. L. REV. 997 (1981)*

The law of corporate opportunities is among the least satisfactory limbs of doctrine in the corpus of corporate law. Not only are the common formulations vague, but the courts have articulated no theory that could serve as a blueprint for constructing meaningful rules. . . . In this Article, we examine the theoretical underpinning of the corporate opportunity doctrine, and suggest relatively clear rules to implement it.

We begin by asking why there is any need for a corporate opportunity doctrine. According to the formulation of most courts, if a business opportunity is determined to be a corporate opportunity, then a corporate fiduciary—such as a director, officer, or controlling shareholder—may not take or "usurp" it for his own benefit, unless proper consent is given.[2] Thus, a corporate opportunity is defined to be, as against fiduciaries, a corporate asset. The reasons for forbidding its appropriation are the same as those for generally forbidding corporate agents and fiduciaries from unilaterally taking corporate property for themselves. . . .

* * *

2 The vast bulk of the case law asks whether the project appropriated is a corporate opportunity, and upon concluding that it is, holds that the defendant is at fault for taking it. . . . In recent years, however, a few decisions have adopted a different linguistic convention: they separate the question whether a "corporate opportunity" is involved from that whether, if there is, it may nevertheless be appropriated. . . . Miller v. Miller, 301 Minn. 207, 222 N.W. 2d 71 (1974). . . .

The new mode of speech both reflects and creates confusion in the thinking of those who use it. In the *Miller* case, for example, the court offers no convincing reason for its two-step analysis: the factors discussed in the second step seem just as relevant to determining whether the opportunity should be classified as a "corporate" one as those applied in the first step. The new methodology in fact adds only a new layer of confusion to an already murky area of law, without forwarding the analysis in any significant fashion.

Of course, the problem repeatedly faced by the courts has *not* been this question of philosophy or economic policy—whether corporate fiduciaries should be able unilaterally to take whatever corporate assets they feel are proper compensation for their efforts—but rather the more difficult problem of determining which business opportunities ought to be considered corporate ones. Serious policy issues arise when the concept of corporate opportunity is broadened or its application is unclear. Suppose, for example, it were to include *any* opportunity to acquire a profitable business (no matter what the corporation's existing business), even when the diverter is not a full-time executive but an outside director. As the loss to the corporation from being deprived of the opportunity becomes less certain (because the opportunity is more remote and therefore less likely to be exploited by the corporation), as the possibility of the diverter's developing the opportunity more successfully than would the corporation increases, and as the rewards to the diverter change from an increase in fulltime remuneration for full-time work to an entrepreneurial reward for an uncompensated director, the balance of social convenience changes and may suggest different rules.

In our examination of the problem of identifying corporate opportunities, we suggest what we think are relevant considerations and feasible rules. Our study rests upon two assumptions that are not generally reflected in the present doctrine. First, we submit that different considerations and rules should be employed for close corporations than for publicly held corporations. Second, we believe that in the latter case, rules should depend upon whether the appropriator is (1) a full-time officer or executive, (2) only an outside director or a part-time executive of more than one corporation, or (3) a parent corporation.

I. Close Corporations

* * *

A. Relevant Differences Between Close and Public Corporations

The basic choice to be made . . . to define the corporate opportunity doctrine is between a categorical approach and a selective approach. . . . The categorical approach would define corporate opportunity in sweeping terms to include all possible active modes of making a profit, and would take a strict stance towards proposed exceptions and defenses. It would prohibit an officer or executive, for example, from taking any other active business opportunity—at least without the consent of the corporation. The selective approach would define corporate opportunity more narrowly, by criteria that relate each opportunity to the operations, needs, or expectations of the firm. It would require the fiduciary to show only that the opportunity he took does not fall within the criteria. On this approach, insiders would be denied some active business opportunities, but permitted to accept others.

In our view, it is desirable to use the selective approach for close corporations and the categorical approach for public corporations. . . .

The ability of the stockholders of private corporations to select the fiduciaries to whom they have entrusted their capital, and to police their management's contributions to (and diversions from) the enterprise is much greater than the selecting and monitoring capacities of shareholders in public corporations. . . . Accordingly, such investors have less need of categorical strictures on such diversions.

Moreover, both the scope of the duties and the nature of the compensation of the managers differ between the two types of corporation. The duties of the executives of a public corporation normally require full-time application of their managerial talents and energies and leave no room for active participation in the development or operation of other businesses. Correspondingly, their compensation arrangements are such that neither equity nor efficiency requires them to be allowed to take covert indirect compensation as they see fit. But for many close corporations, other expectations may be more reasonable. The participants may sometimes agree, or assume in the initial arrangements, that their managing colleagues are not to work only for the particular corporation, but are free to engage in other activities. . . .

Finally, differences between the opportunity sets of the two types of enterprise imply different constraints on their managers. A publicly held enterprise may fairly be treated as large and flexible enough to accept any new investment opportunities that offer an appropriate return per unit of risk. Hence, its opportunity set embraces virtually any business in which its executives might want to invest and take an active role. The opportunity set of a close corporation is not nearly so broad. Market imperfections and transaction costs may preclude or impede such corporations' efforts to accept projects unrelated to their existing experience or talent or beyond their existing financial capacity. There may be many businesses that the officers of a closely held enterprise may seek to develop on their own time, but that would not deprive the enterprise of any opportunity it could reasonably hope to exploit.

* * *

. . . Hence, less rigid rules than the categorical ones we shall propose in later Parts of this Article should govern participants in close corporations. What those less rigid rules should be is another question. In general, we believe that in this context only modest alterations are needed in the guidelines provided by existing law.

B. The Governing Principles and the Modifications Implied for the Existing Law of Close Corporations

1. Opportunities Developed with Corporate Assets.—We start with the core principle that a participant cannot take for himself any opportunity to the development of which assets of the corporation have been applied. In this context the concept "assets" includes "hard" assets like cash, facilities, and contracts, and "soft" assets like goodwill, working time, and corporate information. The principle rests on the same considerations that forbid appropriations of the assets themselves, but adds the remedy of tracing the misappropriated assets into their product—a conventional remedy in the law of trusts.

Generally speaking, the case law accepts and applies this principle more consistently when hard assets are used than when soft assets are involved. The use of hard assets is often dispositive of the usurpation issue. . . .

It is relatively easy to conclude that repeated appropriation of corporate contracts, or use of corporate facilities to do research, or of corporate cash to purchase equipment, options, or the like, is a sufficient application of a corporate asset to preclude diversion of the resulting opportunity. But the concept "corporate asset" and its relationship to the opportunity being diverted become less clear when what is involved is the time of an executive or information about a new project discovered by an officer during, but not strictly within, the course of his employment. In these matters, the rule operates somewhat unpredictably in practice. This is apparent from cases dealing with the question whether information acquired by an officer, sometimes in the fulfillment of his duties, sometimes merely collaterally by reason of his position, and at other times wholly "on his own," may be appropriated by him, along with the associated opportunity.

* * *

2. Principles Based on Rational Expectations.—Not all opportunities available to close corporations are discovered or developed by use of corporate assets; an opportunity may become available without any such expenditures. Under what circumstances are participants then precluded from exploiting the opportunity for themselves? In large part, an answer to that question is suggested by focusing on the expectations that rational participants may be deemed to have held at the beginning of the venture.

When a close corporation is formed, the participants rarely envision all the contingencies against which they would have contracted had they foreseen the future. More important, it is fair to assume that if the participants had contemplated the possibilities that later materialized, they would have contracted to prevent some of them from occurring. For example, they probably would have contracted against the appropriation by only some of the participants of projects that are essential to the continued viability of the enterprise. But they might very well have permitted appropriation of opportunities wholly unrelated to the business of the enterprise, even if letting the corporation take them might avoid its insolvency. A more inclusive but still reasonable expectation to impute to the venturers is that their company would be entitled, as against the individual participants, to new projects that were within the corporation's line of business, or within its set of functionally related operations, whether or not the project was "essential" to prevent injury to the corporation. And finally, we can suppose that they would have protected their collective right to opportunities that the corporation would reasonably expect to acquire, such as the renewal of a lease, or that it has taken overt steps to obtain, as by negotiating, or merely by making studies or inquiries—that is, opportunities in which it has an "interest" or "expectancy."[42]

---

42 Our assumption that the participants would normally expect the corporation to have a prior claim to all functionally related projects, even if those projects were not "essential" to the continued prosperity of the enterprise, merits additional analysis. In the case of a small, closely held enterprise, the cost of adding something wholly new—something not in the same line of business—to the venture, expressed as a percentage of the cost of the total enterprise, is apt to be considerably greater than in the case of large, publicly held enterprises. The costs involved in acquiring new talent, space, and equipment, in shifting organizational structures, and in making new external financial arrangements for the type of novel addition to the business of a close corporation than [sic] an insider might acquire for himself are relatively

On the premise that the law should vindicate these imputed expectations, we propose that the following guidelines, which the case law often acknowledges, should govern the taking of business opportunities by participants in close corporations.

(1) If the disputed opportunity is functionally related to the corporation's business, then, whether or not it is "necessary" or of "special value," individual participants may not take it.

(2) If the corporation has an "interest" or "expectancy" in the opportunity, individual participants may not take it.

(3) If the participants consent in advance or contemporaneously to diversion of the new project, an individual participant may take it, even though the taking would otherwise run afoul of (1) or (2); provided, however, that nothing less than express contemporaneous consent will permit the taking of functionally related opportunities whose acceptance is "necessary" to prevent loss or injury to the corporation.

(4) If the new project is not covered by the preceding rules, it may be taken by some individual participants without sharing with the others and without the consent of the others.

The open-ended texture of these guidelines leaves great and perhaps excessive leeway for judicial discretion in administering them and for participants in planning under them. To bring the guidelines into somewhat sharper focus, we offer suggestions about their key notions: (a) "functional relationship" between a new project and the corporation's business; (b) "interest" or "expectancy" in a new project; (c) "necessity" or "special value" of a new project; and (d) "consent" that permits diversion of a corporate opportunity.

(a) Functional Relationship.

* * *

The case law conception of "line of business," which is analogous to functional relationship, is ephemeral, being sometimes as broad as the corporate charter and other times limited by the firm's actual operations. The kernel of validity in the line-of-business test is probably the insight that a firm—especially a small business—is more likely and easily able to expand its current business operations than to enter into new operations. An opportunity to expand into a related operation is thus a particularly appropriate one to prohibit a firm's executives from taking. Because projects within a corporation's existing line of business seem more likely to have special value if

---

greater than similar costs would be for a large public enterprise. Correspondingly, the risks—expressed in terms of variations in total return—are apt to be greater. It is thus reasonable to suppose that the original venturers would have been least likely to worry about entitlement to wholly new kinds of businesses.

On the other hand, it is also reasonable to suppose that the original venturers would have worried most about diversions of opportunities within the corporation's line of business, and with respect to them would have paid very little attention to the distinction between projects that were essential or necessary and those that merely enhanced profits. If a new project "fits" the old business in the sense of embodying operating functions that are synergistically related to the old business and offering better or similar risk-return tradeoffs, there is no rational basis for believing that the original venturers would have assigned it to the corporation only if it were "necessary" or of "unique value."

exploited by it, the line-of-business test may simply be an attempt to articulate more specifically opportunities that are likely to be so valuable to the corporation that executives should be automatically prohibited from taking them.

But to recognize the inspiration of the line-of-business test does not minimize the major problems of interpretation that its application presents. . . .

(b) Interest or Expectancy.—Defining corporate opportunities as those in which the corporation has an "interest" or "expectancy" is of more ancient vintage and is more frequently encountered in the courts than is definition by reference to line of business, but it gives us equally faint guidelines. The concept of an interest or expectancy, which the courts have come to view more broadly in recent years, is fundamentally an extension of the concept of corporate property. It means, however, something much less tenable than ownership—less than a legal right to exclude independent third parties from acquiring the project, and less even than contingent contractual claims. Notwithstanding the rhetoric of the opinions, an interest or expectancy is not legally "property," even though it may be economically capitalizable and of sufficient value to be salable in arm's-length transactions. On the other hand, an interest or expectancy must be more certain than a "desire" or a "hope."

The case law offers few useful criteria for determining when an interest exists. Indeed, the criteria may vary with the context. . . . Moreover, the cases have reached contradictory conclusions regarding the existence of an interest in contexts that are not relevantly distinguishable. Because so many considerations enter into its application, the concept is of little help in deciding particular cases or predicting the outcomes of the next ones.

* * *

(c) Necessity.—Occasionally the current doctrine determines whether an opportunity is a corporate one according to whether it is "necessary" for, "essential" to, or of "special value" to, the venture. Under the case law, a corporation is deprived of such an opportunity if the opportunity is related to its line of business and the consequences of deprivation are so severe as to threaten the *viability* of the enterprise, as by diverting its initial business opportunity. The cases also find an opportunity to be necessary if being deprived of it merely *injures* the corporation's business by causing a loss in the ongoing conduct of its affairs or a contraction in its operation. Loss of an opportunity necessary for continued viability is a meaningful injury against which it is reasonable to believe that all participants would have contracted, in the initial position, by adopting a no-diversion rule. But loss of less critical opportunities is not so clearly a possibility of this type. Contraction of the ongoing enterprise, or economic loss, may be perceived as simply points on a continuum that extends to expansion of the enterprise or to increments in profits gained through the exploitation of new projects. Accordingly, it is difficult to identify a sound economic reason for a definition of corporate opportunity that distinguishes sharply between the failure to maintain the current condition of the business and the failure to improve it.

* * *

(d) Consent.—As we have noted, in close corporations it is feasible to allow a role for the contemporaneous consent of the participants. . . .

It may also be feasible in a given case to show that from the beginning it was or should have been understood by all the participants that some would participate in the management of the enterprise, but would have other active business interests, sometimes even related to the venture at hand. In such cases, a coherent, principled doctrine may properly permit the taking of projects even within a corporation's line of business. Case law reaches results consistent with this view, but unfortunately the courts seem disposed to approach the issue in doctrinal terms as involving a choice between the "interest or expectancy" and "line-of-business" tests, instead of resorting directly to an inquiry into what expectations would have been rational in the given case.

* * *

3. The Irrelevance of Corporate Incapacity and Similar Defenses.—The principles we have proposed omit reference to that last refuge of courts seeking to adjust the law of corporate opportunity to the rational expectations of the participants in close corporations—the concept of fairness. The case law gives this concept no principled content and seems designed to leave the courts with boundless discretion, in this context, the discretion generates much uncertainty about the operational meaning of the legal rule, but no offsetting benefits.

Our proposed principles also leave no room for some of the other variables that frequently appear in the opinions. There is a substantial body of case law that permits officers to divert corporate opportunities when some showing is made that the corporation is unable to take the opportunity because of limitations in its charter or contracts, external legal constraints, its inability to finance the acquisition, or the unwillingness of the persons offering the opportunity to deal with the corporation.

As courts have pointed out on several occasions, if financial disabilities or third-party refusals to deal with the corporation are accepted as tests, the inevitable result will be to permit the diversion. This is true because courts must resolve the legal issues on the basis of a set of facts largely within the control of the diverter. . . .

There is no reason to allow the diverters to exploit opportunities that they claim the corporation is unable to exploit, if the claimed inability may be feasibly eliminated. To permit claims of disability to become the subject of judicial controversy when they can only be disproven by outsiders with great difficulty and at considerable expense is to tempt participants to actions whose impropriety is visible but rarely subject to effective challenge. Availability of the defense of corporate incapacity reduces the incentive to solve corporate financing and other problems.

* * *

II. Public Corporations

A. Full-Time Officers or Executives

1. The Categorical Prohibition.—Although the selective approach to the fiduciary principle may properly govern the relationship between managers and investors in private corporations, it is inadequate for public corporations. We submit that, despite the cost of the categorical approach, there is good reason to apply it to executives of public corporations. Accordingly, a full-time executive of a public corporation should be prohibited from taking any other active business opportunity.

* * *

2. *Comparison with Case Law Principles.*

* * *

The traditional standards for determining whether a particular opportunity is a corporate one fail to take adequate account of these realities of the modern public corporation. The interest or expectancy test rests on the premise that only projects for which there is some evidence of a current likelihood that the corporation would acquire or develop them are within the legitimate expectations of investors. However tolerable it may be to use imminent expectations to test the propriety of takings of opportunities in the close corporation context, for public corporations, and most particularly for larger firms, a more or less continuous interest in growth stimulates constant receptivity to new projects. Although public corporations may not accept every project that comes to their attention, they are potentially receptive to all profitable projects, whether called to their attention or not. Hence, a definition of "corporate opportunity" that depends on narrow notions of likelihood of acquisition does not meet the legitimate expectations of investors in public corporations.

Similarly, the line-of-business test is not consonant with economic learning and experience. One may fairly question why courts should presume a publicly held corporation to be confined to the line or lines of business in which it currently operates. Why should it be assumed that an enterprise that starts out in the electronics business is precluded from moving profitably into the beer-bottling business? Diversification commends itself to financial theorists as a way to increase investment returns per unit of risk, and in light of the takeover and conglomerating process of the past fifteen years, seems equally to commend itself to businessmen.

Matters are not helped by adding another variable from the world of close corporations to the definitional process—the necessity or special value of the particular opportunity to the corporation's business. That variable has little utility in cases involving close corporations; it has none where public corporations are involved.

Finally, the defense of corporate incapacity is, if anything, even less tenable in the context of public corporations than it is in close corporation cases. As noted earlier, the courts frequently permit officers to appropriate an opportunity that is within the corporation's line of business or in which it has an expectancy, if the corporation lacks the ability to exploit it because of financial, legal, or other impediments. As with close corporations, the case law on the corporate incapacity defense is not uniform for public corporations. The defense has even less merit in this context, however, since it inevitably depends on self-serving managerial claims that there exists no viable way to overcome the stated corporate disability; and it is virtually impossible for public stockholders to negate such claims. The allowance of the defense thus tempts the officers to fail to exercise their best efforts to make the corporation able to overcome the disability.

* * *

B. Outside Director and Part-Time, Multicompany Executives

Though a broad rule on corporate opportunities is appropriate for full-time officers or executives, different considerations apply for directors who are not executives of the corporation. . . .

. . . Outside directors typically are neither paid a salary nor expected to devote much time, let alone full time, to the affairs of the corporation. Therefore, a major premise of the prohibition against active business ventures by full-time officers does not apply to outside directors. They are not disentitled, by reason of their directors' fees or commitments to the corporation, to participate actively in other ventures. Indeed, they are often made outside directors precisely because they are executives of other corporations.

. . . Sufficient protection is offered to public investors if [the outside director] is subject to the limited restraint of a prohibition against use of the corporation's resources, including information, to develop or acquire personal business opportunities. . . .

III. Publicly Owned Parent companies and Partially Owned Subsidiaries

In this Part, we consider the proper policy to take toward business opportunities that could be allocated either to one of two or more affiliates of a publicly owned corporation, or to the public corporation itself. Though parent corporations ought to be treated as fiduciaries with respect to their subsidiaries, the corporate opportunity problem is significantly different in this context than in the others we have analyzed because the interests of the parent corporation's public investors must be taken into account. Unlike full-time executives of a corporation, the parent's public investors are not agents of the subsidiary whose compensation reflects a significant basis for categorically denying them access to opportunities. Moreover, as investors, they have legitimate expectations that their enterprise will have opportunities of its own. A categorical rule denying the parent any opportunities would deprive its public stockholders of benefits to which they may have legitimate claims. The entitlements of the subsidiary's and the parent's public stockholders impel a solution that permits both groups to acquire or share in the rewards of at least some opportunities.

* * *

The traditional approach uncritically imports the ambiguous doctrines developed for close corporations. This approach makes no analytical contribution to the problem in this special context, and in practice it generally favors the parent. Given the imprecision of the rules for determining the ownership of an opportunity and the unevenness of nonjudicial sanctions such as bad reputation, the parent's managers are not unlikely to succumb to temptation. And this will happen more readily when, as a key Delaware decision suggests, the matter is viewed by the courts as one of business judgment.[148]

* * *

Notes and Questions

1. Surprisingly few law review articles attempt to address comprehensively the area of corporate opportunities. In addition to the article excerpted above, one can read Chew, *Competing Interests in the Corporate Opportunity Doctrine*, 67 N.C. L. REV. 435 (1989).

2. Professors Brudney and Clark state as a categorical rule that persons cannot take for themselves opportunities to which they have applied the assets of the corporation. As Professors Brudney and Clark recognize, when dealing with intangibles such an executive's time, or information that might come to an executive through his or her job, it is not always clear what is a company asset. Even with tangible property, however, Professors Brudney and Clark may overstate the case. The problem is not determining the appropriateness of the defendant's conduct; the question is one of remedy. To illustrate, suppose a executive takes home a company "laptop" computer to draft a business plan for a new venture unrelated to anything involving her work for the company. We might agree that the conduct was wrong; but should the company be entitled to the new business simply by virtue of her using the computer? Suppose the only company property she used was one floppy disk? Professors Brudney and Clark refer to the remedy of "tracing," which requires one who converts another's property not only to give back what he or she took, but also any profit made with the misappropriated items. For example, if one took money and bet it on a lottery ticket, the misappropriator would have to give up the winnings. When one uses corporate property to develop an opportunity, however, is the profit the entire opportunity, or merely a proportion of it based upon the ratio of corporate to non-corporate inputs?

3. Professors Brudney and Clark toss off a host of terms and principles for determining if something is a corporate opportunity. This might leave one dazed upon a first reading, especially when the authors bounce back and forth between what courts currently do and what the authors recommend.

One thing that might help to organize the relevant factors in this area is to visualize a triangle. At one point of the triangle, we have the opportunity; at the second point, we have the agent who took the opportunity; and at the third point, we have the corporation. The various tests and factors used in the cases, and discussed by Professors Brudney and Clark, for determining if there is a corporate opportunity involve the three relationships created by these three points.

148 Sinclair Oil Corp. v. Levien, 280 A.2d 717 (Del. 1971).

This is easiest to see for the line of business and necessity tests. These involve the relationship between the corporation and the opportunity: Does the opportunity involve the same type of business as the corporation conducts (or, as Professors Brudney and Clark would put it, is there a functional relationship between the opportunity and the corporation's business)? Is the opportunity essential (or has a special value) to the corporation? The interest or expectancy test also fits here. This test, while vague, picks up situations in which the corporation was seeking or negotiating for the opportunity or had some property interest (such as a lease) in the opportunity.

The second leg of the triangle is the relationship between the agent and the corporation. Notice how Professors Brudney and Clark would use different approaches depending on whether the defendant was a full time executive or an outside director.

Finally, there is the relationship between the opportunity and the agent—in other words, how did the agent learn of the opportunity? Here is where one gets into the use of corporate information discussed by Professors Brudney and Clark. In this area, one might distinguish three situations: (i) the opportunity learned of as part of the job (as when the corporation assigns an agent to look for an opportunity and he or she then takes it for him- or herself, or an opportunity which a third party originally brought to the agent in order for him or her to present to the corporation); (ii) the opportunity learned of completely independent of anything to do with the agent's job; and (iii) the opportunity not discovered as part of the job, but which the agent would not have learned of but for his or her employment (such as where the employment puts the agent at the right place and at the right time to learn of the opportunity, or allows the agent to meet the third party who provides the opportunity).

Of course, to identify the relevant factors is not to say where one should draw the line as to what is or is not a corporate opportunity. Professors Brudney and Clark's principal goal was to suggest such lines. In taking the expansive approach they did, have they given sufficient attention to the interests of corporate agents?

4. Professors Brudney and Clark note the possibility that consent might allow the agent to take what would otherwise be a corporate opportunity. If the defendant is a director, then consent involves a conflict of interest situation. Should one employ the same test(s) used in dealing with conflict of interest transactions when reviewing consent to take an opportunity? If so, how can one decide if such consent is fair to the corporation?

D. The Interests of Other Constituencies

1. *The Doctrine Introduced*

American Bar Association Committee on Corporate Laws, *Other Constituencies Statutes: Potential for Confusion*, 45 Bus. Law. 2253 (1990)*

INTRODUCTION

The Committee on Corporate Laws of the Section of Business Law of the American Bar Association continuously reviews legislative and judicial developments in corporation law and the provisions of the Revised Model Business Corporation Act (the "Model Act") to determine whether the Act gives appropriate recognition to evolving developments in corporation law. The Committee has reviewed the so-called "other constituencies" statutes enacted during the last several years by at least twenty-five states to determine whether or not the Model Act should include such a provision. These statutes variously authorize (and, in one state, require) directors to take into account the interests of other "constituencies"—persons or groups other than shareholders—in performing their duties, including the making of change-of-control decisions.

* * *

HISTORICAL BACKGROUND

A recurring debate concerning corporations and their role in American life has centered on the persons to whom corporations owe a duty and have accountability, and whose interests the management and directors of a corporation may or must serve. In the early 1930s, Professor E. Merrick Dodd of Harvard Law School and Professor Adolf A. Berle of Columbia Law School engaged in a classic debate on this subject in the pages of the Harvard Law Review. Dodd asserted that public opinion increasingly viewed the corporation as an "economic institution which has a social service as well as a profit-making function."[1] ...

Professor Berle took strong exception to this viewpoint. While sympathizing with the idealism of Professor Dodd and suggesting that the law might be moving in the direction of recognizing the claims of groups other than shareholders, he repudiated the notion that the management of corporations should have responsibilities beyond the interests of the shareholders. . . .[2]

* * *

1 Dodd, *For Whom Are Corporate Managers Trustees?*, 45 Harv. L. Rev. 1145, 1148 (1932).

2 Berle, *For Whom Corporate Managers are Trustees: A Note*, 45 Harv. L. Rev. 1365, 1372 (1932). . . .

THE LAW BEFORE OTHER CONSTITUENCIES STATUTES

There have been some cases in which courts have appeared to recognize the proposition that corporations have responsibilities that go beyond shareholders and embrace creditors, employees, communities and "other constituencies." In none of the cases examined, however, did it appear that the court countenanced director action which favored one or more of the other constituencies at the expense of shareholders, and in no case were the statements of the court acknowledging such responsibilities a part of its holding. However, it has long been clear that a corporation may properly expend corporate funds, for instance, for employee outings or other employee benefits; for charitable and community purposes in areas where it had operations; and to assist suppliers in staying in business, all at the expense of shareholders (in the sense that they had an equity in the funds used) on the theory that such expenditures advanced the long-term interests of the corporation.

In *Dodge v. Ford Motor Co.*,[11] the Michigan Supreme Court dealt squarely with a situation in which it was alleged that directors had subordinated shareholder interests to other interests. In that case, the directors, dominated by Henry Ford, refused to pay dividends on the apparent grounds that the company had made too much money, and that "a sharing [of the company's profits] with the public, by reducing the price of the output of the company, ought to be undertaken." The court affirmed the primacy of the shareholders' interests in this fashion:

> . . . it is not within the lawful powers of a board to shape and conduct the affairs of a corporation for the merely incidental benefit of shareholders and for the primary purpose of benefiting others, and no one will contend that, if the avowed purpose of the defendant directors was to sacrifice the interests of shareholders, it would not be the duty of the courts to interfere.

The surge of contested takeovers has provided the occasion for careful and repeated consideration of the extent to which directors may give heed to groups and interests other than shareholders by arguably the most sophisticated corporate courts in the country, the Supreme and Chancery Courts of Delaware. Several recent opinions of the Delaware Supreme Court discuss the extent to which a board of directors, in responding to a takeover bid, may consider the effect of a possible takeover on constituencies other than shareholders.

In *Unocal Corp. v. Mesa Petroleum Co.*,[14] the court declared that a takeover defense must be "reasonable in relation to the threat posed" in order to "come within the ambit of the business judgment rule . . . ." The directors' determination of reasonableness, said the court, "entails an analysis . . . of the nature of the takeover bid and its effect on the corporate enterprise." Among the concerns that the directors may consider are "the impact on 'constituencies' other than shareholders (i.e., creditors, customers, employees, and perhaps even the community generally) . . . ."

---

11 204 Mich. 459, 170 N.W. 668 (1919).

14 493 A.2d 946 (Del. 1985).

Nine months later in *Revlon Inc. v. MacAndres & Forbes Holdings, Inc.*,[17] the Delaware Supreme Court described the prerogative of a board of directors to take account of the interests of "various corporate constituencies" in more limited language by adding the requirement that "there be some rationally related benefit accruing to the shareholders." . . . Nonetheless, said the court, "such concern for non-stockholder interests is inappropriate when an auction among active bidders is in progress, and the object no longer is to protect or maintain the corporate enterprise but to sell it to the highest bidder."

* * *

We believe the Delaware courts have stated the prevailing corporate common law in this country: directors have fiduciary responsibilities to shareholders which, while allowing directors to give consideration to the interests of others, compel them to find some reasonable relationship to the long-term interests of shareholders when so doing. In Delaware, this principle is modified when the decision is made to sell the company, at which time the directors may consider only the interests of shareholders. . . .

RECENT ENACTMENTS

Pennsylvania in late 1983 was the first state to adopt a statute that specifically authorized directors to consider the interests of groups other than shareholders in making decisions. Since then, as of the date of this writing, another twenty-four states have adopted similar laws . . . .

All of the statutes incorporate one or more of the following provisions:

1. The directors may[30] consider the interests of, or the effects of their action on, various non-stockholder constituencies.

2. These constituencies may include employees, customers, creditors, suppliers, and communities in which the corporation has facilities.

3. The directors may consider the national and state economies and other community and societal considerations.

* * *

DISCUSSION

The proponents of other constituencies statutes correctly recognize that many groups in addition to shareholders have a continuing and important economic stake in the welfare of corporations with which they have relationships. Often the shareholder's interest in the corporation is transitory, frequently a matter of days or weeks, while that of a manager or other employee may embrace a career and that of a community far longer. Similarly, a supplier may be almost wholly dependent upon one corporate customer for its economic viability, and a corporate customer may also have a measure of dependence upon its supplier. A community and its desirability as a cor-

---

17 506 A.2d 173 (Del. 1986).

30 . . . Connecticut has adopted a formulation which *requires* that directors consider other constituencies.

porate home and a residence for its citizens may depend upon one or a handful of corporations. A friendly or unfriendly change of control of a corporation can create severe hardships for many of these constituencies.

* * *

The issue then becomes whether state corporation laws, and, in particular, a broadening of the interests that directors may consider, constitute an efficient and desirable way to provide protections for non-shareholder groups. The Committee has concluded that permitting—much less requiring—directors to consider these interests without relating such consideration in an appropriate fashion to shareholder welfare (as the Delaware courts have done) would conflict with directors' responsibility to shareholders and could undermine the effectiveness of the system that has made the corporation an efficient device for the creation of jobs and wealth.

While legislatures may not have intended it, adding other constituencies provisions to state corporation laws may have ramifications that go far beyond a simple enumeration of the other interests directors *may* recognize in discharging their duties. Directors might have a duty to oppose a transaction with whatever means are available because it would have a demonstrably adverse impact upon one or more of the constituencies (e.g., the acquirer plans to move the headquarters from the small town in which the company had been rooted for decades resulting in community disruption and loss of jobs). Or directors might be called upon to decide how much of the premium over market price being paid in an acceptable transaction should be allocated among the various constituencies (e.g., how much should accrue to communities in which plants might be closed; how much should be allocated to the terminated hourly employees; and how much should be allocated to a supplier who might lose her market).

The confusion of directors in trying to comply with such statutes, if interpreted to require directors to balance the interests of various constituencies without according primacy to shareholder interests, would be profoundly troubling. Even under existing law, particularly where directors must act quickly, it is often difficult for directors acting in good faith to divine what is in the best interests of shareholders and the corporation. If directors are required to consider other interests as well, the decision-making process will become a balancing act or search for compromise. When directors must not only decide what their duty of loyalty mandates, but also to whom their duty of loyalty runs (and in what proportions), poorer decisions can be expected.

If directors have, or may have, recognized legal duties to other constituencies, perhaps a new class or classes of plaintiffs will have access to the courts to redress perceived breaches of those duties or to challenge directors' failures to take various competing interests into account. An interpretation of these statutes to the effect that directors owe enforceable duties to constituencies other than shareholders would signal a major shift in the premises underlying traditional corporation law and might deter suitable candidates from undertaking board responsibilities.

Furthermore, any articulation of a director's duties that extended them to other constituencies without primacy being accorded shareholder interests would diminish the ability of shareholders to monitor appropriately the conduct of directors. . . .

. . . [T]he reallocation of wealth is a function for which directors are not especially suited and one beyond the general pale of their perceived mandate from society. Such allocations of wealth (which essentially a balancing of the interests of various constituencies would be) are *political* decisions. Absent the vesting of enforceable rights in those whose interests would have to be acknowledged, directors would not be accountable for their conduct in preferring the interests of one constituency over others.

* * *

Notes and Questions

As this piece suggests (but often loses sight of), there are really two questions with respect to directors considering the interests of constituencies other than the corporation's stockholders: (i) Must the directors do so (in other words, is there an enforceable legal duty on the board toward groups other than the stockholders)? and (ii) May the directors do so (in other words, would the directors breach their duty to the shareholders by looking out for other constituencies in the absence of a legal duty to do so)?

By and large, the second question has come up in the context of corporate charitable giving and, more recently, in actions opposing corporate takeovers. After all, it is a rare case that a manager, when faced with shareholder litigation over general business decisions, will make the sort of "profit be damned" statements that Henry Ford did. The ability to finesse the issue in the charitable giving cases by hypothesizing some long-run business benefit—as well as statutory authorization from legislatures that did not want to play "Grinch"—had historically resulted in the subject receiving more academic debate than judicial resolution. In the takeover context when the shareholders are selling out, however, the long range benefit argument becomes more difficult. Hence, the recent wave of other constituency statutes came about as a response to the increasing takeover battles of the 1980s.

The mandatory duty question has appeared in a variety of contexts. Recall in the excerpt at the very beginning of this chapter, Professor Eisenberg stated that directors are under three duties: care, loyalty, and a duty to act lawfully. Naturally, if directors engage in criminal conduct—for example, authorizing the corporation to engage in bribery or price fixing—they face the same criminal liability as any other individual violating these laws. Should this conduct, however, also violate the directors' duty to the corporation? Suppose the directors reasonably believed that the corporation would profit from the illegal conduct and would not get caught. For a discussion see Beveridge, *Does a Corporate Director Have a Duty Always to Obey the Law?*, 45 DEPAUL L. REV. 729 (1996). Turning to third party civil claims, directors, as mentioned earlier, are presumably under the same duty as any other individual to use care in order to avoid personal injury to foreseeable victims. What, if any, duties, however, do directors have to avoid financial injury to various parties—such as creditors, employees and customers—dealing with the corporation? In the absence of a contractual undertaking by the directors to such parties, we would seem to be dealing with the question of whether such parties are the beneficiaries of a fiduciary duty. The traditional answer, as the ABA Committee explains, is generally that they are not. We now turn to a more detailed exploration of the policy considerations involved in this answer.

---

2. *Policy Critique*

Jonathan R. Macey, *An Economic Analysis of the Various Rationales for Making Shareholders the Exclusive Beneficiaries of Corporate Fiduciary Duties*, 21 STETSON L. REV. 23 (1991)*

* * *

II. *THE THREE CRITICISMS OF NONSHAREHOLDER CONSTITUENCY STATUTES*

A. The Residual Claimant Argument

The most well-known argument supporting the proposition that fiduciary duties should be owed exclusively to shareholders is derived from the insight of modern financial theory that shareholders retain the ultimate authority to control the corporation because they have the greatest stake in the outcome of corporate decisionmaking. The idea here is that, despite the fact that corporations are merely complex webs of contractual relations—and despite the fact that shareholders do not "own" the modern, publicly held firm in any meaningful sense—the ultimate right to guide the firm (or, more precisely, to have it guided on their behalf) is retained by the shareholders because they are the group that values it most highly.

* * *

As Easterbrook and Fischel have observed:

> As the residual claimants, the shareholders are the group with the appropriate incentives . . . to make discretionary decisions. The firm should invest in new products, plants, etc., until the gains and costs are identical at the margin. Yet all of the actors, except the shareholders, lack the appropriate incentives. Those with fixed claims on the income stream may receive only a tiny benefit (in increased security) from the undertaking of a new project. The shareholders receive most of the marginal gains and incur most of the marginal costs. They therefore

have the right incentives to exercise discretion [or to have it exercised on their behalf].[9]

* * *

... [I]t is simply incorrect to say that the shareholders are the only group with the correct incentives to decide whether to adopt project C or project A or B. Nor does society benefit by exclusively allocating fiduciary duties to the shareholders. It is possible to manipulate the numbers in ... examples—and the actual projects selected in the real world—to transfer wealth from the fixed claimants [, i.e., bondholders,] to the residual claimants [, i.e., shareholders,] while *reducing* rather than increasing the overall value of the firm. Imagine, for example, that the firm is selecting between two projects, "D" and "E." Project D presents a 50% chance of producing absolutely nothing and a 50% chance of producing a present value payoff of $1.5 million at the end of period one. Project E presents a 100% chance of producing a present value payoff at the end of period one of $1 million. Ex ante, the overall value of the firm is maximized by selecting project E, since that produces a present expected value of $1 million [($1 million x 100%)] while project D produces a present expected value of only $750,000 [($1.5 million x 50%)]. The shareholders [in a situation in which fixed claimants receive $1 million], however, would prefer project D to project E, since under project E there is no chance that the shareholders will realize any payoff at all, while under project D there is a 50% chance that the shareholders will realize something, (i.e. $500,000). Thus, if the shareholders are left in complete control, they will have incentives "to adopt various strategies with the effect of transferring wealth from bondholders to shareholders, such as choosing risky investment projects and withdrawing assets from the firm." As the above example suggests, some of the strategies that shareholders can adopt to transfer wealth from the fixed claimants and other constituencies to themselves reduce the value of the firm and reduce overall societal wealth as well.

* * *

Thus, the argument that shareholders, because they have the greatest incentive to maximize the value of the firm, should be the sole beneficiaries of the legal protection afforded by fiduciary duties is incomplete. It does not explain why the interests of other claimants should not be respected, at least as to those decisions that have the potential to affect their interests directly.

B. The "Too Many Masters" Argument

The second and perhaps the most common argument made against nonshareholder constituency statutes is that such statutes, to the extent they effect any change whatsoever in existing law, simply confuse the legal landscape by forcing directors to

9 ... [Easterbrook & Fischel, *Voting in Corporate Law*, 26 J.L. & ECON. 395, 403 (1983).]

attempt an impossible task—pleasing a multitude of masters with competing and conflicting interests. . . .

In one view, the "too many masters argument" implies that nonshareholder constituency statutes make life more difficult for corporate managers and boards of directors. The better view is that such statutes simplify life for incumbent managers of the large, public corporation. After all, virtually *any* management decision, no matter how arbitrary, can be rationalized on the grounds that it benefits *some* constituency of the corporation.

* * *

. . . The benefits to the constituencies are, at best, weak. Strong support for this assertion lies in the fact that not only are these statutes (with a single exception) permissive, but they also do not afford standing to sue to any of the nonshareholder constituencies that they purportedly are designed to benefit. . . .

But the "too many masters argument" is overstated. Corporations traditionally have been able to issue multiple classes of common and preferred stock. And corporate managers and directors have discharged fiduciary duties to all of these claimants simultaneously. . . .

C. The Real Concern: Shareholders as the Group with the Most Acute Need for Fiduciary Duties

The real drawback of nonshareholder constituency statutes is that they fail to recognize that shareholders face more daunting contracting problems than other constituencies. These acute contracting problems vindicate the traditional common law rule that managers and directors owe their primary fiduciary responsibilities to shareholders. Nonshareholder constituencies can protect themselves against virtually any kind of managerial opportunism by retaining negative control over the firm's operations. Workers, bondholders, and even local communities can protect their interests by contracting for the right to veto future proposed actions by management. By contrast, the shareholders must retain positive control over the actions of the firm in order to realize the full potential value of their shares.

Merely because nonshareholder constituencies decline to contract for the right to veto certain transactions does not mean that they are unable to do so. Rather, the absence of contractual protection for nonshareholder constituencies may simply reflect the fact that such constituencies are unwilling to pay for such protection in the form of lower wages or lower interest rates on debt.

Workers are perhaps the group with whom one sympathizes the most when thinking about the possible benefits associated with nonshareholder constituency statutes. Unlike shareholders, who are concerned with the overall profitability of the firm in which they have invested, workers are concerned with wages, pensions, hours, and working conditions. From a contracting perspective, wages and hours pose few, if any, contracting problems. Workers could potentially protect their wage expectations with pension guarantees, golden parachutes, successor clauses, stipulated cost of living adjustments, and other straightforward provisions. . . .

. . . Moreover, should unforeseen contingencies arise that cast doubt on the efficacy of contractual protection, courts can protect workers by construing their employment contracts in light of the original purposes behind the agreements. Gap-filling by modern judges in interpreting contracts provides workers with the same sorts of protection that fiduciary duties provide for shareholders.

It might be argued that rank-and-file employees lack bargaining power, and that at-will employment contracts are likely to reflect this lack of bargaining power. . . .

This argument is flawed and without merit. If workers lack bargaining power in their employment relationship, changing the law to add a fiduciary duty to this relationship will *harm* workers, not help them. This is because extending the reach of fiduciary duties to rank and-file employees will not change any fundamental imbalance in the allocation of bargaining power between workers and their employers that already exists. . . .

Thus, if workers with little bargaining power being paid $8.00 per hour were made the beneficiaries of a new set of fiduciary duties, their employers would simply respond to the additional costs of the new legal responsibilities associated with these duties by reducing the wages or benefits of those same workers by the amount of the additional costs. This is what it means to have unequal bargaining power.

* * *

The above arguments apply with even more force to bondholders. First, bondholders can draft elaborately detailed contracts to protect themselves from transactions that upset the original understanding between themselves and the firm. For example, bond indentures often limit the ability of an issuer to borrow, merge, pay dividends, repurchase stock, issue preferred stock, sell assets, or engage in transactions with affiliate companies. . . .

* * *

III. *GAP-FILLING FOR NONSHAREHOLDER CONSTITUENCIES*

The familiar retort to the preceding argument is that shareholders and the corporate managers who serve them are endlessly creative. As such, no matter how elaborate the guarantees, without the broad-based gap-filling provided by fiduciary duties, management's newly devised strategies will undermine whatever contractual protection nonshareholder constituencies negotiate.

An interesting variant on this argument has been made in an important article by Columbia University's Professor John Coffee.[32] He argues that the hostile takeover itself is best viewed as a shareholder strategy for reneging on the original bargain between nonshareholder constituencies (particularly managers) and the firm:

32 Coffee, *Shareholders Versus Managers: The Strain in the Corporate Web*, 85 MICH. L. REV. 1 (1986).

> [T]he hostile takeover can be seen not simply as a mechanism that compels a management to accept that level of business risk that shareholders deem appropriate, but as a means by which shareholders outflank the safeguards managers obtained to protect the promises of deferred compensation and job security [that shareholders have given to managers]. Thus, what appears from the bidder's perspective to be a process of purging organizational slack looks from the manager's viewpoint more like deceptive reneging on the original understanding.

The ex post reneging argument seems flawed for two reasons. First, as noted above, nonshareholder constituencies can draft contracts that protect them against the consequences of future, unforeseen contingencies. Foreseeable contingencies such as hostile takeovers and corporate restructuring are even easier for nonshareholder constituencies to deal with contractually. Poison puts for bondholders and golden parachutes for workers have the potential to almost completely protect nonshareholder constituencies.

Second, it is inaccurate to suggest that absent nonshareholder constituency statutes, only shareholders enjoy the protection afforded by judicial gap-filling. An impressive body of literature indicates that modern judges should and do go a long way toward filling in unstated terms and conditions in long-term relational contracts such as those forged between nonshareholder constituencies and public corporations. . . .

* * *

For nonshareholder constituencies, the starting point for this judicial gap-filling process must be the contract itself. It may be an employment agreement, a collective bargaining agreement, a bond indenture, or a standard form contract between a firm and its suppliers or customers. For shareholders, it is widely recognized that the "contract" they enter establishes that managers have a duty "to make corporate decisions so as to maximize the value of [their] shares . . . ." Fiduciary duties are a corporate governance device uniquely crafted to fill in the massive gap in this open-ended bargain between shareholders and corporate officers and directors.

Recent attempts to expand the scope of managements' fiduciary duties to nonshareholder constituencies are therefore misguided. . . . [T]o the extent that such duties are legally enforceable, they shift the focal point of the analysis of the relationship away from the actual contract between the relevant constituency and the firm. Allocating fiduciary obligations to nonshareholder constituencies takes the judicial gap-filling process out of its proper framework, depriving judges of any coherent basis for allocating rights and responsibilities within the firm.

* * *

IV. *THE LOCAL COMMUNITY*

Local communities constitute a possible exception to the above analysis because, unlike nonshareholder constituencies, they may have no preexisting contractual relationship with the firm that can provide the basis for reconstructing the original understanding between the parties in the event of future conflict. . . .

. . . Where there is no agreement, creating an amorphous, open-ended fiduciary duty to the local community in which the firm operates is impractical.

Creating such a duty transforms the top managers of public companies from private businessmen into unelected and unaccountable public servants. A decision to elevate the interests of a local community above the interests of a firm's shareholders is nothing less than a decision about how to allocate wealth within society. . . .

Expanding the scope of a firm's fiduciary duties to include local communities, as with other nonshareholder constituencies, is unnecessary. Local communities have unique access to the political process. . . .

Notes and Questions

1. When asked why directors should owe their duty to the shareholders rather than to parties such as creditors, employees or the like, most individuals (assuming they agree with the proposition) will say this is because the shareholders "own" the corporation and, hence, the directors work for the shareholders. Why does Professor Macey blow past this rationale in less than one sentence? Recall the discussion in Chapter I of the view that the corporation is simply a nexus of contracts between various participants in a productive endeavor. As Professor Macey states, under this view there is no ownership of the firm; rather there are simply different claims to its earnings.

Rejection of the ownership rationale, however, carries with it some potentially disorienting corollaries. Why then should only the shareholders vote to elect directors; why not, instead, have representatives of labor, creditors, consumers and the community on the board? In fact, boards of public German companies have had labor representatives. *See* Vagts, *Reforming the "Modern" Corporation: Perspectives From the German*, 80 HARV. L. REV. 23 (1966). Professors Easterbrook and Fischel in their article quoted by Professor Macey attempt an answer. They note that shareholders (actually common shareholders) are "residual claimants"; which is to say that shareholders only get money from the firm after everyone else—employees, lenders, suppliers—gets paid. This, in turn, means that shareholders face the greatest impact from "marginal" profits and losses. In other words, since the shareholders stand last in line, the first dollar of loss from the corporation comes out their pocket and, since the shareholders are entitled to everything above certain fixed claims, the next dollar of income will go into their pocket. Hence, the argument runs, the shareholders have the best incentives for efficient decisions.

One problem with this rationale is that it presumes a solvent corporation. By contrast, if the corporation has liabilities equal to or greater than its assets—either because the shareholders inadequately capitalized the company to start with, the company has undergone a period of losses, or the shareholders have withdrawn their capital from the company—then the shareholders would have very skewed incentives. As discussed before, losses would not impact the shareholders, while gains could. This explains why creditors of a corporation in financial difficulty may insist on contractual terms giving them some control. It also has impacted some court opinions, which state that directors and controlling shareholders of an insolvent corporation owe a fiduciary duty to creditors (or that creditors can gain the benefit of the fiduciary duty that directors owe to the corporation). For a discussion see Morris, *Directors' Duties in Nearly Insolvent Corporations: A Comment on* Credit Lyonnais, 19 J. CORP. L. 61 (1992). Notice that once we start talking of the duty controlling shareholders might owe to creditors, the doctrine of piercing comes back to mind.

2. Professor Macey rejects the "too many masters" argument based in part upon the fact that directors owe duties to owners of various classes of stock and have managed to discharge these obligations simultaneously. In fact, however, decisions of the board which impact different classes of stock differently—as can occur with recapitalizations, sales of the business, or just dividend and corporate investment decisions—have been a frequent source of litigation. Recall that Mr. Marsh identified this as an area of possible conflict of interest.

3. Professor Macey argues that the real reason for an exclusive fiduciary duty in favor of shareholders is because they least can protect themselves by complete contracting for every contingency. Notice how this incorporates the view of fiduciary duty as a gap filling device (or default rule). Professor Macey recognizes, however, that the long-term contracts of creditors, employees and others can also have gaps, but asserts that the implied covenant of good faith and fair dealing can cover such gaps. What then is the difference between this covenant and fiduciary duty? The following excerpt takes a further look at this argument.

Morey W. McDaniel, *Stockholders and Stakeholders,* 21 STETSON L. REV. 121 (1991)*

* * *

VI. *ANSWERING THE CRITICS' ARGUMENTS*

* * *

12. *Stakeholders can protect themselves by contract.*

That is easier said than done. The future is unknown and unknowable. No contract can anticipate every future contingency, especially over long periods. Indeed, no contract can specify an exact response for every known contingency. . . . Moreover, ex ante contracting can produce lengthy and complicated contracts that curtail managerial discretion and introduce rigidity and inflexibility into intrafirm relationships.

The debate over contractual versus fiduciary protection for stakeholders comes down to a debate over ex ante versus ex post protection and who gets the superior benefits of ex post protection. If stakeholders must protect themselves ex ante by contract, stakeholders must forecast the future and suffer the consequences if they guess wrong. When the contract turns out to be incomplete, stakeholders must incur the costs and uncertainty of litigation to have a judge fill any gaps. Stockholders, by comparison, do not have to predict the future or turn to the courts because managers who run the corporation are on the scene to protect stockholders as the future unfolds. Stockholders are in the enviable position of having agents in the boardroom who can act with the benefit of hindsight. Put another way, stakeholders are on the outside with a piece of paper (maybe) for protection, while stockholders have agents on the inside for protection. Stakeholders want some inside, ex post protection, too.

. . . Finally, if self-protection by contract is such a good idea for other constituencies, maybe it is a good idea for stockholders, too. Managerial fiduciary duties to stockholders could be repealed, and stockholders could contract for their own protection like everyone else is urged to do.[127]

Note

Mr. McDaniel set forth an extended argument for a fiduciary duty to corporate bondholders in *Bondholders and Stockholders*, 13 J. CORP. L. 205 (1988). For an argument in favor of a duty to employees see O'Connor, *Restructuring the Corporation's Nexus of Contracts: Recognizing a Fiduciary Duty to Protect Displaced Workers*, 69 N.C. L. REV. 1189 (1991). For a broader review of "corporate social responsibility" see the symposium on this topic in 30 HASTINGS L.J. 1247 (1979).

---

127 Ironically, of all the corporate constituencies, stockholders are the one group most able to protect themselves. Stockholders have the vote and elect the directors. . . .

A different contractual model of the corporation might treat managers not as agents for stockholders (or anyone else) but as independent contractors who hire capital (debt and equity) and labor for their own account. In this model, stockholders would have to protect themselves ex ante by contract just as others are supposed to do.

E. Enforcement of Fiduciary Duty: The Derivative Suit

1. *Demand on the Board and Deference to the Board's Judgment Regarding the Suit: The Doctrine Introduced*

Dennis J. Block, Stephan A. Radin, and James P. Rosenzweig, *The Role of the Business Judgment Rule in Shareholder Litigation at the Turn of the Decade*, 45 Bus. Law. 469 (1990)*

* * *

THE PRE-LITIGATION DEMAND REQUIREMENT

. . . [A] shareholder derivative action is a lawsuit brought by one or more minority shareholders on behalf of a corporation to remedy an alleged wrong to the corporation. . . . The action is two-fold in nature: "First, it is the equivalent of a suit by the shareholders to compel the corporation to sue. Second, it is a suit by the corporation, asserted by the shareholders on its behalf, against those liable to it." . . . The derivative action may involve a corporate claim against persons not affiliated with the corporation or against directors, officers, employees, or other agents of the corporation. Damages recovered in the suit are paid to the corporation.

The law in all jurisdictions is that, prior to filing a derivative action, a shareholder generally must demand that the corporation's board of directors cause the corporation to pursue the claim alleged in the action. . . .

Demand is required for several reasons. First, and most important, demand reflects the fundamental tenet of corporate law which holds that the business and affairs of corporations are managed by or under the direction of directors rather than individual shareholders. . . .

Second, the demand requirement "enables corporate management to pursue alternative remedies, thus often ending unnecessary litigation." . . . Finally, the demand requirement "affords corporate directors reasonable protection from the harassment of litigious dissident shareholders who might otherwise contest decisions on matters clearly within the directors' discretion," and thereby discourages "strike suits" brought "not to remedy wrongs to the corporation, but to induce settlements beneficial to the named plaintiff or his counsel."

It cannot be overemphasized that the rationale underlying the demand requirement is in no way diminished by the fact that causes of action having merit may exist which the corporation has not pursued or may not be inclined to pursue. A board of directors may decide against bringing an action, for example, where "the litigation costs and the adverse effect on the business relationship between the corporation and the potential defendant might outweigh any potential recovery in the lawsuit." . . .

DEMAND FUTILITY

The demand requirement will be excused and the shareholder plaintiff will be permitted to proceed with litigation on behalf of the corporation in cases where the role of the directors in the challenged conduct (or the alleged domination and control of the directors by the alleged wrongdoers) is such that demand would be "futile." Certain general principles emerge from the case law, both before and after the Delaware Supreme Court's landmark 1984 decision in *Aronson v. Lewis*.[26]

***Demand Futility Before* Aronson**

Prior to 1984, courts considered demand futility on a (for today) surprisingly infrequent basis, and focused primarily upon whether a corporation's directors were sufficiently disinterested to render an objective business judgment, and not upon the business judgment underlying the demand. . . .

* * *

Delaware's Two-Prong* Aronson *Test

The Delaware Supreme Court used its 1984 decision in *Aronson v. Lewis* to set forth a more specific standard for determining demand futility. The *Aronson* test focuses not just upon directorial interestedness but also upon the merits of the challenged conduct:

> [I]n determining demand futility the Court of Chancery in the proper exercise of its discretion must decide whether, under the particularized facts alleged, a reasonable doubt is created that: (1) the directors are disinterested and independent [or] (2) the challenged transaction was otherwise the product of a valid exercise of business judgment.

* * *

Following *Aronson*, . . . it is settled that, under Delaware law, demand will not be excused merely because a majority of directors are named as defendants, approved the challenged transaction, . . . failed to take corrective action prior to the filing of the lawsuit, refused to reconsider a challenged transaction or rejected a prior demand, . . . [or] are alleged in conclusory language to be dominated and controlled by those benefiting from the challenged conduct . . . .

The Importance of Delaware's Two-Prong Aronson *Test Outside of Delaware*

The two-prong test established by the Delaware Supreme Court in *Aronson* has had a substantial impact upon shareholder litigation outside as well as within Delaware . . . .

* * *

26 473 A.2d 805 (Del. 1984).

The Proposed Universal Demand Requirement

The drafters of the American Bar Association Section of Business Law Committee on Corporate Laws' Model Business Corporation Act and the American Law Institute's corporate governance project, Principles of Corporate Governance: Analysis and Recommendations, have proposed a very different approach to the demand requirement from that employed in Delaware. Rather than utilizing an *Aronson*-type (or any other) analysis, the current drafts of the Model Business Corporation Act and Principles of Corporate Governance provisions propose a "universal" demand requirement mandating demand in all cases except those in which a requirement that a shareholder make a demand (and then wait for a board response prior to filing a law suit) would result in irreparable injury to the corporation. . . .

The proposed Official Comment to the Model Business Corporation Act explains that the rationale underlying the universal demand rule is two-fold. First, even if a board of directors does not include a majority (or even any) disinterested directors, there is still no reason not to give the board an opportunity "to reexamine the act complained of in the light of a potential lawsuit and take corrective action." Second, requiring demand on a universal basis will save litigants and courts the time and expense they would otherwise incur in litigating the demand futility issue. The drafters of the Model Business Corporation Act also note that "requiring a demand in all cases does not impose an onerous burden" upon shareholders.

* * *

THE CORPORATION'S RESPONSE TO A DEMAND

Once a pre-litigation demand is made, a board of directors must make an informed decision regarding how to respond to the demand. . . . The board may determine "to accept the demand and prosecute the action, to resolve the grievance internally without resort to litigation, or to refuse the demand."

* * *

THE SCOPE OF JUDICIAL REVIEW IN DEMAND REFUSED CASES

* * *

The law in virtually every jurisdiction which has addressed the issue is that a determination by a board of directors to refuse a pre-litigation demand will be evaluated in accordance with business judgment rule standards, just like any other business decision by a board of directors.

* * *

DEMAND EXCUSED CASES, CONTRASTED

Standing in contrast to the usual case where demand is required because shareholder plaintiffs are unable to plead facts demonstrating a reasonable doubt concerning either disinterestedness or the inapplicability of the business judgment rule to the subject matter underlying a particular litigation is the relatively rare case where demand is excused because shareholder plaintiffs can plead such facts. A board faced with a derivative complaint in a demand excused case may, however, appoint a "special litigation committee" consisting of disinterested directors to determine what action should be taken with respect to the litigation.

If a special litigation committee determines to seek dismissal, some courts hold that the business judgment rule does not protect that decision; such courts require more detailed judicial scrutiny of the committee's decision prior to terminating any action brought by a complaining shareholder. Delaware, for example, has developed a two-step test pursuant to which the court (i) reviews the committee's independence and good faith and the bases supporting its conclusions, with (unlike demand required cases) the corporation bearing the burden of proof on these issues, and (ii) exercises its own "independent business judgment" concerning the merits of the committee's decision to seek dismissal if the court in its exercise of discretion deems such review appropriate in the particular case.[207] In New York, however, judicial review of the merits of a special litigation committee's decision to seek dismissal is limited to the independence of the committee's members and the appropriateness and sufficiency of the committee's investigation. Judicial review of the substantive aspects of the decision to seek dismissal is not permitted. . . .

The differing rules governing actions in which demand is excused and actions in which demand is required and refused reflects the fundamental differences between these two categories of cases. Demand required cases involve boards consisting of a majority of disinterested directors, while demand excused cases involve boards which do not have a majority of disinterested directors capable of objective decision-making. . . .

THE MODEL BUSINESS CORPORATION ACT

As discussed earlier, the drafters of the American Bar Association Section of Business Law's Model Business Corporation Act and the American Law Institute's Principles of Corporate Governance: Analysis and Recommendations have proposed a universal demand requirement mandating demand in all cases except those in which requiring a demand would cause irreparable injury to the corporation. The Model Business Corporation Act nevertheless carries forward the distinction between demand required and demand excused cases for purposes of judicial review of motions to dismiss by disinterested directors. . . .

* * *

The Model Business Corporation Act accordingly adheres to a business judgment rule standard of review in cases where a board consisting of a majority of disinterested directors determines in good faith and with due care that prosecution of the demanded litigation would not serve the best interests of the corporation. The Model Business Corporation Act is thus consistent with present law, both within and outside of Delaware.

---

207 . . . Zapata Corp. v. Maldonado, 430 A.2d 779, 788-89 (Del. 1981).

* * *

Notes and Questions

1. This piece mentioned two approaches—Delaware's and New York's—taken in response to motions by special litigation committees to dismiss derivative suits. A third approach, followed by at least one jurisdiction, simply ignores any recommendation of dismissal coming from a committee of directors, when a majority of the board which appointed the committee are defendants in the action.

2. The remainder of the article which followed the excerpted portion above contrasted and criticized a tentative draft of the ALI's *Principles*. In the following piece, Professor Coffee, who served as reporter for the portion of the *Principles* dealing with derivative suits, explains and defends the philosophy behind the approach taken in the final version of the ALI document.

John C. Coffee, Jr., *New Myths and Old Realities: The American Law Institute Faces the Derivative Action,* 48 Bus. Law 1407 (1993)*

* * *

A COMPARISON OF THE ALI AND DELAWARE TREATMENT OF DERIVATIVE ACTIONS

THE DELAWARE PROCEDURE

* * *

Doctrinally, the real bite in the Delaware formula is its waiver rule, which faces the plaintiff with a "Catch 22"-like dilemma: If the plaintiff does not make demand on the board, the plaintiff must overcome the *Aronson* test; but if the plaintiff does make demand, the plaintiff thereby concedes the disinterestedness of the board. Because of this constructive "waiver" of all challenges to the board's objectivity, plaintiffs who make demand may only attack the board's rejection of demand by raising the functional equivalent of *Aronson's* second prong and attacking the good faith and reasonableness of the board's investigation. Sometimes (but rarely), plaintiffs have succeeded in challenging the reasonableness or good faith of the board's response to demand. Still, there is a sufficient disincentive in the Delaware "waiver" rule as to produce an entirely predictable consequence: Plaintiffs today seldom make demand in Delaware, but instead litigate the issue of whether demand was excused.

Delaware's demand rule also results in a substantial amount of collateral litigation and sometimes can be a trap for the unwary. For example, issues arise as to (i) whether a skeptical or protesting letter from a shareholder constitutes a demand (thereby waiving the issue of board independence) or only a request for information; (ii) whether a non-specific letter from a shareholder is too indefinite to constitute a demand (and thus requires no board response); (iii) how long after demand the plaintiff must wait for a response before filing its action; (iv) how broadly a demand letter relates when there are multiple issues; and (v) what effect does demand have when there is a subsequent change in the composition of the board. Nonetheless, the shareholder plaintiff usually faces an unattractive choice: either (i) not make demand and thereby accept the burden of convincing the court that seemingly respectable directors should be deemed too biased even to deserve an opportunity to respond to demand, or (ii) make demand and thereby acknowledge the applicability of the business judgment rule to the directors' decision whether or not to reject demand (and, for most practical purposes, concede the outcome of the case).

* * *

THE ALI'S ALTERNATIVE APPROACH

Demand and Demand Rejections

The ALI's approach to the derivative action differs fundamentally at the outset from that of Delaware by abandoning the traditional distinction between "demand required" and "demand excused." Instead, section 7.03 requires demand in every case. In instances where "irreparable injury" would otherwise result, demand may be made after the filing of the action.

* * *

[B]y making demand obligatory, the ALI approach shifts the focus from the *potential* capacity of the board to evaluate the derivative action to its *actual* response to the demand. . . .

* * *

. . . Here, section 7.04(a) governs both the particularity with which the plaintiff must plead its case and how the plaintiff must respond to the rejection of the demand.

* * *

[I]n substance it establishes both who can reject demand and what the plaintiff must plead to overcome that rejection. In essence, it contains the following rules:

1. Rejection of demand by the board only will be given legal effect if a majority of the board's directors are both not "interested" in the action and "capable of objective judgment in the circum-

stances." Both these tests are marginally more rigorous on defendants than the Delaware standard for demand futility, but they will not disqualify outside directors absent concrete specific evidence indicating bias or a lack of objectivity.

2. If the transaction is a self-dealing transaction that the *Principles* elsewhere subject to a limited fairness review, then the directors' rejection of demand is correspondingly made subject to an objective standard of fairness (i.e., could the directors "reasonably have determined that rejection of the demand was in the best interests of the corporation"). In addition, the disinterested directors also must satisfy the business judgment rule by adequately informing themselves.
3. Conversely, in a simple business judgment case, the rejection of demand will be dispositive unless the board's response fails even the deferential test of the business judgment rule.

Therefore, the ALI's two principal departures from Delaware law are (i) universal demand, and (ii) an explicit dichotomy between a "reasonableness" standard of review (applicable largely to fair dealing cases and cases involving knowing violations of law) and a "business judgment" standard (applicable to duty of care cases and certain fair dealing cases where a business judgment standard governs). Under both the ALI and Delaware approaches, there is, however, one procedural similarity: the plaintiff need not actually prove anything to survive the demand rejection stage. In Delaware, the judicial determination is made on the basis of the pleadings, and the plaintiff need raise only a "reasonable doubt" by pleading particularized facts. Similarly, under the ALI approach, the plaintiff's obligation at the demand stage is to raise by particularized pleadings a "significant prospect" that (in a fair dealing case) the board "unreasonably" rejected demand.

* * *

SPECIAL LITIGATION COMMITTEES

. . . Once past the demand rejection stage, Part VII's procedures thereafter largely parallel the Delaware "special litigation committee" procedure. . . . Procedurally, section 7.09 requires only: (1) the use of a two or more member committee, (ii) the assistance of counsel "capable of exercising independent professional judgment under the circumstances;" (iii) an adequate evaluation of the action; and (iv) the preparation of a report or other written submission setting forth the determinations of the board or committee in sufficient detail to permit judicial review. . . .

The key substantive ALI provision at this litigation committee stage is set forth in section 7.10, which once again provides for a bifurcated standard of judicial review. Basically, if the gravamen of the action is a violation of the duty of fair dealing, or if the action alleges a "knowing and culpable violation of law" (or other violation of the duty of care to which the business judgment rule is not applicable), then the court may dismiss the action based on the litigation committee's report only "if the court finds, in light of the applicable standards under Parts IV or V, that the board or committee was adequately informed under the circumstances and reasonably determined that dismissal was in the best interests of the corporation, based on grounds that the court deems to warrant reliance." The last clause — "based on grounds that the court deems to warrant reliance"—does not require that the court employ its own "independent business judgment" (as in *Zapata*), but it does preclude the court from simply deferring to the asserted greater expertise of the board or committee.

In contrast, if the gravamen of the action involves the duty of care or some other duty that would be reviewed under the business judgment rule, then a business judgment standard similarly governs the court's review of the determinations of the board or committee and its justifications for dismissal of the action. . . .

* * *

WHY SHOULD THE DUTY OF LOYALTY BE TREATED DIFFERENTLY FROM THE DUTY OF CARE?

. . . The standard academic answer has been that judicial competence is lesser in the [latter] case, and thus the prospect of judicial error is greater in cases where a conflict of interest is absent. Clearly, when a business decision proves erroneous, multiple explanations for that failure are possible. It could be that the decisionmaker was negligent, but, conversely, the truth may be that a risk that was accepted knowingly and prudently simply came to an unfortunate fruition. . . .

In contrast, within the context of the duty of loyalty, the possibility of non-culpable error is much smaller. When a corporate fiduciary fails to disclose a conflict of interest to disinterested directors, the chances are much greater that the fiduciary did so opportunistically, not innocently. . . .

Although the differing competence of courts in handling duty of care versus duty of loyalty actions represents the conventional justification for focusing the derivative action on duty of loyalty claims, another justification may be even more important. Within the corporate context, the duty of care is at least partially self-policing. Thus, less need exists for legal institutions to generate additional deterrence. To the extent that both the corporation and its managers operate in reasonably competitive financial, product, and labor markets, the cost of negligent errors will be borne, at least partially, by those who commit them. Any incentive to slack is at best marginal. Because there is little incentive to commit negligent errors (and because real stupidity tends to reveal itself, thereby increasing the probability of detection), the usual logic of the deterrence theory, which focuses on the magnitude of the gain and the difficulty of detection, does not require substantial penalties for negligence.

In the case of duty of loyalty violations, however, the likelihood of detection is lower, and the magnitude of the expected gain is higher. Not only can self-dealing be concealed, but it tends to become self-perpetuating. Once a manager has engaged in one unfair self-dealing transaction, there is less social or moral inhibition to dissuade that manager from engaging in similar transactions. In addition, other managers may detect the self-dealing behavior and emulate it. In short, unlike simple incompetence, self-dealing can be contagious and can corrupt the organizational culture.

Given this greater likelihood that undetected self-dealing will lead to recidivism, the deterrent gains from a derivative action contesting duty of loyalty violations seem greater.

* * *

DOCTRINAL CONSISTENCY: WHERE DOES THE ALI POSITION COME FROM?

As a historical proposition, no generalization about American corporate law is safer or sounder than that the fiduciary duty of loyalty has long been subject to judicial oversight. . . . Beginning in the 1950s with the adoption of the Model Business Corporation Act, a number of states enacted "sanitizing" statutes, which established procedures for the approval of "interested director" transactions. In general, courts and commentators have read these statutes, not as eliminating the issue of fairness, but as shifting the burden on the plaintiff to prove unfairness. What has not changed, at least in most jurisdictions, is the idea that a court still can review the fairness of a self-dealing transaction. Thus, the common law's baseline is that fairness remains relevant, even if a transaction is approved after full disclosure by disinterested directors.

This was the position adopted by the ALI in Part V (Duty of Fair Dealing) of the *Principles*. . . .

Given this position in Part V, Part VII [(dealing with derivative suits)] comes into better focus as simply an attempt to maintain consistency between the substantive right and the procedural remedy. If Part V provides that full disclosure and disinterested approval do not alone immunize a self-dealing transaction (if its terms are outside the range that the board reasonably could have concluded were fair to the corporation), then Part VII could not provide for a business judgment standard of review of the demand rejection decision without overriding Part V.

* * *

Notes and Questions

1. Professor Coffee's defense focuses on the different responses proposed by the ALI to demand rejection depending on whether the suit involves an alleged breach of the directors' duty of care or their duty of loyalty. The two arguments he makes find support in earlier academic literature. For an article which takes the argument that there is greater need for deterrence in the loyalty context all the way to suggesting abolition of the duty of care see Scott, *Corporate Law and the ALI Corporate Governance Project*, 35 STAN. L. REV. 927 (1983). For a dissent see Cox, *Compensation, Deterrence, and the Market as Boundaries for Derivative Suit Procedures*, 52 GEO. WASH. L. REV. 745 (1984). For a more extended discussion of the relationship between dismissing self dealing suits upon board recommendation and the scheme of the conflict of interest statutes see Buxbaum, *Conflict of Interest Statutes and the Need for Demand on Directors in Derivative Actions*, 68 CAL. L. REV. 1122 (1980).

2. The reader who finds the rules in this area convoluted is not alone. Is there some reason for this complexity? Perhaps if we focused on the purpose for the rules, things could become clearer.

Messrs, Block, Radin and Rosenzweig list three purposes for the demand requirement. The second is to allow the directors to pursue alternatives to litigation. If this is a purpose, why not always require demand? After all, how much burden is it to write a letter to the board? Moreover, the board, no matter how implicated in wrongdoing, might always repent and take appropriate action. On the other hand, does this rationale support dismissing suits months or even years after the plaintiff files, even if he or she did not make a demand? If the board really wanted to take some action to resolve the matter, could it not have done so once it found out about the suit? What about the third rationale, the prevention of so-called strike suits (in other words, meritless suits brought to extort settlements)? How does demand serve to prevent this? In fact, perhaps Messrs. Block, Radin and Rosenzweig should have quit with their first rationale: The purpose of demand is to allow the board to decide whether or not there should be a suit. Futility then involves the situation in which the law does not want the directors to make this decision. Put another way, if the court is going to ignore the directors' determination regarding the suit, then it is a futile exercise to ask the board to make a decision.

The ALI's and Model Act's universal demand requirement obviously simplifies the demand rule. Yet, then one must decide how to respond to the board's rejection of demand: Will the court respect what the board decided or ignore it? Is there any reason to expect this poses any different challenge than dealing with demand futility?

This suggests that the purpose of these rules is to frame the central issue of derivative suits: When should the court let the directors and when should it let an individual shareholder decide whether it is in the corporate interest to bring a lawsuit? Still, this does not answer why the rules are so convoluted. The next three article excerpts look more deeply at the policies in this area. The first is generally supportive of current rules; the next two are critical. That is not, however, why these pieces are here. Rather, each looks primarily at one of the three decisionmakers—the plaintiff shareholder (or more realistically, his or her attorney), the board of directors, and the court—involved in determining if a proposed derivative suit would be in the corporation's best interest.

2. *Policy Critique*

Jonathan R. Macey and Geoffrey P. Miller, *The Plaintiffs' Attorney's Role in Class Action and Derivative Litigation: Economic Analysis and Recommendations for Reform*, 58 U. Chi. L. Rev. 1 (1991)*

* * *

I. The Role of the Entrepreneurial Attorney

Over the past decade a number of scholars, including most prominently Professor John Coffee, have recognized that the single most salient characteristic of class and derivative litigation is the existence of "entrepreneurial" plaintiffs' attorneys. Because these attorneys are not subject to monitoring by their putative clients, they operate largely according to their own self-interest, subject only to whatever constraints might be imposed by bar discipline, judicial oversight, and their own sense of ethics and fiduciary responsibilities. In this section we begin by describing the economic rationale for class action and shareholder's derivative lawsuits. We then discuss the role of the entrepreneurial attorney in such lawsuits by placing it in the context of the economic theory of agency, and by contrasting it with the role of the attorney in standard litigation in which the client exercises a substantial degree of influence over the attorney's actions.

A. The Economic Rationale for Class Action and Shareholder's Derivative Litigation

* * *

The economic rationale for the [Federal Rule of Civil Procedure 23] (b)(3) class action—as a method for overcoming free-rider and other collective action problems—stands in sharp contrast to the rationale for the shareholder's derivative suit. Shareholder's derivative actions are not premised on collective action problems in the *litigation*. On the contrary, they presuppose the existence of a corporate form that is already organized to overcome such collective action problems. The corporation has standing and is fully competent to bring legal actions to redress injuries to its rights. The problem, rather, is with collective action *within* the corporate form itself. As scholars since Berle and Means have observed, corporate managers typically have only a small ownership stake in the firms they manage. Thus, their interests deviate from those of shareholders: they may prefer to consume excessive perquisites or practice their golf whereas shareholders would want them to work diligently at maximizing profits.

The shareholder's derivative suit is one of many devices in corporate law for controlling these conflicts between managers and shareholders. Many cases arise in which a corporation has an enforceable legal claim against others for harm to the cor-

---

* Reprinted with permission.

poration. Like other matters affecting the corporation, pursuit of the claim is left initially to the managers. But if the suit would potentially harm the managers' personal interests, the managers may be unwilling to prosecute the claim, even when doing so would serve the best interests of the corporation. The classic case is the action for breach of fiduciary duty against corporate directors. Obviously the directors cannot be trusted to cause the corporation to sue themselves. The derivative action allows a representative shareholder in such circumstances to take over the litigation from recalcitrant managers and prosecute it on behalf of the corporation. Unlike the class action, in which the relief is given to the plaintiff class members, any relief recovered in a derivative action (net of expenses including attorneys' fees) is returned to the corporation.

* * *

B. The Role of the Entrepreneurial Attorney in Class Action and Shareholder's Derivative Suits

* * *

2. Application of agency cost theory to class and derivative cases

* * *

a) *Monitoring*. Members of the plaintiff class in a large class action or shareholder's derivative suit often have claims so small that the litigation is a matter of relative unimportance to them. . . .

[C]ollective action and free-rider effects allow the plaintiffs' attorney in class and derivative cases to operate with nearly total freedom from traditional forms of client monitoring.

* * *

c) *Incentives*. Finally, consider incentive effects in class and derivative litigation. . . . Unfortunately, there is a substantial deviation of interests between attorney and client. The nature of the conflict varies depending on the type of litigation involved and the procedure used in the jurisdiction for determining the attorney's fee. . . .

In "common fund" cases, where the plaintiffs' attorney generates a fund for the benefit of the class, the majority of American courts award fees out of the fund based on the lodestar calculation. Under this approach, the hours reasonably expended by the lawyer are multiplied by the lawyer's reasonable hourly fee to calculate a lodestar. . . . Attorneys in these cases thus have an incentive to run up excessive hours, delay the litigation unnecessarily, or even to exaggerate the number of hours expended in order to obtain a larger fee. . . .

The other method of calculating attorneys' fees in common fund cases, which has become more popular recently, is the "percentage" method, in which fees are awarded based on some fixed percentage of the fund. There are obvious incentive problems with this arrangement as well. First, plaintiffs' attorneys will earn windfall profits, at the expense of the class members, in cases presenting large damages and low proof costs.

* * *

The second incentive problem in percentage-of-the-recovery cases is settlement. Attorneys compensated on a percentage method have an incentive to settle early for an amount lower than what might be obtained by further efforts. The attorney who puts in relatively few hours to obtain an early settlement is likely to earn a much greater compensation per hour of effort than an attorney who expends greater efforts and litigates a case to the point where the plaintiffs' recovery is maximized. Again the plaintiff class loses.

* * *

. . . Defendants . . . typically wish to minimize the sum of three costs: the costs of the relief on the merits, the costs of their own attorney's fees, and the costs of the plaintiffs' attorney's fees. Defendants are typically indifferent about how the total cost of litigation is distributed among these elements. Plaintiffs' attorneys, on the other hand, have an interest in increasing their own fees, even at the expense of a reduction in the relief afforded to the putative client. Thus the conditions are present for a bargain under which the plaintiffs' attorneys agree to a lower overall settlement on the merits of the litigation in exchange for a higher fee.

* * *

. . . The next section discusses one way in which the system has adjusted for these problems: by allocating the authority to make decisions regarding the litigation to someone other than plaintiffs' attorney.

II. Regulations Allocating Litigation Authority

* * *

B. Control of Derivative Litigation

. . . In the derivative context the problem is not that the client—the corporation—is uninterested and disorganized. To the contrary, the client is typically both highly organized and very interested. Rather, the problem is that the client is under the control of parties—namely corporate managers—who are hostile to the litigation. If the client were allowed free rein to control the lawsuit, the derivative action would be vitiated as a corporate control mechanism: the corporate management would routinely cause the suits to be dismissed or compromised on terms favorable to them but not necessarily favorable to the corporation or its shareholders.

In an attempt to alleviate this problem, the regulatory system divides control of the litigation between the corporation and the derivative plaintiffs' counsel. This allocation of control manifests itself in rules governing director demand and special litigation committees. These rules allow the corporate management to control the litigation when such control would be in the best interest of the corporation. When management control ceases to be in the corporation's interest, the rules permit the derivative plaintiffs' attorneys to take over. We believe that these rules work reasonably well as a means of controlling the entrepreneurial attorney.

1. Director demand

* * *

a) *Demand required cases.* From the standpoint of economic analysis, the demand requirement appears quite justifiable as applied to cases in which the directors are not so personally interested in the litigation as to make them unreliable champions of the corporate interest. It seems obvious that corporate directors are better situated than plaintiffs' attorneys to initiate and control litigation to enforce corporate rights.

The directors have a greater stake in the corporation and accordingly are in most cases aligned in interest with the shareholders. Directors usually own some stock in their corporations and are interested in preserving their reputational capital by not being associated with firms that perform poorly. Representative shareholders, on the other hand, may have only a minimal interest in the corporation, especially if their shareholdings are small or part of a highly diversified portfolio. Moreover, representative shareholders, like named class plaintiffs, typically exercise virtually no control over the activities of the plaintiffs' attorney. The real party in interest is an attorney with no stake in the corporation at all other than an interest in extracting a fee from it.

The directors possess far greater expertise to evaluate the corporation and its affairs than do plaintiffs' attorneys. This expertise can be used to analyze whether litigation would be in the corporation's best interest. It is not difficult to imagine cases in which, while the corporation may have a potential right of action against another person, the best interests of the shareholders would not be served by immediate recourse to the courts. The potential defendant may be involved in complex and long-term relationships with the corporation—relationships that provide opportunities for adjusting disputes cheaply and effectively outside the formal legal process. Litigation may harm the corporation because sensitive business information will have to be disclosed in discovery. Litigation will tie up time and energies of corporate managers that might better be spent on other tasks. There are many good reasons of business judgment for a corporation not to bring suit even though it may have a colorable right of action, or even though an outside attorney considers the matter sufficiently promising to warrant bringing the suit on a contingent basis.

Finally, the directors are chosen by shareholders, whereas the plaintiffs' attorney is a volunteer. There is no reason to suppose that the plaintiffs' attorney is the best person to conduct the litigation simply because she happened to identify it and indicated a willingness to take it on. Thus, other things equal, it would appear preferable to allow the directors to pick the attorney, rather than permitting an attorney to acquire the right to litigate the corporation's claim simply by volunteering.

These reasons provide overwhelming support for a rule requiring a plaintiffs' attorney to make a demand on the directors before bringing a derivative suit in situations where the directors do not face a conflict of interest in their decision. If the directors decide to institute suit after receiving the demand, the action is taken over by the corporation, which is presumably better situated to bring the action than plaintiffs' counsel. If the directors refuse the demand, this determination is ordinarily final unless the shareholder can establish that directors did not act out of informed business judgment.

* * *

b) *Demand excused cases.* Where, however, the directors are personally interested in and hostile to the litigation, they cannot be relied on to serve the best interests of the corporation. The demand requirement ceases to serve its intended purpose. The classic case, as already noted, is that in which the directors or other top corporate managers are the potential defendants in a suit for breach of fiduciary duty. . . .

Delaware corporate law, like that of other states, copes with this situation in a relatively sensible fashion by excusing demand when the plaintiffs' well-pleaded allegations, taken as true, raise a reasonable doubt as to (1) the disinterestedness or independence of a majority of the board, or (2) the directors' exercise of proper business judgment in approving the challenged transaction. Stated as a general rule, this approach appears to be quite carefully crafted to carve out a limited territory in which the benefits of director demand are outweighed by the possibility that interested directors will abuse their rights under the demand requirement to the detriment of the corporation. In these situations, it is better for the litigation to be turned over to the derivative plaintiffs' attorney for zealous prosecution.

* * *

2. Special litigation committees

. . . Even if demand is excused as futile, however, corporate managers may seek to reenter a derivative lawsuit at a later date by constituting a special litigation committee of presumptively impartial directors that may then seek to wrest control of the litigation away from plaintiffs' counsel.

* * *

Zapata has something to recommend it, in that the court attempted to devise a reasonable compromise that would maximize the likelihood of outcomes beneficial to the corporation.

* * *

However, the rule in *Zapata* suffers from several shortcomings. First, the court did not articulate with any precision the substantive standard that a trial court should apply in exercising its own business judgment. Thus, there is an unfortunate element of indeterminacy in the *Zapata* test. . . .

Second, the idea that a trial court can exercise "business judgment" is anomalous. Trial judges are not business people; they do not possess the practical experience and exposure to the special needs of the corporation that characterizes the business judgment of corporate managers. . . .

* * *

A more appropriate rule for evaluating the recommendations of special litigation committees could easily be crafted using the common jurisprudential devices of substantive standards and burdens of proof. The appropriate substantive standard is whether the benefits to the corporation of continuing the litigation exceed the costs of doing so. Observe that this standard is quite different from an analysis of the merits of the litigation. In many cases the standard could be met even though the corporation has a relatively low probability of success on the merits. If, for example, the corporation has only a 20 percent chance of victory, but stands to win a net judgment (after deducting the fees of the plaintiffs' attorney) of $10 million if it does win, then the approximate value of the case to the corporation ex ante is $2 million. In such a case, the derivative litigation should be dismissed only if the costs to the corporation from continuing the litigation exceed $2 million. These costs would not include attorneys' fees, the major component of expenses in most standard litigation settings, because no fees will be owed if the case fails and the fees in the event of success are already included in the calculation.

* * *

Application of this substantive standard depends on difficult questions of proof and complex factual inferences. Thus much turns on the burden of proof. In our view, the burden should be on corporate management to demonstrate that the costs of continuing the litigation exceed the benefits.

* * *

III. Regulation of the Named Plaintiff

* * *

2. The contemporaneous ownership rule in derivative suits

. . . In general, to qualify as a representative plaintiff in a derivative suit, an individual must not only own stock at the time the suit is brought but must also have owned the stock at the time of the alleged wrong to the corporation. This rule . . . tends to require that the interests of the representative plaintiff be aligned with those of the corporation during all relevant periods of the controversy.

The rationale for the contemporaneous ownership rule, however, appears questionable at best. No discernible harm to the corporation can arise simply from the fact that a given plaintiff may not have owned the stock at the time of the alleged harm. Such a plaintiff has the same interest after the fact as all other shareholders, including those who happen to have held their stock for a longer period. And since the representative plaintiff's principal role is to act as key to the courthouse door, there would appear to be little harm to the corporation even if some element of conflict could be established.

The most plausible current justification[224] for the contemporaneous ownership rule would appear to be a concern with avoiding litigation that might harm the corporation. . . . The greatest danger, according to this view, is the nonmeritorious "strike suit" brought by entrepreneurial attorneys solely for settlement value. The justification for the contemporaneous ownership rule, then, is that it deters strike suits by discouraging attorneys from purchasing shares themselves or causing someone they know to purchase shares in order to act as representative plaintiff—in other words, it discourages them from "manufacturing plaintiffs in order to initiate strike suit litigation."

This argument, however, is not particularly plausible. Most observers agree that strike suit litigation is relatively uncommon. Defendants in class action and derivative litigation are typical repeat players, in that they are vulnerable to frequent lawsuits brought by entrepreneurial attorneys. It would not appear particularly desirable for such defendants (or their insurers, as the case may be) to settle cases for their nuisance value, because doing so would predictably establish a reputation as an easy mark and thus generate even more frivolous litigation. Moreover, a plaintiffs' attorney who brings a strike suit incurs substantial risk; she must fund and staff the litigation subject to a high probability of nonsuccess at the end. The true strike suit, where it occurs, is unlikely to be overly costly for defendants because the plaintiff would be likely to settle at a very low figure.

To the extent that the strike suit is a problem in derivative cases, the contemporaneous ownership rule appears to be a poorly designed regulatory tool for handling the difficulty. It is overinclusive: bona fide derivative suits may be deterred if the plaintiffs' attorney must identify a contemporaneous shareholder. It is also underinclusive: to the extent strike suits are possible, the contemporaneous ownership rule does not prevent them. A plaintiffs' attorney wishing to engage in a strike suit simply has to expend additional resources to identify a contemporaneous shareholder. These additional expenses might deter some strike suits, but so would any other means for increasing the costs of class and derivative litigation. If the goal is to increase costs, it would seem more efficient to impose some sort of direct tax on the plaintiffs' attorneys,[227] because doing so avoids the socially inefficient transactions costs of searching for an appropriate representative plaintiff.

Further, if the goal is to deter frivolous litigation, the most direct approach would be to sanction litigation when it is frivolous. Sanctions are now widely available

---

224 The original jurisdiction for the rule in federal courts was apparently a fear of collusive diversity jurisdiction. . . . This rationale is obviously inapplicable to state court jurisdiction, and appears to have little merit for federal court derivative litigation given that plaintiffs' attorneys can search for representative plaintiffs with suitable citizenship even under a contemporaneous ownership rule; the only difference is that the search costs will be higher.

227 Indeed, in some states a de facto tax may be applied to class and derivative litigation in the form of statutes providing that the plaintiff may be required to post a bond if her financial stake in the corporation is below some minimum threshold. As of 1988 such statutes were in effect in 14 states. . . . Even where they are in effect the statutes play little current role in contemporary litigation.

under Rule 11 of the Federal Rules of Civil Procedure, which allows the trial court to fine attorneys who file pleadings that are not well-grounded in law or fact. Although not without problems of its own, Rule 11 appears to provide a potentially more carefully tailored regulatory response to the problem of frivolous litigation or strike suits than does the blunt instrument of the contemporaneous ownership rule.

* * *

Notes and Questions

1. Professors Macey and Miller mention two additional rules impacting derivative suits. In footnote 227, they refer to a requirement that the plaintiff post a bond to cover the corporation's and defendants' expenses. Several factors account for the limited impact of these statutes which the two authors note. For example, in New York, a plaintiff may avoid the requirement by having the holders of five percent of the corporation's stock join the suit. While plaintiffs rarely succeed in reaching this number, the threat that the plaintiff will demand the shareholder list and communicate to the stockholders in an effort to secure such support often deters the board from demanding the plaintiff post bond. The California corporations statute only requires a bond if the court finds no reasonable possibility that the suit will benefit the corporation or its shareholders. Obtaining such a finding can require a major evidentiary hearing.

The two authors are unable to find a persuasive rationale for the rule that the plaintiff stockholder must have held his or her shares at the time of the wrongdoing. Would such a shareholder receive some sort of windfall by being able to bring a derivative suit? After all, he or she did not hold stock that declined in value by virtue of the defendants' wrong. On the other hand, the fact that one cannot bring a derivative suit does not prevent one from benefiting by the increase in share value resulting if any other stockholder successfully prosecutes the action to corporate recovery. Hence, if windfall is the rationale, does the rule prevent it? Moreover, might the price of stock reflect the prospect for a successful action, thereby removing any element of windfall for the non-contemporaneous shareholder?

2. Professors Macey and Miller suggest that the problem with individual shareholders deciding whether the corporation should sue is not meritless strike suits brought to extort settlement, but rather inferior incentives possessed by the plaintiff's attorney. Their example helps clarify the point. If a suit has a 20% chance of recovering $10 million, the corporation should not bring the suit if its expected costs exceed $2 million. These costs can include the obligation of the corporation, if it does not prevail, to indemnify the directors under statutes discussed earlier, and the various business costs outlined by Professors Macey and Miller. Note, however, that the plaintiff's attorney normally does not pay these costs. Hence, his or her calculations as to the value of the suit will not match the corporation's. Might this justify the statutes which require the plaintiff to post a bond covering the corporation's expenses? Notice this would require the plaintiff to pay all the company's expenses, while the plaintiff's attorney only obtains a portion of the recovery as fees. Unfortunately, then the incentive structure deters bringing suits which are worthwhile from the corporation's standpoint.

3. Professors Macey and Miller clarify the basic rationale behind the demand rule and futility exception: Directors can decide best if the corporation should bring a suit, except if they are the wrongdoers the corporation should sue. Professors Macey and Miller conclude that the Delaware formulation of the demand rule is carefully crafted to implement this rationale. The next two articles raise two problems with this happy assessment: First, suppose some directors are wrongdoers and some are not; can we trust the non-defendant directors to determine the corporate interest in a possible suit against their colleagues? Second, how do we know if any directors really are wrongdoers at the outset of a lawsuit?

James D. Cox and Harry L. Munslinger, *Bias in the Boardroom: Psychological Foundations and Legal Implications of Corporate Cohesion*, 48 Law & Contemp. Probs. 83 (1985)*

* * *

II

SOCIAL AND PSYCHOLOGICAL CAUSES OF DIRECTOR BIAS

A. Uncertainty and Director Bias

. . . The theory advanced here is that directors edit the decision choices posed by the derivative suit in a manner which precludes consideration of the suit's favorable effects. Editing is a well-documented approach decisionmakers utilize to simplify and reduce to manageable proportions inherently complex decisions. The near perfect record of defendants before special litigation committees suggests that such independent directors engage in editing. As a consequence of editing, the directors' evaluation of the suit is made, not in response to the corporation's interests, but as a result of the directors' social and psychological drives.

* * *

2. *Choice Editing.* Natural aversion toward risk can hardly explain the consistent behavior of directors in seeing only downside potential in derivative suits. A possible explanation may be found in natural forces that arise in decisionmaking, whereby indi-

viduals seek to keep an inherently complex problem within their limited processing capacity. When confronted by a multifaceted, inherently complex choice such as the choice to continue or terminate a derivative suit, decisionmakers edit the problem by simplifying the information relied upon to make a choice. The most frequent form of editing entails evaluating a current problem in terms of the decisionmakers' prior experience, understanding, or belief respecting problems of that same general type. Important bias is introduced by such simplifications because of the well-recognized tendency of decisionmakers to give insufficient attention to material differences between the choice at hand and the experience drawn upon in the simplification. For example, directors confronted with a demand can be expected to draw upon their personal experiences and general beliefs about the probability of success in derivative suit litigation when assessing the present suit's impact on the corporation's interest. These attitudes are not likely to be positive.

A cornerstone of the boardroom culture is a near fanatical concern for "the liability of today's director," which is documented by studies of director attitudes that repeatedly identify fear of personal liability as a paramount concern about service on the board. . . . [D]irectors not only feel threatened by such litigation, but they also share the view that most shareholder litigation against managers is extortionate, yielding handsome fees to the suit's representative and bestowing small benefits on the corporation. . . . Such a view of the derivative suit can only introduce a very solid source of decision bias to the choice between the suit's continuance and its dismissal.

An even more robust source of bias, which arises through the directors' editing of the complex choice of continuing or terminating the suit, is the directors' affinity with the defendants and their particular concern that the defendants not be subjected needlessly to the opprobrium and inconvenience of litigation. . . .

* * *

B. Social Needs and Director Service

* * *

The process by which board members are selected, the criteria by which their candidacy and continued service are evaluated, and the motives and rewards that impel nominees and directors to serve on the board all interact to form a highly cohesive group of mutually attractive individuals. All available evidence suggests that the strength of this attraction among the directors and the value they each place upon their membership in the group are extremely high. For example, the selection criteria generate boards of directors who have highly similar backgrounds, goals, talents, and work experience: a high cohesive, cooperative set of directors who share corporate attitudes and loyalties. In addition, the shared perception of mutual agreeableness enhances the interpersonal attraction among ingroup members and this enhanced mutual attraction creates even more conformity. The very high nonmonetary personal value that directors place on continued membership on these highly prestigious boards tend to multiply the overall cohesion of the group even more. Finally, enhanced self-esteem derived from being singled out for membership in the select group and the increased attention associated with continued group membership contribute importantly to ingroup cohesion within the boardroom and special litigation committee. Taken together, these studies all suggest that powerful psychological factors are at work within the boardroom, creating a cohesive, loyal, conforming ingroup that will support its members for positive and negative reasons, under low and high levels of motivation and group values.

C. The Board, Self-Validation, and Bias

Prior or ongoing interaction between individuals, called interpersonal familiarity in the psychological literature, has been repeatedly demonstrated to be a source for strong biases favoring a familiar ingroup and correlatively disfavoring a threatening or unfamiliar outgroup. Ingroup bias is generated by the tendency to raise or reinforce one's own self-worth by magnifying differences between a person's ingroup and a threatening outgroup. In the small group or committee, ingroup bias is an analog of ethnocentrism among large populations and nations. Both psychological research and real world experience support the conclusion that ingroup bias is a remarkably prevalent and robust phenomenon, one that is caused by many psychological factors, including hostility, conflict, competition, importance of the group differences, and familiarity with the environment. Each of these factors is present in the directors' evaluation of an "outsider's" suit against their colleague. Intergroup comparison is a common device for self-validation, and provides the source for the intergroup bias described in this section.

* * *

2. *The Corporate Context.* In the context of the shareholder suit, several forces are at work that cause the directors to identify themselves and the defendants as a discrete group and the plaintiff as a disfavored outgroup. Consequently, directors can reasonably be expected to exhibit intergroup discrimination of the type described above. The directors called upon to evaluate a derivative suit against their colleagues are not, and generally have not been, isolated from the suit's defendants. As members of the board of directors they continue to interact with the defendants, who usually remain directors or officers of the corporation. Even members of a special litigation committee who were appointed *after* the derivative suit was initiated are legally bound under the organic requirements for committee membership to serve as directors on the full board. The new special litigation committee members and the defendant directors therefore serve as colleagues on the same corporate board in addressing an array of nonderivative suit issues. Consequently, the judges and those to be judged associate on a regular basis in discharging their many tasks as corporate directors during the preliminary derivative suit skirmishes. In doing so, they share a mutual duty to serve the corporate interest, and they often adopt a common view of that corporate interest. Analogous studies suggest that the effect of these shared experiences is not only to bond the directors and the defendants together but also to form a basis upon which the directors can be expected to give greater weight to the defendant's values, attitudes, and perceptions than to those of outgroup members like the plaintiff. . . .

* * *

We are careful to observe that the studies examined do not conclude that directors are biased or that their well-documented proclivity to shield colleagues from derivative suits is the product of such bias. Indeed, this precise question remains unexplored in the social psychology literature. Also, even given our description of the many biasing agents, these studies do not tell us whether natural psychological bias is so strong that it cannot be overcome by the advocacy of plaintiff's counsel or by the directors' knowledge that their evaluations will be reviewed by a court. Minimally, however, these factors strongly suggest there is bias in the boardroom favoring colleagues and disfavoring the derivative suit plaintiff. Furthermore, the preceding description offers no support for current assumptions that "outside" directors can be expected to act impartially, absent family or financial relationship with the defendants or a direct involvement in the underlying transaction.

* * *

Notes and Questions

1. One additional source of bias not mentioned in this piece is that the defendants, assuming they constitute a majority of the board, will pick the members of the committee charged with looking into a derivative suit. What would be the expected result of a trial in which one side could pick the jury?

2. For additional articles which criticize judicial deference to directors when it comes to actions against their colleagues see Coffee & Schwartz, *The Survival of the Derivative Suit: An Evaluation and a Proposal for Reform*, 81 COLUM. L. REV. 261 (1981); Dent, *The Power of Directors to Terminate Shareholder Litigation: The Death of the Derivative Suit?*, 75 NW. U. L. REV. 96 (1980).

3. The third player in derivative litigation, besides the plaintiff shareholder and the board, is the court. The next excerpt looks at two roles the court might take: Assessment of whether the board should make the decision regarding the corporate interest in a suit against any of its members, and a judicial determination as to whether such a suit is in the corporation's best interest. The former role lies at the heart of the futility exception to the demand requirement; the latter role finds its genesis in the Delaware Supreme Court's *Zapata* decision.

Franklin A. Gevurtz, *Who Represents the Corporation? In Search of a Better Method for Determining the Corporate Interest in Derivative Suits,* 46 U. PITT. L. REV. 265 (1985)*

* * *

1. *Defendant Directors*

It seems too obvious to state that directors who are named as defendants cannot be expected to determine the corporation's interest uninfluenced by their own. Yet courts and commentators who wish to preserve a role for "disinterested" directors have been forced to rethink the obvious by a gambit they otherwise would open up to the plaintiff. A rule which automatically disqualified any director named as a defendant could (unless the directors are replaced) allow the plaintiff to preclude a role for the board by the simple expedient of suing all or most of its members. Those directors who did not participate or profit in the purported wrongdoing may be alleged to have breached their duty of care to the corporation by approving, acquiescing in, or not moving to correct the acts of the ones who did.[32] These allegations may never be proved, yet the plaintiff will be able to continue the suit.

Frustrating as this result may be, no one has proposed a satisfactory alternative. Least acceptable is the approach followed by some courts which allows defendant directors to decide whether the suit serves the corporation's interest so long as those directors did not profit from the challenged acts. . . . It makes no sense to assert that defendants who did not profit in the challenged transaction can somehow be considered disinterested. If a cause of action is stated against the passive directors for not opposing the transaction, they have a clear interest, financial and otherwise, in seeking dismissal.

In defense of these decisions, perhaps the courts viewed the allegations against the passive directors as without merit. In that case, the courts should at least dismiss the complaint against those directors before allowing them to exercise any judgment on the corporation's interest in pursuing the action against the remaining defendants. . . .

Before becoming too optimistic of such a simple solution, however, one must examine whether the likely claims against the passive directors are susceptible to early dismissal. Unless those claims can be dismissed on the pleadings (or even on summary judgment), the plaintiff will have succeeded in precluding the board from determining

32 . . . *Barr v. Wackman* [36 N.Y.2d 371, 329 N.E.2d 180, 368 N.Y.S.2d 497 (1975)] provides a prototype case of this pleading. In *Barr*, the plaintiff alleged that five directors of Talcott National Corporation (who were also its principal officers) agreed, in exchange for employment contracts and other personal consideration, to aid Gulf and Western Industries in acquiring Talcott on terms substantially less favorable to Talcott than a merger already negotiated between the two companies. This plan was allegedly carried out through various actions taken by Talcott's board, including abandonment of the merger, support of a less favorable tender offer for Talcott's shares, and authorization of various employment contracts for the principal officers. The eleven outside directors of Talcott—who did not personally benefit from these transactions—were alleged to have failed to exercise due care in authorizing and approving them.

the corporation's interest in the lawsuit. After all, once the case is tried, it is too late for the board to decide it was against the company's interest to bring it.

* * *

Another procedure was recently adopted by the Delaware Supreme Court in *Aronson v. Lewis*. It instructed the Chancery Court to require that demand be made unless the allegations against the directors create a "reasonable doubt" whether they are protected from liability by the business judgment rule. The probable result of this decision will be confusion. If the plaintiff does not allege facts which, if proved, establish the inapplicability of the business judgment rule, then the complaint can be dismissed on the merits regardless of whether demand was made. If, however, the plaintiff pleads such facts, then it is impossible to understand how the trial court is to examine those pleadings further to decide whether or not a "reasonable doubt" exists as to the applicability of the defense.

2. *Nondefendant Directors*

* * *

b. *The Impracticality of Searching for Independence*

One response to bias is to argue that the courts can determine which directors are independent and which are not. Such a determination, however, is rendered impractical by the inherent dilemma in which it will place the courts. Unless they simply ignore structural bias, extensive adjudication will be required to determine (if that is even possible) whether the directors can exercise independent judgment. Such extensive adjudication, however, would frustrate the whole purpose of allowing the board to terminate litigation which is against the corporation's interest.

The issues involved in determining bias may be as difficult as the issues raised by the underlying claims and could easily require the development and presentation of extensive evidence. Take, for example, bias caused by possible dominance of management over outside directors. As discussed above, a number of studies found such dominance to be typical in the corporations surveyed. Proof that outside directors will be unable to exercise independent judgment in a specific case, however, will require more than reference to general studies. Evidence concerning the manner in which the outside directors came to be on the board—including who suggested their nomination and what expectations management may have had as to their independence—would be relevant, as would any evidence that management possessed the power to force the removal of those directors. Also relevant would be evidence concerning any economic relationships the outside directors have, or hope to have, with the corporation, as well as social or other relationships between the outside directors and the management defendants. In addition, the voting pattern of the board in response to management proposals could be examined. This, in turn, could easily lead into a morass of side issues concerning the merits of a wide variety of past board actions.

* * *

The alternatives to this extensive adjudication are either to preclude the directors' say when the claim is against any of their colleagues or simply to ignore structural bias and limit the meaning of independence to the lack of any blatant self-interest. The courts have generally taken the latter approach, even though the result is to make a mockery of any assurances that the corporate interest would be protected by the scrutiny of independent directors.

* * *

C. *The Courts*

* * *

Unfortunately, neither when it comes to initiation nor settlement does the exercise of the courts' judgment provide a satisfactory solution to determining the corporation's interest. The problem is not, as some courts and commentators suggest, that judges lack the expertise to make these decisions. Individual judges are probably as capable as anyone to weigh the various costs against the gains incurred in litigation and settlement.[146] Instead, the problem lies in the adversarial process by which judicial decisions are reached. The result of this process, if the decision is hotly contested, will be to create extensive litigation over the wisdom of decisions that have as their purpose the termination of litigation. . . .

The question whether it is in a company's interest to pursue a derivative lawsuit raises a number of difficult factual and legal issues which the court will need to address in exercising its judgment. First, there must be an assessment of the probability of the plaintiff's success in the action, which, of course, means considering the various factual and legal questions involved in deciding the merits of the claim. Further, the size of the recovery in the event of success may be estimated. This requires review of the defendant's ability to pay in addition to the amount of damages likely to be awarded. The probable recovery must be weighed against the various costs to the corporation. That involves more than simply estimating the total costs of attorney's fees and other out-of-pocket expenses which the company might ultimately pay. In addition, difficult factual and legal issues may be raised in determining the extent of the corporation's obligation to indemnify the defendants, the coverage provided by any insurance, or the propriety of large expenditures by the company in defense of the action. Further issues may be raised regarding the existence and extent of various intangible costs of litigation to the company. For example, if it is claimed that distraction of corporate personnel is one of the costs justifying dismissal, there may be a question not only as to the exact amount of the time lost by employees, but also as to the impact such lost time will actually have. Similar questions can be raised concerning claimed effects of the suit on employee morale and the corporation's public reputation.

---

146 . . . Indeed, many settlement conferences demonstrate that judges often have a more realistic understanding of the burdens involved in litigation than do numerous businessmen.

* * *

While the *Zapata* decision did not resolve a number of questions as to how a court is to obtain and weigh the data needed to evaluate these issues, it suggested that the normal adversary process will be followed.[165] The result will be to create extensive and costly litigation over whether the burden of the suit outweighs its benefit. Initially, each of the factual issues listed above could mandate substantial discovery. . .

Once discovery is completed, the presentation of evidence to the court will require something more than a "mini" trial. This is well illustrated by examining the amount of evidence heard by special litigation committees in their attempts to determine whether to pursue a derivative suit. These committees often report hearing extensive testimony over the course of investigations which may span several months. . . . If the court is to exercise its independent judgment on the corporate interest, it should hear for itself the testimony presented to the committee. Moreover, it should allow the plaintiff an opportunity to cross-examine the company's witnesses and to present his or her own evidence. The result will be for the court to take longer than the committee to hear evidence on the issue.

The length of hearings conducted to determine whether the court should approve the settlement of a derivative action can also provide a useful comparison. Some of these hearings have been as long as major trials. . . .

To require such extensive and costly litigation in order to determine whether further litigation is against the corporation's interest hardly seems to be a sensible approach. The whole point of considering the motion to dismiss is to prevent the corporation from being burdened by the costs of undesirable litigation, not to add to those costs. To make things worse, the costs of this phase of the lawsuit will be borne directly by the company. It is the company, not the defendants, who will presumably make and defend a motion to dismiss on the ground that the suit is against the corporate interest.

* * *

Undoubtedly, such extensive adjudication as outlined above is not really what the Delaware Supreme Court or others who advocate similar solutions have in mind. It is difficult to see, however, what viable alternatives exist if the courts are to exercise their independent judgment to determine the corporation's interest. Prior to *Zapata*, several courts suggested a more limited exercise of judicial judgment. Under this approach, they would no longer automatically defer to the recommendation of directors on the sole condition that those directors be nominally independent and act in good faith. Instead, the courts would reserve the right to reject a recommendation of dismissal if they found it to be unreasonable. Admittedly, this standard would curtail possible litigation over the merits of the decision to dismiss, although it might not eliminate it altogether depending on how rigorously the court undertakes the reasonableness

165 The court stated that the motion to dismiss should be handled in a manner "akin to proceedings on summary judgment." . . . However, the court further cautioned that the moving party must show there is no material issue of fact and left open the possibility of a trial on any factual issues raised. . . . Given the numerous areas for dispute outlined above, it would be a rare case when, under any reasonable application of the standard, no material issue of fact could be found.

review. The price for limiting review to reasonableness, however, is to undermine almost completely the protection of the corporation from litigation decisions made under the influence of structural bias.

There is a wide range of cases in which a decision whether or not to sue would be reasonable regardless of which way one concluded. Indeed, it is a rare case in which a claim is so one-sided that a lawyer should advise his or her client that it would be unreasonable not to bring suit. In this broad range, an exercise of judgment is called for. Yet the danger of structural bias is that instead of objective judgment, the directors' decision will be based on the interests of the defendants. This danger will not be cured by a court review limited to reasonableness since decisions in this range will pass that test. The end result, therefore, will be to deprive the corporation of any objective assessment of its interest in proceeding with claims against its directors except in the rare case in which the claims are overwhelming.

* * *

Notes and Questions

1. Perhaps instead of looking to the individual plaintiff shareholder to determine the corporation's interest, we might turn to the entire body of stockholders for a vote on the issue. In fact, some jurisdictions require demand on the shareholders prior to filing a derivative suit unless the plaintiff has some good excuse (such as ownership of a majority of shares by the alleged wrongdoer). Authorities in these jurisdictions differ on whether either the burden of contacting numerous stockholders, or the inability of the shareholders to legally ratify the challenged board action (for example, because it constitutes waste or fraud), constitutes a good excuse.

In a widely held corporation, how well informed and careful can we realistically expect the stockholders to be if asked to vote on the question of whether it is in the corporate interest to pursue an action against its directors? In a corporation in which there are a few shareholders, who are also the directors, what would one expect the result of such a vote to be? For a discussion of demand on shareholders see Leavell, *The Shareholders as Judges of Alleged Wrongs by Directors*, 35 TUL. L. REV. 331 (1961).

2. Is there any alternative to having the individual plaintiff shareholder (or his or her attorney), the directors who include among their number the alleged wrongdoers, the court, or the entire body of shareholders, decide whether the suit is in the corporation's interest? Both the Cox and Munslinger and Gevurtz articles recommend judicially appointed independent decisionmakers.

3. *Reality Check: Who Wins in Derivative Litigation?*

Roberta Romano, *The Shareholder Suit: Litigation without Foundation?*, 7 J.L. ECON. & ORG. 55 (1991)*

* * *

2. Direct Benefits from Shareholders Suits

2.1 Sample Construction and Description

This study consists of all shareholder suits brought from the late 1960s through 1987 . . . against a sample of 535 public corporations, randomly selected from firms currently traded on the New York Stock Exchange (NYSE) and over-the-counter (OTC) in the National Association of Securities Dealers Automated Quotation National Market System, and from firms that have ceased trading in those markets. . . .

* * *

Ninety-nine firms (19 percent of the sample) experienced a shareholder suit. There were 139 suits. . . .

* * *

2.2 Lawsuit Dispositions

Most lawsuits (83 of 128 resolved suits) settled. This aspect of shareholders litigation is unremarkable; most civil suits settle. . . . Shareholder-plaintiffs, however, have abysmal success in court. Only one suit had a judgment for the plaintiff (upholding some of the plaintiff's claims in a ruling on stipulated facts), and in one other suit a state supreme court reinstated a complaint that had been dismissed by the trial court. This is a success rate of 6 percent of adjudicated cases, but plaintiffs actually won no judgments for damages or equitable relief.

The settlements exhibit two striking features. First, only half of all settlements have a monetary recovery (46 of 83). Second, awards are paid to attorneys far more frequently than to shareholders (75 of 83). In seven cases (8 percent) the *only* relief was attorneys' fees. Moreover, financial recoveries are highly skewed: the average recovery in 39 settlements that can be valued is $9 million, while the median is $2 million.[11] These recoveries are approximately 1.3 percent of firm assets (median: 0.5 percent). One interpretation is that most fiduciary breaches involve minor harm to shareholders. But the settlement pattern is consistent with another, more troubling explanation, that a significant proportion of shareholder suits are without merit.

---

11 All amounts are in 1988 dollars. The range is from $226,000 to $118 million.

Settlement funds vary substantially by type of action. The average recovery in derivative suits ($6 million) is about half that in class actions ($11 million).[12]. . .

. . . Eleven derivative suits with a monetary recovery averaged $0.18 a share ($0.15 net of attorneys fees). This is approximately 2 percent of the stock price on the day prior to the lawsuits' filing. . . .

* * *

. . . In 25 lawsuits, settlements afforded structural relief. (There was a monetary recovery as well in four of these suits.). . . .

Settlements modified board composition in nine suits. . . . In five cases, a small number of outside directors was added to the board. . . . Moreover, in all but one settlement, the incumbent board, not the plaintiff, was to select the new directors. In three cases, however, the settlement included a change in the board's majority. . . . However, the lawsuit was scarcely the motor force for change: these suits were brought by shareholders waging proxy fights against management. . . .

The remaining structural settlements afforded even more cosmetic organizational change. Eight involved minor modifications of executive compensation plans or independent board review of compensation practices; seven adopted restrictions on defensive tactics against hostile takeovers (primarily prohibitions on greenmail); and five placed restrictions on self-interested transactions.

* * *

2.3 Stock Price Effects

. . . Using well-established event study methodology, stock price effects of lawsuit filings and terminations can be measured. . . .

The data do not provide compelling support for the proposition that shareholders experience significant wealth effects from litigation. . . .

* * *

. . . The small per share recovery as a percent of market value is not a cause of the statistical insignificance: the event study methodology is well-specified for 1 percent abnormal returns with daily data. . . .

Fischel and Bradley examined stock price reactions to reported judgments in derivative suits on management motions to dismiss (either for plaintiff's failure to make demand, or a special litigation committee's recommendation to drop the suit). They find a significant negative abnormal return on the day suits are terminated and a positive though insignificant abnormal return when suits are not dismissed. . . . These

---

12 Of the monetary recoveries, there are 12 derivative suits and 29 class actions. In three suits, class and derivative claims were separately settled; these suits are separately counted for this discussion. Settlement awards compared by lawsuit subject parallel the difference by type of action, as the awards in financial disclosure and acquisition suits ($11 million and $9 million, respectively), which tend to be class actions, are much higher than those in executive compensation and self-dealing suits ($490,000), which are typically derivative claims.

data suggest that the market views derivative suits positively, given its adverse reaction to suit termination and positive valuation of suit continuance, although the authors conclude instead that the suits have no significant wealth effects.

In this study, the average residuals and [(portfolio cumulative average abnormal returns)] CARs when derivative suits are dismissed are also negative but always insignificant. When derivative suits settled, the average residuals are negative and insignificant . . . . Despite nuanced differences in findings and analysis, Fischel and Bradley's assessment seems correct: the wealth effects of shareholder litigation are negligible. . . .

* * *

3. Indirect Benefits of Shareholder Suits

Lawsuit settlements are not the sole measure of litigation benefits. It is possible that when a shareholder suit is filed a corporation reorganizes on its own, leaving little for litigation to achieve, as was acknowledged in three lawsuit settlements. . . .

To probe these propositions, three key organizational factors, which are the focus in most structural settlements, are examined for changes during litigation—cash compensation and turnover of top management, and board composition . . . . To control for changes that would occur regardless of litigation, a paired sample was constructed that matched lawsuit firms with sample firms that had not experienced a lawsuit and had the same four-digit Standard Industrial Classification (SIC) code. . . .

3.1 Does Litigation Produce Coasian Adjustments in Firm Organization?

Changes in top management or their compensation following the commencement of a shareholder suit would be key indicia of incentive realignment induced by litigation. Litigation appears, however, to have no impact on insiders' compensation packages. Cash compensation of top executives of lawsuit firms grew more rapidly than that of their matches. . . .

. . . Top management of lawsuit firms turned over significantly more frequently than did their matches: 55 percent of lawsuit firms experienced a change in CEO or Chair in the years surrounding the litigation while only 31 percent of the matches experienced a change. . .

The significance of changes in the year before the suit is filed can be attributed to the transaction underlying the suit and the board's effectiveness in disciplining management . . . rather than the lawsuit. The subsequently higher turnover rate for sued firms may also be attributed to events other than litigation, such as firm profitability, for we might expect the difference in turnover to be significant *after* the suit's resolution rather than during its course, if litigation is the cause, as the disposition could signify management's blameworthiness. To test for this possibility, a maximum likelihood estimation logit regression was estimated, with the dependent variable the dichotomous variable indicating whether the CEO or Chair changed during the lawsuit years, and the independent variables profitability the year before the lawsuit (as measured by change in unexpected earnings and, alternatively, by earnings growth) and a dummy variable for litigation. The litigation dummy is highly significant and explains most of the variation in turnover, although prior profitability, as measured by change in unexpected earnings, is also a significant predictor under a one-tailed test. This suggests that the significance of changes in top management after litigation has commenced is evidence that shareholder suits could have some disciplining effect.

* * *

The board stability data are difficult to interpret. They appear to suggest an internal monitoring effect in response to litigation: Board members are held accountable for lawsuits, particularly those with greater merit (those that settled), as they depart in greater numbers from sued firms. But turnover need not be a sign of poor monitors being replaced. It could also indicate that more able monitors are leaving for better opportunities because they disliked being sued. . . .

* * *

4. Conclusion

The data support the conclusion that shareholder litigation is a weak, if not ineffective, instrument of corporate governance.

. . . The principal beneficiaries of the litigation therefore appear to be attorneys, who win fee awards in 90 percent of settled suits.

* * *

. . . A possible interpretation of the data is that managers are so deterred by the prospect of shareholder litigation that suits involve only trivial violations. This proposition cannot be tested against the alternative—that shareholder litigation is by and large an ineffective governance structure—because it is virtually impossible to identify a general deterrent effect as we cannot estimate the number of offenses, and thereby estimate the probability of detection, which is essential for measuring such an effect. Still, the failure to find much in the way of specific deterrence undercuts this proposition, and suggests that general deterrence is weak. This is because without instances of penalized managers, it is unlikely that anyone else will be deterred.

* * *

Notes and Questions

1. A study such as this provokes controversy not because of questions about the accuracy of its results, but rather because of differing interpretations as to their meaning. Professor Romano's conclusion is that the derivative suit serves little purpose other than to provide fees for attorneys. For a similar assessment without the benefit of an empirical survey see Dusenberg, *The Business Judgment Rule and Shareholder Derivative Suits: A View from the Inside*, 60 WASH. U. L.Q. 311 (1982). Along the same lines, Professors Fischel and Bradley concluded, as discussed in the excerpt, that their stock price study showed no favorable impact on stock value from derivative suits. Fischel & Bradley, *The Role of Liability Rules and the Derivative Suit in Corporate Law: A Theoretical and Empirical Analysis*, 71 CORNELL L. REV. 261 (1986). (Notice, however, the disregard by Professors Fischel and Bradley of their own data suggesting a contrary conclusion.)

On the other hand, is Professor Romano too dismissive of the recoveries she reports? An average monetary settlement of $6 million in derivative suits may yield a tiny sum on a per share basis; but is this the relevant comparison? For example, how large is the typical recovery obtained by public corporations in the sort of breach of contract or debt collection actions which such companies file every day against third parties? Does small recovery in such actions mean that the suits against these third parties were meritless or that it was against the corporate interest to bring the suit? Along the same line, does the greater recovery in shareholder class actions suggest less merit for derivative suits? Look at footnote 12 in the article and compare the damages caused by unfair self-dealing or excessive compensation (what the corporation overpaid) to the damages resulting if the board misleads shareholders into overpaying for millions of shares or deprives all the shareholders of a significant premium by blocking a hostile takeover. For a more positive spin on a study of monetary recovery in derivative suits see Jones, *An Empirical Examination of the Resolution of Shareholder Derivative and Class Action Lawsuits*, 60 BOSTON U. L. REV. 542 (1980).

Moreover, even if one agrees with Professor Romano that her data on the outcome of derivative litigation suggests that the plaintiffs had weak cases, does this necessarily mean that there had been no director wrongdoing? Recall, as explained by Messrs. Block, Radin and Rosenzweig, that the effect of the demand rule and respect for the board's litigation decision is to impose a significant barrier to even meritorious shareholder claims. Is there something of a "Catch 22" here: Procedural obstacles to derivative suits lead to few plaintiff victories, while few plaintiff victories, in turn, then become the justification for procedural obstacles to derivative lawsuits?

Finally, what do you think of Professor Romano's effort to measure the deterrent effect of derivative litigation? Would it be relevant to know not only how boards responded in terms of cutting compensation or sacking individuals when sued, but also how boards would behave if there could be no threat of suit? On what data does Professor Romano base her negative assessment of such general deterrence?

2. Assuming Professor Romano's data shows a problem with derivative suits, what is (are) the answer(s)? For example, her data show numerous settlements for non-monetary corporate recovery coupled with fees for the plaintiff's attorney. Given that derivative suit settlements and the award of plaintiff's attorneys fees require judicial approval, why is that not a sufficient protection of the corporate interest? Presumably, the judges in these cases did not share Professor Romano's assessment of the value of the non-monetary reforms. For an exploration of the rules surrounding the settlement of derivative litigation see Haudek, *The Settlement and Dismissal of Stockholders' Actions—Part II: The Settlement*, 23 SW. L.J. 765 (1969). If courts are not up to the task of determining the corporate interest in settlements, might the appointment of independent decisionmakers help?

Chapter IV

Federal Regulation of Insider Trading and Proxy Solicitation

As discussed in Chapter I, most corporate law is state law. As part of the "New Deal" legislation, however, Congress enacted two statutes—The Securities Act of 1933 and The Securities Exchange Act of 1934—to regulate the issuance and trading of "securities" (stocks, bonds, and other investments). This Chapter explores two aspects of those laws which are closely related to the fiduciary duty of corporate officers and directors. The first is trading in stock when one party to the transaction—often, though not always, a corporate officer or director—knows important information impacting the stock's value which the other party does not know. In reading the materials to follow, consider not only the justification for the specific rules, but also why, if at all, this should be a matter of federal rather than just state concern.

A. Rule 10B-5 and Insider Trading

1. *The Doctrine Introduced*

A number of state and federal laws potentially address trading stock based upon undisclosed "inside" information—in other words, information known to one, but not the other, party to the trade. The most important of these laws, however, has become Rule 10B-5. This is a rule promulgated by the Securities and Exchange Commission pursuant to the Commission's authority under Section 10(b) of the 1934 Securities Exchange Act. Section 10(b) makes it unlawful to engage in manipulative or deceptive devices or contrivances in connection with the purchase or sale of a security in violation of rules made by the Securities Exchange Commission. In other words, the Section constitutes a grant of legislative authority to the Commission to make up rules prohibiting manipulative or deceptive securities trading practices. Rule 10B-5, in turn, prohibits making false or misleading statements of material fact, or engaging in acts of fraud or deceit, in connection with the purchase or sale of a security.

Significantly, nothing in either Section 10(b) or Rule 10B-5 explicitly refers to trading on undisclosed inside information. (While Part 2 of Rule 10B-5 prohibits "omissions of material fact," this refers to omissions which make a statement misleading; something that is not the case with trading based upon completely undisclosed information.) Accordingly, the reach of Rule 10B-5 to trading on inside information results entirely from interpretation.

Richard M. Phillips and Larry R. Lavoie, *The SEC's Proposed Insider Trading Legislation: Insider Trading Controls, Corporate Secrecy, and Full Disclosure*, 39 ALA. L. REV. 439 (1988)*

* * *

I. THE DEVELOPMENT OF THE EXISTING INSIDER TRADING DOCTRINE AND THE NEED FOR LEGISLATIVE REFORM

* * *

A. The Parity of Information Standard

Prior to the Supreme Court's decisions in *Chiarella v. United States*[28] and *Dirks v. SEC*,[29] the SEC and the courts had adopted a relatively simple, but now largely discredited, standard for determining who must abstain from trading on the basis of material nonpublic information. According to the SEC and the courts, rule 10b-5 imposed a duty on anyone in possession of material nonpublic information to disclose that information before trading in the securities to which the information related. As the Second Circuit noted in *SEC v. Texas Gulf Sulphur Co.*,[30] "anyone in possession of material inside information must either disclose it to the investing public, or, if he is disabled from disclosing it . . . , or he chooses not to do so, must abstain from trading in or recommending the securities concerned while such information remains undisclosed."

The possession standard was based upon a theory of "equal access" or "parity of information." The basic rationale of the theory was explained by the SEC in its administrative decision in *In re Cady, Roberts & Co.*[32] The SEC reasoned that it was inherently *unfair* to permit persons with special access to confidential corporate information to trade on the basis of such information when it was unavailable to other market participants. The *Texas Gulf Sulphur* court, in adopting the rationale of *Cady, Roberts*, added a further justification for the parity-of-information theory by stating that the federal securities laws should be construed to promote the "justifiable expectation of the securities marketplace that all investors trading on impersonal exchanges have relatively equal access to material information." For this reason, the court stated, the duty to disclose or abstain applies not only to insiders but to "anyone" in possession of such information.

---

28 445 U.S. 222 (1980).

29 463 U.S. 646 (1983).

30 401 F.2d 833 (2d Cir. 1968) (en banc), *cert. denied*, 404 U.S. 1005 (1971).

32 40 S.E.C. 907 (1961).

B. The Chiarella *Decision: The Repudiation of the Parity-of-Information Theory*

In *Chiarella*, the first insider trading decision reviewed by the Supreme Court, the Court rejected the equal access theory in favor of a breach of a fiduciary duty analysis and thus made it clear that the existence of an "unfair advantage" does not by itself give rise to rule 10b-5 liability. Chiarella, a "mark-up man" at a financial printing company, traded in the securities of several companies that were the targets of impending tender offers. . . . Chiarella was convicted on the theory that he had access to material nonpublic information that he knew was not available to the market traders with whom he dealt. . . .

The Supreme Court reversed, holding that "a duty to disclose under section 10(b) does not arise from the mere possession of nonpublic market information." The Court explained that a duty to speak arises not from one's ability to acquire access to information, but rather from a fiduciary or similar "relationship of trust and confidence between parties to a transaction." . . . No such relationship existed, however, between Chiarella and the target company shareholders with whom he traded. He was not their agent, their fiduciary, or a person in whom they placed trust and confidence. He was a complete stranger to them. In fact, he had no contact with the target companies or their insiders; the sources of Chiarella's information were the bidder companies. Thus, without more, Chiarella could not be held to have violated rule 10b-5 when he traded based on confidential market information.

C. The Dirks *Decision: The Constructive Insider and Personal Benefit Test*

Subsequent to *Chiarella*, the SEC attempted to preserve its equal access theory with respect to inside information by arguing that those persons who acquire material nonpublic information from corporate insiders (the "tippees") also acquire the fiduciary duties of their insider sources merely by receiving inside information from them—*ie.*, they "stand in the shoes" of their sources. The Supreme Court disposed of this argument in *Dirks* . . . .

The *Dirks* Court explained that corporate outsiders can acquire the duties of insiders under one of two theories. First, the outsiders can become "constructive insiders"—essentially, consensual fiduciaries—if they enter into a confidential relationship with a corporation through which they gain access to inside information. Thus, accountants, lawyers, underwriters, and others who legitimately obtain confidential information as a result of their relationships with a corporation are subject to the same fiduciary duties as traditional insiders. Second, corporate outsiders, under constructive trust principles, can acquire a fiduciary duty to the corporation's shareholders as "tippees" when they are aware that they have been given confidential corporate information by an insider who has tipped the information in violation of his duty to the shareholders. The Court, however, emphasized that tippees acquire duties under this theory only if their insider sources violate their fiduciary duty to shareholders by personally benefitting from the disclosure and the tippees know or have reason to know of this breach.[45]

* * *

The *Dirks* decision, however, carried a potential for creating loopholes in the coverage of the law. For example, the personal benefit test cannot be satisfied when a friend or relative of a corporate insider secretly trades on information that is confidentially revealed by the insider for the purpose of soliciting his advice. In such a case the insider is not intending to benefit either himself or the friend. He is usually unaware of the trading and feels betrayed. . . . Moreover, neither the personal benefit test nor the constructive insider test reaches trading by outsiders, such as Chiarella, who have acquired and misused information from sources other than the issuer and its insiders. For these reasons, under the theories approved in *Dirks*, rule 10b-5 would not cover many instances of outsider trading that would be not only unfair but also unethical. . . .

D. The SEC's Responses to Chiarella *and* Dirks: *Rule 14e-3 and the Misappropriation Theory*

The SEC attempted to address the potential loopholes left by *Chiarella* and *Dirks* in two ways. First, shortly after the *Chiarella* decision, the SEC promulgated rule 14e-3, which prohibits trading on the basis of nonpublic information regarding tender offers, the single most important type of market information involved in insider trading abuses.[50] . . .

Second, the SEC began to use the so-called "misappropriation theory" more aggressively. The misappropriation theory, first endorsed in Chief Justice Burger's dissenting opinion in *Chiarella*, makes unlawful trading by any person on the basis of confidential information that was stolen or misappropriated from any other person. The significance of the misappropriation theory lies in the fact that the victim of the fraud is the owner of the information, *not* the investors with whom the defendant trades in the marketplace. This theory permits the government to prosecute outsiders who trade on the basis of stolen or misappropriated information even if they have no contact with the issuer of the securities in which they trade and thus have no possible duty to the issuer's shareholders.

* * *

45 The Court's opinion noted that the benefit received by an insider from disclosing inside information in breach of his fiduciary duty may be an indirect, rather than a direct, pecuniary gain. A reputational benefit that will translate into future earnings or even evidence of a "relationship between the insider and the recipient that suggests a *quid pro quo* from the latter" can satisfy the test. Moreover, the mere intent to make a gift of confidential information to a trading relative or friend can suffice. . . .

50 Rule 14e-3 was adopted pursuant to section 14(e) of the Securities Exchange Act of 1934, . . . which authorizes the SEC to define and prescribe means reasonably designed to prevent fraudulent, deceptive, or manipulative acts and practices in connection with any tender offer.

E. The Carpenter *Decision: The Survival of the Misappropriation Theory*

The federal government sought to extend the misappropriation theory in the *Carpenter* case.[57] *Carpenter* involved a scheme to profit by trading on the basis of the probable market impact of articles that were to appear in the *Wall Street Journal's* influential "Heard on the Street" column. . . . R. Foster Winans, a *Journal* reporter who coauthored the column, . . . leaked information about the timing and content of forthcoming articles to several friends and associates, including David Carpenter. . . . Both Winans and Carpenter were convicted of mail, wire, and securities fraud on the theory that they had defrauded the *Journal* by misappropriating the information for their own securities trading. . . .

The Supreme Court . . . unanimously upheld the use of the misappropriation theory in mail and wire fraud prosecutions and also upheld, by a four-to-four vote, the Second Circuit's ruling that the same conduct violated rule 10b-5. The basis for the Court's decision on the mail and wire fraud counts was clear and simple—confidential business information, such as the timing and content of the *Journal's* articles, is a form of "property" as that term is used in the mail and wire fraud statutes. Thus, Winans and his co-conspirators defrauded the *Journal* when they stole the information and used it for trading in the securities markets.

The Court's views on the rule 10b-5 issue, on the other hand, were not revealed by the decision. . . . However, since the definition of "fraud" does not appear to be more narrow under rule 10b-5 than it is under the mail and wire fraud provisions, it is logical to assume that the Justices were equally divided as to whether rule 10b-5 covers fraud that is perpetrated on a person, such as the *Journal*, who is neither an investor nor related to an investor in the securities to which the nonpublic information relates. The dissenting Justices may have believed that it would be stretching the concept of securities fraud too far to determine that rule 10b-5 encompasses situations in which the victim of the fraud is neither an investor nor an affiliate of an investor.

If this in fact was the basis of the disagreement, the Court should have no problem upholding the misappropriation theory under rule 10b-5 in the more typical misappropriation cases brought by the SEC that involve misuse of information obtained from employers or clients who are themselves investors or persons related to investors, such as tender offer bidders and their advisers.

* * *

Notes and Questions

1. The excerpt above mentions three other federal laws applicable to trading on inside information: Rule 14E-3 and the mail and wire fraud statutes. In addition, Section

57 Carpenter v. United States, 108 S. Ct. 316 (1987), *aff'g on securities fraud counts by an equally divided Court* 791 F.2d 1024 (2d Cir. 1986).

16(b) of the Securities Exchange Act requires directors, officers and owners of over 10 percent of a corporation's stock to give to the corporation any profit they make if they both buy and sell (or sell and buy) stock in the corporation within a six month period. In fact, Section 16(b), rather than 10(b), constituted Congress' originally intended weapon against trading on inside information. The notion was that taking the profit out of short swing transactions by defined insiders would avoid the problem of proving that a specific individual possessed material inside information when trading. The growing use of Rule 10B-5 against trading while in possession of inside information seems to have taken much of the wind out of this notion. For consideration of some other possible utility of Section 16(b) see Thel, *The Genius of Section 16: Regulating the Management of Publicly Held Companies*, 42 HASTINGS L.J. 391 (1991); Okamoto, *Rereading Section 16(b) of the Securities Exchange Act*, 27 GA. L. REV. 183 (1992).

2. Twice in the 1980s, Congress amended the Securities Exchange Act to add sanctions against parties engaged in trading based upon inside information. Section 21A creates a treble profit fine, while Section 20A allows limited recovery by contemporaneous traders (in other words, those who sold around the time the insider bought, or who bought around the time the insider sold). Neither of these two sections, however, defines when trading based upon inside information is illegal; rather they simply establish sanctions for such trading if it violates other provisions of the Securities Exchange Act—in other words, *if* the trading violates Rule 10B-5. Still, creation of these sanctions shows Congress must agree that at least some trading on inside information violates the Rule.

3. Given that the original thrust of Rule 10B-5 was not trading on undisclosed inside information, one might ask what was it. Both the language and history of the Rule show how it targets false and misleading statements. In fact, most Rule 10B-5 litigation involves alleged affirmative misrepresentations and half-truths. While the policy behind prohibiting such fraud and deceit (albeit, why through Federal action?) would seem unexceptional, some literature has debated arguable advantages to allowing corporations to make misleading statements despite possible impact on their stock prices. *See* Macey & Miller, *The Fraud on the Market Theory Revisited*, 77 VA. L. REV. 1001 (1991); Ayres, *Back to Basics: Regulating How Corporations Speak to the Market*, 77 VA. L. REV. 945 (1991). Of more practical interest is the question of when silence by a corporation can be misleading. For a somewhat dated discussion see Sheffey, *Securities Law Responsibilities of Issuers to Respond to Rumors and Other Publicity: Reexamination of a Continuing Problem*, 57 NOTRE DAME L. REV. 755 (1982). Still another issue in this area involves determining whether the misstated fact is "material"—in other words, important to a reasonable investor in making a buy or sell decision—so as to trigger liability. For a discussion see Brudney, *A Note on Materiality and Soft Information under the Federal Securities Laws*, 75 VA. L. REV. 723 (1989). Perhaps the most controversial issues in this area, however, do not involve the substance of the prohibition, but rather the availability of a class action remedy. For example, in order to avoid the requirement that each trader prove he or she heard and relied upon the allegedly false or misleading statement—which would make it impractical to have a class action—courts developed the so-called fraud on the market theory. This is simply the idea that false statements will impact share prices in a well developed market, thereby creating the basis for a presumption that traders indirectly relied on the misrepresentation. For a discussion see Macey & Miller, *Good Finance, Bad Economics: An Analysis of the Fraud-on-the-Market Theory*, 42 STAN. L. REV. 1059 (1990); Fischel, *Efficient Capital Markets, The Crash, and the Fraud on the Market Theory*, 74 CORNELL L. REV. 907 (1989). Also, paralleling some of the criticisms of derivative suits is the suggestion that attorneys use securities fraud class actions to extort settlement of meritless claims. *See* Alexander, *Do Merits Matter? A Study of Settlements in Securities Class Actions*, 43 STAN. L. REV. 497 (1991).

---

2. *Policy Critique*

Donald C. Langevoort, *Setting the Agenda for Legislative Reform: Some Fallacies, Anomalies, and Other Curiosities in the Prevailing Law of Insider Trading,* 39 ALA. L. REV. 399 (1988)*

INTRODUCTION

. . . Although the prevailing doctrinal structure is workable in a rough sense, it is neither satisfying nor coherent. Much of the difficulty derives from an unresolved conflict between the values of efficiency and equity. . . .

. . . [T]he restriction of insider trading seems largely emotional in its genesis, a political response to the demand for an appearance of equity in both the securities marketplace and society generally. It is hard to make the case that the typical investor is systematically better off, as far as his or her own particular trading opportunities are concerned, as a result of an insider trading prohibition. Yet, the political rhetoric of insider trading legislation and enforcement is largely directed to such investors (if not the public at large).[6] The resulting regulation thus seems to share the same ideological roots underlying other legal rules that purport to neutralize some of the excessive advantages of economic power, size, and status in order to satisfy those who feel unfairly disadvantaged by the absence of power, size, or status. . . .

* * *

6 Professional investors are far more likely to benefit from insider trading prohibition since they are "next in line" with respect to the opportunity to trade immediately upon disclosure. That group might well exercise some political pressure for insider trading regulation. . . . Yet, this fact seems unconvincing as a complete explanation for regulation. The public fascination with the recent insider trading scandals and the prompt political reaction thereto suggest that legislators sense the opportunity to gain in broader political sense from a regulatory response. . . .

I. Insider Trading as Fraud

The most benign of the doctrinal fallacies is the threshold determination that insider trading in the anonymous marketplace is actually fraudulent. Fraud is a concept, under section 10(b) at least, that includes traditional common-law elements of deception, scienter, reliance, and causal injury; it is narrower than the idea of constructive fraud, a phrase synonymous with breach of fiduciary duty.

When an insider (much less a tippee) executes a trade on a stock exchange or the over-the-counter market, he does so anonymously. The offer to trade carries with it no communicative content as to possession of nonpublic information or anything else. In what sense, then, can it be said that such trading has the capacity to *mislead* those who are trading contemporaneously, or otherwise cause detrimental reliance?

There is no convincing answer: insider trading may be many bad things, but it is unlikely that deception is one of them. The solution arrived at by the Securities and Exchange Commission ("SEC" or "Commission") in the *Cady, Roberts* case—that it is fraudulent because the insider breaches a duty to disclose the inside information before trading—is simply conclusory, begging the question of how the imposition of such a duty prevents deception. . . .

II. The Prohibition of Insider Trading Rests on the Law of Fiduciary Obligation

Having been forced to cast insider trading as a disclosure issue, the courts thereafter had to articulate the nature and basis of an affirmative duty of disclosure to those with whom the insider trades. Who is subject to the obligation? The first definitive answer came from the Supreme Court in the *Chiarella* and *Dirks* cases: such a disclosure obligation arises if (and presumably only if) the trader stands in a direct or indirect fiduciary relationship with those on the other side of the trade.

The Court found support for this limited rule in the common law. It has long been the case that an agent must affirmatively disclose all material information when transacting with his principal. But is this really a relevant concept when trading is in the anonymous marketplace? Functionally, the common-law approach was designed to avoid the detrimental reliance that might result from the trust actually placed in the agent by the principal. In such a face-to-face bargaining situation, self-serving conduct by the fiduciary may in fact be deceptive. Yet, with respect to open-market trading, as noted above, shareholders have no idea with whom they are trading; offers to purchase or sell carry no other communicative content.

At best, fiduciary status is a rough basis from which to conclude that, as a matter of fairness, insiders should not profit from information in their possession while the beneficial "owners" of the corporation are disadvantaged. But even given this thought—which does justify a restriction on trading by fiduciaries—is there any reason to believe the fiduciary classification ought to be the *exclusive* basis for imposing an insider trading restriction? The Court's inference that the common law offered only this one exception to a general rule of *caveat emptor* is a fallacy. In fact, the common law was well on is way in 1934 (or 1942, when rule 10b-5 was adopted) to imposing an affirmative disclosure obligation in any situation where societal precepts of honesty and fair dealing demanded it, and as Justice Blackmun noted in his *Chiarella* dissent, there is no reason to expect that Congress or the SEC would have intended the antifraud statute or rule to lag behind this development.

The Court's restrictive approach probably was not the result of a misreading of the common law, but rather the false assumption that such a limited rule would give the law clarity by providing due notice to those who trade in securities. The cost, however, is clear; a wedge now separates the intuitive sense of when instances of trading on the basis of material nonpublic information are abusive and the doctrinal framework used to decide specific cases involving such trading. . . .

The predictable response of the lower courts to this confinement was the adoption of a new theory of liability not formally foreclosed by the Court's reasoning. The so-called "misappropriation theory"—the theory that a person defrauds his employer or his employer's client when he profits from confidential information entrusted to him—was quickly accepted, at least in the Second Circuit. But this theory is awkward at best, essentially federalizing the law of corporate intellectual property and employee responsibility for securities law purposes without any real justification, except in terms of result—a means of permitting the SEC to reach what intuitively are abusive trading practices that were thought to be unreachable under the post-*Chiarella* fraud . . . theory.

III. The Sole Concern of the Law of Insider Trading and Tipping Is Avoiding Personal Benefit by the Insider

In the *Dirks* case, the Supreme Court—again in an effort to add greater clarity to the law, especially for the benefit of market professionals—refined the fiduciary principle for purposes of the "abstain or disclose" obligation by stating that the essential element of insider trading liability is the attempt by an insider-fiduciary to derive some personal benefit from information entrusted to him. Tipping liability could then be rationalized as a means of prohibiting insiders from being able to do indirectly (profit personally in some pecuniary, reputational, or gift-giving way from the conveyance of information to others) what they are precluded from doing directly (profit by trading). Tippee liability, in turn, would be limited to those situations in which the tippee had notice of the insider's self-serving behavior and could be seen as intentionally assisting it.

This refinement further separates doctrine from reality. The intuitive sense of why the friend of a company's chief executive officer should not trade on the basis of information imparted during a golf outing has little or nothing to do with the determination that the *officer* has somehow gained something from the conversation.[22] Yet, this is the strained thought process *Dirks* demands.

---

22 More to the point, it would seem, is the impression that the tippee profited solely because of his position of access to the information, unrelated to any exercise of skill, diligence, or expertise. A more difficult question arises if the trader obtains the information through blind luck rather than through either connections or trickery. . . . The intuitive answer seems to be that liability is not appropriate, perhaps as much as anything else, because true instances of simple luck may befall anyone, not simply those who know the right people.

The problem is well-illustrated by three related anomalies the personal benefit standard would create if strictly construed. One is the question whether the issuer itself can be liable for insider trading, as when it repurchases its securities in the open market while possessing material nonpublic information indicating that the prevailing market price of its securities is too low. Assuming the managers of the corporation who cause the repurchase have no significant ownership interest in the corporation, does the fact that they act solely in what they perceive to be the corporation's best interests (*i.e.*, that no personal benefit is being sought) preclude the imposition of liability? The answer should be "no" (and the law has traditionally been so understood), but *Dirks* easily can be read to the contrary.

A related anomaly involves communications to investment analysts. If an insider of a corporation conveys inside information to an investment analyst, who in the past has written favorably about the corporation, in order to reward the analyst and keep his favor with respect to future recommendations, it is hard to characterize the situation as anything but a classic "tip." Before *Dirks*, at least, this sort of scenario was clearly a basis for liability. Of course, a creative prosecutor or enforcement attorney today might be able to persuade the fact finder that the (or an) actual motivation behind the communication was an attempt by the executive-insider to promote his standing in the eyes of his superiors, thereby deriving a personal benefit. But suppose the insider was indeed simply doing what he thought was best for "the company." Do both tipper and tippee really avoid liability simply because no personal benefit was being pursued? The intuitive response is that they both should be held liable, but once again *Dirks* hints at the possibility of a different result.

* * *

A third potential anomaly in the law is the problem of remote tippees. If an insider tips a friend, who thereupon tips another person, is there liability for the remote tippee? So long as the remote tippee knows that the information has been obtained improperly, the answer should be "yes." But *Dirks* suggests (although the matter is by no means free of doubt) that tippee liability might end at the point where the insider ceases to obtain the anticipated personal benefit from the initial tip.

On reflection, the false logic in *Dirks* is the assumption that the tipper-tippee liability question can be viewed simply as a derivative form of the basic question of trading liability. It is much more accurate to say that what is wrong with tipping is it violates a fiduciary duty of impartiality—the duty not to discriminate unfairly among investors or classes of investors. A tip unjustifiably favors one shareholder over others, which alone provides the justification for holding both tipper and tippee liable for any resulting profits.

IV. An Anomaly: Authorized Insider Trading

The *Chiarella-Dirks* construct is based on the idea that insider trading liability is imposed because the insider (or derivatively, his tippee) has improperly used corporate property in order to gain a personal benefit. The misappropriation theory simply extends this idea to trading by a fiduciary in securities other than those of an employer or client. In this sense, it is possible to see the disclose or abstain theory articulated by the Court as simply a subset and refinement of the principle against misappropriation.

This brings us to one of the more perplexing anomalies in the law, the possibility that under either of these theories a corporation might be able to authorize trading on material nonpublic information by its insiders. If the essence of liability is the misuse of corporate information for personal gain, it would seem to follow that the board of directors of a corporation (or managers with delegated authority) could properly insulate all subordinates from liability—absent a showing of conflict of interest—by declaring that insider trading is not a breach of fiduciary duty, but rather part of executive compensation. Once again, however, this sort of privatization would effect a radical break with our intuitive notion of the correct solution.

* * *

Notes and Questions

1. Professor Langevoort could perhaps have added to his discussion several other doctrinal anomalies in the Supreme Court's approach to insider trading. As he explains, the Court in *Chiarella* rationalized the insider's obligation to disclose or abstain as based upon a fiduciary relationship between the two parties to the trade. Given that directors and officers have such a relationship with the stockholders of their corporation, this only explains the result when directors or officers purchase based upon inside information consisting of good news about the company. (This assumes they purchase from an existing shareholder rather than a "short seller," in other words, someone contracting to sell shares he or she does not yet own.) Suppose, however, knowing bad news, an insider sells to someone who is not yet a shareholder. This would seem to be a classic instance of an arms-length transaction, yet the Court in *Chiarella* stated that it would not follow its own logic to such a result. Also, in *Dirks*, the Court stated that a tippee could be liable for trading if he or she knew or "should have known" of the insider's breach in passing on the tip. "Should have known" sounds like the language of negligence; yet in *Ernst & Ernst v. Hockfelder*, 425 U.S. 185 (1976), the Supreme Court held that negligence would not support liability under Rule 10B-5. Finally, the Court's rationalization in *Dirks* of tippee liability appears to incorporate an aiding and abetting theory—the tippee is aiding the insider in his or her breach of duty. Recently, however, the Supreme Court rejected aiding and abetting liability under Rule 10B-5 (at least for private actions). *Central Bank of Denver, N.A. v. First Interstate Bank of Denver*, 114 S. Ct. 1439 (1994).

2. If neither the explicit language of Rule 10B-5 nor a coherent doctrinal logic explain the treatment of insider trading under the Rule, then where does the prohibition come from? There are several possibilities. Since Rule 10B-5 refers to fraud, a common law term, perhaps the prohibition comes from the common law. Alternately, perhaps there is something to indicate the prohibition is what Congress had in mind for

Section 10(b). Professor Langevoort seems to find the rationale in the general public's notions of fairness. Finally, one might consider the economic impact of the practice. The following two article excerpts explore these possibilities.

Joel Seligman, *The Reformulation of Federal Securities Law Concerning Nonpublic Information*, 73 Geo. L.J. 1083 (1985)*

* * *

Congress should end this confusion [about the scope of the prohibition of insider trading] and reimpose the "parity of information" approach to fraud liability under federal securities law. This standard was a clearer statement of law, a more effective deterrent on trading while in possession of nonpublic information, and easier to enforce than the duty standard established in *Chiarella* and *Dirks*. . . .

I. BACKGROUND

The insistence in *Chiarella* and *Dirks* that liability for trading on the basis of material nonpublic information attaches only when the trader is subject to a fiduciary or similar duty echoes common law standards applicable to securities traders. It is useful therefore, to begin this analysis by understanding the common law standard and why the federal securities laws have generally supplanted it.

A. THE COMMON LAW

Underlying the common law standard applicable to trading while in possession of nonpublic material information was the notion of caveat emptor. . . . Perhaps the most often cited explanations of why the common law enforced the standard, "Let the buyer beware," are those associated with the 1817 United States Supreme Court opinion *Laidlaw v. Organ*.[46] In *Laidlaw*, the court held that a vendor of tobacco had no duty to inform his vendee of his nonpublic knowledge that a treaty of peace had been signed at Ghent by the American and British commissioners, an extrinsic circumstance likely to affect the price of tobacco. Chief Justice Marshall stated in the key sentence of his six sentence opinion that "[i]t would be difficult to circumscribe the contrary doctrine within proper limits, where the means of intelligence are equally accessible to both parties."

Contemporary commentators have focused on the premise of Chief Justice Marshall's opinion, that "the means of intelligence are equally accessible to both parties," and analyzed it in terms of economic theory. Information concerning future material changes in the supply and demand of goods will affect the allocation of resources. The

---

* Reprinted with permission.

46 15 U.S. (2 Wheat) 178 (1817). . . .

Treaty of Ghent, for example, could be expected to lead to an increase in the demand for American tobacco. This, in turn, initially would increase the price of tobacco, and ultimately because of higher price, likely would lead to increased production. . . . Thus, society has an interest in the accurate reception of market signals regarding future levels of supply and demand at the earliest possible moment. If signals are delayed or not accurately received, tobacco might be priced too low relative to other goods and services, leading to its underproduction and a lower total value received for the production of all goods and services.

Consistent with the economic theory of allocational efficiency, *Laidlaw* encouraged traders to seek out new information about future supply and demand levels. By rewarding those who first learn of information concerning future supply and demand levels, Laidlaw created a financial incentive for traders to speed information concerning future supply and demand level to the marketplace. The opposite legal result, imposing liability on those who trade while in possession of material nonpublic information concerning market conditions, would discourage traders and analysts from expending resources on search costs, slow the acquisition of material information concerning changed market conditions, and lead to an inferior allocation of resources.[49]

Modern economic theory thus provides an intriguing rationalization of the result in *Laidlaw*. But this rationalization does not support the most important application of the *Laidlaw* doctrine in corporate and securities law, that is, application to corporate officers and directors who possess material "inside" information. In this instance, the corporate officers or directors possess information that is not "equally accessible to both parties." The information, typically about such matters as mineral discoveries, new products or product research, or payment of dividends, concerns decisions that would be produced inside the corporation in any event. The common law hardly needed to create an incentive for insiders to undergo search costs to inspire the insiders to learn such data.

The "majority" common law rule concerning insider trading ignored economic effects. Instead, it held that a corporate executive or director could trade securities without informing the shareholder with whom he traded of material nonpublic information obtained while inside the corporation because the corporate insider was not a "fiduciary" or "trustee" of the shareholder. The common law focus on whether a fiduciary or similar relationship existed, as a practical matter, ended thoughtful judicial consideration of the purpose of the rule. . . .

To the extent that courts or subsequent commentators have defended the majority rule, three types of justifications have been advanced. First, partially drawing on

49 The common law recognized important exceptions to the *Laidlaw* doctrine. The *Laidlaw* opinion itself made clear that it would not tolerate deliberate concealment of material nonpublic information[.] . . . A second exception, early recognized at common law, prohibited trading on the basis of wrongfully acquired nonpublic information. . . . This exception is consistent with contemporary economic theory. If traders could exploit material nonpublic information by improperly obtaining it, rather than searching for it, they will reduce their investment in information production. Ultimately, less information will be produced and a less desirable allocation of resources will occur than if traders only had an incentive to search legitimately for new information about material changes in market conditions. . . .

dicta in cases such as *Goodwin v. Agassiz,*[52] a few commentators, notably Manne,[53] and more recently Carlton and Fischel,[54] have argued that profits from insider trading are appropriate compensation for corporate insiders. The initial difficulty with this argument is understanding why so unpredictable a form of compensation is necessary in wage markets that operate on competitive principles. . . .

* * *

. . . A major problem with legitimizing insider trading to compensate corporate insiders (however defined) is that of moral hazard. Corporate insiders would be able to profit just as much from adverse corporate events as from good news. Their personal interests would radically depart from the interest of the shareholders whom, in theory, they serve. Where shareholders seek higher stock prices, the insider's interest would be in a volatile stock price. Insiders would have a personal incentive to delay the publication of news, whether good or bad. Managers might also seek to manipulate corporate press releases or oral communications with the press in order to accentuate stock price volatility. Alteratively, managers might adopt riskier new business ventures than they otherwise would have, thinking that whether the new project succeeds or fails is irrelevant as long as they can trade stock before the news of the outcome of the venture is made public.

* * *

A second justification for insider trading, again most elaborately developed by Manne, is that insider trading will smooth the price changes that occur after the nonpublic information is disclosed to the public. To illustrate, one can hypothesize a stock trading at $28 when managers first learn that a key supplier will charge a higher rate, causing a dramatic decline in corporate earnings. The reduction in earnings will eventually cause a new stock price of $11. If insider trading is forbidden, it may be assumed (all other things being equal) that the stock's price would continue to trade at approximately $28 from the time the managers learned the adverse news until it was publicly announced. Then the price abruptly would plummet to $11. In contrast, if insiders are allowed to sell their stock when they first learn of the adverse news, Manne conjectured that the stock's price would begin falling before the news is announced to the public. New purchasers who buy shares between the time that the adverse news is learned by the firm's managers and the public announcement of that news will suffer a smaller loss than if they had purchased at the higher price that would have occurred if insider trading were strictly prohibited.

52 283 Mass. 358, 186 N.E. 659 (1933). . . .

53 H. MANNE, INSIDER TRADING AND THE STOCK MARKETS (1966); Manne, *Insider Trading and the Law Professors*, 23 VAND. L. REV. 547 (1970).

54 Carlton & Fischel, *The Regulation of Insider Trading*, 35 STAN. L. REV. 857 (1983).

The simple answer to this assertion is that available empirical evidence has consistently documented that insider trading does not have a significant impact on market prices. . . .

* * *

The third justification for the "majority" common law rule permitting corporate insiders to trade without disclosing material nonpublic information appears to have been the most important to common law judges in the pre-1934 period. Plaintiffs were incapable of identifying any harm to the corporation in which they had bought or sold shares caused by the insiders' nondisclosure of material information. . . .

* * *

There are several reasons to be skeptical about this line of reasoning. Inside information, particularly about such matters as a new corporate product or a mineral discovery, can be viewed as corporate business property. The firm has devoted resources to develop the property. Just as a corporate insider is expected to be compensated under a contract and may not "take" corporate property or corporate opportunities, it can be argued by analogy that the insider is not entitled to "take" the benefits of insider information. Otherwise, the insider is violating an agent's duty not to profit secretly in the use of the principal's property and is receiving "unjust enrichment."

In addition, it can be argued that insider trading deprives a blameless shareholder or potential shareholder of the profits he or she otherwise would have enjoyed. For example, suppose an insider is aware of a mineral discovery that will double the firm's stock price from $10 per share to $20 per share. If the insider buys stock at $10 per share from the existing stockholder *A*, the insider has not harmed stockholder *A*. Stockholder *A* was willing to sell at $10 per share in any event. But potential stockholder *B*, who would have bought stockholder *A's* shares at $10 per share, has been harmed. The insider's purchase temporarily pushed the price of the stock above $10 per share. At the least, potential stockholder *B* must pay a higher price for other shares than the shares otherwise would have commanded. At the most, potential stockholder *B* may find the new price too high and may not purchase at all, thereby losing the profit he or she otherwise would have enjoyed as the stock rose from $10 to $20 per share.[79]

The justifications of the "majority" rule did not persuade a significant number of state courts in the pre-1934 period. A small number of jurisdictions instead adopted the "minority" rule which obligated directors or officers to make full disclosure of material nonpublic information before trading with uninformed shareholders or potential shareholders. The reasoning of the "minority" rule cases was no more sophisticated than the reasoning of the "majority" rule cases. . . .

---

79 The most elaborate articulation of this argument appears in Wang, [*Trading on Material Nonpublic Information on Impersonal Stock Markets: Who is Harmed, and Who Can Sue under SEC Rule 10b-5?*, 54 S. CALIF. L. REV. 1217 (1981)]. . . .

There also was an intermediate rule, popularly known as the "special facts" doctrine, which originated in the 1909 United States Supreme Court decision, *Strong v. Repide*.[84] *Strong* emphasized as a special fact the concealment of identity by the defendant who purchased shares from plaintiff employing an agent and a third person's check. The Court in *Strong* also seemed troubled by the fact that the defendant, who was a director, three-fourths owner and chief negotiator for the Philippines Sugar Estates Development Company, had unique control over information concerning whether or not a sale of lands would be made to the Government. While the opinion in *Strong* discussed at some length the "special facts" of that case, it did not clearly articulate a theory. For example, if a dispositive "special fact" in *Strong* was the defendant's possession of material inside information about the land negotiations, then virtually all common law cases concerning insider trading could identify analogous informational advantages possessed by the insiders. . . .

* * *

The emergence of the "minority rule" and "special facts" doctrines loomed larger in the law review literature and the casebooks than it did in the real world. Neither doctrine could be successfully pleaded in the pre-1934 period unless the plaintiff was in privity with the defendant. There was no cause of action for transactions effected through "impersonal" stock markets. . . .

In sum, the Supreme Court's assertion in *Chiarella* that a person can only be liable for trading on the basis of material nonpublic information when he or she is subject to a fiduciary or similar duty is an unpredictable standard, to the extent that the Court meant to refer to state corporate law judicial standards. The "majority" state law rule denied liability even when corporate insiders traded on the basis of corporate nonpublic information. The "minority" and "special facts" doctrines, at least in some instances, imposed liability on corporate insiders. Neither doctrine, however, extended liability to the panoply of people who can be liable according to footnote fourteen of the *Dirks* decision. The Court did not specify which state corporate law judicial doctrine it intended. Instead, in the *Chiarella* opinion, the Court relied on section 551 of the Restatement Second of Torts for the statement that a duty of disclosure is required when there exists "a fiduciary or other similar relation of trust and confidence. . . ."

This was an odd choice of authority. The comment to section 551 explicitly states that "it is not within the scope of this restatement to state the rules that determine the duty of disclosure under the law of business associations. . . ."

B. FEDERAL SECURITIES LAW

* * *

A basic purpose of the 1933 and 1934 securities acts, and relevant amendments, was to prevent corporate insiders, market professionals, and persons participating in takeover transactions from trading while in possession of material nonpublic infor-

84 213 U.S. 419 (1909).

mation. Congress has consistently prohibited trading while in possession of material nonpublic information regardless of whether the prohibited conduct would have been actionable under state common law. In this sense, a limitation of liability under section 10(b) to persons in violation of a fiduciary or similar duty is an exception to the general pattern of the federal securities laws.

The enactment of the corporate disclosure and insider trading provisions of the 1933 and 1934 securities acts occurred after three different congressional hearings had demonstrated that material information often was omitted when new or already issued securities were traded. The primary response of Congress was the enactment of a mandatory disclosure system. Both in the issuance of new securities to the public and in periodic reporting, Congress specified in great detail the type of data that must be disclosed. . . .

In addition to the mandatory periodic disclosure system, several other provisions of the 1934 Act prohibited trading while in possession of material nonpublic information. First, section 16(b) explicitly prohibited any director, officer or beneficial owner of more than ten percent of any class of any equity security from realizing any profit from any purchase and sale or sale and purchase of any equity security of an issuer within a period of less than six months. . . . The legislative history emphasized the need to renew investors confidence in the exchange markets by deterring profitable short swing trading by insiders or large stockholders presumed to have access to inside information.

* * *

Third, section 11(b) of the 1934 Act empowered the SEC to limit dealings by an exchange specialist "so far as practicable to those reasonably necessary to permit him to maintain a fair and orderly market. . . ." The specialist is a securities exchange member who makes a market in an assigned list of securities. Inevitably he has access to two types of material nonpublic information. His physical presence on the exchange floor and knowledge of the broker-dealer firm affiliations of floor brokers often will permit him to predict short-term price trends. He also has sole possession of the "specialist's book" in which are recorded limit orders, or orders to be executed, usually at prices somewhat above or somewhat below the current market price. Since the specialist may trade for his own account, these informational advantages periodically have made specialist "dealing" controversial. Rather than prohibit specialists from dealing while they possess material nonpublic information, Congress in 1934 empowered the SEC to limit specialist dealing to those trades necessary to maintain fair and orderly markets. Under the current regime, specialists should only trade to maintain the "orderliness" (that is, without wide or abrupt price swings), "continuity" (with minimum price variations between successive trades), or "liquidity and depth" (ability to immediately handle large orders without significant price variations) of a market in a stock. While trades for these purposes are required of a specialist and do coincide with their possession of material nonpublic information, trades made purely to exploit material nonpublic information are not permissible.

* * *

In contrast, section 10(b) of the Securities Exchange Act was a residual provision, meant to address forms of fraud not elsewhere specifically covered in the 1933 or 1934 Acts, with little legislative history to guide courts. . . .

II. THE INTEGRITY OF THE MARKET THEORY

The primary policy reason for proscribing trading while in possession of material nonpublic information is to make investors confident that they can trade securities without being subject to informational disadvantages. The goal is to guarantee the integrity of the market. This integrity of the market theory is the key analytical distinction between state and federal securities fraud laws. Where state law focuses on the direct relationship between specific buyers and sellers of securities, federal law also addresses the general impact an individual securities fraud may have on overall investor confidence.

The basis of the integrity of the market policy is both historical and theoretical. In recommending passage of the 1933 securities bill, Roosevelt emphasized that by putting "the burden of telling the whole truth on the seller" the proposed act "should give impetus to honest dealing in securities and thereby bring back public confidence." At the time President Roosevelt wrote these words, the idea of increasing public confidence had a clear significance. New corporate securities which had equalled $6.5 billion in 1927, $6.9 billion in 1928, and $9.4 billion in 1929, had fallen to $644 million in 1932 (and would equal $380 million in 1933). President Roosevelt anticipated that full disclosure of material investment information about new issues would reduce investors' concerns that they could be defrauded or treated unfairly and would help increase sales of corporate securities.[161]

* * *

More recently, the total number of individual owners of corporate stock and mutual funds declined from 30.85 million investors in 1970 to 25.77 million investors in 1975, the only period between 1952 and 1983 in which there was a reduction in the number of investors. . . . There were several causes of the small investors' flight including discouragement after losses in the 1969-1970 market break, high debt security interest rates, and the "back-office" crisis that led to the bankruptcy or merger of several brokerage houses. However, the widely held belief that institutional investors fre-

---

161 New corporate securities issues did increase to over $2.3 billion in 1935 and over $4.6 billion in 1936. . . .

The belief that insider trading would reduce public confidence in the securities markets also was held by a committee of the American Bar Association, which in 1941 recommended the retention of § 16(b) of the 1934 Act because, "[a] persistent cause of lack of public confidence in the exchanges has been the popular impression that they can be traded in profitably only by persons specially informed." . . .

quently received "inside information" that small investors did not was a prominent reason given by investors for their departure from the market.[167]

The assumption that investors will be more willing to purchase securities when compulsory disclosure of material information reduces the incidence of fraud, increases the reliability of estimates of firm value, or reduces the volatility of securities price swings embodies the familiar financial theory of risk aversion. Other things being equal, investors will choose investments with the least risk. To persuade investors to select investments with greater risk, investment sellers must offer a higher expected rate of return.[168] In this sense, increasing investor confidence in the securities markets may have several important economic consequences. By reducing the perceived risk of corporate securities, compulsory disclosure would tend to reduce the risk premiums that issuers selling new securities would have to pay, thus increasing the funds available for economic growth. Reduction of investors' concerns that securities fraud waves periodically may drive down securities price levels will tend to increase propensities to save. And reduction in the volatility of market price swings (caused by investor ignorance of material data) will tend to increase allocative efficiency.

Ironically, two critics of the SEC mandatory disclosure requirements have provided evidentiary support for the theory that compulsory corporate disclosure of material investment information increases public confidence in the securities markets. Stigler

---

167 . . . .

Several commentators believe that this circumstantial evidence does not prove that investors lost confidence in the stock market because of insider trading. . . . Other commentators have observed that it is impossible to measure the extent of the loss of investor confidence in the market that occurs when public investors believe insider trading occurs. . . . The burden should be on those opposed to a "disclose or abstain" rule to demonstrate that investor belief in widespread insider trading does not lead to a reduction in the aggregate level of stock investment.

This is not an easy burden to carry. For example, between mid-1981 and mid-1983, the number of individual Americans who directly owned shares of corporate stock or stock mutual funds increased from 32.26 million to 42.36 million. . . . During that period, the SEC significantly increased the number of insider trading cases it brought. Does this demonstrate that investors no longer would be dissuaded from stock purchasing because of the existence of insider trading? It does not. The issue is what number of investors (or level of aggregate investment) would have obtained in a market absent any legal restrictions on insider trading compared to the current market with imperfect restrictions. Nor do the total number of investors increase or decrease purely because of insider trading restrictions. It can be argued, for example, that the number of investors rose in the 1981-1983 period primarily because of a rising stock market and changes in the tax laws that encourage the formation of Individual Retirement Accounts. The increases in SEC enforcement actions probably sent contradictory messages to the marketplace. On the one hand they signified a likely increase in the incidence of insider trading; on the other, they signified an increase in SEC enforcement efforts (which might in the future reduce the incidence of insider trading).

168 . . . .

. . . Brudney has explained:

A rational buyer (or seller) in a market, who knows that the person with whom he is dealing has material information about the value of the product being exchanged which he could not lawfully acquire, will either refrain from dealing with that transactor or demand a risk premium. If the market is thought to be systematically populated with such transactors some investors will refrain from dealing altogether, and others will incur costs to avoid dealing with such transactors or corruptly to overcome their unerodable information advantages. None of those responses is socially useful. All raise the cost of capital.

. . . .

reported that the variance of price ratios was "much higher" in the 1923-1928 period than in the years 1949-1955. Similarly, Jarrell found that post-SEC new issues had lower variances in return relative to the variance of market returns than pre-SEC new issues. Jarrell also conducted a study of corporate bond default rates and found that default risks and default risk premiums (measured by the yield difference between AAA corporate bonds and risk-free government bonds) declined after the SEC began enforcement of its compulsory disclosure requirements.

Both Stigler and Jarrell argued that post-SEC new issues were less risky than pre-SEC new issues because the Commission's administration of the mandatory disclosure system tended to exclude risky firms. A more plausible explanation of the reduced price variances was that investors were better able to predict firm earnings because the SEC mandatory disclosure system increased the accuracy and completeness of available investment data. Logically, compulsory full disclosure of material investment information should reduce price variances by making it more difficult for issuers to create misleading impressions about their expected earnings. Similarly, a prohibition on trading while in possession of material nonpublic information should encourage full disclosure of material information and maintain investor confidence.

The advantages of encouraging full disclosure to maintain investor confidence are most obvious when one focuses on insider possession of material information. If insiders are forbidden to trade until disclosure occurs there will be no financial incentive to delay disclosure of material information. The insiders will realize, if the law is effectively enforced, that either buying or selling shares while in possession of material nonpublic information about their firms will be punished.

Faster dissemination of material information should improve the market's allocative efficiency. Information on firms with promising probable future earnings will cause the prices of these securities to rise; the market price of securities of firms whose earnings prospects are less promising will decline. In this fashion, society allocates its resources towards investments promising the greatest return and away from less promising firms. Ideally, resource allocation will achieve "Pareto optimality" in which no reallocation of resources could be achieved that would make a single individual better off without harming another individual. Assuming this optimal state is not realizable, it still is preferable to allocate resources to achieve the highest possible level of productivity. By helping to allocate resources to the most productive uses, prompt disclosure of material information contributes to this economic objective.

* * *

Frank H. Easterbrook, *Insider Trading, Secret Agents, Evidentiary Privileges, and the Production of Information,* 11 Sup. Ct. Rev. 309 (1981)*

* * *

C. Fairness as the Source of the Obligation to Disclose

If notions of "duties" do not supply a coherent way to discuss the obligation to disclose, what about notions of fairness? . . .

If arguments about fairness are to be more than discussion stoppers, they must have some content. . . . Is it unfair for a geologist, after studying the attributes of farmland, to buy the land without revealing that the land likely covers rich mineral deposits? If the answer is yes, then fairness means that no one may appropriate the value of information he has created. . . .

I suspect that few people who invoke arguments based on fairness have in mind any particular content for the term. . . . It should be possible, though, to supply a meaning.

1. *Fairness as identical returns.* . . . Suppose there are ten shares of Target Corp. They trade freely for $10. Chiarella knows that a tender offer will be made the next day at $15. He buys one share at $10 and sells the next day for a profit. Nine of the ten original shareholders obtain the $5 gain; the one who sold to Chiarella does not. The difference might be called unfair.

This proposed definition is unsatisfactory. Shareholder 1, who sold to Chiarella, might well have sold no matter what Chiarella did. There is no reason to think that Chiarella's "buy" order, placed through a broker, caused additional investors to sell. If Chiarella's buying did not cause shareholders to part with their shares, then it is not responsible for the difference in returns obtained by the ten shareholders.

* * *

But suppose this is wrong, and insider trading causes some investors to sell in advance of the price rise. Insider trading then reduces the likelihood that an active trader will obtain the highest possible price. If there is a chance that they will be shortchanged as a result of insiders' purchases, shareholders will respond by bidding less for the stock in the first place. The lower price compensates them *ex ante* for the risk. Because many sophisticated buyers are acquainted with the approximate frequency of insiders' purchases, the discount will accurately reflect the odds. If the discount accurately reflects the odds, then it is hard to see any unfairness in the process. (Because all traders, at any given time, deal at the same price, the self-protective moves of sophisticated traders protect the unsophisticated as well.) The stockholders who lose out in one round of insider trading are compensated by the increased gains they obtain if their shares (purchased at a small discount) are not scooped up by insiders and thus appreciate more in other cases.

* * *

3. *Fairness as the absence of wealth transfers.* Insiders who trade obtain gains that otherwise would have gone to the shareholders. . . .

This approach begs the question whether insider trading is a good method of compensating people for productive activity. Sometimes, as in *Chiarella*, the entire value-increasing enterprise would disappear if people (there, the acquiring firms and their agents) were barred from acquiring the stock for less than it would be worth under new ownership. Similarly, there would have been no discoveries of ore in Timmons, Ontario, by the Texas Gulf Sulfur Corp. unless the discoverer were allowed to use its hard-won information to appropriate much of the value of the deposits.

The view that appropriation of gains is unfair may seem more compelling as applied to employees of the firm in whose stock they trade. These traders are on salary; why is not the stated salary sufficient compensation? . . .

* * *

4. *Fairness as equality of information.* The last concept of fairness I consider here is that it is unfair for one person to trade with another unless the two are equally knowledgeable about the subject of the deal. In this view, not only insider trading but also Texas Gulf Sulfur's acquisition of land is unfair. Although this view of fairness seems astonishingly broad, the "equal information" position has its share of adherents.

Justice Blackmun was not among them, and for good reason. One cannot resolve the optimal use-optimal production problem by wishing it would go away. If information must be equalized, there will be precious little to go around. Indeed, the fact that some people can reap rewards by creating and using information provides a great benefit to the ignorant. The informed traders will buy and sell stock until its price is appropriate in light of its risk. . . . The informed traders thus protect the uninformed. Because the price is set by the knowledgeable, it is quite safe to buy stock in ignorance. It would be a colossal waste if the information, so conveniently and cheaply embedded in prices, had to be extracted and presented to everyone who executed a trade on the market.

Justice Blackmun may have intended, however, to argue that trading becomes unfair if one person lacks *access* to information known to another. Victor Brudney has developed the equality of access position with considerable skill.[93]. . . People do not have or lack "access" in some absolute sense. There are, instead, different costs of obtaining information. An outsider's costs are high; he might have to purchase the information from the firm. Managers have lower costs (the amount of salary foregone); brokers have relatively low costs (the value of the time they spent investigating); Sherlock Holmes also may be able to infer extraordinary facts from ordinary occurrences at low cost. The different costs of access are simply a function of the division of labor. A manager (or a physician) always knows more than a shareholder (or patient) in some

93 Brudney, [*Insiders, Outsiders, and Informational Advantages Under the Federal Securities Laws*, 93 HARV. L. REV. 322 (1979).]. . .

respects, but unless there is something unethical about the division of labor, the difference is not unfair.

D. The Real Concerns About Insider Trading

The fairness arguments get us nowhere, and duty arguments must specify a source of the duties. I turn now to some considerations that deal more explicitly with the optimal use-optimal production problem.

1. *Business property.* A thief may not lawfully use stolen information. Disclosure of the information would reduce its value to the rightful owner, and trading on the information would do likewise if it increased the price of the securities and led the market to infer the truth. This is the basis of much trade secret law. . . .

The business property rationale for restrictions on insider trading carries obvious limits. It applies only when secrecy is necessary to preserve the value of information to the firm that created the knowledge. . . .

* * *

2. *Perverse incentives.*

* * *

Michael Dooley asked the right question: If insider trading is undesirable, why do not firms voluntarily curtail the practice?[102] . . . If trading leads to costs from riskier projects and precautions against disclosure of information, the shareholders would willingly ban the practice, obtain the savings, and pay part of the gains to managers to obtain their cooperation. Yet almost no firms attempted to curtail insider trading before the SEC's *Cady, Roberts* decision in 1961.

One possible explanation of the firms' failure to do away with insiders' trading on material information—assuming that would be beneficial—is that they lack adequate enforcement devices. One way to abolish the practice is to ban shareholding by insiders. This works quite well for institutions such as law firms, which avoid trading on clients' information by abstaining; it would be counterproductive for the firms themselves, though, for shareholding helps to induce managers to run the firm in the interest of shareholders. If managers and insiders own shares, it may be exceptionally difficult to separate proper trades from the improper ones that use material inside information. Managers might agree, *ex ante*, that they would forego improper trading; but when the opportunity presented itself they could trade anyway, knowing that they probably would avoid detection.

When most incidents of an undesirable practice escape detection, the only way to deter that practice is to impose very large penalties when the practice is detected. Such penalties generally must be imposed by public prosecution. The size of the optimal penalty could exceed the wealth of the trader; in that case, only jail would be an adequate response. . . . Finally, there may be economies of scale in public enforcement,

102 Dooley, [*Enforcement of Insider Trading Restrictions*, 66 Va. L. Rev. 1 (1980)]. . . .

because enforcers (including the stock markets) may find it possible to program their computers to monitor unusual trading as well as to perform more mundane functions.[107]

These considerations offer support for prohibition of insider trading under some circumstances. Surely the prohibition is desirable when it protects business property. The prohibition probably is desirable in general, because it allows public enforcement to replace inefficient private enforcement. But the conclusion is uneasy, because it depends on conjectures about the magnitude of the costs of insider trading and its prohibition. . . .

3. *Trading and stock prices*. I have addressed only briefly the point, frequently made by those who see little wrong in insider trading, that such trading causes prices to move toward the accurate one for the stock. Trading seems to give shareholders the best of all worlds, solving the tension between optimal use and optimal production of knowledge. Their firms can maintain business secrets, thus fully exploiting the value of information, while insider trading causes stock prices to move to the level they will reach once the news is revealed.

Unfortunately, the tension will not yield so easily. Why does insider trading cause prices to change? An increase in the insiders' demand for stock will not do the trick. The stock of any one firm is only a minuscule portion of the total supply of investment opportunities. People invest in stocks because they anticipate return. They will shift funds around in order to equalize the expected (and risk-adjusted) return from each part of their portfolios. The simple fact that many people start to buy AT&T stock should not affect its price; an equal number of shares are bought and sold. People who have high hopes for a firm's future buy its stock from those who are relatively pessimistic. This process damps out any substantial differences in the expectations of shareholders, who then fall into two classes: active traders who have homogenous expectations, and passive holders who take the price set by the active traders and have no independent expectations about the firm. The upshot is that "stock of firm X" has a highly elastic supply. People can buy arbitrarily large amounts at the going price.

This might seem inconsistent with the observation that, to obtain a lot of stock, people often must pay a premium price. It is not. Purchases often convey information to the market about the prospects of the firms. If the information indicates that the firm's prospects are better than those previously perceived, the price of the shares rises. Large purchases give the market a good deal of information. Traders find out or infer why one person is buying so much, and the new knowledge causes prices to adjust. For this reason, large transactions for technical, portfolio-adjustment reasons should have no effect on price, while smaller purchases based on new information should have an effect, even a dramatic one. This seems to be the pattern in the market.

The insider's trading thus may lead to price adjustments, but only to the extent the insider's secret has leaked to the market or been inferred by traders. . . .

* * *

---

[107] Chiarella was caught because the New York Stock Exchange's computer signalled unusual trading. . . .

Notes and Questions

1. As both Professors Seligman and Easterbrook discuss, the question of when silence equals fraud arises in many contexts beyond stock trading. For a classic discussion of the general common law rules regarding silence and fraud see Keeton, *Fraud—Concealment and Non-Disclosure*, 15 TEX. L. REV. 1 (1936). As Professors Langevoort and Seligman point out, the Supreme Court in the insider trading area seems to be following a common law based rationale—the duty to disclose comes from the fiduciary relationship between the parties to the trade—but ignoring the common law's specific results in the insider trading area. Of course, if all the Rule meant to do was to codify and federalize the common law, one might ask what was the point.

2. Professor Seligman argues that a basic purpose of the securities acts was to prevent trading on inside information and that the acts in large part accomplish this by mandating extensive disclosure by issuers of securities. Specifically, the 1933 Act requires a company seeking to sell its stock, bonds or other securities to the public to register the offering first with the Securities Exchange Commission. Such registration requires the production of documents containing detailed disclosure about the company. The 1934 Act, in turn, requires corporations with publicly traded stock to file periodic (annual and quarterly) reports with the Securities Exchange Commission. These reports continually update the publicly available information about the corporation. Such disclosure may serve to lessen the informational advantages of insiders over other traders. Still, was that their primary purpose? If not, what purpose, if any, does such mandatory disclosure serve? For a consideration of the justifications for mandatory disclosure see Easterbrook & Fischel, *Mandatory Disclosure and the Protection of Investors*, 70 VA. L. REV. 669 (1984); Coffee, *Market Failure and the Economic Case for a Mandatory Disclosure System*, 70 VA. L. REV. 717 (1984).

3. Professors Seligman and Easterbrook both explore what, if any, specific shareholders are hurt by insider trading. Notice that this question impacts not only the broader policy question of whether to prohibit the practice, but also the narrower legal question of who might be able to demonstrate damages in order to bring a private cause of action (at least in the absence of the express right of action found in Section 20A). Both professors generally reject the obvious answer—the shareholder who traded with the insider. Why? Instead, Professor Seligman notes the harm to the shareholders who bought after the insider bought and pay more than they would have, or who sell after the insider sold and receive less than they would have; or worse, who, because of the price move, decided not to buy or not to sell. (Did you see the internal inconsistency here in Professor Seligman's article?) Interestingly enough, these are the parties for whom current law recognizes no cause of action for insider trading; indeed, the Supreme Court has held that parties who do *not* buy or sell lack standing to sue for violation of Rule 10B-5 even in the context of affirmative misrepresentations. *Blue Chip Stamps v. Manor Drug Stores*, 421 U.S. 723 (1975).

4. Professor, now Dean, Manne started the debate about the economic impacts of insider trading in the work cited by Professor Seligman. One of his arguments is that such trading moves the stock price toward a level which reflects the inside information, thus improving stock market efficiency. Professor Easterbrook argues that this will not occur unless other traders guess that insiders are trading based upon inside information. Why does the change in demand caused by the insiders' trades not itself move the price? For a different view on this question see Stout, *Are Takeover Premiums Really Premiums? Market Price, Fair Value, and Corporate Law*, an excerpt from which is reprinted in Chapter VI.

5. Professor Seligman's argument for prohibiting trading on inside information comes down largely to a claim that such trading will make it more difficult for firms to raise capital because it discourages investors. Professor Easterbrook seems to reinforce this concern when he explains how sophisticated traders will discount the price they pay for stock to take into account the risk of lost profits to insiders. On the other hand, why is this a government concern? Why can corporations, who do not want to have their stock discounted in this manner, not prohibit their executives from insider trading and then advertise this fact to the public? Is there what economists refer to as a "lemons problem" here? In other words, purchasers of a product who cannot easily distinguish good from defective items will discount all purchases to reflect the risk of defects—thereby punishing producers of the good products who cannot provide the public with a *credible* assurance of their better quality. Note Professor Easterbrook's explanation as to why firms banning insider trading may not be able to provide such a credible assurance to investors.

On the other hand, this rationale suggests a line of empirical inquiry: Is there presently significant trading on inside information and, if so, has this dried up investment? The following article looks into this question.

---

3. *Reality Check: The Extent of Trading on Inside Information*

H. Nejat Seyhun, *The Effectiveness of the Insider-Trading Sanctions*, 35 J.L. & Econ. 149 (1992)*

* * *

I. INTRODUCTION

This study empirically examines the effects of increases in the level and enforcement of insider-trading regulations in the 1980s on corporate insiders. . . .

---

* * *

. . . During the 1980s, the SEC increased its enforcement effort against insiders by more than sixfold. Moreover, the SEC's efforts resulted in sweeping securities legislations that increase criminal fines from $10,000 to $1 million and jail sentences from five years to ten years. The new laws also enable recovery of treble damages, create a bounty program for informants, hold top management legally responsible for insider trading by any of the firm's employees, and create a right of action for traders who lose to insiders.

* * *

III. EFFECTS OF INSIDER-TRADING REGULATIONS

* * *

This study examines the effects of changes in insider-trading regulations by analyzing changes in (i) overall volume and profitability of insider trading, (ii) trading activity of top executives, and (iii) block trading by all insiders. In addition, insider-trading activity is examined around the time of the *Chiarella* decision and when ITSA [(the Insider Trading Sanctions Act)] and ITSFEA [(the Insider Trading and Securities Fraud Enforcement Act)] became law to determine if changes in regulations produce a temporary effect.

While Congress has been reluctant to explicitly define illegal insider trading, case law has, in effect, defined the insider trading that will result in penalties. Michael Dooley reports that 80 percent of all insider-trading cases brought by the SEC are associated with trading immediately before corporate takeovers or earnings announcements. Consequently, illegal insider trading has come to be associated mostly with trading before takeovers and earnings announcements. To gauge the effects of case law, this study also examines changes in insider trading (i) prior to earnings announcements and (ii) prior to corporate takeover announcements.

The overall sample period from January 1975 to December 1989 is separated into three subperiods. The pre-*Chiarella* period from January 1975 to March 1980 (sixty-three months) is characterized by a relatively lower level of enforcement. This forms the benchmark period. The post-*Chiarella*, pre-ITSA period from April 1980 to August 1984 (fifty-three months) is characterized by increased enforcement by the SEC. Finally, the post-ITSA period from September 1984 to December 1989 (sixty-four months) is characterized by both increased enforcement and increased sanctions. The effects of the changes in insider trading regulations are investigated by analyzing insider-trading activity in these three sub-periods.

IV. DATA AND SAMPLE CHARACTERISTICS

The data used in this study come from the National Archives. The data include all insider transactions in publicly held firms between January 1975 and December 1989.

. . .

* * *

Table 1 shows the sample characteristics of the insider-trading data analyzed in this study, covering the period from January 1975 to December 1989. The sample contains a total of 19,571 firms. Panel A shows that there is a total of 844,399 transactions . . . by insiders involving 9.3 billion shares. . . .

Table 1 does not seem to support the proposition that increased sanctions have deterred insider trading. The number of transactions per month has remained constant over the three subperiods, while the number of shares traded shows a dramatic increase. . . .

V. EMPIRICAL RESULTS

A. *Profitability of Insider Trading*

The empirical results presented in this section document the profitability of insiders' transactions for the three subperiods and also compare profitability across the three subperiods. Insiders' abnormal profits are computed using the familiar market model for twenty-five months around the insider-trading month. . . .

* * *

. . . Overall, Table 2 shows increases rather than decreases in profitability across the three subperiods.

* * *

The evidence in Table 4 indicates that there are no measurable declines in either frequency or profitability of insider-trading activity immediately following increases in the level and enforcement of insider-trading sanctions. In 1981, the frequency of insider trading declines slightly (4 percent) over 1980, while the profitability increases moderately. In 1985, following the passage of ITSA, there is another slight decline in frequency of insider trading (1.6 percent), while there is a substantial increase in the profitability. Finally, after the passage of ITSFEA in 1989, the profitability of insider trading is mostly unchanged, while the frequency of insider trading increases substantially (30 percent).

* * *

VI. CONCLUSIONS AND INTERPRETATIONS

* * *

In spite of the increased statutory sanctions of the 1980s, corporate insiders earned an average of about 5.1 percent (on a dollar-weighted basis) abnormal profits over a one-year holding period between 1980 and 1984, increasing further to 7.0 percent after 1984, compared with 3.5 percent before 1980. During the 1980s, insiders increasingly sold stock before bad news. Moreover, after increases in regulations, data indicate that a larger volume of insider-trading activity was followed by greater favorable abnormal price movements. . . .

Data also show increases in the volume of insider-trading activity over time. On average, the number of shares traded by insiders increased by four times from the pre-1980 to the post-1984 subperiod. Also, the frequency of large-volume insider trading increased after the ITSA became law in 1984. In fact, insiders did not reduce their trading activity even on a temporary basis following changes in regulations.

Evidence also shows that court cases regarding insider trading around the time of earnings and takeover announcements did affect insider-trading patterns. Over time, insiders displayed a greater reluctance to exploit earnings announcements and takeover information. . . . Taken together with increases in overall volume and profitability, the evidence is consistent with the interpretation that greater involvement by the courts have given insiders greater latitude to trade on the basis of increasingly more valuable privileged information not directly covered by case law.

. . . [T]he statutes enacted during the 1980s seemed [not] to provide additional effective constraints on insider trading. This evidence suggests that everyday insider trading does not fall under the definition of legally material information. . . . Whatever the reason, corporate insiders were able to profitably trade on economically important private information not covered by case law.

* * *

Notes and Questions

Some readers may wonder how Professor Seyhun is able to examine thousands of insider stock trades from publicly available records, especially when one tends to think of "insider trading" as an illegal practice and so done in secret. The answer lies in being precise in terminology. If by "insider trading" one is simply referring to purchases and sales of stock by corporate directors, officers and other insiders, there is nothing illegal about that. In fact, Section 16(a) of the 1934 Securities Exchange Act requires corporate officers and directors to report their stock trades to the Securities Exchange Commission—which accounts for the publicly available data. The legal prohibition triggers when insiders trade in their corporation's stock while in possession of undisclosed non-public material information (often referred to as inside information).

Still, Professor Seyhun concludes that insiders often *are*, in fact, trading on undisclosed material information (at least in an economic if not a legal sense); how else to explain their success in trading in their own corporation's stock relative to the other traders in the market. If so, what are the policy implications of this fact? Does this suggest that perhaps Congress was correct in its initial instinct when drafting Section 16(b) that a direct prohibition of trading on material inside information would founder on proof problems for most trades? Prehaps a broader approach to materiality would help. What problem, however, might exist if courts deem simply the insider's better feel for the corporation's health to be material? Notice, incidentally, how the definition of materiality can come to depend, as a practical matter, as much on the SEC's enforcement policy—focusing on mergers and earnings reports—as it does on the doctrinal standard. Finally, if insiders are inevitably favored in trading, and yet corporations seem to raise adequate funds anyway, what does this say about the integrity of the market theory? Still, for a study which found the market tends to discount the stocks of corporations whose insiders trade heavily see Demsetz, *Corporate Control, Insider Trading and Rates of Return*, 76 AMER. ECON. REV. 313 (1986).

B. Regulation of Proxy Solicitation Under Section 14(a)

1. *The Federal Role in General*

Jill E. Fisch, *From Legitimacy to Logic: Reconstructing Proxy Regulation*, 46 VAND. L. REV. 1129 (1993)*

* * *

II. STATE CORPORATION LAW AND THE REGULATION OF VOTING

The primary rules governing shareholder voting are supplied by state corporation law. State law requires that corporations be managed by a board of directors and that the directors be elected by the shareholders. State law also determines which issues, in addition to board election, require shareholder approval and specifies the procedures governing the voting process. Specifically, state law generally requires corporations to hold an annual shareholders meeting at which shareholders elect the directors. At common law, it was necessary for shareholders to attend the annual meeting personally in order to exercise their voting rights. The development of large, widely held corporations rendered this requirement problematic and led to the development of the proxy voting process.

The proxy process allows a shareholder to vote without being physically present at the annual meeting. Proxy voting is governed by agency principles that permit a shareholder to authorize another person to vote on his or her behalf. A proxy can either give the shareholder's nominee discretionary authority or specify the manner in which the shares are to be voted. Although state law originally restricted the use of proxies, their use grew necessary as corporations became unable to secure sufficient shareholder presence to meet the quorum requirements. Eventually, state statutes addressed proxy voting and expressly protected the right of shareholders to vote by proxy.

Under modern practice most shareholders vote by proxy, and personal attendance at the annual meeting is a rare and primarily symbolic gesture. Typically, management

* Reprinted with permission.

will distribute to shareholders a form of proxy that authorizes a corporate official to vote the shareholders' shares in accordance with their instructions together with the notice of the annual meeting that is required by state law. This process is generally used whether or not the election is contested.

The main reason corporations solicit proxies is to satisfy the quorum requirement. Under state law, business may not be conducted at an annual meeting unless holders of a certain percentage of the stock are present. A national corporation may have shareholders spread over fifty states and abroad, making it impossible for many shareholders to attend the annual meeting. Without state law provisions that allow shareholders to be present "by proxy," it would be difficult for the corporation to secure the quorum necessary to conduct business. Shares represented by proxy at the annual meeting are explicitly defined by statute to satisfy the quorum requirement.

Modern state law permits, but does not require, the use of proxies. Moreover, under state law, a corporation is not required to provide a proxy mechanism for shareholders who cannot attend the annual meeting, although a shareholder may make private arrangements to be represented by proxy. In addition, state law does not specify disclosure requirements or procedural rules in connection with proxy solicitation and voting.

These gaps in state law lead to a further complication. Presence at the annual meeting carries with it certain common-law rights, such as the right to nominate a candidate for the board of directors or to propose resolutions or transactions within the authority of the shareholders, such as a shareholder resolution or bylaw amendment. . . .

* * *

[T]he evolution of the conventional corporation from a small business in which many of the investors were local and perhaps active owners to an enterprise owned by a large and widely dispersed group of investors with an ever-diminishing amount of involvement and control over their property . . . diminished the importance of shareholder voting as a means of supervising the management of the corporation because it hampered both the ability of shareholders to attend annual meetings and their ability to become informed about corporate affairs in order to exercise their franchise intelligently. Although proxy voting developed as a means of giving dispersed shareholders an opportunity to vote, voting by proxy required shareholders to delegate their voting power to someone else—usually a nominee chosen by management. This delegation further limited shareholders' effective participation in corporate governance.

The disempowerment of the shareholder may have contributed to the abuses that predated the stock market crash of 1929. In assessing the abuses to which federal regulation should be addressed, Congress identified the ability of corporate insiders to use their power to take advantage of investors as a primary problem. Some of these practices became the explicit target of the federal legislation.

III. The Federal Proxy Rules

Congress entered the regulation of corporate voting by passing the federal securities laws. Section 14 of the Securities Exchange Act of 1934 establishes federal regulation of the proxy voting process. Rather than legislating specific laws to deal with proxy voting, Congress delegated the rulemaking function to the SEC. Section 14(a) does not impose any substantive requirements in connection with a proxy solicitation; it simply makes the solicitation of proxies without complying with the SEC rules unlawful.

* * *

Section 14(a) of the Exchange Act authorizes the SEC to make rules governing the solicitation of proxies "in the public interest or for the protection of investors." The SEC has exercised this authority by promulgating extensive regulations. . . .

Rule 14a-3 of the Commission's proxy rules requires anyone soliciting a proxy, with certain exceptions, to furnish the shareholder with a written proxy statement prior to or concurrent with the solicitation. The proxy statement must include a description of the subject of the solicitation, a list of parties interested in the solicitation, a description of the person or entity making the solicitation, and an explanation of the rules and procedures governing the proxy process. The rules require disclosure tailored to the issue for which proxies are being solicited. For example, if the issue is election of directors, Schedule 14A requires information about the nominee and incumbent directors, including a description of the nominees, the composition of the board of directors, a description of the attendance by incumbent directors at board meetings during the prior fiscal year and a summary of their committee service, and a description of director compensation.

The proxy statement must be pre-filed with the SEC before it may be used to solicit proxies. Rule 14a-6 provides for a ten-day waiting period after the proxy statement is filed before it may be distributed to shareholders. . . .

Special rules apply to solicitation of proxies in connection with the election or removal of directors. Rule 14a-11 requires the identification of all participants in an election contest, both in the proxy statement and in solicitations made prior to delivery of the written proxy statement. Participants include the issuer, its directors, nominees for the position of director, and anyone soliciting proxies or financing the solicitation of proxies. The Rule further requires detailed disclosure relating to all such participants. Participants must disclose their occupation and relationship to the issuer, including sources of funds for any securities purchased with borrowed funds, their criminal record, if applicable, a description of their proposed activities in the proxy contest, and any contribution they have made or will make in furtherance of the solicitation.

The proxy rules also regulate shareholder access to the proxy mechanism. Rule 14a-7 protects the shareholder's ability to oppose management's position through the proxy process. The Rule provides any shareholder who wishes to solicit in opposition to management with the right either to obtain a list of shareholders from management or to have management mail the insurgent's proxy materials to the shareholders. The Rule gives management the option to mail the materials or to provide the list, and if management elects to do the mailing, the shareholder must pay the costs.

Rule 14a-8 gives a shareholder who meets certain threshold requirements the right to require management to include his or her proposal in management's proxy statement. This "shareholder proposal rule" is the rule most fundamentally concerned with shareholder access to the ballot and is considered in more detail below.

Finally, Rule 14a-9 is a general antifraud provision that bars the use of false or misleading statements in connection with the solicitation of a proxy. The Rule applies to all communications, oral or written, that are part of a solicitation subject to Section 14(a). . . . The federal courts have implied a private right of action under Rule 14a-9; most litigation under the federal proxy rules is based on this provision.

IV. Federal Regulation of Ballot Access

Federal law affects shareholder access to the ballot in connection with both issue voting and election contests. To understand this effect, it is necessary to explore further both the federal proxy rules relating to shareholder access and the evolution of those rules.

A. Evolution of Federal Regulation and Rule 14a-8

The SEC's rulemaking under Section 14 initially reflected a perception that the SEC's role would be limited to addressing the problems introduced into the voting process by the replacement of personal attendance with proxy solicitations. In adopting early proxy rules, the SEC described its mission as an attempt to replicate the old-style annual meeting that was personally attended by shareholders. . . .

The proxy rules were designed to enable shareholders to retain, while voting by proxy, the same state and common-law rights of corporate governance that they had exercised previously through attendance and participation at the annual meeting. . . .

The proxy rules reflect this deference to state law. The earliest version of the rules simply required a minimal degree of disclosure and inhibited false and misleading statements. Almost immediately, however, the SEC found that these requirements forced it to consider the issue of ballot access.

Although the right of shareholders to make proposals at annual meetings predated the passage of the federal securities laws, the replacement of personal attendance with proxy voting made it difficult for a shareholder to inform other shareholders of his or her intention to raise such a proposal. Shortly after the SEC had adopted the first proxy rules, the Bethlehem Steel case forced the SEC to consider how its regulation of the proxy voting process impaired shareholder-initiated proposals.

A shareholder of the Bethlehem Steel Corporation informed the management, shortly before the company's annual meeting, of his intention to make a motion at the meeting to amend the bylaws to provide that the shareholders would choose the company's auditors. Management made no mention of the proposed motion in the proxy solicitation materials that were distributed to shareholders. The shareholder complained to the SEC that management's failure to mention the proposed motion made its proxy solicitation false and misleading in violation of the SEC's new proxy rules. Bethlehem responded that it was under no obligation to solicit proxies for a shareholder proposal.

The SEC decided that failure by a company to mention in its solicitation materials an issue that it knew would be raised at the annual meeting rendered the materials false and misleading. It is not clear, however, that this position was supported by existing law, particularly in cases in which the shareholder proposal was completely unrelated to the subject for which management was soliciting proxies. The federal rules did not require management to solicit proxies at all. Arguably, under both state and federal law, management could select the issues upon which it sought shareholder voting authority.

To remedy this problem, the SEC amended its proxy rules. The first amendment, enacted in 1940, required solicitation materials to disclose "any matters which the persons making the solicitations are informed other persons intend to present for action at such meeting." Subsequently, in 1942, the SEC amended the rules to require management to include in its proxy statement any proposed shareholder resolution that was "a proper subject for action by the security holders."

The SEC took the position that the shareholder proposal rule simply implemented the shareholder's rights to ballot access under state law. . . .

It soon became clear, however, that state statutory or decisional law had not fully defined proper subjects for shareholder action. . . .

* * *

Management concerns about abuse of the shareholder right to ballot access compounded the difficulties in determining and applying this ambiguous state law concept of proper subject. Management claimed that shareholder proposals could result in management liability, render the solicitation material libelous, and cause needless expense to the corporation. In the absence of clear state law, the SEC felt an obligation to engage in rulemaking, both to clarify the rights of shareholders to ballot access and to prevent the potential abuses feared by management.

Accordingly, the SEC began exercising its rulemaking power to set forth the circumstances under which shareholders would be entitled to ballot access. Starting with an opinion by the SEC Director of the Division of Corporation Finance and continuing in a series of amendments to SEC Rule 14a-8, the SEC articulated the limits to a shareholder's right to free ballot access. The current version of Rule 14a-8 contains thirteen bases upon which management can exclude a shareholder proposal from the proxy statement as an improper subject.

* * *

D. Nomination of Directors

Closely related to the issue of shareholder ballot access with respect to policy issues is access with respect to director elections. Indeed, the area of director elections seems to be one in which shareholder participation is most legitimate because state corporation statutes vest in the shareholders the authority to elect the board of directors. In spite of congressional concern in 1934 that corporate insiders controlled the election process, a concern to which the proxy regulations appear to be addressed, insider domination of the election process remains pervasive today.

The continued ability of corporate insiders to control director elections can be attributed, in part, to deficiencies in the federal proxy rules. The proxy rules both have failed to provide affirmative access for shareholders to participate in the nomination process and have thwarted shareholder attempts at participation.

The most obvious omission from the federal proxy rules is a mechanism for shareholders to access the nomination process. The SEC took a few tentative steps toward providing such access in the early 1940s. . . . In 1942, the SEC proposed a rule that would have required corporations to include shareholder-nominated director candidates in the corporation's proxy statement. Corporate management criticized the rule on the grounds that it was unworkable; shareholders might nominate unqualified candidates or create ballot confusion by nominating too many candidates. These interferences with effective corporate management could prove costly in connection with the wartime effort. Ultimately the SEC abandoned its efforts to pass the rule.

The SEC has also interpreted other aspects of its rules to prevent direct shareholder participation in the nomination process through use of the proxy to debate election issues. For example, since the 1947 amendments, Rule 14a-8 has allowed management to exclude shareholder proposals that relate to elections for office. . . .

Although the SEC has not interpreted the exclusion to bar general proposals relating to election procedures, such as cumulative voting rights and general qualifications for directors, the provision prevents a shareholder from using Rule 14a-8 to nominate or advocate the election of a particular director. . . .

Lacking direct ballot access under Rule 14a-8, the shareholder's only alternative is a counter-solicitation as governed by Rule 14a-11.[164] Under Rule 14a-11, a shareholder wishing to nominate a director, to criticize an existing director, or to propose changes in director qualifications that would disqualify a member of the current board is relegated to many of the same hurdles faced by a shareholder seeking control of the company.

Thus, although the SEC rules do not prevent a shareholder from nominating a candidate or slate of candidates in opposition to management's choices, they impede the ability of a shareholder to do so. . . .

* * *

VI. THE LEGITIMACY OF THE SEC'S PROXY RULES

As the preceding discussion demonstrates, the SEC's proxy rules are not passive attempts to implement shareholders' state law rights in an increasingly large and impersonal voting system. Instead, the rules change the voting process, both by deter-

164 A counter-solicitation occurs when a group of shareholders propose their own slate of candidates and conduct a solicitation in which they seek proxy authority to vote in favor of their slate rather than the slate nominated by management. . . .

mining issues upon which shareholder democracy is appropriate and by structuring the way in which such democracy can be exercised. The proxy rules' substantive impact on shareholder voting, a subject traditionally relegated to state corporation law, distinguishes them from much of the system of federal securities regulation, which focuses primarily on disclosure.

The dominance of state law with respect to shareholder voting raises the question of whether the proxy rules are a legitimate exercise of the SEC's rulemaking authority—ultimately a question of statutory interpretation. The broad language of Section 14(a) makes it difficult to derive limitations on the SEC's power from an examination of the text of the rule. . . .

* * *

B. The Legislative History of Section 14(a)

* * *

. . . Although the legislative history demonstrates a congressional concern with disclosure, it also shows that the drafters of the Exchange Act hoped to reform the management of business corporations. Increased shareholder participation in corporate governance represented one mechanism for achieving this reform. It is unclear, however, whether the legislation adopted by Congress retained that objective. The dearth of clear evidence regarding Congress's objectives in enacting Section 14(a) makes reliance on legislative history as a basis for evaluating the legitimacy of the proxy rules impossible. . . .

* * *

Apart from the debate over the shareholder list, the legislative history materials contain only a few references to proxy regulation. The most detailed discussion is contained in the Report on Stock Exchange Practices (the "Fletcher Report").[235] The Fletcher Report devotes approximately three pages of discussion to the regulation of proxies. According to the Fletcher Report, the objective of proxy regulation is to provide shareholders with greater information to assist them in the voting process—information about matters such as the financial condition of the company, the major questions of policy to be decided at shareholders' meetings, and the matters for which voting authority is sought through the proxy.

This description in the Fletcher Report suggests that disclosure is the threshold concern of federal proxy regulation. The state law right to elect directors is meaningless unless the shareholders can evaluate the performance of the current board, hence the requirement that the corporation provide shareholders with information on the cor-

---

235 The Fletcher Report, which was published by the Senate Committee on Banking and Currency in June 1934, is a virtual treatise on the then-existing trading and operational practices in the securities and investment banking industries. The report contains both a summary of the problems revealed by the congressional hearings and the manner in which the new federal securities legislation had been drafted to address those problems.

poration's financial condition in connection with the voting process. Shareholders should also understand the nature of the authorization they are being asked to provide in the proxy card. The Report describes a proxy solicitation by American Commercial Alcohol Corporation as an example of a solicitation that fails to disclose to shareholders the nature of the transaction they are being asked to ratify. Finally, the Fletcher Report states that shareholders should be informed as to "major questions of policy." This language is susceptible of two interpretations: (1) it may suggest a role for shareholders as decisionmakers with respect to corporate policy, or (2) it may simply direct that shareholders receive information about corporate policies and objectives in addition to operating results.

The Fletcher Report explains that the SEC's rulemaking process can meet the objectives of proxy regulation. It does not, however, articulate the nature of the rulemaking to be undertaken, apart from a direction that the rules and regulations be designed to protect investors from the abusive use of the proxy process, both by corporate insiders and by third parties who thereby seek to obtain control of the company. The Report, therefore, does not conclusively answer the question of whether the rules should be limited to disclosure requirements.

A second congressional report, the Rayburn Report, contains some of the most frequently quoted language concerning regulation of the voting process. In a section entitled "Control of Unfair Practices by Corporate Insiders," the Report states: "Fair corporate suffrage is an important right that should attach to every equity security bought on a public exchange." The Report goes on to describe these unfair practices. The Report explains that corporate insiders can perpetuate themselves in office by soliciting proxies to secure their re-election without disclosing to shareholders: (1) their interest in the corporation; (2) the management policies they intend to pursue; and (3) the purposes for which the proxies are to be used. Thus, although the language of the Rayburn Report indicates a broad concern with fair voting practices, the abuse articulated in the Report actually concerns disclosures.

Professor Stephen Bainbridge argues that the language of the Fletcher and Rayburn Reports supports the *Business Roundtable*[*v. SEC**] conclusion that Section 14(a) is limited to disclosure and that Congress did not intend the SEC, in regulating the solicitation of proxies, to affect the substantive voting rights of shareholders. . . .

Indeed, Congress could have been much more straightforward if it intended the SEC to regulate substantive aspects of shareholder voting. Congress instead authorized SEC rulemaking solely with regard to the solicitation of proxies. Congress did not authorize the SEC to regulate shareholder voting in general.

Why did Congress draft the statute this way? In 1934, Congress was aware of substantive deficiencies in the voting process; a staffer at the Federal Trade Commission had prepared a draft bill that would have included federal regulation of issues such as cumulative voting, voting trusts, and composition of the board of directors. Moreover, the separation of ownership and control in the large public corporation and the inability of shareholders to affect the operations of their corporations just recently had been

[*905 F.2d 406 (D.C. Cir. 1990).]

identified by Adolf Berle, a member of the committee charged with developing the Stock Exchange legislation, as a major problem in American business. Why then did Congress limit its regulation to the proxy process?

Substantive regulation of voting clearly would have affected the balance of power between shareholders and management, as well as the overall structure of corporate governance. It would have, in effect, displaced at least part of state corporation law with federal standards. The drafters of the federal securities laws in fact considered the adoption of a federal corporation law. President Roosevelt himself viewed federal securities regulation as an effort to redress problems caused by lax enforcement of state corporation law. Richard Whitney, President of the New York Stock Exchange, suggested during the hearings that the inadequacy of state corporation laws caused the abuses about which Congress was concerned, and that a national incorporation law would solve the problem.

Congress's failure to adopt a federal corporation law may reflect, in part, its perception that it lacked the power to do so. Under contemporary theories of constitutional law, whether Congress could regulate corporations directly was questionable. . . .

* * *

Although both the Fletcher and Rayburn Reports demonstrate a regulatory concern with disclosure that is consistent with the regulatory structure of the federal securities laws in general, do the Reports indicate congressional intent to regulate beyond disclosure? The Rayburn Report in particular contains a broad reference to "fair corporate suffrage." Does the use of that language suggest an intention on the part of Congress to inject goals of substantive fairness into the voting process beyond insuring the ability of a shareholder to exercise state law voting rights in an informed manner?

Unfortunately, neither the Reports nor the Congressional debate answer the question. Even if Congress intended to authorize the SEC to address questions of substantive fairness, the Reports do not indicate what Congress mean by "fair." The argument that Congress intended the Exchange Act to regulate more than disclosure is bolstered, however, by examining more closely the problems to which the Act was addressed and the concerns raised during the hearings about insider domination of corporate decisionmaking.

For example, Thomas Corcoran, one of the principal drafters of the Exchange Act, had a broad view of the problems to which the proxy regulation was addressed. Corcoran believed that corporate insiders, through their control of the proxy process, were able both to perpetuate themselves in power and to use the voting process to further their private ends. . . .

* * *

C. Proxy Regulation and Federalism

The foregoing review suggests that the prevailing view in Congress at the time the federal securities laws were passed was that corporate insiders had too much power and were misusing this power at the expense of shareholders. The question this review does not answer concerns the extent to which Congress intended the federal securities laws to provide a substantive remedy to this problem. One additional factor should be considered in determining whether proxy regulation is the appropriate remedy: the role of the federal securities laws in the federalist structure of corporate regulation.

The relationship of the proxy rules to state law is frequently overlooked. Although the proxy rules do not preempt state corporation law, the two regulatory systems rest upon very different organizing principles. Corporate law varies from state to state, and for the most part, the organization and internal affairs of a corporation are subject only to the law of its state of incorporation. Additionally, corporate law is primarily enabling rather than mandatory. . . .

Federal law, on the other hand, applies to publicly held corporations wherever located, subject to certain thresholds on size, number of shareholders, or Exchange listing.[297] The federal regulations are mandatory; firms cannot, for example, adopt charter provisions exempting them from the federal proxy rules. Finally, federal law is administered through the SEC, a specialized agency that brings unique experience and perspective to the regulatory process.

Regulation of corporate issues is effected primarily by one system or the other. Federal law, for example, is the dominant force in the regulation of insider trading, the issuance of new securities, and periodic disclosure by corporations. State law supplies the rules governing directors' duties to their shareholders, the payment of dividends, and the shareholder's right to inspect corporate books and records and shareholder lists. In the area of shareholder voting, however, federal and state laws are highly interdependent because of the development of the proxy voting process. For more than fifty years, during which time the modern public corporation has undergone a substantial transformation in size, range of business, and role in society, both state and federal law have regulated shareholder voting.

The interdependence of the state and federal regulatory systems has several consequences. First, the mere existence of the federal proxy rules may have restrained the development of state corporation law in the area of voting regulation. A state statute that conflicted with the proxy rules might not be valid under the Supremacy Clause. Additionally, the federal rules subdue state motivation to legislate. State legislatures have become accustomed to leaving the regulation of the voting process to the SEC and defer to that agency's expertise. State and federal courts also have grown accustomed to viewing shareholder proxy rights as those rights defined by the SEC rules. In spite of the SEC's statements that its rules simply enable shareholders to realize state law rights, courts are loathe to recognize ballot access, information, or procedural rights that extend beyond those explicitly guaranteed by federal law.

Federal law further constrains experimentation by individual corporations. Because the proxy rules do not contain an opting-out mechanism, a corporation cannot determine how to conduct its proxy solicitation process through charter provisions. . . .

---

297 See Section 14(a) (applying federal proxy rules to solicitations in respect of any security registered under § 12 of the Securities Exchange Act of 1934). A few provisions of the statute even apply to privately held corporations, such as the antifraud provision of Rule 10b-5.

At the same time, the existence of state corporation law has served as a restraint, and perhaps an excuse, limiting the scope of the SEC's rulemaking. . . .

VII. Implications and Conclusions

The interdependence of federal and state regulation of shareholder voting plays an important role in a pragmatic or dynamic approach to interpreting the scope of delegation under Section 14(a) within which the SEC's proper actions must be evaluated. . . .

* * *

[I]f shareholder voting does not reflect an accurate and informed expression of shareholder opinion, business decisions such as choosing management, selecting a new state of incorporation, engaging in a merger, or opting into an anti-takeover statute can be made in circumstances under which they are not value-increasing. Moreover, limitations on shareholder access to the proxy process prevent shareholders from initiating value-increasing changes in the governance structure of their corporation. The market, which is expected to produce efficient business decisions, thereby fails.

Perhaps this market failure motivated congressional regulation of the proxy process. Although Congress did not provide a definition of "fair corporate suffrage," this term may define a voting process in which shareholders are able to voice their concerns and objectives, communicate them to fellow shareholders, and implement them in corporate decisions. A dynamic interpretation of Section 14(a) considers the evolution of federal regulation of voting within the context of the modern corporation. . . .

In particular, although the model supports a theory of regulation that extends beyond disclosure and operates substantively to empower shareholders at the expense of management, the theory is not inconsistent with congressional intent to steer clear of corporate internal affairs. State law can be relied upon to regulate corporate governance without generating a race to the bottom, as long as the choice of governance structures by shareholders is a real choice. Viewed in this light, substantive regulation of the proxy process does not preempt the operation of state corporate law, but rather enhances it.

This enhancement provides both a basis for evaluating the legitimacy of the SEC's proxy regulations and a blueprint for future regulatory activity. The foregoing suggests that, based on Congress's concern with insider abuse, Congress intended to authorize the SEC to remove the barriers erected by management to shareholder participation in corporate governance. SEC rules designed to enhance shareholder participation, such as allowing shareholders access to the proxy mechanism, or to facilitate the ability of shareholders to communicate with each other thus are legitimate. Rules that curtail shareholder participation by limiting the number of proposals a shareholder can make, preventing shareholders from communicating freely or acting in concert to effect a change in corporate governance, or providing management the ability to control the voting agenda are not. Furthermore, the SEC has not been empowered to adopt a general theory of corporate governance. The SEC has neither the expertise nor the authorization to decide if corporations should respond to social policy concerns, or if shareholder-initiated proposals will unduly interfere with management discretion. Congress has reserved precisely those issues for state law.

* * *

The extent to which the federal proxy rules frustrate shareholder democracy has been chronicled extensively elsewhere.[319] In spite of its continued re-examination of the regulatory system and its never-ending series of amendments, the SEC continues to limit shareholder participation in corporate governance both through sins of commission and omission in connection with its proxy rules. Accordingly, the rules remain an unauthorized and misbegotten regulatory endeavor.

* * *

Note

As Professor Fisch points out, most litigation under the proxy rules involves claims of misleading solicitations in violation of Rule 14A-9. (Gee, imagine what general elections would be like if political ads were subject to such strictures. Why is there less First Amendment concern for corporate elections? For a discussion see Symposium, *The First Amendment and Federal Securities Regulation*, 20 CONN. L. REV. 261 (1988).) Rule 14A-9, however, has attracted little commentary. In contrast, the shareholder proposal provision (Rule 14A-8) has generated considerable debate. The following two article excerpts stake out some of the positions.

2. *Shareholder Proposals*

Alan R. Palmiter, *The Shareholder Proposal Rule: A Failed Experiment in Merit Regulation*, 45 ALA. L. REV. 879 (1994)*

* * *

For more than half a century, the SEC's shareholder proposal rule has been a corporate curiosity. A glaring inroad into management's control over the process and content of the solicitation of shareholder proxies, Rule 14a-8 mandates that public companies subsidize access to the company's proxy mechanism for shareholders who offer "proper" proposals. If a shareholder proposal satisfies the rule's daunting agency-

319 See, for example . . . Black, [*Shareholder Passively Reexamined*], 89 MICH. L. REV. [520], 536-42 [(1990)]. . . .

made conditions, management must include it in the company-funded proxy statement and give the body of shareholders a chance to vote on it. If the proposal does not, management can effectively block shareholder access to the proxy machinery for initiating corporate reforms.

The history of Rule 14a-8 offers, in microcosm, a study of federal involvement in the shareholder-management relationship of the American public corporation. Emerging from the Great Depression, the SEC promulgated the rule in 1942 to catalyze what many hoped would be a functional "corporate democracy." During the 1950s, sensing that "what is good for GM is good for America," the agency added layers of conditions to the rule and gutted meaningful shareholder access. Later, as Vietnam and Watergate led Americans to question their political institutions, federal courts and the SEC opened the 14a-8 door for shareholders to join in the questioning of America's corporate institutions. In the 1980s, as America turned inward, the Reagan-inspired SEC sought to squelch access by social/political activists and enlarge the role of shareholders seeking governance changes. . . .

* * *

. . . From the beginning, Rule 14a-8 jurisprudence—both in quality and quantity—has rested almost exclusively with the agency, not the courts or Congress. At the heart of the rule is its mandatory no-action procedure, which assigns to the staff of the SEC's Division of Corporate Finance the task of mediating *all* Rule 14a-8 interpretive disputes. Since 1947 the rule has required management to submit for SEC no-action review every shareholder proposal it intends to omit from the company's proxy materials. Rarely do disappointed proponents seek judicial review. In fact, until 1990, only thirteen reported court cases (about one every four years) arose out of the hundreds of annual 14a-8 exclusions. When courts do hear disputes under the rule, their review is often case-specific and generally deferential.

. . . The history of the SEC as arbiter of a proper dialogue between shareholders and management under the rule has been tumultuous. Since its promulgation five decades ago, the rule itself has undergone no less than fourteen revisions. Lately, the agency's interpretive flip-flops in no-action letters have become legion. Over the last decade, with the most minimal of explanations and without any formal rulemaking, the agency has openly reversed itself on the propriety of proposals raising such matters as executive compensation, tobacco production, board composition, and employment policies. And, without acknowledging the shift, the SEC staff is now thirty percent more likely to permit the exclusion of proposals urging greater corporate social responsibility than was the case ten years ago. Adding to the confusion, the federal judiciary has joined the ruckus, in recent cases chastising (and mirroring) the agency's aimless vacillation. In short, the rule is today in chaos.

Until recently, the stakes presented by Rule 14a-8 and the consequences of the SEC's erratic and desultory performance have been low. During its first four decades, shareholder proposals faced near certain defeat by wide margins at the ballot box. As of 1981, only two contested shareholder proposals of the thousands submitted had ever won. The rule's subsidized access to the company's proxy materials amounted to little more than a nuisance for corporate management and a slight burden on the SEC staff. Based on management's statement of costs, I estimate that annual compliance costs total about $15 million.[15] The SEC has estimated its regulatory costs to be equivalent to one staff[-person] year.

In the late 1980s institutional shareholders brought Rule 14a-8 out of its quaint and curious shell, employing the rule as a potent tool for corporate governance reform. They proposed such changes as limits on golden parachutes and executive pay, repeal of staggered boards, redemption of poison pills, reduction of supermajority voting requirements, opting out of antitakeover statutes, establishment of confidential voting, and greater roles for outside directors. Some recent proposals have won outright; others have led managers to negotiate settlements rather than face the embarrassment of a shareholder rebuff. Over the last couple of years, the rule has served as a springboard for direct shareholder access to directors and management.

* * *

I. The Current Rule

* * *

A. Anticongestion Conditions

Many of the rule's access conditions seek to ensure an orderly solicitation process so that shareholder proposals do not choke the company-funded proxy mechanism or interfere with management's solicitation efforts. Some protect the solicitation process without regard to a proposal's content: the proponent's submission must be submitted four months before the annual meeting so that management has time to include the proposal or seek SEC review; the proponent can submit only one resolution per meeting; and the proposal and accompanying statement cannot exceed 500 words—approximately two double-spaced typewritten pages.

Other requirements seek to avoid shareholders converting management's proxy solicitation into an open forum in which shareholder proposals could swamp or confound management's solicitation: the proposal may not substantially duplicate another shareholder proposal that management already plans to include; the proposal may not be counter to a proposal that management plans to submit at the meeting; the proposal may not nominate directors or officers;[28] and the proposal may not relate to specific

---

15 In 1992, shareholders submitted a total of about 900 proposals, half of which were included in companies' proxy statements. Assuming costs of $30,000 per included proposal and $4000 per excluded, total compliance costs amounted to $15.3 million.

My estimates of costs are based on company estimates from the early 1980s. In response to an SEC inquiry, companies estimated the administrative and legal costs of excluding a proposal to be between $2000 to $4600, and the printing, mailing, and administrative costs of including a proposal to be between $18,760 to $44,000.

28 . . . It's an anomaly that the rule excludes the most significant shareholder function in corporate governance—the election of directors. Without the exclusion, however, "firms might be forced to list as candidates innumerable small investors with no significant support." . . .

amounts of cash or stock dividends.[29] Consistent with management's control of the proxy solicitation process, the rule permits management to state in the proxy statement and on the proxy card its opposition to a shareholder proposal, thus giving management the last word.

B. Anticrackpot Conditions

Other provisions of Rule 14a-8 filter out vexatious, illegal, deceptive, and unintelligible proposals. . . .

Some of the anticrackpot exclusions are content-neutral: the proponent must have owned (beneficially or of record) at least one percent or $1000 worth of the company's voting securities for at least one year; the proposal may not substantially be the same as a prior unsuccessful proposal submitted in the last five years that failed to garner a vote of at least three percent on its first try, or six percent on its second try, or ten percent after three tries; and the proponent must appear at the shareholders' meeting and continue to own a qualifying number of shares.

Other exclusions, based on the proposal's content, carry out the state law mandate that shareholder communications relate to the shareholder's interest as such: the proposal may not relate to the redress of the proponent's personal claim or grievance; the proposal may not be beyond the company's power to effectuate; the proposal may not be moot; the proposal may not seek to have the company violate any law; and the proposal may not violate the federal proxy rules, including the antifraud provisions of Rule 14a-9 which prohibit false or misleading solicitations. The SEC staff has also used the antifraud provision to justify exclusion of proposals that are "vague and indefinite." The "crackpot" exclusions have not created significant controversy.

C. Merit-Based Exclusions

The most frequently used (and most litigated) of the grounds for exclusion purport to test the content of the proposal against the state law scheme of centralized corporate governance: the (c)(1) "proper subjects" exclusion; the (c)(5) "substantially related" exclusion; and the (c)(7) "ordinary business" exclusion.

The first draft of the rule released for comment in 1942 did not include any "limitation whatsoever upon the shareholder as to what was proper for proposal at the annual meeting." To address the stated concern of management that an open-ended rule would allow "libelous" or "scurrilous" materials to be placed in the proxy statement, the new rule mandated inclusion of any shareholder proposal that was "a proper subject for action by the security holders."

In 1954, following the Commission's successful challenge of the exclusion of a shareholder proposal seeking greater shareholder supervisory powers in *SEC v. Transamerica Corp.*,[46] the Commission codified in the rule its view that "the laws of

---

29 . . . In adopting this exclusion, the SEC stated its concern that "several proponents might independently submit to an issuer proposals asking that differing amounts of dividends be paid." . . .

46 163 F.2d 511 (3d Cir. 1947) . . . .

the issuer's domicile" determine the "proper subject[s]" for action by shareholders. Among the agency's most established assumptions is that state law permits only precatory shareholder resolutions that request, but do not demand, board action.

The two other "merit" exclusions purport to define the scope of shareholders' state-based rights to initiate corporate reforms under a regime of centralized corporate decision-making. Under subsection (c)(5), the proposal must relate to operations that account for at least five percent of the firm's total assets, gross annual sales or net annual earnings, or be "otherwise significantly related" to the firm's business. The exclusion is the culmination of a four-decade debate on the propriety of proposals dealing with social/political causes. The SEC added it in 1972 to provide a more "objective standard" than the prior exclusion of proposals submitted primarily for the purpose of promoting "general economic, political, racial, religious, social or similar causes." According to the SEC, matters relating to ethical issues, such as political contributions and carrying on business in South Africa, may be significant even though not from a purely financial standpoint.

Under subsection (c)(7), the proposal may not relate to the firm's "ordinary business operations." The SEC adopted the exclusion "to relieve the management of the necessity of including in its proxy material security holder proposals which relate to matters falling within the province of management." . . .

The "significantly related" and "ordinary business" exclusions create a near-perfect bureaucratic Catch-22. A proposal can be neither so general that it is unrelated to the firm's business or so specific that it is a matter of ordinary business. The merit exclusions thus supply the SEC with sufficient textual ambiguity to construct a regime of censorship in which the agency has virtually complete administrative freedom.

II. Justifications For The Rule

* * *

A. Mandated Access and Informed Voting

The SEC originally justified subsidized access as a means to carry out the congressional directive that the SEC regulate deceptive practices in management's solicitation of proxies. On the theory that a management proxy statement would be misleading if it failed to state the subject and supporting justifications for shareholder proposals that management anticipated at the upcoming shareholder's meeting, the rule requires management to include such proposals, along with the proponent's supporting statement. . . .

Under this view, the extent of management's 14a-8 obligations, like the rest of federal proxy regulation, hinges on state law voting rights . . . .

. . . State corporate law uniformly permits shareholders to offer resolutions at shareholders' meetings and to amend the corporate bylaws. Like voting, these are mandatory rights, not subject to opt-out or amendment.

* * *

The point is important. Rule 14a-8, like federal proxy regulation in general, mandates subsidized access to ensure the effectiveness of shareholder state-based control rights in the face of the practical impediments of proxy voting in public corporations.

B. The 14a-8 Subsidy and Suboptimal Shareholder Participation

Subsidized access alleviates the collective action and free-rider problems that the management-dominated proxy mechanism creates for public shareholders who would initiate corporate reforms. Faced with the costs of moving fellow shareholders to collective action and a state law system that makes reimbursement by free-riding shareholders both voluntary and dubious, shareholder reform initiatives would be suboptimally produced unless subsidized.

* * *

. . . Corporate reimbursement of solicitation costs is discretionary and available, as a practical matter, only if the dissident gains control of the board of directors. . . .

* * *

Some critics of Rule 14a-8 argue the collective action and free rider impediments that may have justified the rule for individual proponents no longer justify the rule in the wake of its use by institutional shareholders. The problems of suboptimal production, however, still exist even for larger shareholders.[71] . . .

The SEC and commentators have defended the Rule 14a-8 subsidy as producing "significant revisions of corporate policy, even where the proponent shareholder has owned few shares." Lewis D. Gilbert, a pioneer and lifetime advocate of shareholder activism, used Rule 14a-8 to urge public companies to adopt more liberal dividend policies and consistent financial accounting[74]—visionary ideas with which modern finance economists now agree. . . .

---

71 . . . Consider the numbers. A contested proxy solicitation for a large public company costs about $5 million. Even if we assume in this age of institutional activism that a highly desirable proposal (and request for reimbursement) would stand a 60-40 chance of succeeding, a rational institutional proponent would not undertake the effort unless it promised an expected increase in share value that offset the expected costs of the contest. In our example, with a 60% chance of reimbursement, the expected value to the shareholder of the reform would have to be greater than $2 million—a significant increase in share value.

74 . . . Professor Ryan recounts Gilbert's story:

> Lewis D. Gilbert, a small shareholder (by virtue of a bequest) in the Consolidated Gas Company of New York, was a pioneer of shareholder activism. Angered by the ritualistic lack of meaningful content at the company's annual meeting in 1932, his response was to broaden his holdings in order to change both the nature of the shareholder meeting itself and the ways in which directors were allowed to run the corporation. He was chiefly concerned with undeclared dividends and with installing accounting and other monitoring devices to make directors more answerable to the shareholders.

. . . With his brother, John, the Gilberts became ardent users of the new Rule 14a-8. Their share of 14a-8 submissions increased from 47% during the period from 1948 to 1951 to 65% in 1955. . . . Two decades later they were still going strong.

To the extent the rule subsidizes shareholder discourse on externality-reducing proposals —whose value may not immediately or ever be reflected in share prices—the rule acts as a tax on public companies and their shareholders. The Rule 14a-8 tax, however, increasingly falls broadly on those who benefit from greater social utility. Rising institutional equity ownership has spread indirect corporate ownership to a wider range of Americans, so that today there is a significant identity between equity owners and beneficiaries of social-enhancing gains. To turn an old adage on its head: "What's good for America is good for Wall Street."

Professors Schwartz and Weiss argued that the rule led management to take actions, such as South African disinvestment and broader representation on GM's board, "tied directly to or seemingly stimulated by shareholder proposals."[80] . . .

* * *

III. Critique Of The SEC's Limits On The Rule 14a-8 Forum

* * *

B. An Inappropriate SEC Role: The Case Against Merit Regulation

The Rule 14a-8 "proper subject" exclusions stand on different ground [from its other exclusions]. As applied by the SEC, they are beyond the agency's institutional competence. They engage the agency in the vain exercise of evaluating the merits of social/political proposals, they are inconsistent with state law, they are at odds with the avowed federal disdain for merit regulation of corporate governance, and they mock the agency's renewed faith in shareholder control. In short, the SEC's attempts to pass on the propriety of shareholder proposals illustrate the intractable problems of administrative licensing of speech based on its merits.

1. *The SEC is institutionally incapable of passing on the merits of shareholder initiatives.* —The SEC's recent inconstancy paints a sad portrait of a bureaucracy aimlessly in search of purpose. SEC staff, moved by what the popular press considers newsworthy or by personal political views on recent corporate governance trends, seems quite unable to delineate which initiatives shareholders should be able to consider and which ones they should not. . . .

* * *

In all fairness to the SEC staff, the current rule's attempt at merit regulation lays on the staff the impossible task of deducing what should be of interest to investment-minded and public-minded shareholders and what should not be of interest. . . .

---

80 *See also* Donald E. Schwartz, *The Public-Interest Proxy Contest: Reflections on Campaign GM*, 69 MICH. L. REV. 419 (1971)(explaining the impact of Campaign GM). Campaign GM, a proxy solicitation effort, sought to create a shareholder committee on social responsibility and to enlarge the board to add women, Blacks, consumer advocates, community activists, and ecologists. Though the Campaign garnered less than 3% of the vote, GM management within three years added a black community leader, a woman, and a scientist to the board. GM also held annual conferences on "Progress in Areas of Public Concern" and sent lengthy reports of these conferences to its shareholders. . . .

2. *The SEC has been unable to assess the merits of social/political proposals.*—The most dramatic and prominent example of SEC inconstancy under the rule has been the agency's shifting approach to social/political proposals. . . .

* * *

3. *The SEC's merit-based restraint of shareholder initiatives is inconsistent with state law.* . . . State corporate law does not specify any limits on the content of shareholder resolutions or bylaw changes except that they be consistent with the corporate statutes and the articles of incorporation. The few courts to face the issue have assumed wide shareholder latitude to make nonbinding, precatory recommendations on any subject related to maximizing shareholder value. In fact, under state law shareholders may vote selfishly or altruistically, as they choose.

In the related context of shareholder inspection rights, state courts have interpreted the "proper purpose" requirement for access to shareholder lists to encompass a broad definition of wealth maximization. For example, a recent Delaware case permitted a shareholder to request a list "for the purpose of communicating with fellow stockholders with respect to the alleged economic risks of Chevron's business activity in Angola," even though the requester's position was "only marginally related to the economic interests of the corporation" and might even be viewed by other shareholders as "useless" or "bizarre."

Nowhere do the inspection statutes or state courts mention a "substantiality" test or limit access when the topic of shareholder communications is related to "ordinary business." Not surprisingly, state courts have said it is irrelevant to a shareholder's state inspection right that the SEC has not cleared the shareholder's 14a-8 proposal.

4. *The SEC's "proper subject" review is paternalistic merit regulation.* . . .

* * *

If management is correct that a shareholder proposal interferes with management prerogatives or is otherwise nonmaximizing, management has at its disposal the means to say so and shareholders the means to agree. . . .

* * *

IV. A Proposal To Abandon Rule 14a-8 Merit Regulation

* * *

Abandoning the current "proper subjects" exclusions and substituting a numerical cap raises at least three principal objections.

1. *The excessive-litigation argument.*—The first objection . . . is that eliminating SEC review of the propriety of proposals "would result in costly and time consuming litigation." . . . [T]he fear would seem to be that under an easy-access rule, management would resort to state courts to block proposals that previously SEC staff would have blocked.

Will there be more state court litigation, and if so, would it be a bad thing? . . .

* * *

. . . [O]ne would expect more satisfying answers [from state courts] than the SEC staff's sometimes contradictory, usually unsubstantiated, and always conclusory no-action positions—hardly inspiring the confidence of a well-considered judicial opinion on a novel corporate device. . . .

* * *

2. *The ubiquitous "social/political gadfly" argument.*— A recurrent theme . . . is . . . that social/political gadflies will abuse subsidized access to the proxy mechanism. My proposed easy-access rule would abandon this fifty-year old suspicion. And why not? I see nothing pernicious with a particular corporation opting for different models of profit-maximization. Many investors readily make this choice. The Delaware courts have told us, for example, that the shareholders of Time Inc. invested in a "corporate culture" in which journalistic integrity could come before maximizing share prices. Today, mutual fund investors choose "green" funds that explicitly invest in companies that seek to combine environmental responsibility and profits.

* * *

But even if more social/political proposals end up on the ballot than under the current rule, it is difficult to see the harm. If they force management to define a position or alert shareholders to a dimension of their investment they had not considered, it is hard to see how the corporation is hurt. An expanded rule would offer shareholders, in an area of increasing identity between equity ownership and political citizenship, another means of political discourse. The costs are minimal, the gains potentially large.

* * *

George W. Dent, Jr., *SEC Rule 14a-8: A Study in Regulatory Failure,* 30 N.Y.L. Sch. L. Rev. 1 (1985)*

* * *

II. A Critical Analysis Of Rule 14a-8

Although the SEC has not recently articulated any formal justification for the shareholder proposal rule, commentators have advanced many defenses. Most are based on the intention of Congress to promote disclosure and shareholder democracy or on the alleged indirect benefits of shareholder proposals.

A. Disclosure Theory

The original justification for requiring inclusion of shareholder proposals in proxy statements was that it would be misleading for management to omit a proposal and yet state that it knew of no other business expected to come before the meeting. This justification can be attacked on several grounds. First, the Commission has not followed this principle consistently; rather, it has required inclusion of a proposal even if management neither made such a statement nor requested discretionary authority to vote on matters not described in the proxy statement. Second, if the disclosure theory were consistently applied, it would require inclusion of all shareholder proposals, but the rule has always had several exceptions, and no one has ever argued that disclosure principles require including all proposals.

More important, disclosure principles embrace the concept of materiality. Requiring disclosure of all information in the world would be both impossible and pointless. The concept of materiality has been used in securities law to separate important information from the unimportant. According to the Supreme Court: "An omitted fact is material if there is a substantial likelihood that a reasonable shareholder would consider it important in deciding how to vote." Applying this test often requires guessing how a hypothetical reasonable shareholder would react in a hypothetical situation. Forty years of experience solves this problem with respect to shareholder proposals: Since no shareholder proposal opposed by management has ever come close to receiving approval of a shareholder majority, nothing about such a proposal is material. . . . One cannot argue that many shareholders consider shareholder proposals significant even though they vote against them. Their rejection is too consistently overwhelming to admit such an argument. . . .

* * *

B. "Fair Corporate Suffrage"

* * *

Does shareholder democracy demand more than an opportunity to vote on matters shareholders consider material? Does it require that minority shareholder groups be heard through shareholder proposals? . . . Precepts of political democracy do not demand anything like shareholder proposals. Even states that permit voter initiatives insist that proponents show substantial support before their initiative will be placed on the ballot, and the federal government and most states do not even permit voter initiatives. . . .

The weakness of the shareholder democracy defense of rule 14a-8 is apparent not only in the lack of voting support for shareholder proposals but also in the domination of shareholder proposals by a few agitators. In 1982 nearly half of all shareholder proposals were submitted by just five individuals, two of whom were brothers working as a single team. Often an individual has purchased a single share of stock in several companies just to be able to make shareholder proposals. The concerns of these proponents are not shared by most shareholders. Many social proposals have virtually nothing to do with being a shareholder, but merely reflect the political views of one citizen. Yet these proponents can impose the costs of their publicity games on fellow shareholders who overwhelmingly reject their proposals and who have never agreed to foot this bill. . . .

* * *

C. Indirect Effects of Rule 14a-8

Supporters of rule 14a-8, perhaps uneasy over the weakness of disclosure theory and shareholder democracy as defenses for the rule, have more recently stressed the alleged indirect benefits of the rule as compared with its slight costs. . . .

* * *

A variation of this theme is that the rule forces management to defend and perhaps reconsider its policies. Although the rule sometimes provokes a detailed response, that is not always true. In any case, why *should* management be compelled to defend virtually any policy that a shareholder cares to question? Since the law already demands disclosure of all material information, any defense of management policies compelled by the rule would not be material—i.e., important to a reasonable shareholder. To oblige management to defend policies of interest to only a few shareholders might be acceptable if it were cost free, but of course it is not. This justification of the rule shows more clearly that it imposes not only mundane costs on the corporation (such as printing and secretarial work) but also demands on the time of managers who are already overburdened. This obligation should be rejected for the same reason that the SEC has rejected disclosure aimed at specific groups—the responses are of interest to only a few shareholders but the costs must be borne by all shareholders and will probably outweigh the benefits. . . .

* * *

Rule 14a-8 is also defended for benefitting the broader public by capturing the public's interest and motivating politicians. According to this view Campaign GM "won," even though it gained only 2% of the shareholder vote, because it "forced General Motors into a debate on public policy issues." The factual basis for this defense can be questioned. First, shareholder proposals rarely entail substantial public debate and, when they do, the rule may not be crucial to spurring the debate. Campaign GM was a novelty, capturing much coverage in the press; rarely does a shareholder proposal attract any public attention at all. Because Campaign GM was backed by such media celebrities as Ralph Nader, it probably would have generated substantial publicity even without a proxy contest. . . . The prospect of provoking public debate through a shareholder proposal has diminished since managements have become more sophisticated in responding to them. In 1970 General Motors stirred up much of the publicity Campaign GM sought by fighting its proposals tooth and nail. In 1971 GM quietly agreed to include all Campaign GM's proposals, refused to wage a publicity war, and simply let shareholders defeat the proposals by an even wider margin than in 1970. Thus the publicity value of the rule is minimal, even if publicity value could ever justify the rule.

The last, and perhaps the most common current justification for rule 14a-8, is that shareholder proposals, even though invariably defeated when opposed by management, often cause management to change its positions. Such changes could occur in several ways: management might make changes to deter submission of a proposal, to render moot a proposal already submitted, or to comply with a proposal even after it has been defeated, or management might decide to support a proposal. One could question whether the rule has prompted many changes. Rarely can one prove that changes were induced by shareholder activities or, even if they were, that shareholder proposals in corporate proxy statements were a necessary element of that influence. Intuition suggests that distribution (or the threat of it) of a proposal that shareholders are sure to reject overwhelmingly does not influence managers much. Indeed, changes ascribed to the rule often occur after resounding defeat of a proposal. If managers want certain changes, one would think that they would make them before circulation of the proposal. Perhaps the adversarial context of shareholder proposals prompts managers to oppose them even though in a less adversarial context they might be more receptive.

* * *

. . . Indeed, the defense of rule 14a-8 based on the corporate changes it has produced reveals the fundamentally antidemocratic operation of the rule—even though shareholders resoundingly defeat a proposal, management adopts some or all of the proposal. This is not shareholder democracy, but pressure group politics, and the SEC has no business encouraging it.

* * *

Notes

1. Professor Dent's criticism of the shareholder proposal rule predates the remarkable change in the fate of shareholder proposals, as noted by Professor Palmiter, when those proposals come from large institutional investors. For a modification of his views to take into account this change see Dent, *Proxy Regulation in Search of a Purpose: A Reply to Professor Ryan*, 23 GA. L. REV. 815 (1989).

2. As these two excerpts suggest, much of the controversy over shareholder proposals involves those which raise social issues. This harkens back to the earlier exploration of the directors' ability or duty to take into account the interests of groups other than the stockholders. To what extent should the analysis change when dealing with the shareholders, rather than the directors, as the decisionmaker? Professor Palmiter asserts that the shareholders have the right to be altruistic. Should those holding a majority of the stock have the right to sacrifice profit maximization over the objection of the minority? In fact, the leading case suggesting a duty of profit maximization,

Dodge v. Ford Motor Co., 204 Mich. 459, 170 N.W. 668 (1919), involved decisions by Henry Ford, who was not only a director and president of the company, but also its majority stockholder.

Shareholder interest in so-called social issues not only raises questions under Rule 14A-8, but also under Rule 14A-9. Specifically, must management disclose arguably immoral or illegal conduct by the corporation (such as pollution or overseas bribery) in its annual proxy statement? Is such conduct important to a reasonable shareholder in deciding how to vote, and so material? For a discussion see Roiter, *Illegal Corporate Practices and the Disclosure Requirements of the Federal Securities Laws*, 50 FORDHAM L. REV. 781 (1982).

Chapter V

Special Problems In Closely Held Corporations

At several points, articles excerpted in this anthology have employed a different analysis of the question before them when dealing with closely held corporations—in other words, companies with few shareholders. For example, several writers took the position that limited liability may not be an economically efficient arrangement for closely held companies. Consistent with this view, we saw that piercing the corporation to impose personal liability upon shareholders was entirely a phenomenon of closely held firms. In terms of internal affairs, Professor Eisenberg differentiated closely and publicly held corporations as far as the need for mandatory rules. Recall, as well, that Professors Brudney and Clark argued for different rules regarding corporate opportunities when dealing with closely held corporations versus public firms. We now turn to a more comprehensive look at closely held corporations. This begins with a detailed examination of the subject raised by Professor Eisenberg: To what extent does and should the law facilitate private contractual arrangements among the owners of a closely held corporation?

A. Ex Ante Governance Arrangements Which Deviate From Traditional Corporate Norms

1. *The Doctrine Introduced and Critiqued*

Edwin J. Bradley, *Toward a More Perfect Close Corporation—The Need for More and Improved Legislation,* 54 GEO. L.J. 1145 (1966)*

* * *

INTRODUCTION

The associates in a close corporation usually wish to assume partnership characteristics and to be free of the obligation to map out their organization along the lines associated with a widely held company. To put matters in focus, the parties' freedom

* Reprinted with the permission of the publisher, copyright © 1966, Georgetown University.

of action in the partnership form should be recalled. The Uniform Partnership Act tells us that each partner has an equal voice in the running of the business . . . . Profits are to be shared equally. All of this, however, is subject to the agreement of the parties. They may provide for the management of the partnership business at their fancy and agree on the division of its profits as they choose. Thus, one associate might be designated the managing partner with exclusive authority to act on behalf of the firm and the partners, and to manage the normal operations of the business. Matters of importance could be reserved to the full body of partners to be decided on a unanimous consent or eighty per cent basis. . . . There can and probably will be some agreement on the actual distribution of profits or their use in the business. . . . Since the parties enjoy the fullest freedom of contract when doing business under the partnership form, the agreement in the above areas is unquestionably valid and enforceable.

The parties, however, may be dissatisfied because of the risk of unlimited liability. Assuming their bargaining position with creditors is strong enough after the formative years of the enterprise, the partners should be able to incorporate and do business without pledging their own personal credit. How will obtaining a corporate charter affect that freedom of contract which marked their partnership relationship? . . .

Traditionally the corporation statute does not endow the associates with the same freedom to establish their own ground rules in contract if they do not wish to embrace whatever rules of thumb might be found in the statute. . . .

If our businessmen attempted to outfit themselves with a corporation managed as was their partnership and subject to the same terms and conditions for the employment of the partners and distribution of the profits, the effort would fail unless they resorted to intricacies and deviousness of such proportions that they would believe their counsel was merely trying to earn a fee. They would be astounded to learn that a most dangerous thing would be to sit down and attempt to spell out lucidly and forthrightly their agreement as they did in the partnership agreement. Their forthright agreement that one shareholder shall have the sole right to manage the business, that certain shareholders shall be retained for their lives as officers at agreed upon salaries, and that profits shall be divided in specified ways, would be of doubtful enforceability.

Efforts to accomplish partnershiplike arrangements have sometimes been rebuffed *in haec verba* by the courts. In *Jackson v. Hooper*,[14] the corporation had two shareholders. They agreed in an elaborate document that they would operate in the manner of a partnership. In deference to the statute they named themselves directors, and a third "dummy" [director] was selected. The dummy chose one of the "partners" as his ventriloquist and voted with him. Hence, the lawsuit. The court took the tack that the parties should not be allowed to ride off in both corporate and partnership directions, as if they were somehow two different worlds:

> The law never contemplated that persons engaged in business as partners may incorporate, with intent to obtain the advantages and immu-

14 76 N.J. Eq. 592, 75 Alt. 568 (Ct. Err. & App. 1910).

> nities of a corporate form and then, Proteus-like, become at will a copartnership or a corporation, as the exigencies or purposes of their joint enterprise may from time to time require.

. . . [C]ases like *Jackson v. Hooper* led to the fact that in the very first [legislative] effort to rescue close corporation arrangements from rude invalidation by uncomprehending courts, the salient provision was:

> Except in cases where the shares are . . . generally traded . . . no written agreement to which all of the stockholders have actually assented . . . and which relates to any phase of the affairs of the corporation, whether to the management of its business or division of its profits or otherwise, shall be invalid as between the parties thereto, on the ground that it is an attempt . . . *to treat the corporation as if it were a partnership or to arrange their relationships in a manner that would be appropriate only between partners.*[17]

This statute attempts in general terms to give recognition to the contractual base of the close corporation. . . .

Nothing short of explicit permission may safely be relied upon when the client is risking so much. The statute ought to provide the close corporation with the contractual malleability of the partnership, but to do that it probably is not enough to say so only in general terms.

In order to see more particularly the types of agreements which a statute should specifically authorize, it is helpful to examine both the problems which close corporation associates face in maintaining control of their enterprise and some of the arrangements they have utilized to overcome these problems.

Shareholder Agreements Affecting The Composition of The Board Of Directors

THE . . . TWO-MAN CORPORATION

* * *

Equal Shareholdings

The two-man company generally has been able to operate within the conventional corporate framework without undue harassment so long as the voting shares are evenly divided. The board of directors may be fixed at an even number and each shareholder issued half of the voting shares, thus forcing agreement in the first instance on equal director representation for each side under straight voting. After the first board is chosen, the evenly divided voting stock will either all have to be voted for each side's nominees or the incumbents will remain in office for failure of the shareholders to elect successors. The evenly split board inherently gives each side a veto at the

---

17 N.C. Gen. Stat. § 55-73(b) (1965). (Emphasis added.) . . .

board level. This gives the parties the identical control situation they would have had under the partnership form since each will have a veto and the running of the business will require unanimity. . . .

But where [corporation statutes require a minimum of three directors] . . . the need for an even number of directors necessitates four directors. This creates problems. . . . In *Gearing v. Kelly*,[25] one of the two plaintiffs, who composed a fifty per cent faction, refused to attend board meetings after the resignation of one of her faction's directors. The two directors representing the other faction along with the plaintiff would have constituted a quorum and the board vacancy would have been filled legally. Since the plaintiff was outnumbered two to one by the other faction's directors, she did not attend the board meeting in order to block a quorum and thus avert the shift of power to the other faction. The two directors met and purported to fill the vacancy. The lawsuit initiated by the plaintiff for a declaration of the illegality of the fourth director's election was dismissed. Plaintiff was said to be an unworthy applicant for the exercise of the equity court's precious jurisdiction. She had caused the unseemly situation of director paralysis by her stubborn refusal to attend the board meetings.

* * *

Proper planning would have protected the plaintiff in *Gearing v. Kelly* against the takeover by the other faction. But statutory permission for two directors would make that planning much easier. If each faction is represented by one director, the risk from resignation, death, or failure to attend meetings is minimized and fairly easy to plan for.

Disproportionate Shareholdings

When shares are held in disproportionate amounts in a two-man corporation, the built-in veto power is missing. This suggests that as far as possible voting shares ought to be held in equal amounts. This may be done without difficulty. First of all, corporation statutes traditionally do not prevent sales of stock at different prices to different stockholders. One stockholder may acquire one hundred shares of stock for 100,000 dollars, and the second the same number of shares for 10,000 dollars. There are no nonconsenting shareholders to complain and trigger the equitable controls which exist. Creditors' rights are unaffected. This arrangement requires heroic action by the predominant capital contributor who is called upon to make a gift to his associate. Unless the second shareholder contributes technology or other intangible property (prescinding from family situations) there is more likely to be resort to other arrangements involving the use of debt and senior classes of stock. *Obre v. Alban Tractor Co.*[33] illustrates the possibilities. Obre and Nelson pooled equipment and cash for the purpose of forming a corporation to engage in the dirt-moving and road-building business. Obre transferred equipment appraised at over 63,000 dollars and cash to

25 11 N.Y.2d 201, 182 N.E.2d 391, 227 N.Y.S.2d 897 (1962).

33 228 Md. 291, 179 A.2d 861 (1962).

make his total contribution 65,000 dollars. Nelson's contribution was equipment and cash having a total value of 10,000 dollars.

The court noted that the parties carefully planned the capitalization to reflect their intention to share control from the outset and ownership eventually. The resulting capital structure gave each an equal number of voting common shares capitalized at 20,000 dollars. Thus Nelson received voting common stock exclusively for his 10,000 dollar contribution. Obre likewise received an equal amount of voting common stock for 10,000 dollars but, in addition, received 20,000 dollars par value, nonvoting redeemable preferred stock plus the corporation's unsecured notes at five per cent interest payable in five years. There are many variations on this theme.[35] . . .

Classification of stock can be of great aid where the capital contributions are to be unequal and the use of debt or preferred stock is undesirable for credit reasons or because the parties may not want prior claims on profits or assets. For instance, one stockholder would receive all of the class A voting common for 100,000 dollars, and the other would receive all of the class B voting common for 10,000 dollars. These shares would be equal in every proprietary respect (dividends, liquidation rights, preemptive rights, etc.), but each class would have the right, as a class, to elect the same given number of directors to the board. Under a well-drawn modern corporation statute, this should mean that each would be able to elect himself to a two-man board.

* * *

Where there is a disproportionate capital contribution and stock classification is not desired, perhaps because of Subchapter S inhibitions, how is the same "veto" or per capita voting effect to be achieved?

In *Benintendi v. Kenton Hotel, Inc.*[42] the stock was split two-thirds to one-third. The implications of a split of this kind, in a corporation governed by classic "norms," require careful defensive planning for the minority shareholder. While under the partnership form our one-third capital contributor would have an equal voice in the management of the partnership business, in the "orthodox" corporation voting is on a per share basis, election of directors is by a shareholder plurality, and other shareholder action is taken by majority vote or a greater proportion, but never exceeding two-thirds. Our one-third holder is thus wholly at the other shareholder's mercy. Since management is by a board of directors, and that board has boundless prerogatives and discretion as long as it exercises a loyal business judgment, the law gives insufficient protection against dismissal from employment and a stingy dividend policy. The two-thirds stockholder and others of his selection may be receiving a large, though reasonable salary, while the one-third stockholder receives none and no dividend to boot . . . . If anything left after salaries is put to legitimate use in the business, a suit for the mandatory payment of dividends is a forlorn cause.

---

35 *See, e.g.*, Herwitz, *Allocation of Stock Between Services and Capital in the Organization of a Close Corporation*, 75 Harv. L. Rev. 1098 (1962).

42 294 N.Y. 112, 60 N.E.2d 829 (1945).

In the face of such an intolerable situation the need for some arrangement protecting the minority shareholder becomes obvious. One such device, albeit unsuccessful in *Benintendi*, is a requirement of unanimity.

Unanimity Arrangements

If the shareholders must elect directors by unanimous vote then no nominee will be elected unless shareholders vote for one another. This forces agreement in the beginning and prevents the election of successors so that incumbents remain in office. The risks are deadlock, and forced dissolution . . . . These risks, however, should be a matter solely for the judgment of the shareholders; they should not be a matter of paternalistic preaching by either the courts or the legislature. The Freudian slip in the infamous *Benintendi* case, which held unanimity arrangements at the shareholder and board levels to be contrary to statutory norms of pluralities, majorities, and representative democratic government for corporations, was the reference to the provisions being "almost as a matter of law, unworkable." Such a position fails to account for the millions of partnerships which have operated essentially this way for centuries.

Unanimity on other matters protects against unwanted charter amendments, bylaw amendments, mergers, dissolution, sale of the assets, and other actions requiring shareholder vote. At the board level, unanimity affords a veto on matters related to the management and control of the business of the corporation, and provides protection in matters such as guarding a shareholder's employment with the corporation and blocking changes in the business believed to be unwise.

* * *

Cumulative Voting

To protect the minority holder of stock, a combination of the two-man board and cumulative voting is awkward, but it does work sometimes. Cumulative voting should be the rule in the close corporation statute unless the parties agree to the contrary. No argument against it based on the obstructionism of a minority shareholder makes sense in a close corporation, especially when the proper stress is put upon the importance of arrangements unanimously arrived at. . . .

THE FIVE-MAN CORPORATION

. . . The associate in a five-man organization shares with his counterpart in the two-man firm the problem of finding ways to effectuate fully agreements as to control and profit sharing; he has an additional problem, however, of protecting against the formation of alliances within the stereotyped corporate framework.

As noted previously even if our business venturers are in accord at the organizational stage of the enterprise that each is to participate equally in the control and management of the business, they must grapple with the fact that it is not as simple as merely providing for the same, no matter how formal the agreement might be. They must contend with the statutory complexities fashioned for the large, publicly held corporation. Since management under that scheme is lodged for expediency's sake in a committee called a board of directors, it is imperative to insure compliance with their agreement that each shareholder be placed on the board.

In order to achieve representation on the board for each associate, many of the devices mentioned earlier in connection with the two-man corporation are equally effective in the context of the five-man corporation. Five classes of stock, each carrying the right to elect one director might be issued. . . .

Voting Agreements

* * *

May the shareholders simply agree that each is to vote for the others as directors, or for the nominees of another shareholder?

Agreements to vote stock in a certain way, for specified people or as agreed upon in a specified way or in accordance with a procedure agreed upon (arbitration) have usually been upheld by the courts. The relief afforded is quite another matter, although a vital one. *Ringling Bros.-Barnum & Bailey Combined Shows, Inc. v. Ringling*[62] serves to emphasize the fact that attention must be directed to the enforceability of voting agreements as well as to the permissibility of such agreements. In that case two of three shareholders agreed to vote their stock in unison, as agreed upon by the two or in accordance with the decision of a named arbitrator. The arbitrator determined how the stock should be voted because the parties were unable to agree. The Delaware Supreme Court held the agreement valid but confined the relief to the nullification of the votes cast by the breaching party. The court did not order the shares of the breaching party be voted in accord with the decision of the arbitrator, thus refusing specific enforcement of the agreement.

Voting agreements are markedly superior to unanimity as a way of assuring election of each owner to the board because deadlock is avoided. Furthermore they provide greater flexibility and avoid the necessity of classes of stock.

The Model Act should therefore expressly permit such agreements. Just as important is a provision for the specific enforcement of these agreements. . . .

Absent such legislatively supplied certainty, if each owner is to be sure of his election to the board as agreed upon, the precariousness of the availability of the remedy of specific performance forces counsel to supply a built-in means of assuring performance of the promise to vote a certain way. . . . [T]he irrevocable proxy and the voting trust [are] two devices developed to provide such assurance . . . .

* * *

Irrevocable Proxies

A proxy is ordinarily revocable, but it can be made irrevocable. If one of the shareholders is given a proxy to vote the stock of the others as part of the consideration for the promises of the voting agreement, the proxy should be irrevocable. A proxy given

62 29 Del. Ch. 610, 53 A.2d 441 (Sup. Ct. 1947).

for the benefit of the proxy holder as security for the performance of the promises should be irrevocable. No property interest in the shares is necessary. But the agreement doubtless was a *sine qua non* for the investments of the parties, and there may be cross-options to buy the stock. Proxies given as the means of effectuating shareholder voting agreements ought to be irrevocable under Sections 138 and 139 of the second *Restatement of Agency.*

. . . Hopefully, proxies will be held irrevocable when affixed to shareholder agreements. The better situation would be statutory precision and concreteness. . . .

Voting Trust

The voting trust developed as a result of the uncertainty as to the irrevocability of proxies. If the record owner of the share renounced the agency and terminated the proxy authority, the purposes for which the voting agreement was formed were frustrated. The voting trust was contrived to make the agreement impervious to unilateral repudiation. To form a voting trust the stock of the participating shareholders would be transferred to a trustee for the purpose of voting the stock as provided for in the trust agreement. The owner would retain all of the beneficial and economic attributes and incidents of shareholders. They [sic] might even retain the right to determine how the shares should be voted for purposes other than board elections.

Initially the threat of insiders or unscrupulous corporate raiders grabbing permanent control of the corporation by means of a voting trust, terminable only on unanimous consent, led some courts to hold all voting trusts to be illegal, while other courts insisted on a "proper purpose." Statutes now generally permit their formation, but fear of harm to investors and minorities has resulted in a requirement of publicity by actual transfer of the shares on the books of the corporation to the trustee and deposit of the agreement with the corporation. A time limitation of ten years is common . . . . Since the purpose of both the irrevocable proxy and the voting trust is to assure the enforcement of shareholder voting agreements, one might inquire into the differences and similarities between these arrangements.

* * *

If A, B, C, D, and E agree to give A an irrevocably proxy, is that a voting trust or the "same thing" as a voting trust? Certainly its result is the same. If A, B, C, D, and E agree to vote the stock together as decided upon by eighty per cent . . . and then agree to confer upon the entire group an irrevocable proxy to vote the stock as decided upon by four of the five, is that a voting trust? It clearly achieves the same result as a voting trust. If the focus is put on the separation of voting power from ownership of the stock, everything depends on how the agreement is looked at. If one stockholder is isolated, it is possible to say that he has transferred his voting privilege to the group for the decision of four out of five on how it is to be voted. His stock can be voted against his will at any time. Looking at this from the group vantage point, all of the shareholders are party to the proxy, and they have not surrendered to anyone else the decision on voting the stock.

Is it to make a difference, in puzzling out the distinction between the voting trust and voting pool *cum* irrevocable proxies, whether an outsider is brought into the picture? In *Ringling* the two stockholders agreed to vote the stock together, as they would agree or as determined by a named arbitrator. If the arbitrator were to be given a proxy to effectuate his decision, would that be a voting trust? . . .

Obviously this muddled situation has to be resolved not by the pursuit of the "essence" of the voting trust, but by treating both the voting trust and the voting agreement with an irrevocable proxy in the same way. If a definitional approach is insisted upon, then a voting trust would be defined as a voting agreement with an irrevocable proxy included.

The court in *Abercrombie* [*v. Davis**] was completely correct in its visceral feeling that the voting pool with irrevocable proxy carries the same dire implications for minority shareholders as the secret voting trust. Substantively, the irrevocable proxy attached to a voting pool representing control raises the same specter of opportunity for acquisition of a permanent control with minimal investment. A voting pool with irrevocable proxies may be used to exploit shareholder disinterest through the formation of an impregnable voting alliance. In fact the voting trust was invented because the proxy was revocable.

* * *

. . . In the close corporation the riddle of the voting trust and the voting agreement *cum* irrevocable proxy need not be resolved. Voting agreements with irrevocable proxies and voting trusts, unanimously arrived at, should be released from limitation as to time. No public policy is served by a time limitation when all shareholders are parties to the agreement. There is no minority group on whose behalf protection is needed from sluggish, inefficient, or oppressive majorities. And the notion of rescuing the parties from themselves is too paternalistic to be worth considering. The devices should be put on a parity. The use of one or the other should be a matter for the parties to decide upon.

* * *

A voting trust or voting agreement participated in by less than all of the shareholders of a close corporation should be illegal. . . . Intramural factions and alliances are improper unless their outcropping is the result of the control arrangement unanimously agreed upon, and should never be allowed to be hardened into shatterproof trusts or voting pools. . . .

* * *

Shareholder Agreements Affecting The Management And Control Of The Business

Election of the board of directors is the first stage in planning a close corporation. . . . Even though the associates succeed in having themselves or their representatives

[*130 A.2d 338 (Del. 1957).]

elected to the board, they are still threatened with being consistently outvoted by alliances which are formed at the board level. But if in order to avoid such an occurrence the shareholders dare to agree among themselves in a way which impinges upon the directors' autonomy as decreed by the state, they offend public policy.

This mentality is well illustrated by a line of New York cases although that state has no monopoly on the problem. In *McQuade v. Stoneham*[104] an agreement among less than all of the shareholders divided certain corporate offices among the participants. This agreement was held illegal as offensive to the legislative norm that the business of a corporation, including selection of officers, shall be managed by a board of directors.

In *Clark v. Dodge*[106] the two stockholders agreed that the minority holder, the plaintiff, should be the general manager of the corporation for his lifetime. In specifically enforcing the agreement the court made two distinctions between the case and *McQuade*. In *Clark* all of the shareholders were parties to the agreement, and the invasion of board power was not a major deprivation of the board's statutorily conferred functions. . . . Nevertheless, to assert that the contract deprived the board of only a minor part of its managerial integrity, when in fact it was stripped of the right to name or replace the chief executive officer of the corporation, is ingenuous at best.

Any hopes that the *Clark* case had restored full contractual freedom to the close corporation were dispelled in *Long Park, Inc. v. Trenton-New Brunswick Theatres Co.*[107] This case involved an agreement among all of the shareholders that the class A corporate shareholder should have the exclusive management of the corporation's business. This went too far, the court held, and was not the slight and harmless impingement upon board power sustained in the *Clark* case, and the agreement was not enforced. The result of these decisions was great uncertainty as to what inroads into board control could legally be made by an agreement among all of the shareholders.

* * *

Close corporation statutes should demolish the mischievous heresy that the uninhibited control and management of the business and affairs of a corporation by a board of directors is part of the "essence" of a corporation. . . .

The recent legislative forays into the no man's land of the close corporation do come to grips with this problem. . . .

The New York statute provides:

> A provision in the certificate of incorporation otherwise prohibited by law as improperly restrictive of the discretion or powers of the board in its management of corporate affairs shall nevertheless be valid:

104 263 N.Y. 323, 189 N.E. 234 (1934).

106 269 N.Y. 410, 199 N.E. 641 (1936).

107 297 N.Y. 174, 77 N.E.2d 706 (1948).

> (1) If all the incorporators or holders of record of all outstanding shares, whether or not having voting power, have authorized such provision in the certificate of incorporation or an amendment thereof. . . .[112]

Does this provision authorize doing away entirely with the board of directors? The draftsmen say that it does and that it was intended to overrule cases like *Long Park* and to codify *Clark v. Dodge*. But, it would take a daring draftsman to advise his clients to make large investments while counting on the belief that the New York courts will hold that this section tolerates total sterilization of the board. Prior to the enactment of the statute, this was said rather emphatically to be illegal, and the statute does not emphatically change that result.

* * *

The question of the enforceability of agreements between fewer than all of the shareholders has been the subject of a recent case, *Wilson v. McClenny*,[135] which arose under the North Carolina statute. The statute provides:

> An agreement between all or less than all of the shareholders, whether solely between themselves or between one or more of them and a party who is not a shareholder, is not invalid, as between the parties thereto, on the ground that it so relates to the conduct of the affairs of the corporation as to interfere with the discretion of the board of directors, but the making of such an agreement shall impose upon the shareholders who are parties thereto the liability for managerial acts that is imposed by this chapter upon directors.

The *McClenny* case shows how eagerness to validate close corporation arrangements can lead to a Pavlovian, judicial word-matching application of the statutes. In that case the five promoters of an insurance corporation entered into a written agreement which provided that each of them was to become a director; plaintiff was to be the president, and others were given offices. Salaries were fixed and secrecy was imposed. After plaintiff aided in the organization of the corporation (he was a retired president of another insurance company) and made loans to it, he was dismissed as president by the board; he sued for breach of contract.

The case does not involve a typical close corporation problem. There was no close corporation to begin with. Four thousand shares were sold to public stockholders. The agreeing parties did not have it within their power as shareholders to carry out the commitments without using proxies solicited from public stockholders to control the board. The corporation had thirteen directors. . . . Plaintiff's resignation was forced when the other parties to the contract announced their possession of proxies covering

112 N.Y. Bus. Corp. Law § 620(b).

135 262 N.C. 121, 136 S.E.2d 569 (1964).

a majority of the shares. The court held that the statute validated the contract absent fraud. One may wonder why there was not fraud on the other directors and public shareholders through the secrecy provision and practice. But the important difficulty with the case is that the statute does not cover this agreement. The statute validates, as the court itself said, a contract between stockholders "to vote *their* stock in a specified manner." The statute in no way bears upon agreements to use the power of proxies to insure the retention of officers by promoters or insiders. These agreements are so insidious and frought with peril for minority shareholders that they should be illegal.

New York recognized this danger and did not by its legislation overrule *McQuade*. One section of the statute[138] authorizes voting agreements among fewer than all of the shareholders, but another[139] requires unanimous shareholder participation in contracts which restrict director discretion. . . .

* * *

Notes and Questions

1. The various techniques discussed by Professor Bradley remain the staples of planning for control in a closely held corporation. Since his article, however, state corporation statutes have evolved to make such planning easier than it was in 1966. For example, fewer state statutes now require a minimum of three directors (especially if the corporation has fewer than three shareholders). Statutes generally validate unanimous vote requirements—albeit, placement of such requirements in a shareholders agreement, rather than in the corporate articles or bylaws, may still raise problems as to their validity in some jurisdictions. The latest version of the Model Business Corporations Act calls for specific enforcement of shareholder voting agreements and makes proxies irrevocable if held by a party to a shareholders agreement which so provides. (By contrast, despite the arguable authority of the Restatement of Agency provisions cited by Professor Bradley, many jurisdictions without the new Model Act have taken a narrower view of when a shareholder loses the power to revoke his or her proxy in breach of a promise not to. For instance, the Delaware corporations act only makes a proxy irrevocable if coupled with an interest either in the stock to be voted or in the corporation; neither of which, for example, an arbitrator under a voting agreement may have).

2. From a policy standpoint, Professor Bradley's article returns us to two broad issues raised in Chapter I—what are the appropriate default rules, and what, if any, rules should be mandatory—in this instance, when dealing with closely held corporations.

With respect to default rules, compare the equal voting and equal profit default rules under the Uniform Partnership Act, with the voting and profit in proportion to

---

138 N.Y. Bus. Corp. Law § 620(a).

139 N.Y. Bus. Corp. Law § 620(b).

stock holdings rules in corporate law. The Partnership Act also prohibits salaries barring contrary agreement and requires, unless otherwise agreed, unanimity for decisions outside the ordinary course of business—such as selling the venture. This stands in contrast to a majority rule approach under corporate law. Which rules are more likely to reflect the wishes of parties in a closely held business who neglect to specifically agree on such questions? Professor Bradley calls for cumulative voting barring contrary agreement. Cumulative voting allows any shareholder to place all his or her votes (the number of shares owned, multiplied by the number of directors to be elected) on less than enough individuals to fill all the vacancies (for example, by placing all the votes on just one person). This can enable minority shareholders to vote themselves onto the board, thereby mirroring, to a certain extent, the partnership rule allowing all partners to participate in management unless otherwise agreed. For a formula showing how many directors one can elect with a given fraction of the stock by using cumulative voting see Mills, *The Mathematics of Cumulative Voting*, 1968 DUKE L.J. 28. A few jurisdictions have cumulative voting as a default rule (for all corporations, not just closely held); while a few go so far as to create a mandatory rule giving shareholders the right to cumulate their votes. Since the effectiveness of cumulative voting depends on the number of director positions up for election, majorities can undermine the technique by reducing the size of the board or staggering the directors' terms. For a criticism of cumulative voting see Axley, *The Case Against Cumulative Voting*, 1950 WIS. L. REV. 278.

Compare Professor Eisenberg's approach to mandatory rules in the closely held corporations context to Professor Bradley's. For example, notice the different attitudes toward time limits on voting trusts and voting agreements. Professor Eisenberg's prime concern is with the inability of parties to such agreements to judge future events, whereas Professor Bradley's concern lies in prejudice to non-parties. Hence, Professor Bradley criticizes a North Carolina court for enforcing a shareholder agreement in a widely held corporation. What is the best way to address Professor Bradley's concern about prejudice to non-party shareholders from an agreement among a shareholder faction:

(i) limit the legality of shareholder agreements to a defined class of close corporations;

(ii) require the agreement to have the consent of all shareholders in order to be valid; or

(iii) make the agreement enforceable as between the parties to the agreement, while allowing non-parties to challenge the agreement if they feel aggrieved?

3. Professor Bradley discusses some of the early statutes directed toward validating shareholders agreements in closely held corporations. The following article describes and criticizes the spread of such acts.

Dennis S. Karjala, *An Analysis of Close Corporation Legislation in the United States*, 21 ARIZ. ST. L.J. 663 (1989)*

* * *

III. A GENERAL OVERVIEW OF SPECIAL CLOSE CORPORATION LEGISLATION IN THE UNITED STATES

. . . [S]pecial close corporation statutes in the United States can be roughly divided into two types. One type simply provides, for nonpublic companies, that certain shareholder agreements shall not be invalidated on the ground that they interfere with the discretion of the board of directors. Because North Carolina was the first state to adopt such a statute, I term this type the "North Carolina approach" to close corporation legislation. States following the North Carolina approach define the close corporation eligible for special treatment only indirectly, as any corporation whose shares are not publicly traded. This strategy avoids many of the definitional problems that plague statutes of the second type. States following the North Carolina approach attempt, in the single provision that constitutes their close corporation legislation, to deal only with the problem of internal governance. The problem of minority shareholder oppression is relegated to the general law provision on involuntary dissolution and the equitable powers of the courts.

The second type of special close corporation statute defines a "close corporation" explicitly, and certain of its provisions apply solely to the defined entity. Delaware was one of the first states to adopt such a statute, and I thus term this type the "Delaware approach" to close corporation legislation. Although statutes following the Delaware approach vary widely in detail, most of their provisions are directed toward solving the internal governance problem. Some of these statutes, however, address problems of minority shareholder oppression as well.

A. The North Carolina Approach

* * *

All states following the North Carolina approach require that shareholder agreements be unanimous and in writing. Four states follow North Carolina in permitting such agreements to be either in the articles (charter), bylaws, or other written agreement. Four others require that the agreement actually be in the articles. . . .

B. The Delaware Approach

* * *

1. Defining the Close Corporation

In defining the class of close corporations subject to special legislation, statutes patterned after the Delaware statutes apply one or more of four qualifications: (1) limitations on the number of shareholders, (2) prohibitions against public offerings of stock, (3) requirement of a stock transfer restriction, and (4) election of close corporation status by the shareholders. . . .

2. Substantive Provisions under the Delaware Approach

The substantive provisions of the special close corporation statutes following the Delaware approach are difficult to summarize because of their great variety. . . .

* * *

The statutes of the remaining ten states that follow the Delaware approach to special close corporation legislation are sufficiently similar to be discussed as a single group. Their statutes approach the internal governance problem through a North Carolina equivalent aimed solely at statutorily defined close corporations by providing that written close corporation shareholders agreements are not invalid on the ground that they interfere with board discretion. . . .

In addressing the oppression problem, most of these statutes explicitly permit the articles to provide for dissolution at will by any shareholder, but variety begins to emerge in the grounds they provide for involuntary dissolution where a right to dissolution has not been reserved. . . .

Of all the special close corporation statutes that have adopted the Delaware approach, only those of California and Texas appear to have considered the potential conflict between the increased informality authorized by the statutes and the desire of participants in the venture for limited liability. Both expressly provide that failure to observe certain formalities shall not be a factor in determining shareholder liability for corporate obligations.

IV. An Evaluation Of Special Close Corporation Legislation

* * *

A. The Benefits of Special Legislation

* * *

1. Internal Corporate Governance

A flexible general corporation law permits deviations from board management by provisions in the articles of incorporation and authorizes other nontraditional features such as supermajority voting, deadlock-breaking devices, and share transfer restrictions. Under such a statute, incorporators can tailor instruments of incorporation adequately to meet the foreseeable needs and desires of the parties. Nearly all of the special close corporation legislation is enabling and elective; that is, it permits deviations from the traditional forms by those who elect to make use of it. These special close corporation statutes do nothing more for parties who know what they want and who hire a competent lawyer to effect their desires in appropriate legal instruments than do flexible general corporation statutes. Even a limited statute like that of North Carolina is therefore necessary only where the courts have drawn a particularly hard line against deviations from traditional corporate norms and need a nudge from the legislature to correct their thinking.

* * *

B. Drawbacks of Special Legislation

1. Negative Implications and Effect on General Law

The adoption of special close corporation legislation can raise problems the drafters may not have fully considered. Singling out one class of corporation for special treatment inevitably carries with it the negative implication that such treatment is unavailable for others. If courts regard special close corporation statutes as providing flexibility in determining forms of internal governance, for example, they may return to the discredited "statutory norms" approach to interpreting the general corporation law, notwithstanding the need for flexibility in that arena as well.

The negative implication problem can arise even under a modest North Carolina approach to close corporation legislation. The North Carolina statute provides that unanimous *written* shareholders agreements are not invalid on stated grounds. Many close corporations operate very informally, however, and do not reduce important agreements to writing. By expressly validating written agreements, the statute invites an interpretation that oral agreements among close corporation shareholders are not enforceable.

Under Delaware-approach statutes, the negative implication arises most often with respect to corporations that are either not eligible for, or have not elected, close corporation status. The policy concerning close corporation management is to permit as much contractual freedom to make business arrangements as is consistent with the legitimate interests of third parties and society as a whole. That policy dovetails only incompletely with the eligibility requirements the current statutes impose, such as the number of shareholders and the existence of share transfer restrictions. Refusal to enforce voluntary arrangements that do not unfairly affect third party rights restores the very arbitrariness special legislation is designed to overcome. Yet, enforcing such arrangements in the same way for ineligible as for eligible companies would deprive the statutes of much of their substance.

* * *

2. Conflicts with Third-Party Rights

. . . Certainly, unless third-party rights intervene, it is difficult to envision a policy basis for refusing to recognize unanimous agreements voluntarily entered into by the parties, notwithstanding deviation from a "statutory norm." Most courts now recognize the need for more flexibility in their resolution of internal disputes among participants in close corporations, even in jurisdictions wholly lacking in special close corporation legislation. Informality inevitably accompanies much actual close corporation operation, and the courts are properly forgiving of informal operation when third party rights are not at stake, but legislatures should not sanction or encourage such informality with special legislation.

Many of the special close corporation statutes, for example, expressly authorize management without a board of directors. Viewed solely as a matter of internal governance, decisionmaking by boards of directors at formal meetings with recorded minutes may appear to be a vestige of public company law that serves no purpose in the close corporation context. Every corporation, however, including those closely held, enters into transactions with third parties who are not privy to its special methods of operation. A corporation, whether or not it is closely held, is a legally separate entity that cannot speak for itself. Someone must act on the corporation's behalf, and those dealing with the corporation must have a means of confirming that the person purporting to act for the corporation has the authority to do so. One advantage of the standard corporate formalities is that they provide a uniform and widely accepted method for determining who has authority to do what on the corporation's behalf.

Operation without a board or pursuant to some other unusual structure can complicate corporate transactions, because other parties to such transactions must investigate unusual incorporation papers or agreements that establish the unusual structure. The parties may even require the assistance of counsel in doing so. Moreover, after operating without corporate formalities, the participants in the corporation themselves may forget that they really intended to have a corporation. When shareholders start acting like a partnership and a party dealing with them is confused into thinking they are a partnership, the courts may well treat the shareholders as partners and deny them the limited liability they sought when they took the trouble to incorporate.

The reasoning behind decisions to deny limited liability is often sound. The privilege is based on a meaningful separation of the corporate entity from its shareholders, especially a separation of corporate from personal assets. While deviations from traditional corporate governance will inevitably occur from time to time in close corporations, corporation statutes should not foster management structures that increase the risk of commingling assets to the extent that the limited liability privilege will be denied.

3. Fractionation of Corporation Law

* * *

Special close corporation legislation, even if uniform from state to state, requires . . . decades of development before courts can iron out the interpretive problems inevitable in any new statute. Moreover, as shown by the above brief summary, the various statutes that currently exist reflect highly individualistic, even idiosyncratic, views of the nature of the close corporation and its needs. There is also little reason to expect that competition among the states will eventually lead to uniformity among the close corporation statutes as it has among general corporation statutes. No state has emerged as the "Delaware" of close corporation law, primarily because the statutes now in existence do not serve any real purpose.

Notes and Questions

1. Professor Karjala contends that special close corporation statutes are unnecessary in order for parties with skilled attorneys to avoid following undesired corporate norms. Contrast Professor Bradley's concern about the complex nature of corporate planning compared with the direct approach of drafting a partnership agreement. Should setting up a closely held business require the assistance of counsel familiar with the subtle devices of corporate planning? On the other hand, do close corporation statutes, which require a special election, avoid the need for advice from a knowledgeable attorney? One might note, moreover, that, primarily because of tax considerations, the drafting of a partnership agreement is no longer a straightforward undertaking.

2. One disadvantage asserted by Professor Karjala to flow from special close corporation statutes is that courts may draw a negative implication from the act when dealing with a company which is not a statutory close corporation. For a recent example of this see the Delaware Supreme Court's decision in *Nixon v. Blackwell*, 626 A.2d 1366 (Del. 1993).

3. Professor Karjala worries about prejudice to third parties from informal management structures. In fact, one reason shareholders may choose not to take advantage of statutory provisions allowing close corporations to dispense with a board of directors is to avoid hassles from third parties whose contract forms call for a board resolution. Still, is the loss of convenient proof of authority a factor parties can weigh for themselves when, as shareholders, they decide to follow informal management practices and when, as third parties, they decide to enter contracts with such firms?

Professor Karjala also raises the specter that management informality might lead to piercing. For arguments that close corporation statutes are unsound because shareholders should not be able to obtain limited liability if they also want partnership style management see Fessler, *The Fate of Closely Held Business Associations: The Debatable Wisdom of "Incorporation,"* 13 U. C. DAVIS L. REV. 473 (1980); Mitchell, *Close Corporations Reconsidered*, 63 TUL. L. REV. 1143 (1989). Professor Karjala does not go this far, but worries that informal management practices may lead to informal financial practices (commingling assets) that justify piercing. Is there any empirical basis for the fear that management informality leads to financial irregularities which periodic meetings would avoid? Is this a concern shareholders can weigh for themselves? More broadly, what sort of shareholders would wish to make use of statutory close corporation provisions and why? A majority shareholder does not need such provisions in order to run the company as he or she wishes (including creating unanticipated risks for the company's creditors). Rather, these provisions allow the use of various agreements designed to protect the minority from the majority's power under traditional corporate norms. Recall that the target of piercing is the dominant shareholder—who loses, not gains, power from these provisions.

4. Why has no state, not even Delaware, emerged as the "Delaware" of close corporation law? One factor is that the added expense of incorporating in one jurisdiction and qualifying to do business in another (and thus paying fees to both) is disproportionately greater for a small corporation only operating in one state than for a large corporation whose multistate operations means it inevitably does business in states other than its state of incorporation. For a discussion of competition for close corporation charters see Ayers, *Judging Close Corporations in the Age of Statutes*, 70 WASH. U. L. Q. 365 (1992).

5. One way to resolve the debate between Professors Bradley and Karjala over the utility of special close corporation legislation might be to examine the extent to which firms make use of such statutes. This suggests another look at empirical data.

---

2. *Reality Check: The Utilization of Special Legislative and Contractual Arrangements*

Mike Harris, Comment: *Assessing The Utility Of Wisconsin's Close Corporation Statute: An Empirical Study*, 1986 WIS. L. REV. 811*

* * *

Wisconsin recently became the twenty-second state to adopt legislation specifically tailored to the needs of close corporations and the first state to enact legislation modeled on the close corporation supplement to the Model Business Corporation Act (MBCA). . . .

* * *

This Comment reports the results of an empirical study undertaken to explore the utility and potential impact of Wisconsin's recent close corporate legislation. . . .

I. METHODOLOGY

The study employed two different methods to gather information about Wisconsin corporations. First, the study examined 500 articles of incorporation filed in the

Wisconsin Secretary of State's Office from December 1, 1983 to April 30, 1984. These articles were randomly selected from the approximately 3,000 articles filed during the five-month period immediately preceding the effective date of the Wisconsin close corporation statute. . . .

Second, the study gathered information about Wisconsin corporations through use of questionnaires designed to evaluate corporate size and exercise of certain bylaw provision options. These questionnaires were mailed to the registered agents of the 500 corporations whose articles provided the data for the articles survey. Ninety-eight corporations responded to the questionnaires . . . .

* * *

II. Results

A. *Most Wisconsin Corporations are "Close" Corporations*

1. SMALL PARTICIPANT GROUPS SERVING SEVERAL CORPORATE ROLES

The study indicated that the typical Wisconsin corporation involves a small number of participants. . . . Almost all of the multi-shareholder corporations responding to the bylaw survey had fewer than ten shareholders and fewer than five officers.

. . . Three out of four corporations operated with a board of directors equal in size to the number of shareholders. . . .

* * *

2. RESTRICTIVE CO-OWNERSHIP

* * *

The bylaws survey indicates that share transfer restrictions commonly are placed in the bylaws or shareholder agreements. Most of the bylaws placed restrictions of one or more types on share transfer.[52] . . .

* * *

III. Analysis

Based on the foregoing discussion of incorporation practices, Wisconsin close corporations may be classified into two broad groups. In the most common type of corporation, the participants appear to engage in little detailed planning before drafting

---

52 (29/44 = 66%). O'Neal estimated that at least half of United States corporations use share transfer restrictions. . . . A 1952 study of Iowa corporations indicated that about half used share transfer restrictions. . . .

the corporate documents. . . . [S]treamlined articles of incorporation[76] and bylaws are drawn up with minimal special drafting beyond perhaps share transfer restrictions. . . .

Participants forming the second type of Wisconsin close corporation actively alter or supplant the normal corporate structures to meet their other needs. Although specially drafted articles provisions and bylaw minority shareholder veto provisions received infrequent use, a small but significant proportion of shareholder groups adopted shareholder agreements. While these agreements were not studied in detail, their existence suggests that some Wisconsin close corporation shareholders felt the need to clarify their corporate relationship beyond the general language typically contained in corporate articles and bylaws. The enforceability under Wisconsin general incorporation law of shareholder agreements which infringe upon traditional board functions is unclear. The Wisconsin general incorporation statutes require that restrictions on the board's management authority appear in the articles of incorporation, and dicta in *Capital Investments v. Whitehall Packing Co.*[82] suggests that shareholder agreements that seriously impinge upon the board's discretion may be contrary to Wisconsin public policy. . . .

The Wisconsin close corporation statute . . . guarantees the enforceability of the private contractual arrangements between the shareholders.

Yet, despite the prevalence of close corporations in Wisconsin and the advantages available under the close corporation statute, the statute appears to receive little use. Examination of 1,000 Wisconsin articles of incorporation filings made during the fourteen months following the effective date of the special statute revealed only five percent elected statutory close corporation status.

The newness of the Wisconsin close corporation statute obviously contributes to the small proportion of statutory close corporation elections. Two factors suggest that unfamiliarity with the new legislation does not in itself explain the low usage rate of the Wisconsin statute. First, data from other states indicate that close corporation statutes remain infrequently used even several years after adoption.[90] Second, because attorneys appear to be involved in most Wisconsin incorporations,[91] close corporations are usually formed after consultation with persons who should be familiar with recent changes in the law.

* * *

76 Most of the corporations used the twelve-section incorporation form of approximately 300 words which is available from the Wisconsin Secretary of State's Office, Form 2. (290/500 = 58%). Many of the articles studied which were not filed on Form 2 contained fewer provisions than the Secretary of State's form. . . .

* * *

82 91 Wis. 2d 178, 280 N.W.2d 254 (1979).

90 Examination of 11,974 Arizona articles of incorporation filings for the two years following the enactment of the Arizona close corporation statute indicated less than 1% elected close corporation status. . . .

A study of 2,128 Texas articles of incorporation filed five to six years after the 1973 enactment of the Texas special legislation showed only 4.65% of the Texas corporations chose statutory close corporation status. . . .

* * *

91 Lawyers appeared to be consulted during 73% of the Wisconsin incorporations included in the study [undertaken for this Comment]. . . .

Notes and Questions

The question raised by this study, as well as other studies cited in footnote 90 which reached similar results, is why so few closely held corporations elect to become statutory "close corporations." Professor Karjala's answer is that the statutory election does not accomplish much of anything. As both Professor Karjala's article and this Comment point out, essentially what these statutes do is to prevent a shareholder who entered into an agreement which impinges on the board of directors' normal authority from turning around and seeking to have a court declare the agreement void for offending public policy. Hence, the utility of the statutory election depends on (i) how much risk there is that a court, in the absence of the statutory election, might invalidate the shareholder agreement, and (ii) how useful are shareholder agreements which seek to control decisions which the board of directors normally has the authority to make. The conventional wisdom is that modern courts will uphold shareholder agreements even without a statutory election. Notice, however, the date of the *Capital Investments* decision cited in the Comment. True, the warning there was only dicta; but in a transaction often involving a significant investment for the parties, should an attorney advise them to take a chance if there is a low cost way to achieve legal certainty? Perhaps then the answer lies in the data that the individuals forming most of the corporations studied seemed not to have engaged in detailed planning—hence, they do not need an election to ensure the validity of a shareholder agreement which they did not bother to make. This, in turn, however, raises a new question: Does the failure to engage in detailed planning for a closely held corporation reflect the lack of necessity for such planning, or does it reflect the participants' (or their attorney's) overlooking this necessity? This brings us to consideration of what happens when minority shareholders fail to protect themselves by contract.

B. Ex Post Resolution of Dissension in Closely Held Corporations

1. *The Doctrine Introduced and Critiqued*

Robert B. Thompson, *Corporate Dissolution and Shareholders' Reasonable Expectations*, 66 Wash. U. L.Q. 193 (1988)*

This article honors F. Hodge O'Neal for more than forty years as a teacher and scholar. The topic is one that Professor O'Neal has nurtured for some time as part of legal writings that have made him the foremost authority on close corporations and oppression of minority shareholders. . . .

* * *

The traditional corporate norms, oriented as they were toward publicly held corporations, proved unsuitable for close corporations .... Closely held enterprises tend to entail more intimate and intense relationships.... Such an enterprise is not just a vehicle for investment of the participants' monetary capital but also serves as a vehicle for investment of their human capital by providing everyday employment. Shareholders in a close corporation usually expect both employment and a meaningful role in management. Further, they often have additional bonds, such as family or other personal relationships, that are interwoven with business ties and influence what they hope and expect to derive from the enterprise.

In a close corporation setting, the norm of free transferability of shares is illusory. Because of the size of the business and the small number of participants there is no ready market for interests in the enterprise. Indeed, because of the close personal relationship that characterizes the closely held business, the participants often affirmatively restrict who can join the enterprise in order to avoid being stuck in an intimate relationship with someone with whom they are not compatible.

In this intimate, illiquid relationship the corporate norms of centralized control and majority rule can easily become instruments of oppression. When harmony between participants breaks down, a minority participant may find that the majority interests can manage the affairs of the corporation in unexpected ways. For example, most participants in close corporations receive a return on their investment as salary for services rendered to the corporation instead of as dividends paid on their capital investment. Such an arrangement saves the enterprise taxes and costs the participants nothing so long as the shareholders deprived of the dividends are also officers and directors who receive salaries. Yet, the employment of officers is one of those functions left to the board of directors; after a falling out, those in control of the board can terminate minority shareholders' employment as officers and thereby deprive them of a return on their investment.

The permanence of the corporate existence compounds the minority's dilemma. The minority participant who has fallen out with the majority faces the prospect of the majority having indefinite use of any capital he or she has contributed to the enterprise with no immediate return. Further, the minority may get no return in the long-term if the majority is able to siphon off corporate assets in the form of salaries or rents and the courts use the business judgment rule to refrain from interfering with those decisions.

* * *

... [M]odern legislatures and judges recognize that the intimate, illiquid close corporation investment requires some modification of the permanence normally associated with corporations. The freedom of contract concerning management arrangements that is now permitted to participants in close corporations can lead to deadlock or stalemate for which the parties did not adequately plan. In the absence of such contracts, centralized power and majority rule create a likely potential for abuse of minority shareholders. Investors often fail to anticipate the failure of their enterprise, or they demonstrate an overly optimistic trust in those with whom they are undertaking the venture....

II. Broadening Grounds For Corporate Dissolution

* * *

B. Dissolution on Deadlock

Almost all states have statutory provisions authorizing a court to dissolve a corporation upon deadlock in director or shareholder voting. However, restrictions in these statutes discussed below prevent them from providing a dissolution remedy except in extraordinary situations of shareholder dissension in a close corporation.

Deadlock, not Dissension. The triggering event in some deadlock statutes is defined narrowly to apply to a corporation "having an even number of directors who are deadlocked in the management of the corporation." Such a statute may not apply to a corporation deadlocked because its charter, its bylaws or a shareholders' agreement requires unanimity or a high vote for director action, and no faction can get the necessary vote. Other statutes authorize dissolution on director deadlock without reference to an even number of directors; under this kind of statute courts have held that a deadlock resulting from a high vote requirement in a shareholders' agreement meets the statutory requirement. . . .

Most state statutes now permit dissolution to be sought if there is a deadlock among shareholders, even if the directors are not deadlocked. Thus, if a corporation's shares are equally divided between two shareholders or groups of shareholders, but one group has control of the board of directors, the shareholder or group out of power can petition for dissolution. A significant limitation on this right in most states is that the shareholder deadlock must have continued for a specified period of time, usually two consecutive annual meetings.

Available only to Holders of a Specified Percentage of the Corporation's Stock. In a few states, the right to petition for dissolution because of director or shareholder deadlock is limited to holders of twenty-five percent or some higher percentage of the company's stock.

Irreparable Injury. Most state statutes listing director deadlock as a reason for dissolution require that the deadlock threaten irreparable injury to the corporation. . . .

While the irreparable injury requirement is common for state statutes authorizing dissolution for deadlock among directors, only a few statutes impose a similar requirement for dissolution based on deadlock among shareholders.

Judicial Discretion. A mere showing of deadlock does not result in dissolution under the dissolution-on-deadlock statutes. The statutes describe the circumstances in which courts may grant dissolution, and judges have interpreted the grant of authority as permissive rather than mandatory. Courts list a number of factors they consider in exercising this discretion, and the determination may well overlap factors which a court would consider in connection with irreparable injury. Profitability has been a controversial factor. Several courts have denied dissolution largely because the corporation was operating profitably. In repudiation of one such decision, the New York legislature modified its statute to provide that "dissolution is not to be denied because it is found that the corporate business has been or could be conducted at a profit."

* * *

C. Dissolution Based on Misconduct by Those in Control of the Corporation.

Most American jurisdictions now permit a shareholder to petition for dissolution on grounds which involve misconduct by those in control of the corporation. Illegality, fraud, misapplication of assets or waste are listed as grounds for dissolution in most states. . . .

The inclusion of "oppression" or similar grounds as a basis for involuntary dissolution has opened up a much broader avenue of relief for minority shareholders in close corporations wracked with dissension. Oppression as a ground for dissolution was included in the Illinois and Pennsylvania corporations acts of 1933, in the Model Business Corporation Act by 1950, and in the Companies Act of 1948 in the United Kingdom. Thirty-seven American states now include oppression or a similar term in their corporations statutes.

* * *

In defining oppressive conduct courts have used several phrasings. Some courts describe oppression as "burdensome, harsh and wrongful conduct . . . a visible departure from the standards of fair dealing and a violation of fair play on which every shareholder who entrusts his money to a corporation is entitled to rely." Other courts link the term directly to breach of the fiduciary duty of good faith and fair dealing majority shareholders owe minority shareholders . . . . A third view ties oppression to frustration of the reasonable expectations of the shareholders. The highest courts in several states have adopted disappointment of reasonable expectations as the best guide to defining oppression, and this idea is now included in some state dissolution statutes. . . .

These standards for determining oppression are not contradictory, as conduct that violates one may also violate the others. Breach of a majority shareholder's fiduciary duty, for instance, is likely to be considered a departure from standards of fair dealing and also conduct which frustrates a reasonable shareholder's expectations. . . .

* * *

D. Dissolution Based on Broader Grounds

The increasing legislative and judicial tendency to define oppression by reference to the reasonable expectations of shareholders and to include terms like "unfairly prejudicial" in statutes have pushed the focus of the dissolution remedy beyond fault of the controlling shareholders. Some states explicitly contain "no fault" grounds for dissolution in their statutes. California and North Carolina, for example, authorize a petition for dissolution if necessary to protect the rights or interests of complaining shareholders. . . .

* * *

III. Shareholders' Reasonable Expectations As A Basis For Granting Relief To Minority Shareholders

Reasonable expectations has become a vehicle both for broadening the reach of "oppression" in involuntary dissolution statutes and for interpreting the no fault grounds for relief. Since 1980, courts in a half dozen states have adopted reasonable expectations as the basis for judicial relief, and two states have included reasonable expectations in their statutes.

* * *

IV. Considerations Shaping Relief Based On Reasonable Expectations

* * *

Expectations need not be evidenced by a written instrument. In a close corporation, the parties' entire business bargain is not completely set forth in the corporation's charter or bylaws or even in a separate signed preincorporation or shareholders' agreement. . . . Expectations, therefore, must be gleaned from the parties' actions as well as their written documents. Courts permit expectations to be established outside of formal written agreements, but the minority shareholder retains the burden of proving the existence of the expectations.

Expectations must be important to the investor's participation. The New York Court of Appeals has stated: "oppression should be deemed to arise only when the majority conduct substantially defeats expectations that, objectively viewed, were both reasonable under the circumstances and were central to the petitioner's decision to join the venture . . . .

The judicial decisions tell us that denial of a shareholder's continued employment or of a proportionate share in the return on the capital invested in an enterprise is significant enough to warrant relief if the parties' expectations were for each shareholder's active participation in the enterprise. In contrast, the Oregon Supreme Court held that preventing a corporation's forty-nine percent owner from examining corporate records and failing to notify him of corporate meetings was not sufficiently serious conduct to justify dissolution or the granting of any equitable relief. . . .

Expectations must be known to the other parties. Frustration of subjective hopes and desires will not trigger relief. . . .

The relevant expectations are those that exist at the inception of the enterprise, and as they develop thereafter through a course of dealing concurred in by all shareholders. Expectations of participants may change during the evolution of an enterprise and courts should examine the whole history of the participants' relationship. This is not to say that the primary emphasis should not be on the participants' original business bargain; in a close corporation the most significant bargaining occurs at the initial stage of the enterprise. . . .

. . . [I]n a leading North Carolina case the court refused to give a limited reading to the expectations of a shareholder who had inherited minority interests in family enterprises in which his brother had inherited the controlling interests. . . .

If shares have been received by inheritance or gift, the donor's wishes may have some bearing on whether the donee's expectations are reasonable. . . .

Expectations move the focus away from the defendant's wrongdoing and toward consideration of whether the plaintiff's rights and interests have been prejudiced. The increasing use of the reasonable expectations standard reflects a move away from an exclusive search for egregious conduct by those in control of the enterprise and toward greater consideration of the effect of conduct on the complaining shareholder, even if no egregious conduct by controllers can be shown. . . .

There remains some disagreement on the extent to which plaintiffs' misconduct provides the basis for denying relief. The decisions reflect a lessening of judicial willingness to provide relief as the minority shareholder's conduct becomes more objectionable. . . . When majority shareholders point to the minority's conduct as the reason for the majority's act, for example, claiming that the minority shareholder was fired because of a lack of sales or ineffective job performance, courts nevertheless have provided some relief if termination would frustrate the parties' expectations. When the unsatisfactory job performance can be traced to more affirmative and egregious misconduct of the minority shareholder, however, courts are less sympathetic. . . .

* * *

Corporations to which a reasonable expectations standard should be applicable. The linking of the reasonable expectations standard (and the oppression remedy in general) and the close corporation has occurred for the most part without a specific definition of the close corporations to which the standard is to be applied. In fact, most statutes which provide "oppression" as a ground for involuntary dissolution are open to shareholders in all corporations even though the remedy is almost always used by a shareholder in a close corporation. A few of the more recent statutes restrict the oppression ground to defined close corporations. . . .

* * *

The effect of a shareholders' agreement on reasonable expectations. . . . The principle issues thus far litigated have been whether a petition for involuntary dissolution triggers a buy-sell agreement previously entered into between the parties and whether the buyout formula or the amount stipulated in the agreement controls the remedy to be awarded in the involuntary dissolution proceeding.

* * *

. . . A controlling shareholder should not be able to engage in conduct prejudicial to a minority shareholder and then force the minority shareholder to sell out at a price set in an agreement entered into when relations were harmonious and intended only to govern share transfers in other circumstances.

Courts can prevent a minority shareholder from utilizing an involuntary dissolution proceeding to circumvent a buy-sell agreement. In two cases, courts refused to order involuntary dissolution where no misconduct by majority shareholders was established and instead enforced a buy-sell agreement. . . .

V. Reasonable Expectations And Alternative Remedies To Dissolution

The broadening of the grounds for involuntary dissolution has been accompanied by an increased use of remedies which are alternatives to dissolution. This linkage should not be entirely surprising; the availability of remedies perceived as less drastic than dissolution undoubtedly has contributed to the breakdown in judicial (and legislative) resistance to granting relief. . . .

Alternative remedies adopted by legislatures and courts include: Appointment of a provisional director, appointment of a custodian, ordering a buyout of one shareholder, or some other form of relief such as ordering a change in the corporation's charter or bylaws. Within this array of remedies the buyout has captured judicial attention . . . .

* * *

One of the most important questions in fixing the price of stock being transferred in a buyout is whether a court should discount the value of the stock, once determined, because the stock is a minority interest or because stock in a close corporation does not have a market. . . . Courts in New York, California and elsewhere have fairly consistently held that a minority discount should not be applied in a buyout resulting from an involuntary dissolution proceeding. A California court noted that such a discount would be inappropriate since the purchase is by controlling shareholders or the corporation; to apply such a discount would be to further oppress minority shareholders aggrieved by the controlling shareholders' misconduct. . . .

Even though courts generally have not discounted stock because it constitutes a minority interest, they have not demonstrated the same reluctance in applying a discount for lack of marketability. . . .

* * *

Note

The late Professor O'Neal's treatise, *Oppression of Minority Shareholders* (in which Professor Thompson joined as a co-author for the second edition), is the classic reference in this field. One particularly useful portion of this treatise is a list of the causes of oppression as revealed in reported cases and by discussions with experienced practitioners. The last cause listed is the failure of participants to obtain preventative legal services and the inability of many lawyers to adequately supply such services. Compare this with the frequent lack of detailed planning found in the study of Wisconsin corporations.

Frank H. Easterbrook, and Daniel R. Fischel, *Close Corporations and Agency Costs*, 38 STAN. L. REV. 271 (1986)*

* * *

III. THE ROLE OF CORPORATE LAW IN THE ABSENCE OF A SHAREHOLDERS' AGREEMENT

A. *Does the Rule of Law Matter?*

* * *

. . . The rule matters most frequently, though, when parties are ignorant of it until a dispute arises; then they are bound by whatever the standard term happens to be. Many commentators have argued that such ignorance is widespread and that the law of closely held corporations is defective because it fails to protect ignorant investors, particularly minority shareholders, who do not know enough to protect themselves by contract. The extent to which minority shareholders are ignorant of problems they might face and thus fail to protect themselves is impossible to tell. . . . Certainly participants in closely held corporations are better informed about their legal rights and obligations than participants in either partnerships or public corporations. Investors in close corporations often put a great deal of their wealth at stake, and the lack of diversification (compared with that of investors in publicly held firms) induces them to take care. Partnerships can arise by operation of law without any express agreement between the parties; closely held corporations exist only as a result of formal documents and (typically) the assistance of an attorney. The attorney is a specialist provider of information; questions that never occur to the parties have been addressed and solved long ago by others, and attorneys transmit this accumulated expertise. This process of learning (through counsel) from the mistakes of others seems to work reasonably well in assuring intelligently specialized contractual terms for closely held corporations. The ignorance theory predicts that investors in closely held corporations would fail to provide for restraints on alienation, but this is not the case.

According to our argument, if the organizing documents of a firm fail to provide, say, for dissolution at the will of any investor while at the same time providing for restraints on alienation, this implies that the parties desired the latter type of provision but not the former. Still, the failure of the parties to include a particular contracting term is ambiguous. It may mean that the parties did not want the term, but it *could* mean that they were ignorant. We cannot get much information from the frequency of a given device, either. If 90 percent of all close firms explicitly provide that dissolution is unavailable, this may mean that the other ten percent forgot this beneficial provision or that the other ten percent have an organizational difference that makes this provision unwise.

Drafters of the organizing documents of a closely held corporation cannot avoid a tradeoff. On the one hand, they must provide some protection to minority investors to ensure that they receive an adequate return on the minority shareholder's investment if the venture succeeds. On the other hand, they cannot give the minority too many rights, for the minority might exercise their rights in an opportunistic fashion to claim returns at the majority's expense. The drafters also must worry about the chance that judges will err in misconstruing the scope of the minority's entitlements. The right of dissolution at will and the imposition of strict fiduciary duties—the two entitlements whose omission is most commonly chalked up to ignorance—create precisely these types of problems. In light of the potential costs of these protections, it is conceivable, indeed certain, that there will be situations where all parties decide that they are better off without them. This makes it inappropriate to imply such terms as a rule. . . .

B. *Unconditional Buy-Out Rights*

* * *

. . . [C]ourts have been reluctant to grant involuntary dissolution. In *In re Radom & Neidorff, Inc.*,[43] to take one well-known example, the court declined to dissolve a profitable firm at the request of one of two equal shareholders, even though the other refused to sign salary checks and did not to contribute to the running of the business. Other courts have also been reluctant to order involuntary dissolution of profitable corporations despite allegations that those in control have acted wrongfully. These decisions leave most commentators somewhere between perplexed and apoplectic. Why should investors be locked forever in mortal combat, dragging down profitable businesses?

The answer is closely related to the reason why people do not put dissolution provisions in their contracts to start with. If it is easy to dissolve a firm, there will be more deadlocks, more claims of oppression. . . .

* * *

Doubtless, a minority shareholder who has not bargained for any contractual protection will be in a relatively weak bargaining situation in the event of genuine oppression. The likely outcome of a private settlement in this situation will be a sale by the minority to the corporation or other shareholders on unattractive terms. Some commentators, sympathetic to the potential plight of minority shareholders, have advocated relaxing the standards for involuntary dissolution and allowing a minority shareholder to obtain dissolution whenever his "reasonable expectations" have been frustrated. . . . John Hetherington and Michael Dooley have gone further and argued that shareholders in closely held corporations should have the absolute right to force the corporation or other shareholders to purchase their shares at an agreed upon price or, failing agreement, at a price fixed by the court. Only the automatic and nonwaivable buy-out right, Hetherington and Dooley argue, will solve the "unique" problems of illiquidity and exploitation faced by minority shareholders in closely held corporations.

---

43 307 N.Y. 1, 119 N.E.2d 563 (1964).

These proposals, particularly the automatic buy-out rights, implicitly assume that existing law does not adequately constrain the ability of those in control to take actions to the detriment of the minority and that allowing shareholders to force dissolution of the firm is costless. Neither assumption is accurate. The restrictive rule of involuntary dissolution based on fault does not leave the minority shareholder without any remedy but rather limits its use to egregious cases. . . .

The costs of automatic buy-out rights make it unlikely, however, that this right will be optimal for all investors in closely held corporations. Few firms other than banks and open-end mutual funds hold the liquid financial assets that permit withdrawal of investments on demand. When the firm holds illiquid assets, the right to withdraw capital is restricted to avoid having to sell firm-specific assets at distress prices. . . .

A right to withdraw capital from a firm that has no liquid assets and that does not have an active secondary market in shares also creates difficult (costly) problems of valuation. . . .

Each of the effects of a right to withdraw capital from the firm—the possibility of having to sell firm-specific assets at distress prices and the uncertainties in valuation—encourages opportunistic behavior by minorities. The automatic buy-out right, in other words, gives minority shareholders who have a relatively smaller stake in the venture the ability to impose costs on other investors that is absent under a fault standard for involuntary dissolution. Minorities can use this bargaining advantage to extract a disproportionate share of benefits from other investors. . . .

An unconditional right to withdraw capital from the firm also may be prejudicial to creditors. Under the rule of limited liability, creditors look only to the assets in the corporate treasury for satisfaction. If any shareholder can withdraw assets from the corporate treasury for any reason, the likelihood that a particular extension of credit will not be repaid increases. Creditors will demand compensation for the new risk. . . .

Ex ante, therefore, it is unlikely that an unconditional right to withdraw capital from the firm is desirable even from the perspective of minority shareholders. It would give them greater protection against opportunistic behavior by the majority, but at the cost of greater transaction costs as deadlocks multiply, an increase in the price of equity and debt capital, and perhaps the denial of any opportunity to invest. We therefore think it wise to observe what people actually do when they negotiate buy-out rights. Typically shareholders do not have extensive rights to withdraw capital from the firm. They may do so only on certain events such as termination of employment, retirement, or death.

The failure of the parties themselves to provide routinely for a right to withdraw capital from the firm has important implications. It suggests, for example, that it would be inefficient to impose this provision on shareholders in closely held corporations and not allow them to opt out. It also suggests that courts should not readily infer a right to withdraw capital from the firm on behalf of minority shareholders.

C. *Strict Standards of Fiduciary Duty*

* * *

Courts rarely interfere with the decisions of managers of publicly held firms. It could be argued that judges should treat the acts of managers of close corporations with suspicion, however, because of the absence of the disciplinary effects of the stock market and other market mechanisms. One rationale for the business judgment rule is that managers who make errors (and even those who engage in self-dealing) are penalized by market forces while judges who make errors are not. Thus managers have better incentives to make correct business decisions than do judges. But if neither managers nor courts are disciplined by market forces, this justification has less force. On the other hand, the smaller number of participants in closely held corporations ensures that managers bear more of the costs of their actions and facilitates contractual arrangements between the parties to reduce the likelihood of self-dealing. The differences between publicly and closely held corporations, in other words, do not suggest unambiguously that the level of judicial scrutiny should vary or, if it does, in which direction.

Now courts might use the same *standard* of review for the two types of corporations but apply it differently based on the structural differences in corporate organization.

. . .

. . . For example, a general fiduciary rule in publicly held corporations is that managers cannot engage in self-interested transactions unless they convince a court or disinterested decisionmakers within the firm that the transaction is beneficial. The same rule could be applied in closely held corporations, but its application would vary because of differences between the two types of firms. For example, the decision to terminate an employee in a publicly held corporation is a classic example of the exercise of business judgment that a court would not second guess. In a closely held corporation, by contrast, termination of an employee can be a way to appropriate a disproportionate share of the firm's earnings. It makes sense, therefore, to have greater judicial review of terminations of managerial (or investing) employees in closely held corporations than would be consistent with the business judgment rule. The same approach could be used with salary, dividend, and employment decisions in closely held corporations where the risks of conflicts of interest are greater.

Many courts, however, apply a unitary business judgment rule in reviewing employment, salary, and dividend decisions in closely held corporations. One defense of this result is again to create incentives for parties to protect themselves by contract or otherwise (for example, by arbitration). Although application of the deferential business judgment rule no doubt is harsh in some cases, it does have the advantage of limiting the judicial role to enforcing, rather than writing, contracts between the parties.

. . .

If a court is unavoidably entwined in a dispute, it must decide what the parties would have bargained for had they written a completely contingent contract. The difficulties that result when a court misses this point are illustrated by the much applauded case of *Donahue v. Rodd Electrotype Co.*[61] The closely held corporation purchased the shares of its long-time manager, who had been with the firm for 35 years but was 77 years old and in poor health. He no longer owned a controlling stock interest. The con-

61 367 Mass. 578, 328 N.E.2d 505 (1975).

trolling shareholders (the founder's sons) wanted him to retire and authorized the purchase of some of his shares. The remaining investor (the only one unrelated to the controlling family) then demanded that the corporation purchase her shares on the same terms. The corporation refused, stating that it did not possess adequate funds. The ensuing suit alleged that the controlling shareholders breached a fiduciary duty by causing the corporation to purchase some shares while refusing to extend the same benefit to other investors.

The trial court found that the price paid per share was less than either the liquidating or book value, that the purchase did not alter control or prejudice plaintiff or creditors in any way, and that the directors acted in good faith in approving the purchase. . . .

The Supreme Court of Massachusetts reversed. Shareholders in closely held corporations, the court wrote, owe each other the utmost duty of good faith and loyalty, a higher duty than their counterparts in publicly held corporations. This higher duty requires controlling shareholders who use their positions to confer benefits on themselves to do the same for all investors. Thus the controlling group's purchase of shares breached its fiduciary duty. . . .

Grave reflections on the plight of minority investors in closely held corporations and stirring proclamations of the fiduciary duty of the majority fill the opinion. Completely overlooked in all of this rhetoric was any consideration of the basic question—which interpretation of fiduciary duties would the parties have selected had they contracted in anticipation of this contingency? Although no one can answer such a question with certainty (precisely because the parties did not), it is most unlikely that they would have selected a rule requiring an equal opportunity for all. Buy-out arrangements on contingencies such as retirement are common in closely held corporations. Such agreements provide some liquidity and ensure that the identity of the managers and the investors remains the same, reducing agency problems. At the same time, the limits minimize the costs of requiring cash payouts or disrupting hard-won patterns of investment. No comparable commonly used agreement requires a firm to purchase all shares if it buys any. . . .

* * *

Not surprisingly, courts have found the equal opportunity rule of *Donahue* impossible to administer. It is hard to imagine, for example, how closely held corporations could function under a requirement that all shareholders have an "equal opportunity" to receive salary increases and continue in office regardless of their conduct. Yet this is the logical implication of *Donahue* which holds that the business justifications for unequal treatment are irrelevant. In light of this threat to the day-to-day functioning of closely held corporations, it was predictable that subsequent courts would either refuse to follow *Donahue* or limit its scope. In *Wilkes v. Springside Nursing Homes, Inc.*,[64] for example, the court that decided *Donahue* stated that an employee and shareholder of a closely held corporation could be fired or denied a salary increase if

64 370 Mass. 842, 353 N.E.2d 657 (1976).

there was a legitimate business purpose for the action that could not be furthered without disadvantaging the minority. The court in *Wilkes* inquired into the business purpose of the conduct at issue, precisely what it had forbidden in *Donahue*. . . . This standard, which gives some but not absolute protection to the minority, is in all likelihood closer to the bargain the parties would have reached themselves if transactions costs were zero.

Understanding fiduciary duties as implied terms in contractual agreements sheds light on the question whether minority shareholders owe fiduciary duties to the majority. Unanimity agreements, which exist in many closely held corporations, create a risk of deadlock. A minority shareholder may refuse to attend meetings so that a quorum does not exist or refuse to consent to corporate acts, paralyzing the firm. Although this right helps minority shareholders protect themselves against opportunistic behavior by the majority, it creates incentives for the minority to behave opportunistically toward the majority to extract disproportionate concessions.

Would fiduciary duties diminish the net costs created by the minority's ability to exercise veto power? Several courts have held that fiduciary duties are beneficial on net.[65] The issue is difficult because any constraint on the minority's veto power increases the probability that the majority will be able to exploit the minority notwithstanding the minority's bargained-for protection. One guide is whether the decision at issue might have a disproportionate effect on the minority. Thus a minority shareholder in a closely held corporation with a super-majority voting or quorum requirement would be justified in failing to attend a meeting and blocking the election of a new director who might act adversely toward him but might not be justified in failing to attend a meeting to authorize the purchase of a machine in an arms-length transaction. The veto in the former situation is consistent with the purpose of the protection, while the same action in the latter situation is much more likely to be evidence of opportunistic behavior.

D. *The Partnership Analogy*

That closely held corporations are really "incorporated partnerships" is a common refrain. The participants in the venture view each other as partners; therefore, the argument runs, they should be governed by the law of partnerships. Equal sharing rules, automatic buy-out rights, and strict fiduciary duties are fundamental principles of partnership law and thus, proponents of the partnership analogy contend, should also be fundamental principles of the law of closely held corporations.

There is something to the analogy. We have conjectured elsewhere, and there is now some evidence, that participants in smaller firms who are unable to reduce risk by diversifying their investments are more likely to contract for equal sharing rules and to opt for other principles that constrain managers' discretion. Still, there are problems with pushing the analogy to partnerships too far. First, at least with respect to automatic buy-out rights, the analogy is based on a misstatement of partnership law. Although

65 *See, e.g.*, Smith v. Atlantic Properties, Inc., 12 Mass. App. 201, 422 N.E.2d 798 (1981) (minority shareholder's use of veto power unreasonable). . . .

partnership law allows any partner (unless all agree otherwise in advance) to disinvest at any time and dissolve the firm, the withdrawing partner may be liable in damages for "wrongful" termination and may be able to disinvest only on disadvantageous terms. Thus the Hetherington and Dooley proposal for automatic buy-out rights in closely held corporations, although supposedly based on partnership law, actually goes well beyond existing doctrine.

Second, the assumption that participants in closely held corporations want to be governed by partnership law is itself questionable. The participants incorporated for a reason. Perhaps the reason was only limited liability or favorable tax treatment, and in all other respects they wanted to be treated like partners. But this is not the only possibility. Corporate law is different from partnership law in many ways, and the venturers may desire to preserve these differences. . . . Proponents of the partnership analogy assume that participants in closely held corporations are knowledgeable enough to incorporate to obtain the benefits of favorable tax treatment or limited liability but ignorant of all other differences between corporate and partnership law. There is no support for this assumption once you realize that people have to jump through a lot of formal hoops (assisted by counsel) to incorporate but could become partners by accident.

The right inquiry is always what the parties would have contracted for had transactions costs been zero, not whether closely held corporations are more similar to partnerships than to publicly held corporations. The failure to recognize the limited role of analogical reasoning can have significant consequences. The court that decided *Donahue* was apparently so concerned about establishing the similarities between closely held corporations and partnerships that it never considered the possibility that its rule of equal opportunity might be inconsistent with the observed behavior of participants in both partnerships and closely held corporations. Both types of firms must provide some mechanism for dealing with retirements or terminations in situations where the firm will continue to exist. Most firms could not survive if the purchase of the interest of a retiring member required that everyone else be given the opportunity to sell out at the same price. Because the court never asked what the parties would have intended, it missed the boat.

Participants in business ventures are free to reflect their wishes explicitly in a written contract. Both partnership and corporate law enforce private decisions. When the parties do not or cannot contract explicitly, it will often be difficult to discern what they would have done if contracting were costless. This subtle inquiry is not made any simpler by asking whether closely held corporations are really partnerships. This latter focus simply puts everyone off the scent; indeed, it may be perverse because it directs attention away from the questions of why people formed the corporation and why, having done so, they did not adopt partnership-like rules by contract. Even if the parties did not consciously decide to opt out of the partnership rule, all this means is that they were asleep. What reason have we to think that if they were awake they would have selected the partnership rule?

* * *

Close corporations differ in size, and the larger ones will find it worthwhile to incur greater costs of transacting. (A one percent chance of encountering a problem is worth more to a $10 million firm than to a $100,000 firm.) Larger firms routinely have detailed provisions for handling deadlocks or buying out the shares of retiring employees, even though smaller firms may leave these issues unaddressed. Courts should observe how the larger firms tackle a given problem. These firms are the most likely to surmount any transaction cost hurdle and to spend the most time dealing with the problem once they have elected to do so. The solutions these larger firms offer may be copied and applied to other close corporations, unless there is some reason to think that the proper solution is a function of the firm's size. If larger firms elect not to address a subject through contract, then it is best to conclude that the presumptive rule does not need tinkering.

* * *

Notes and Questions

1. Compare the confidence Professors Easterbrook and Fischel express in attorneys setting up closely held corporations with the experience suggested by Professor O'Neal's work and the Wisconsin corporations study. One consistency between the Wisconsin study and Professor Easterbrook and Fischel's claim is the common presence of restrictions on the shareholders' ability to transfer their stock. Do such restrictions show thoughtful planning, or simply a form book response to one isolated concern—transfer of shares to strangers—found in the closely held corporations context? What do such restrictions do to prevent or handle the common squeeze-out of minority stockholders, removed from employment and deprived of dividends, described by Professor Thompson? Does the presence of an attorney assure thorough consideration of the various differences in default rules implicated when choosing between corporate and partnership business forms? For example, can you specify the difference in default rules which impact the prospect for oppression of minority interests in one form versus the other? For some possibilities see Gevurtz, *Squeeze-outs and Freeze-outs in Limited Liability Companies*, 73 WASH. U. L.Q. 497 (1995); Hillman, *The Dissatisfied Participant in the Solvent Business Venture: A Consideration of the Relative Permanence of Partnerships and Close Corporations*, 67 MINN. L. REV. 1 (1982).

2. Professors Easterbrook and Fischel point to the liquidity problem created if owners can demand the firm buy out their interests at any time. Yet, what are the alternatives? The common existence of share transfer restrictions, not to mention the lack of willing buyers for a minority interest in a closely held corporation run by strangers (even without such restrictions), typically prevents the sale of shares from providing an out for the dissatisfied minority stockholder. Professors Easterbrook and Fischel point to the relief minority shareholders may obtain from the court if they can show fault on the part of the majority. Is there any problem with forcing parties to prove fault in order to obtain a divorce from a business relationship racked with dissension? How much will such litigation cost? How confident can we be of a court's ability to determine fault after hearing a lot of "who did what to who first" testimony from squabbling stockholders in a closely held (and often family held) business? Is there some lesson here from marital law?

3. Professors Easterbrook and Fischel applaud the *Wilkes* business purpose test. For a contrary view see Mitchell, *The Death of Fiduciary Duty in Close Corporations*, 138 U. PA. L. REV. 1675 (1990).

4. Professors Easterbrook and Fischel suggest looking to actual experience to see what parties agree. The following study provides some possible insights in that regard—although it involves agreements reached after rather than before dissension.

---

2. *Reality Check: The Results of Dissension Litigation*

J.A.C. Hetherington and Michael P. Dooley, *Illiquidity and Exploitation: A Proposed Statutory Solution to the Remaining Close Corporation Problem*, 63 VA. L. REV. 1 (1977)*

* * *

B. Survey of Decisions

The Tables in the Appendix report the final disposition of the fifty-four reported cases decided since 1960 dealing directly or primarily with suits for involuntary dissolution of close corporations. Table I contains the cases in which the plaintiff was unsuccessful; Table II contains the cases in which the complaint was sustained on appeal or some form of affirmative relief was granted. . . .

The information presented in the Tables concerning the relative share ownership of the parties, the nature of the business and its condition . . . was obtained from the court's opinion or from counsel; the information concerning the nature of the dispute and the judicial disposition of the case . . . was published in the reported opinions; and the final disposition of the dispute . . . was obtained from counsel.

The final dispositions in the twenty-seven cases in Table I are as follows: one party bought out the other in fourteen cases; the business was sold to a third party in two cases, and was liquidated in three. There was no change in ownership in six cases, and in two cases the result is unknown.

In Table II the results are similar: a buyout of one party by the other party occurred in seventeen cases; in three instances the business was sold to an outsider, and in six it was liquidated. There was no buyout or other change in one case.

When the results in all the cases are tabulated, it appears that defendants bought out plaintiffs in twenty-six cases and plaintiffs bought out defendants in three instances; in two instances the data do not show which party bought out the other. The business was sold to an outsider in five cases and was liquidated in nine. There was no buyout or other change in seven cases.

* * *

The most striking result of the survey concerns the effect of dissolution decrees on viable firms. In only six instances out of the seventeen [sic] cases in Table II in which dissolution was actually ordered did liquidation follow the court's decree. Three of those firms were in a barely marginal or deteriorating financial condition; one company operated a profitable apartment hotel which was sold to outsiders; and two operated successful services businesses. In one of these latter two cases, the parties went into business separately after dissolution, and in the other the defendant continued in a competing firm which acquired at least some of the dissolved firm's business; the plaintiff in that case retired. Similarly, liquidation occurred in three cases in which the court denied dissolution in its final reported opinion. Two of these cases involved failing or unsuccessful businesses, and in the third, a network of family corporations, each representing a separate business, was dissolved and the various enterprises apportioned among the shareholders. These results plainly show that dissolution decrees do not cause the liquidation of viable firms. In all nine cases where liquidation occurred, the firm was either not profitable or its business was continued in some form after the liquidation.

By far the most frequent resolution of the disputes in these cases was a buyout of one party by the other. Buyouts occurred in fourteen of the cases where the plaintiff was unsuccessful on appeal, and in seventeen of the cases in which he prevailed, for a total of thirty-one of the fifty-four cases surveyed. The results indicate that the single most important determinant of whether a buyout occurs is the financial condition of the firm. . . .

In the overwhelming majority of the thirty-one buyouts, defendants bought out the plaintiffs. In the great majority of cases, the defendants were operating the business prior to the litigation so that their purchase of the plaintiff's interest meant the continuation of present management. The infrequent instances of buyouts by plaintiffs would indicate that dissolution litigation is rarely used as a takeover tactic and that most plaintiffs are in fact attempting to liquidate their investment.

Five firms, four profitable and one unprofitable, were sold to outsiders as going concerns. Plaintiffs succeeded on appeal in three of the four of these cases involving profitable firms; they lost in one case involving a profitable firm and in the one case in which the firm was unsuccessful. The effect of the judicial decision in these cases on the final resolution of the business conflicts is unclear. In the cases where the plaintiff succeeded, it seems reasonable to infer that the court's action expedited the sale to outsiders, but no reason clearly appears why one party did not buy out the other. (If both wanted to sell, why did they go to court?) Where the plaintiff was unsuccessful, sales to outsiders were presumably beneficial to both parties; certainly this is true in the two instances involving unsuccessful firms. Clearly, the judicial decision had little effect on the outcome. In all six cases in this category, as well as in the thirty-one buyout cases, the dispute was effectively resolved through the market mechanism, not through the courts.

The only cases in the survey in which the courts' decisions seem to have significantly influenced the course of subsequent events are those in which no change occurred after the litigation. In six of the seven cases in this category the plaintiff lost on appeal, and in the one case in which he succeeded in the reported appeal, he subsequently lost at trial. In each of these cases the defendant was in control of the firm prior to the litigation. Since there was no deadlock, and plaintiff was unable to state or to establish a claim, the defendant was under no pressure to buy him out and apparently chose not to do so. There is no clear basis in the data for distinguishing these cases from the twelve cases in which the defendant bought out the unsuccessful plaintiff. One would expect that in the cases where buyouts occurred, the plaintiffs were able to induce sales either by lowering their price or by harassing the defendants.

III. The Case for Legislation

A. In General

Dissolution proceedings for profitable companies thus function primarily as a price-fixing mechanism for an eventual buyout, but a more cumbersome, inefficient, and costly means of achieving that end is difficult to imagine. . . .

* * *

Notes and Questions

Based upon their results, Professors Hetherington and Dooley advocated an automatic buy-out right for shareholders in a closely held corporation—the criticism of which we earlier encountered from Professors Easterbrook and Fischel. A less extreme corollary to these results might be to change the statutory remedy provided for oppression. If the result of an order of dissolution generally is a buy-out rather than liquidation, why not short-circuit the process and have the court, if it finds relief appropriate, simply order a buy-out rather than dissolution? In fact, as Professor Thompson noted, this is what has happened under many statutes. On the other hand, are there some differences in outcome, even if in both cases we end up with a buy-out? With dissolution and liquidation, there is an opportunity, seen in the Hetherington and Dooley results, for the plaintiff to acquire the business, whereas what will decide who gets the firm if the court orders a buy-out? Also, compare what will determine the buy-out price under the two schemes.

Chapter VI

Special Problems In Mergers And Acquisitions

We now turn to four problem areas which have generated significant controversy, and hence considerable literature, in the area of mergers and acquisitions. The first involves a controlling shareholder's sale of stock at a price greater than available to other shareholders. The next concerns the legal impact of the different forms available for structuring a sale or combination of an incorporated business. The third occurs when a majority shareholder forces minority stockholders to sell their shares. Finally, we look at efforts by the board of directors to prevent third parties from purchasing enough of the corporation's outstanding shares to take control despite the board's objection.

A. Sale of Control at a Premium

Einer Elhauge, *The Triggering Function of Sale of Control Doctrine*, 59 U. CHI. L. REV. 1465 (1992)*

* * *

I. THE AMORPHOUS NATURE OF CURRENT DOCTRINE

Absent special circumstances, the general rule is that the owner of a controlling block of stock is free to sell it at a premium price unavailable to the noncontrolling shareholders. What constitutes those special circumstances has never received a clear comprehensive answer in the case law. One can, to be sure, categorize the circumstances under which control sellers have been held liable into three exceptions to the general rule permitting unshared premium control sales. But, as we will see, each exception is more amorphous and open-ended than the one before it, and the exceptions could, if read broadly, easily engulf the general rule.

A. Sales to Suspected Looters

Sellers receiving a control premium have been found liable if, at the time they sold control, the sellers had reason to suspect the buyers planned to use the control to loot the corporation. Where the circumstances raise such a reasonable suspicion, the control seller must investigate the prospective buyer and, if the investigation confirms the suspicions, the seller cannot sell the controlling block of stock to that buyer.

One difficulty in applying this exception is whether the duty to investigate should be considered affirmative or instead conditional on suspicious circumstances. The bulk of the courts have concluded the duty is conditional: where the circumstances known to the seller do not raise a reasonable suspicion, no special investigation is required. But two courts have concluded that the duty to investigate should apply even absent suspicious circumstances.

* * *

One important issue, which has so far split the courts, is whether a large control premium should alone be sufficient grounds for finding reasonable suspicion. The potential for undermining the general rule is clear. If the existence of a substantial premium suffices to establish a reasonable suspicion, then in effect the duty to investigate applies affirmatively in most cases.

* * *

B. Sales of Office

It is considered a "sale of office," and per se illegal, for corporate fiduciaries who are not selling a controlling block of stock to accept payment for installing particular individuals into corporate positions. But it is generally legal for the seller of a control block to agree, as part of the sale of control, to insert the control buyer's nominees into corporate offices.

The latter rule is grounded on the premise that the buyer of the control block would eventually be able to vote his nominees into office at the next shareholder meeting. Accordingly, courts reason that forbidding agreements to insert the buyer's nominees would serve no useful purpose. . . .

The main doctrinal problem with allowing control sellers to transfer offices has been determining what percentage of the corporate stock suffices to constitute a control block. Under the bright-line position advocated by Judge Friendly, agreements to transfer offices should not be valid unless the block sold constitutes over fifty percent of the voting stock. But other judges and courts have held that blocks of less than fifty percent can suffice if they constitute "working control."

* * *

Avoiding the costs of adjudicating working control is an important advantage of the bright-line position. But this advantage is offset by an important disadvantage. . . . Buyers of control blocks under fifty percent would have to either pay for a special shareholders meeting, delay buying control until the next annual meeting, or risk non-control for some months. And if the block in fact sufficed to provide working control, these costs, delays, or risks would be unnecessary.

* * *

. . . [H]ow can courts in sale of control cases decide what percentage of the corporation's stock is large enough to provide working control? The New York courts have held that 3 percent is not enough, but that 9.7 percent might be. The exact dividing line remains unclear.

Other than gut intuition, it is hard to see what guides these results under the current doctrinal framework. It is surely not whether the seller in fact exercised working control, because any shareholder who possesses the influence to arrange the seriatim resignation of the board of directors certainly exercises actual control. . . .

Another line of judicial opinions potentially has more far-reaching significance. This line suggests that office transfers incidental to control sales are invalid if the payment to the control seller exceeds the premium the control block alone commands, and thus in part reflects payment for the office transfer. One possible limitation, suggested by some cases, is that this line might invalidate transactions only if the relevant contract designates a separate payment for the transfer of offices. But this limitation has no substantive significance. Even without such separate designation, agreements to transfer offices have economic value and will inevitably affect the price paid for a control block; part of the premium is thus always payment for the office transfer. If this economic reality is recognized, this line of cases could easily turn the sale of office exception into a vehicle for reversing the general rule whenever, as often happens, an immediate transfer of offices is provided.

C. Sales of Corporate or Collective Opportunities

Finally, courts have sometimes held controlling shareholders liable when a control transaction effectively "diverts" a corporate or collective opportunity. Corporate opportunities are business opportunities that "belong" to the corporation. The concept of collective opportunities has more potential sweep, including any opportunities that "should," or "ought to," be developed for all the shareholders. The meaning of these terms is, as we will see, fraught with difficulty.

1. Diverted business opportunities.

The most celebrated case involving the diversion of a corporate business opportunity is *Perlman v Feldmann*,[34] which concerned a corporation that manufactured steel during the Korean War. Because of ethical price guidelines then in place, there were widespread shortages of steel. These ethical guidelines prevented the corporation from increasing its profits by raising steel prices to the levels that steel users would pay. Feldmann and his family, however, realized healthy profits by selling their control block (thirty-seven percent of the stock) at a premium to a syndicate of steel users, who presumably intended to use their purchased control to sell themselves steel at the ethically fixed prices.

34 219 F2d 173 (2d Cir 1955).

The court held the control sellers liable on the ground that they had "siphon[ed] off for personal gain corporate advantages to be derived from a favorable market situation." . . . [T]he *Perlman* exception has generally been interpreted to embrace liability only when the sale of control diverts, or allows the diversion of, a corporate business opportunity: here the opportunity to maximize corporate profits from the steel scarcity.

The difficulty with this interpretation is that there was no proof that any corporate business opportunity had actually been diverted. The court dismissed this difficulty, stating: "The corporate opportunities of whose misappropriation the minority stockholders complain need not have been an absolute certainty. . . . If there was possibility of corporate gain, they are entitled to recover." But this dismissal undermines the court's distinction, for any sale of control raises the risk that the control buyer will divert corporate business opportunities, or otherwise exploit corporate control, to profit at the corporation's expense.

* * *

2. Converted offers.

Another line of corporate/collective opportunity cases concerns offers made to the corporation that are converted into sales of the controlling shareholders' stock. In the typical case, the buyer first offers either to buy corporate assets or to effect a corporate merger, but the controlling shareholder declines this offer and instead sells the buyer her controlling block of stock. A profit that could have accrued to the corporation and to all the shareholders proportionate to their holdings is, in this manner, effectively diverted to the original controlling shareholder. The cases are split on the question of whether the control seller is liable in such circumstances.

Some cases finding such control sellers liable seem to turn on the seller's failure to disclose the buyer's offer to the corporation or the other shareholders. But, where the seller is truly a controlling shareholder, nondisclosure seems generally immaterial. A controlling shareholder could fully disclose a buyer's initial offer to the corporation, but then exercise her control to have the corporation formally reject the merger or sale of assets. The real question in such cases is substantive: whether the controlling shareholder should be able—with or without disclosure—to exercise her control to prevent the corporation from accepting the buyer's offer and instead sell only the shareholder's control block.

Another basis for liability is the notion that, because the buyer inquired first about purchasing (or merging with) the corporation, the sale of a control block took a "corporate" or "collective" opportunity. This conclusion, however, seems to beg the question. Why should it matter whether the buyer inquired first about buying the control block or about buying corporate assets? In either case, one could well conclude that all the controlling shareholder took was the opportunity to sell the controlling block of stock, and this certainly "belonged" to the controlling shareholder rather than to the corporation. Or, conversely, one could say that in any case where the buyer does first inquire about purchasing the control block, the seller should know that the buyer is really interested in controlling corporate assets and, accordingly, the seller should first offer the buyer (or other potential buyers) a corporate merger or sale of assets. How the offer was pitched seems substantively irrelevant.

* * *

II. THE TWO DOMINANT SCHOOLS OF ACADEMIC CRITIQUE

* * *

A. Dispensing With Conclusory Arguments

Many scholars use arguments based on intuition or formal categorization to reach conclusions about sale of control doctrine. Adolph Berle started the ball rolling by arguing that control was a "corporate asset" and that any control premium thus "belongs," and must be paid, to the corporation.[61] . . .

* * *

These claims provide fruitful grist for classroom discussion but are all vulnerable to opposing intuitions or categorizations. One can argue that a corporation cannot "own" the power to control itself and that the power to control a corporation is not an "asset" the corporation can put on its balance sheet, but is rather an attribute of stock ownership. . . .

* * *

Pursuing this debate is, however, unhelpful. One can go round and round about whether control is a corporate asset. . . . One should move directly to the policy arguments underlying each school.

B. The Equal Sharing School

The equal sharing approach provides that, whenever a control block is sold, the noncontrolling shareholders must be given an opportunity to sell the same proportion of their shares at the same premium price. A controlling shareholder could not, for example, sell her entire fifty percent control block to a buyer offering $50/share. Instead, each shareholder would be entitled to the opportunity to sell fifty percent of his holdings at $50/share. If all take the opportunity, the controlling shareholder could only sell a twenty-five percent block and would remain a twenty-five percent shareholder. If the controlling shareholder insists on selling all her shares, the sale of control could proceed only if the noncontrolling shareholders consent or the control buyer purchases 100 percent of the shares.

An ingenious argument for this approach was developed by William Andrews. He began by observing that control transfers can either benefit or harm the corporation.[68] A control buyer might, for example, believe that once in control he can increase

61 . . . Adolph A. Berle, Jr., *"Control" in Corporate Law*, 58 COLUM. L. REV. 1212, 1221 (1958).

68 See Andrews, [*The Shareholder's Right to Equal Opportunity in the Sale of Shares,*] 78 HARV. L. REV. [505], 527 [(1965)].

the corporation's efficiency: this would enhance corporate value and benefit all the shareholders. Or a buyer might instead intend to use control to loot the corporation, engage in self-dealing, or take corporate opportunities: this would divert value from the corporation to benefit the buyer at the cost of the noncontrolling shareholders. An equal sharing rule, Andrews then argued, tends to permit the beneficial control transfers and selectively screen out the harmful transfers.

Andrews reasoned that the rule would prevent a sale of control only when the buyer will not purchase one hundred percent of the corporate stock, the seller insists on selling her entire control block, and the noncontrolling shareholders withhold consent to a sale of the control block. These obstacles should not, he felt, pose an insurmountable problem if the control transfer would enhance corporate value. The value-enhancing purchaser should be happy to buy (at the same premium price) as many shares above the control block as he can, because the more he owns, the more he profits from the increase in corporate value. If he lacks the funds, he should still be able to get financing for the extra share purchases by persuading the capital markets that the control transfer will enhance corporate value. If the capital markets mistakenly fail to provide financing, the original controlling shareholder should be willing to remain a proportional shareholder if she believes the transfer will increase corporate value. And, if all else fails, noncontrolling shareholders should be willing to consent to the control transfer if they believe corporate value (and thus the value of their shares) will be enhanced. The equal sharing rule would thus block a control transaction only if the control buyer will not commit enough funds to purchase the whole corporation, and her plans to increase corporate value convince neither the capital markets, nor the original controlling shareholder, nor the noncontrolling shareholders. In such circumstances, Andrews concluded, it is doubtful the control transfer would have enhanced corporate value.

* * *

C. The Deregulatory School

In contrast to the equal sharing school, the deregulatory school argues that the law should never require the controlling shareholder to share premium control sales with the noncontrolling shareholders.[80]. . . The main point is that, for a variety of reasons that follow, an equal sharing rule would, in fact, discourage many productive transfers of control.

First, even if everyone believes the buyer intends value-enhancing action, both the control buyer and the control seller have sound reasons for avoiding the divided or incomplete control that often follows a pro rata sale of the control block. Suppose, for example, the original owner of a thirty percent control block and all the other shareholders participate in the sale of a thirty percent control block to a purchaser. Such a pro rata purchase means that the buyer gets a thirty percent block but is left to contend

80 The strongest proponents are Frank Easterbrook and Daniel Fischel. *See* Easterbrook and Fischel[, *Corporate Control Transactions*], 91 YALE L.J. . . . 698 [(1982)] ("Any attempt to require sharing simply reduces the likelihood that there will be gains to share.").

with another shareholder (the original controlling shareholder) who remains holding a twenty-one percent block. The supposed control buyer thus ends up with a large opposing shareholder who can disrupt the buyer's effective control. The control seller ends up with large stockholdings in a corporation she cannot control.

* * *

A control buyer will thus pay less for the uncertain control that follows a pro rata sale than he would pay to have the clear control that comes with having the only control block. For the same reason, the control seller will value a large, but noncontrolling, block of stock at less per share than she would value a controlling block. She will thus demand a higher per share premium to sell a pro rata share of her control block than she would demand to sell the whole control block. With the price buyers are willing to pay reduced, and the price sellers are willing to accept increased, a pro rata rule will result in fewer beneficial control transfers.

Second, it may not be feasible for control buyers aiming to enhance corporate value to buy one hundred percent of the corporation's stock. Capital markets might sometimes be imperfect, refusing to finance sound corporate plans. . . . [L]ike noncontrolling shareholders, those providing debt capital can never have the same confidence in the plan as the control buyer because only the latter enjoys the advantage of knowing he will be positioned to protect his investment. . . . Lenders may thus refuse to finance control transfers that offer sound investments to control buyers, or lenders may demand risk-adjusted rates of return greater than the control buyer receives or can afford to pay, given the stock premium demanded by the sellers. . . .

Third, even if they can raise the capital, control buyers often have legitimate reasons to be unwilling to purchase one hundred percent of a corporation. They may be unwilling to purchase all the shares themselves because they can enjoy lower risks by diversifying their investments among various corporations. . . .

Fourth, value-enhancing sales of control may often require an unequal division of the premium. Controlling shareholders may, because they reap benefits from nonshareholder relations with the corporation, insist on a price greater than the average value of the shares under the control buyer's management. In such cases, a productive control transfer can occur only if the original controlling shareholder receives more per share than the noncontrolling shareholders. . . .

To be sure, in the above situations one could theoretically still complete beneficial control transfers under equal sharing rules by asking the noncontrolling shareholders to consent to an unshared premium control sale. But even if the noncontrolling shareholders view the control transfer as beneficial, there are two problems with requiring their consent. One is that although beneficial control transfers will benefit all the shareholders, the parties will have to bargain over the distribution of the gains created by the transfer. Often this bargaining will break down due to strategic behavior or be stymied by the transaction costs of getting all the shareholders to consent. Two, free-rider problems are likely to prevent individual shareholders from consenting even though it would be in the noncontrolling shareholders' collective interests to consent.

. . .

In addition to stressing that sharing rules may discourage value-enhancing control transfers, the deregulatory school questions whether equal sharing rules do much to prevent abuses of control. Existing owners of control blocks can, after all, abuse their control without ever selling it. That control transfers are sometimes followed by control abuses does not mean that the control transfers increased the number of control abuses that would have resulted.

Easterbrook and Fischel further argue that looters are hard to detect in advance and that the penalties directly imposed on looters could simply be increased to deter looting more effectively. . . . Easterbrook and Fischel advocate relying more on stock market prices to determine whether the transaction leaves the noncontrolling shareholders worse off than before. If the stock market price of noncontrolling shares has not decreased, or if the noncontrolling shareholders receive a price greater than the stock market price that prevailed before the transaction, Easterbrook and Fischel conclude the control transaction should be legal.

* * *

The stock market prices on which Easterbrook and Fischel prefer to rely are often relevant to determining whether a control transfer was harmful. But relying solely on an ex post assessment of stock market prices would be unwise. Unrelated factors and trends affect the stock market and may result in an increase for a particular corporation's stock despite a new post-transfer abuse of control. . . .

More generally, relying on stock market prices is a two-edged sword. In their examples, Easterbrook and Fischel use the stock market test to identify only cases where liability should not attach. Consistency would, however, indicate that they should also be willing to conclude that liability *should* attach whenever, after a control transaction, the stock market price of the noncontrolling shares declines. . . .

III. MIXING APPROACHES TO OPTIMIZE OVERDETERRENCE AND UNDERDETERRENCE

* * *

The two rules have different advantages and disadvantages. The equal sharing approach would lessen underdeterrence of harmful transfers of control at the cost of increasing overdeterrence of beneficial transfers. . . .

The deregulatory approach, conversely, would lessen overdeterrence of beneficial transfers, but worsen underdeterrence of harmful transfers. . . .

Much of the modern debate between the equal sharing school and the deregulatory school can thus be seen as turning on empirical questions about the magnitude of the over- and underdeterrence associated with the two rules. If most control transfers enhance corporate value, then underdeterrence is relatively less important and overdeterrence is comparatively more important. . . .

Collecting the necessary empirical data is, however, problematic. A particularly difficult problem is that the present frequency of harmful and beneficial transfers may simply reflect current doctrine. For example, a recent study shows that the stock market price of minority shares generally increases when a majority control block is sold. Ronald Gilson, Bernard Black and Larry Ribstein have all suggested that this study supports the deregulatory approach over the equal sharing approach. And the ALI relies on the same study to propose a significant relaxation of fiduciary duties in sale of control cases. But the *reason* the minority shares generally benefit from the majority block sale may be that current doctrine often imposes an equal sharing requirement. Indeed, if the doctrine is functioning properly, we would expect that the sales of control that presently get completed are generally beneficial because most of the harmful ones have been screened out. A currently high frequency of beneficial control transfers does not mean that control transfers would generally be beneficial *if* a deregulatory approach were implemented.

* * *

In any event, focusing on empirical data concerning the general frequency of beneficial and harmful control transfers may not be relevant. The legal regime need not simply accept the general case mix presented to it. With a preliminary sorting, it can segregate cases into two classes—one where the control transfers are mainly beneficial, and another where the control transfers are mainly harmful—and then apply a different rule to each class of cases. All that is needed is a doctrine that can roughly sort control transfers based on the likelihood that they will benefit or harm the corporation, and then trigger the appropriate rule.

* * *

Moreover, the whole point of having a doctrinal trigger that sorts cases into two different types of categorical rules, each of which has different under- and overinclusions, is to avoid case-by-case assessments of the ultimate issue. The equal sharing rule is invoked not because it constitutes the best means of assessing whether the control transfer was value-enhancing, but because the incentive structure prevailing under the equal sharing rule tends to screen out unproductive transfers *without* requiring difficult case-by-case assessments. This incentive structure may hinder productive transfers too frequently to apply the equal sharing approach across the board. But in those cases where a rough initial sorting can determine that the mix of cases includes many non-productive transfers, the equal sharing rule may do a better job of screening out those non-productive transfers than case-by-case assessments ever could.

* * *

The triggering doctrine thus need not sort perfectly. It can be successful as long as it roughly sorts cases into the groups that are best dealt with by the equal sharing and deregulatory approaches. That, I argue next, is precisely what current doctrine does.

* * *

IV. THE TRIGGERING FUNCTION OF CURRENT DOCTRINE

* * *

A. Explaining Sale to Suspected Looters Cases

The line of looting cases is both the easiest and the hardest to explain in terms of its triggering function. It is the easiest because the courts' concern with the increased risk of corporate harm is so apparent. Moreover, the courts' willingness to impose a duty to investigate on the control seller, rather than just relying on the legal enforcement of the buyer's fiduciary obligations, suggests judicial awareness of the inability of ordinary fiduciary duties to eliminate underdeterrence.

* * *

B. Explaining Sale of Office Cases

Understanding the triggering function of sale of control doctrine also helps make sense of the doctrine's sale of office cases. As we saw in Section I.B., these cases cannot be explained in terms of whether or not a payment was actually made for the transfer of offices, because in fact part of the premium must always reflect payment for the immediate office transfer. This is true whether the control block transferred constitutes three, ten, thirty, sixty, or even ninety percent of the corporation's stock.

The doctrine makes more sense, however, if understood as applying the sale of office label, and thus imposing the equal sharing duty, whenever the control transfer seems likely to increase the risk of control abuse. The greater the investment interest of the buyer, the less likely that he will want to place people who will harm the corporation into corporate offices, and the less benefit to the equal sharing approach. The smaller the investment interest of the control buyer, the more likely it is that abusing control will be profitable, and thus the more advantageous the equal sharing approach will be.

* * *

C. Explaining Diverted Opportunity Cases

Triggering function theory is most useful in explaining the cases most difficult to explain (or cabin) under the current doctrine: the diverted opportunity cases. As elsewhere, the formal labels applied by the courts reflect policy conclusions. The courts are more likely to label an opportunity "corporate" or "collective," or to conclude that it was "diverted" by the sale of control, if the control transfer appears to increase the risk of control abuse. Where no such increased risk is posed, opportunities that might otherwise appear similar are labelled differently, and the equal sharing approach is not triggered.

1. Diverted business opportunities.

* * *

Where a market shortage is created by price controls [as in *Perlman*], the rewards of diverting corporate products to a customer who is a controlling shareholder are so great that they substantially increase the risk that such diversions will occur. The circumstances also decrease the feasibility of legal remedies against the buyer because it would be hard to win a suit alleging that it is unfair self-dealing for the controlling shareholder to sell itself the corporate product at the ethically fixed price. . . .

* * *

The incentives to self-deal and the feasibility of post-transfer litigation are different for the typical sale to an interested customer. Normally, a market price for the corporate product exists, and the controlling shareholder cannot hope to reap a great profit by selling the corporate product to itself without selling so far below the market price that a self-dealing claim will be easy to prove and win.

* * *

2. Converted offers.

The central issue concerning allegedly converted offers is whether it should matter which offer the buyer makes first. . . . [T]o the extent how the offer was pitched *is* relevant, it seems to cut in the opposite direction. Buyers who first make an offer for all the corporation or all its shares have signalled a willingness to purchase the entire corporation. This suggests not a buyer planning to abuse control, but a buyer with benign motivations. A buyer who offered to buy only the control block would be more worrisome. It is thus not surprising that few cases have actually followed *Brown v. Halbert's*[*] suggestion that unshared premium control sales cannot be made when the buyer first offers to merge or purchase the corporation.

* * *

Notes and Questions

Professor Elhauge gears his policy discussion toward the objective of discouraging transfers of control to owners who will act detrimentally to the corporation, while encouraging (or, at least, not discouraging) transfers to owners who will improve management. This is a goal of allocative efficiency—moving resources to their most valued use. Might the law, however, also legitimately be concerned with distributional equity—in other words, the fair sharing of profits between different claimants? This was the goal of the *Brown* decision, criticized by Professor Elhauge, in which the court condemned the majority stockholder's restructuring a sale in which all stockholders could have shared pro-rata, into a deal in which the defendant received more per share than minority owners.

[*76 Cal. Rptr. 781 (1969)]

B. De Facto Merger Doctrine

Ernest L. Folk, III, *De Facto Mergers in Delaware:* Hariton v. Arco Electronics, Inc., 49 VA. L. REV. 1261 (1963)*

I. BACKGROUND

The Delaware Supreme Court's recent decision in *Hariton v. Arco Electronics, Inc.*,[1] represents a decisive moment in the development of the *de facto* merger doctrine. This concept has been invoked in connection with two typical techniques of corporate combination other than mergers themselves—sales of corporate assets and stock acquisitions. The archetypal argument . . . is that the transaction, despite attempts to give it another form, is indeed a merger, and therefore certain incidents characteristic of statutory mergers must be attached to it. The usual object of such arguments . . . is to enjoin the transaction for want of adequate consideration or to enforce shareholder voting or appraisal rights. In Delaware, a merger requires a . . . vote of the shareholders of all participating corporations, with appraisal rights for dissenters. A sale of assets, on the other hand, requires only the consent of a majority of the selling corporations' shareholders, with no appraisal rights, and nothing more is needed for a stock acquisition than the approval of the board of directors. Thus, the *de facto* merger concept is primarily a function of the differing features of mergers, assets sales, and stock acquisition. By treating the last two as covert mergers, the doctrine makes certain consequences of amalgamation identical whatever formal technique is used.

* * *

C. *De Facto Mergers: The Pennsylvania Approach*

The pivotal case of recent years, *Farris v. Glen Alden Corp.*,[19] articulates an approach which the Delaware decisions, culminating in *Hariton*, reject . . . . At the time that case was decided, Pennsylvania recognized appraisal rights for shareholders of most corporations participating in a merger and for shareholders of a corporation selling all or substantially all of its assets other than in the regular course of business. In *Farris,* Glen Alden agreed to purchase the assets of List. . . . Glen Alden agreed to issue a large block of its shares to List, and List in turn agreed to dissolve and distribute the stock to its shareholders. A Glen Alden shareholder sued to enjoin the transaction, asserting that it was a *de facto* merger which failed to comply with Pennsylvania merger requirements. The Pennsylvania Supreme Court, in granting the injunction, held alternatively that (1) the transaction was in substance a merger, and (2) even if it

1 188 A.2d 123 (Del. 1963), *affirming* 182 A.2d 22 (Del. Ch. 1962).

19 393 Pa. 427, 143 A.2d 25 (1958).

were not, the nominal purchaser (Glen Alden) was the real seller, whose shareholders consequently had an appraisal right under the sale-of-assets statute.

The *de facto* merger holding was based on a variety of factors which the court found in the transaction, including a complete change in the nature of the corporation's business, the doubling of the size of the successor corporation, a shift in control of the board of directors to the selling corporation, the purchaser's assumption of the seller's liabilities, a reduction of the proportionate interest of the purchasing corporation's shareholders in the successor corporation plus a sharp drop in the book value of their shares, and the fact that the selling corporation dissolved and distributed the shares it received to its shareholders. Evidently, in the court's view, no one of these factors alone can transform an assets sale into a merger, but the court did not disclose the precise combination of factors which would. Indeed, some of the factors are to be found in many assets sales of impeccable legitimacy.

* * *

(1) The fact that a purchaser's post-transaction business is completely changed evidently weighed heavily in the Pennsylvania court's finding that the combination brought about a substantial change in the nature of the shareholder's investment. However, this may be a completely inappropriate consideration. The very reason for a sale of assets may be not only to enable the purchaser to expand the business it is presently engaged in, but also to allow it to diversify, perhaps moving from a declining into a growth industry. The fact that the change of business takes place by combination, rather than by a charter amendment or internal expansion, seems immaterial, and those who would use the *de facto* merger doctrine to ensure the same results whatever the form might well consider that a change of business by means other than corporate combination would grant none of the rights the *de facto* merger doctrine does. Nor is change of business an identifying mark of a covert merger, for many mergers leave the type of business unchanged. . . .

(2) An increase in the size of the purchaser was also stressed in *Farris*. But size is not necessarily material, because some size increase is an inevitable result of any assets [purchase]. . . .

(3) Another factor relied upon by the Pennsylvania court in *Farris* was that the purchaser assumed the seller's liabilities. To give weight to this factor is subtly to commit the logical fallacy of saying that because every merger entails the assumption of liabilities, every assumption of liabilities implies a merger. From the standpoint of creditors and, more generally, of the public, it is desirable for the purchaser to assume the seller's liabilities, particularly in light of the confusion about the rights of the seller's creditors after an assets sale. Indeed, the problem is one of encouraging purchasers to shoulder liabilities, not of discouraging it. . . .

(4) In *Farris*, despite the nearly equal size of the two corporations, the purchaser's shareholders had a much smaller proportionate interest after the transaction. However, this point is inconclusive. Whenever the purchasing corporation issues shares for assets . . . the proportionate interest of the old shareholders is necessarily diluted, and it is natural for existing shareholders, particularly in a close corporation,

to wish to guard against this. But this reasoning, extended logically, would mean that whenever a purchaser uses its own shares to buy another corporation's assets (as all sale-of-assets statutes permit), there is a *de facto* merger. However, if the assets transferred are approximately equal in value to the original assets of the purchasing corporation and yet the seller acquires an excessive proportion of the purchaser's shares, the facts may point to an excessive consideration calling for judicial inquiry. Nevertheless, were this the case in an avowed merger, the same sort of inquiry would be in order. Hence, this factor is logically irrelevant to the *de facto* merger issue.

(5) The fact that the book value per share of the purchaser's old shareholders was markedly diminished by the asset acquisition may be disposed of in a similar fashion. The implication again is that the purchaser gave an excessive consideration which may be traceable to fraud, breach of duty, pressing needs of the purchaser which induce it to part with a large consideration, or a legally permissible misjudgment on the part of the purchaser's directors.

(6) The *Farris* court also considered the mandatory dissolution of the seller to be an important factor in its decision. . . .

(7) A final point stressed in *Farris*—that the nominal seller's directors succeed to a large majority of the purchaser's board posts—also goes to the issue of an excessive consideration.

In sum, these individual factors seem only marginally relevant, at best, to the question when a sale of assets becomes a *de facto* merger. . . . Factors . . . (4), (5), and (7) might create a breach-of-duty issue, especially if it were shown that the seller was controlled by directors, officers, or large shareholders of the purchaser. In such a situation the remedy is not to find a merger but to redress the self-dealing.

A further question is whether some combination of these factors points to a concealed merger . . . . First, if each factor standing alone is only marginally persuasive, grouping together a number of them is not certain to carry conviction. . . .

Second, a *de facto* merger test based on some combination of factors is unsettling to the security of transactions when it is impossible or difficult to state the disqualifying factors, for no objective standard is available for measuring a proposed transaction in advance. Moreover, every sale of assets is potentially subject to a lengthy hearing probing every possible "factor" pointing to a *de facto* merger. Even if the disqualifying factors can be precisely designated, litigation is no less likely to result. Of course, the more disqualifying factors the courts find, the less flexible will be the sale-of-assets procedure. For example, a rule which forbids coupling a sale of assets with a mandatory dissolution of the seller is clear and easy to apply, but its effect is to force every corporate fusion into the mold of a merger. However, even such an apparently straightforward rule creates uncertainty. Is a sale of assets invalid if it is followed by a dissolution of the seller at some later date? The two steps, if such they are, are not formally part of a corporate fusion plan, but a court operating under such a rule must consider whether there is "really" an arrangement which must be interpreted as a *de facto* merger. Finally, the greater the uncertainty, the greater is the chance of unscrupulous shareholders using their enhanced bargaining position to force concessions.

Third, assuming that some of these factors are indicative of a "real" merger, it is questionable whether a court on its own should declare standards supplementary to whatever standards the statute provides. The *Farris* excursion left so much uncertainty that the Pennsylvania legislature promptly came to the rescue with a special rule which was, at least, clear cut. The spirit of the Delaware cases, especially *Hariton,* is to eschew such a judicial attempt. The *Hariton* decision reflects the belief that the value of maintaining objective standards in this area—the simple statutory formalities and traditional equitable requirements—outweighs any possible benefits of turning up a merger lurking under some assets sale. This is the real significance of the court's invocation of the "equal dignity" and "independence" of each of the statutory techniques for achieving a corporate combination. Apparently, the Delaware court is loath to compel the amalgamators to travel only one of the roads opened by the legislature.

A partial assessment of the *Hariton* principle is now in order. Its holding, and the doctrine it radiates, is sound. By requiring only adherence to form and minimum standards of fairness, it affords an objective test facilitating corporate planning and at the same time avoids the inherent complexities of a judicial test which seeks a "real" merger beyond the form of the transaction. In addition, it does suitable obeisance to a modern idol of the market-place, "flexibility," for it leaves open some route other than a strict merger for the consolidation of corporations. Dissenting shareholders seeking a buy-out may suffer if *Hariton* means that most fusions will use the sale-of-assets technique, but there is nothing to show that these interests are so compelling that a court, *absent statute*, should voluntarily give them precedence over the equally weighty competing interests so well served by *Hariton*. But even beyond this, the *Hariton* case points to a judgment, not previously articulated by the Delaware courts, on some profoundly basic questions, to which we now turn.

C. Hariton*'s Hidden Premises*

1. *The Shareholder's Appraisal Remedy.* Whenever a court holds that a sale of assets is a *de facto* merger, it necessarily recognizes appraisal rights for shareholders of all corporations involved, since they are a characteristic incident of any merger. In holding "plainly correct" the contention that the sale in *Hariton* "has achieved the same result as a merger," the Delaware court displays, consciously or unconsciously, a profound distrust of appraisal rights, although not a word of this appears in the opinions. In large measure, then, the soundness of *Hariton* turns on the validity of the appraisal remedy and, more particularly, of judicially extending it to a class of transactions for which such a remedy is not expressly granted.

Although it is unnecessary to explore fully the pros and cons of appraisal rights,[73] several points may be mentioned in the context of *de facto* mergers. First, appraisal rights may severely impair the ready cash of the corporation, especially when it is seeking to step up business performance through an amalgamation. Indeed, if the dissenters own a large number of shares, they may block the transaction altogether, although his-

---

73 This has been done thoroughly and entertainingly in Manning, *The Shareholder's Appraisal Remedy: An Essay for Frank Coker*, 72 YALE L.J. 223 (1962).

torically the remedy was designed to allow corporate combinations to be carried out. Second, the recognition of appraisal rights results in somewhat arbitrarily carving out a group of transactions—usually mergers—for special treatment, since appraisal rights do not apply in other situations where the shareholder is realistically "hurt" or his investment changed just as much. Apart from the infinite variety of directors' business decisions which can affect a shareholder's interest adversely, there are a number of "fundamental corporate changes" which generate no appraisal right, such as corporate purchases of assets for stock, sales of stock for cash which in turn is used to purchase assets, amendments of the articles of incorporation, dissolution with distributions in kind, and sales of controlling blocks of shares. If the theory of the appraisal remedy is to aid the injured shareholder, appraisal rights should be available in many instances other than mergers, particularly if a shareholder injury is defined as a change in the nature of his investment or in his relationship to the corporation and the other shareholders. . . .

If such conceptualistic grounds are insufficient for an express legislative enactment, they should be equally unpersuasive for a court asked to recognize a class of transactions with an extra-statutory appraisal right attached. Indeed, policy considerations play a large role in a court's decision to embrace or reject the *de facto* merger concept, and in making its choice the court impliedly passes judgment on the validity of appraisal rights. A court adopting the *de facto* merger concept should carefully consider whether this is the best way to protect shareholder interests. A court rejecting it, on the other hand, should be assured that it has other tools to protect the affected interests. . . .

2. *The Nature of the Shareholder's Investment.* Another premise underlying *Hariton* runs even deeper than its distrust of the appraisal remedy. Stated negatively, it is a rejection of the idea that a shareholder's investment is exclusively defined in terms of his relationship to a unique business enterprise so that (1) he cannot be forced against his will into a relationship with a different enterprise or (2) at least is entitled to sever his original relationship at the corporation's expense. Appraisal rights on mergers and assets sales are consistent with this idea. On analysis, it is a strict application of the corporate entity concept. Aside from occasional appraisal rights for certain charter amendments or on liquidation, or a very rare extension of such rights on a purchase of assets, this idea has not been recognized in "internal" changes in the corporation in which the shareholder originally invested, no matter how great the impact on his investment. Hence, a total change in the business, if not through a "fundamental corporate change" but through internal evolution or a revolutionary decision to alter course, yields no appraisal rights, for the corporate entity remains the same for "legal purposes." On the other hand, such rights cannot be denied where one corporation merges with another doing an identical business, even though the shareholder's investment is unchanged or improved. Consequently, a doctrinaire insistence on the corporate entity concept, here as elsewhere, should be avoided.

The basic premise implicitly adopted in *Hariton* may perhaps be stated more affirmatively. One does not invest in a unique corporate entity or even a particular business operation,[80] but rather in a continuous course of business which changes over a long period of time. Certainly the best investments are growth investments—investments in enterprises which change with time, technology, business opportunities, and altered demand; and the worst investments are those which diminish in value because the type of business has lost importance and the corporation has been unable to adapt to the changed conditions. Although a shareholder's enthusiasm dwindles when an enterprise changes internally for the worst, no one suggests that he should have an option to compel the return of his investment. Viewed this way, the fact that the change—for better or for worse—comes through marriage, whether by merger or assets sale, seems purely incidental. The fact that the corporate entity in which one invested disappears as a result of a merger or of a sale of assets coupled with dissolution is also beside the point. One's investment may gain immortality when it takes a new form, *i.e.*, a share in a successor enterprise. The fact is that, closely held corporations aside, an investment in a corporation is really an investment in the judgment, business acumen, integrity, and vigor of management, whose personnel and policy change over time. Management ability may have its finest hour in negotiating and implementing arrangements which conceptually change the shareholder's investment and his original relationship to the corporation and its shareholders, but which actually improve his investment.

This is not meant to be a paean in praise of management. It does not mean that management (with or without a majority or more of the shareholders) should be omnipotent. . . . It does seem, however, that an unrealistic importance has been attached to the investor's interest in changes in corporate form. Certainly, "fundamental corporate change" is too undiscriminating a basis on which to adopt a *de facto* merger concept, and in so far as *Hariton* rejects such a basis, the decision seems entirely sound.

* * *

IV. CONCLUDING UNSCIENTIFIC POSTSCRIPT

* * *

B. *Creditors*

Although the Delaware courts at one time invoked *de facto* merger in creditor cases, its use there is not equivalent to its use in *Farris*. It is logically consistent to sustain a corporate fusion vis-à-vis shareholders and at the same time hold that creditors of a corporation selling its assets may claim against the successor corporation. Such a situation is a *de facto* merger only in the sense that a merger incident, the automatic assumption of liabilities, attaches to a transaction which is not technically a merger. . . . Furthermore, assuming statutory compliance, creditors [of a corporation selling its

80 The business can be drastically changed by the corporation without giving shareholders a vote on the matter, let alone appraisal rights. Thus, the articles of incorporation may be drafted with an indefinite number and variety of business "purposes," and the directors may decide when they want to change course. If the articles are not so broadly phrased, an amendment can be added to give the necessary authority.

assets] will generally be protected, since the sale-of-assets plan often requires the purchaser to assume the seller's liabilities. If either an assets sale or an exchange of shares is followed by dissolution, there is a statutory requirement that creditors must be paid or otherwise provided for. In short, *Hariton's* rejection of the *de facto* merger doctrine forebodes no prejudice to creditor interests; it is concerned primarily with rights and relations among shareholders.

Nevertheless, in neither a sale of assets nor an exchange of shares is the purchaser *compelled* to assume the other corporation's obligations. The theory, of course, is that on a sale of assets other assets have replaced those with which the corporation parted, and on an exchange of shares the creditors would retain their priority, this time in relation to a new shareholder. But if theory and fact conflict in a particular case, the courts could, under traditional theories of creditor protection, allow claimants to go against the purchaser. Such a remedy, however, should not be confused with the *de facto* merger doctrine.

* * *

Note

Professor Folk identifies two rights of a corporation's shareholders potentially dictated by the manner in which management structures a corporate acquisition or combination: The right to vote on the transaction and the right to demand the corporation cash any shareholder out at a price fixed by appraisal. The following two articles further explore these two rights. The first broadens the focus by asking when shareholders ought to be able to vote on any transaction. The second updates developments in the area of appraisal rights since Professor Folk wrote.

Lynne I. Dallas, *The Control and Conflict of Interest Voting Systems*, 71 N.C. L. Rev. 1 (1992)*

II. The Development of Shareholder Voting Rights

A. *The History of Voting Rights*

* * *

1. Contract-Partnership Theory

The contractual theory analogized corporations to partnerships. Shareholders constituted the corporation; directors of the corporation were merely their "agents."

Although early charters and state corporation statutes included management clauses providing that the corporation's business affairs be conducted by the board of directors, the power of management was nevertheless perceived to be derived from shareholders. . . .

Even broadly worded management clauses were viewed as limiting directorial authority to "ordinary business transactions." In addition, such clauses did not appear to deprive the majority of shareholders of "the power of directing the general policy of the corporation, and of deciding upon the propriety of important changes in the company's business."

The majority of shareholders, however, could decide matters only within the original objectives and purposes of the corporation. Borrowing from partnership law, corporate law required that "fundamental" or material changes, outside these purposes and objectives, be dependent upon the unanimous consent of shareholders. Such changes included modifications in the nature or extent of the corporation's business from that set forth in its charter, a sale of all its assets, a merger or consolidation of its business, or dissolution. . . .

2. Entity Theory

Courts moving away from the contractualist's position refused to enjoin changes even if shareholders did not unanimously approve them. . . . For example, courts construed original charters to authorize "new and additional enterprises of a nature similar" to those included in the charter or not "so foreign to the purposes and scope of the charter." Therefore, unanimous shareholder consent was not required for the corporation to engage in these new activities. . . .

* * *

The power of shareholders . . . shifted to the board of directors. Directors were not agents of the shareholders; their power was considered "original and undelegated" by shareholders. The courts construed directors' powers granted in management clauses as neither conferred nor revocable by shareholders. Moreover, courts interpreted these clauses to confer exclusive authority over more corporate decisions to the board of directors.

By the late nineteenth century, the unanimous consent requirement for fundamental changes hindered the expansion of corporations into other businesses as well as mergers and consolidations. State legislatures enacted statutory provisions permitting these changes to be made with a lesser vote of shares if the board of directors also concurred with the change. New York adopted one of the earliest of such statutes in 1893; by 1926 virtually all states had adopted similar statutory provisions or reached the same result through court decisions. . . .

. . . Moreover, contrary to their historical roots, explicit statutory provisions that had been designed to change the common-law requirement of unanimity to majority rule disenfranchised the majority of shareholders from deciding all but the changes described by those provisions.

* * *

B. *Traditional, Newly Adopted, and Proposed Voting Rights*

As any corporations textbook explains, shareholders, under state statutes, have the right to vote on "fundamental" changes. These changes consist of mergers, a sale of substantially all corporate assets, changes in the corporation's articles of incorporation, and dissolution. In most cases management must first initiate and approve these transactions. The shareholders' rights thus are essentially veto rights, and hereinafter will be referred to as "shareholder veto rights." Shareholders also have the right to elect and remove directors and in most cases change the corporation's bylaws, without initiation or approval by management.

* * *

III. The Rationale for Veto Rights Under State Law

The existing system of shareholder veto rights rests on the assumption that shareholders have control over "fundamental" or "organic" changes. This section will demonstrate that the current system of voting rights under state law does not [in fact] rest on such a coherent conceptual framework. . . .

A. *The Lack of Veto Rights Over Fundamental or Organic Changes*

* * *

1. Economic Structure

Because shareholders are investors, their perspective of fundamental change often focuses on changes in the economic structure of the corporation. Commonly understood, the corporation's balance sheet, namely its capitalization, reflects the economic structure of the corporation. Decisions affecting a corporation's capitalization involve the issuance or repurchase of shares, issuance or retirement of debt, and issuance of dividends or retention of earnings.

Of these decisions, shareholders have only limited veto rights with respect to the issuance of shares. In addition, these rights exist only when the corporation's articles have not previously authorized the shares to be issued (it is commonplace to authorize large numbers of shares in advance) or when a corporation listed on the New York Stock Exchange increases its outstanding shares by twenty percent or more. . . .

Shareholders do not have veto rights over fundamental changes even if one defines economic structure differently. For example, one may describe structure by reference to the nature of the corporation's business. A decision to make a drastic change in the business, however, such as through the acquisition of the assets of another corporation for non-stock consideration (thus avoiding merger veto rights) or the reinvestment of earnings in a new business, does not require a shareholder vote. . . .

In essence, shareholders do not have veto rights over changes in economic structure. While they have veto rights over mergers, sales of substantially all corporate assets, and dissolutions that have a substantial impact on economic structure, they have no veto rights over other changes, such as debt levels, asset purchases, and stock repurchases, that may have the same or greater impact on that structure.

* * *

3. Control/Power Structure

Additionally, shareholders have no veto rights over various changes in the control/power structure. One may define control structure in formal terms by reference to the corporation's organizational chart describing the hierarchy within the firm. . . . [S]hareholders do not have veto rights over many changes that can affect this organization of authority within the firm. One may also define control structure by reference to rules determining the authority of directors, controlling shareholders, and minority shareholders. Although shareholders have voting rights on articles and bylaw amendments, the directors' independent authority over bylaw changes can result in a change of control without the shareholders' consent. . . . Subjects on which shareholders have veto rights under the existing system, such as various article amendments and the sale of substantially all corporate assets, do not involve changes in the control structure.

* * *

B. *Explanations of Shareholder Veto Rights*

The subsection explores recent explanations of shareholder veo rights by important legal scholars. . . .

* * *

Professor Eisenberg, in his influential book *The Structure of the Corporation*, . . . emphasized the word "structure," which encompassed decisions affecting the "control apparatus" and the "structure of the business" [in determining when shareholders should have voting rights]. The "control apparatus" consisted of ground rules for control, such as cumulative voting and the election and removal of directors. Although he did not define decisions affecting the "structure of the business," he distinguished these decisions from other business decisions involving matters outside the ordinary course of business by asking whether making these decisions required "investment" skills, or "business" skills. Mergers and dissolutions required a shareholder vote because the skills required to make such decisions were similar to the skills needed to determine whether to "invest" in the business.[125]

* * *

125 Professor Eisenberg explained:

[T]he skills involved in formulating a decision to merge with Corporation B or to liquidate Corporation B are similar to the skills involved in formulating a decision to invest in Corporation B, and are quite different from the skills needed to formulate an advertising campaign, conduct employee relations, or make steel. . . .

. . . [D]efining structural decisions by reference to investment or business skills . . . does not distinguish among such transactions. Investment skills are involved when a shareholder decides to invest in a corporation because of its policies with regard to such matters as leverage, dividends, and the nature of the corporation's business, matters over which shareholders have no veto rights. In addition, it is incorrect to characterize the decisions Professor Eisenberg attributes to managers as involving only business skills. Investment skills are also necessary to make important decisions concerning such matters as advertising, employee relations, and steel production.

Unlike Professor Eisenberg, Professors Easterbrook and Fischel, in a frequently cited 1983 article on voting rights,[131] did not focus on differing skills or "structure" to explain shareholder veto rights, but assumed that such rights are explained by the possibility of large gain or loss because of the size of a transaction. For large transactions, shareholders have an incentive to overcome collective action problems. Professors Easterbrook and Fischel expressed concern about the lack of expertise of "passive financial investors" to make "major business decisions," but concluded that shareholder veto rights are presumably efficient because of their durability and uniformity across state statutes.

. . . Unfortunately, Professors Easterbrook and Fischel did not compare the economic significance of transactions that require a shareholder vote and those that do not. For example, shareholders do not have the right to vote on the acquisition of substantial assets or the issuance of excessive debt. Professors Easterbrook and Fischel also did not explain why shareholders have the right to vote on some amendments to corporate articles and bylaws that do not involve the possibility of large gain or loss to shareholders. . . .

In the context of a discussion of the de facto merger doctrine, Professor Gilson asserted in 1986. . . .[138]. . . that "corporate structure" consists of the "interplay of statutory, judicial and market elements." According to Professor Gilson, one should reference this structure, particularly market forces, to answer the question whether events that raise similar economic risks should be treated the same legally. For example, shareholders of an acquiring corporation do not need appraisal rights, whereas shareholders of a selling corporation do, because management of the selling corporation will not be subject to the discipline of markets after the transaction (a final period problem).

Professor Gilson's . . . attempt to explain shareholder appraisal rights by reference to the adequacy of judicial remedies or market forces is a valid hypothesis, although it does not provide an explanation for existing rules. Gilson explains the difference in appraisal rights between shareholders of the acquiring and selling corporations on the basis of whether management will or will not be subject to market forces after the transaction. In a sale of assets transaction, however, the final period problem arises for shareholders of the acquiring corporation when the consideration for the assets is a controlling block of stock, but appraisal rights are unavailable to them. Such analysis

---

[131] Frank H. Easterbrook & Daniel R. Fischel, *Voting in Corporate Law*, 26 J.L. & Econ. 395 (1983). . . .

[138] Ronald J. Gilson, THE LAW AND FINANCE OF CORPORATE ACQUISITIONS, 577-78 (1986).

also does not explain the lack of appraisal rights for shareholders of the selling corporation when the consideration for the assets is cash. For many transactions, moreover, appraisal rights are available for shareholders of both constituent corporations irrespective of which one management ultimately controls. Explaining voting rights on the basis of the final period problem (or the absence of market discipline) also would not encompass shareholder veto rights for amendments to articles and bylaws. . . .

As the preceding discussion demonstrates, shareholder veto rights are not based on a coherent system in which shareholders have the right to vote on fundamental or structural changes, variously defined. . . .

* * *

IV. A Theoretical Understanding of Voting in the Corporate System

* * *

B. *Appropriate Scope of Shareholder Voting Rights*

* * *

1. Voice and Exit as Decision-Making Mechanisms

* * *

In the economic arena, a bias exists in favor of exit over voting or voice. . . .

In the economic arena, arguments concerning the superiority of exit to voice have been confined largely to consumer goods; the same arguments, however, do not necessarily apply to stock. For example, some have claimed exit shows preferences more directly than voice. . . . While this argument may be somewhat persuasive with respect to simpler products—although even here exit does not convey whether the dissatisfaction is with price, quality in performance, or aesthetics—the message given to management through selling or not buying more complex products is unclear. The ambiguity of the message is particularly severe with respect to stock, which reflects an investment in a vast enterprise.

An economist might respond that the message simply is that the shareholder is dissatisfied with the expected return on her investment; by the mere act of selling, the shareholder does not convey her assessment of the manner in which the company has erred. Management may misread her assessment in the absence of voice. . . .

So, as the product purchased becomes more complex, the message given to management through exit becomes less precise. Voting is an alternative to exit permitting a direct and more articulate expression of preferences. The value of voting in this regard exists regardless of the market's ability to price shares accurately.

* * *

One can argue that while voting provides a wider range of choices with respect to the policies and activities of a particular corporation, exit provides a wider range of choices among corporations. Primary reliance on exit encourages persons to migrate to corporations with policies they prefer; different persons will migrate to different corporations. The majority voting construct does not give persons holding majority views the incentive to exit; rather they will impose their views on corporations through voting. All corporations eventually will reflect the same general views; shareholders with less widely held views will not find compatible corporations in which to invest.

Two problems arise with this argument, aside from its debatable assumption concerning efficient markets. First, exit is an imperfect mechanism for the expression of approval or dissent on a wide range of issues. Shareholders may choose one corporation over another because they prefer on balance the policies of that corporation. This choice means that they may actually prefer some policies of the corporation from which they exit. Exit does not provide a means for shareholders to endorse the positive policies of the corporation they leave or to disapprove those policies of the corporation in which they then invest.

Second, the ambiguity of the messages sent by exit provides management with leeway to avoid responding to shareholders' concerns. This lack of responsiveness will be more likely with respect to certain policies that benefit management, or with which management has a conflict of interest. Voting, therefore, generally provides a wide range of choices for shareholders and fosters greater managerial accountability.

* * *

Further differences between exit and voice are important. First, exit provides choices that are limited to existing alternatives, whereas voice provides a mechanism for choosing among future courses of action. Shareholders may exit when a corporation has entered into an unfortunate transaction, but they suffer losses on the sale of their shares. If shareholders can vote in advance on the transaction, their vote may prevent or alter it. Moreover, the specter of shareholder voting causes managers to consult shareholders before proposing certain transactions. Consultation is less likely to occur if the shareholders' only recourse is to exit.

* * *

The comparison of exit and voice demonstrates that voting is particularly useful in certain circumstances. First, voting on specific topics is desirable because of the ambiguity of the message inherent in exit. If the shareholders' dissatisfaction is general and nonspecific, however, exit may be more appropriate, depending on one's assessment of the efficiency of markets in disciplining managers. Second, shareholder voting is preferable to exit on control issues (such as cumulative voting provisions) and conflict of interest issues (such as executive compensation and interested transactions). Because of the ambiguity of the message given by exit, managers are likely to resist interpretations that will result in changes that may adversely affect them. . . . Finally, voting is particularly useful when making decisions on a more inclusive value scale is desirable. Thus, voting on social responsibility proposals is better than exiting. . . . One should also note that voting is more important in closely-held corporations because exit is more difficult.

2. Comparison of Voting and Judicial Oversight of Corporate Behavior

Voting and judicial action provide needed checks and balances on the corporate governance system that management administers. . . .

Both voting and judicial oversight have advantages. Voting permits the shareholders to review a transaction in advance and requires disclosure before a transaction becomes binding. Judicial oversight occurs after the fact, but it permits consideration of the nature of the power relationship between the parties and the evaluation of unanticipated problems.

Each method also has disadvantages that are, in part, offset by the availability of the other to assure accountability. . . .

Judicial oversight has its own problems, including numerous procedural obstacles such as demand requirements and motions to dismiss by litigation committees. It becomes substantially illusory when courts apply the business judgment rule and is expensive and time consuming. Voting . . . decreases the necessity of judicial oversight by permitting shareholders to review important transactions before they occur, especially in situations where breaches of duty are most likely to happen or where the potential harm to shareholders may be most severe.

* * *

Notes and Questions

1. Professor Dallas points up the inability during the earlier history of corporate law of a majority of the shareholders to change, over the objection of the minority, the nature of the business undertaken by a corporation. This reflects something called the ultra vires doctrine: The notion that a corporation only has the power to undertake activities in furtherance of the purpose(s) stated in its articles of incorporation. In fact, the original rationale behind requiring a corporation to state its intended business in its articles, and then voiding efforts to extend corporate activities beyond the stated purpose, may have been only partially to protect minority shareholders against change in the nature of their investment. Another concern seems to have been to prevent the accumulation of economic power by the growth of corporations (something now more the province of the antitrust law). As Professor Folk noted, it is possible to avoid ultra vires limits by having articles give the corporation broad purposes; for example, statutes now commonly allow the articles to state the purpose as simply the carrying out of "any lawful business." Indeed, some modern statutes abandon any requirement for articles to state anything about a purpose. For a discussion of the historic decline of shareholder unanimity requirements, the ultra vires doctrine, and other impediments to corporate consolidation see Horwitz, Santa Clara *Revisited: The Development of Corporate Theory*, 88 W. VA. L. REV. 173 (1985).

2. Professor Dallas addresses the question of when a shareholder vote should be required. Another question is what vote should approval take. For example, what are the trade-offs between requiring unanimity, a supermajority, or merely a simple majority vote to approve a transaction?

Robert B. Thompson, *Exit, Liquidity, and Majority Rule: Appraisal's Role in Corporate Law,* 84 GEO. L.J. 1 (1995)*

* * *

The conventional explanation describes appraisal rights as part of a tradeoff implemented at the turn of the century to facilitate the growth of American business. The nineteenth-century common law required unanimous shareholder consent before a corporation could make radical changes, such as mergers. Unanimity might suffice for an intimate group of investors (characteristic of most businesses through the nineteenth century), but it is a significant limit on the adaptability of larger business and sometimes permits recalcitrant shareholders to frustrate beneficial changes. Legislatures, therefore, passed statutes authorizing fundamental changes by a supermajority vote, and often included appraisal rights permitting the minority to exit from these changed enterprises. The focus was on facilitating desirable corporate changes while providing liquidity to those who chose not to continue in a business fundamentally different from the one in which they had originally invested.

The appraisal remedy we see today serves an entirely different purpose from the original remedy. . . .

* * *

II. THE RISE AND FALL AND REINCARNATION OF APPRAISAL

* * *

C. *The Context in Which Modern Appraisal Appears*

. . . Modern appraisal cases typically arise from a transaction in which a majority shareholder has structured a merger or other transaction to kick the minority out of the enterprise. There are very few cases today like early merger cases in which the majority planned an expansion or other fundamental change in the enterprise and offered the minority the chance to come along, but the minority elected appraisal as a way out of the new venture.

In the decade after *Weinberger* [*v. UOP, Inc.**], there were 103 reported decisions involving appraisal, a substantial increase over the nineteen state court appraisal cases found by Professor Seligman in the previous decade. Of the eighty identified

---

[*457 A.2d 701 (Del. 1983)]

transactions involved in those cases,[105] more than eighty percent involved cash-outs; only six arose in transactions between independent corporations in which shareholders had the opportunity to continue. This is a substantial change from the early years of appraisal, when most cases appeared to involve unrelated corporations and even those that raised possible conflicts were not cash-outs.

* * *

III. The Uneasy Fit of Appraisal Rules and The Current Use of The Remedy

* * *

A. *Legal Rules Defining the Reach of Appraisal*

* * *

1. Denying Appraisal When Shares Are Widely Traded

The withdrawal of appraisal rights for shares that are widely traded is perhaps the most noticeable change since Manning's call to scale down the remedy. . . . About half of the states (covering the great majority of publicly held corporations) now withdraw appraisal if the corporation's stock is traded on a stock exchange or is held by 2000 shareholders. . . .

This exception clearly derives from the first period of appraisal in which the primary purpose of the remedy was to give the minority shareholders a way out of a corporation that had taken off in a different direction. Professor Folk's reporter's notes for the 1967 insertion of the market exception into Delaware's statute explicitly refer to the unnecessary liquidity purpose for appraisal when markets can better perform that function. Of course, to the extent that this exception turns on one's confidence in the substitute, a lack of confidence in the market would suggest a broader appraisal remedy. . . .

Under this view, the debate over the market exception collapses into the larger debate over efficient markets. Yet, appraisal's reincarnation as a check on majority self-dealing makes resolving this efficiency debate unnecessary. The more relevant point is that the price in an efficient market will provide no compensation for the self-dealing. As Professor Fischel has pointed out, if those in control of a corporation propose a transaction that is bad for the corporation but good for the other transacting entity in which the controllers have a larger interest, the market's reaction will send the price of the corporation's shares lower, giving no protection against the self-serving behavior.

Delaware and a few of the states with market exceptions partially respond to this concern by including an exception to the exception. . . . Even if there is a market for the corporation's shares, appraisal rights are reinstated if the shareholders receive cash or illiquid shares. . . .

---

105 Many of the transactions generated multiple decisions either of the same case or related cases arising from the same transaction. . . .

* * *

2. Withdrawing Appraisal from Shareholders of Surviving Corporations (and Some Disappearing Corporations)

During the modern period, most states have withdrawn appraisal from shareholders of surviving corporations in a merger if there is no substantial change in the enterprise. This threshold is often defined as an increase in the number of shares beyond twenty percent of the pre-existing number. If the investment of the surviving corporation's shareholders has not really changed, the law suggests that there is no sufficient reason to provide an exit, with its attendant costs to the remaining shareholders. This change, first introduced in Delaware in 1967 in what Folk called a "major innovation in American corporate law," was likely another response to Manning's attack on appraisal, its costs to the corporation, and its misuse by minority shareholders in a traditional merger transaction.

* * *

3. De Facto Mergers and the Reach of Appraisal

* * *

In contrast to Delaware's limitation of appraisal, California's statutes broaden the transactions in which appraisal is available. California defines business reorganization to give equivalent treatment to alternative business means of accomplishing the same fundamental change. . . . The ALI's corporate governance project, perhaps influenced by its California reporters, use [sic] this broader definition to codify the de facto doctrine in limited circumstances. The ALI provides liquidity after fundamental changes when the existing shareholders will not have control of the new corporation.

* * *

Notes and Questions

1. For an attempt to consider what purposes appraisal statutes should serve see Kanda & Levmore, *The Appraisal Remedy and the Goals of Corporate Law*, 32 UCLA L. Rev. 492 (1985).

2. How should courts compute the value of shares pursuant to appraisal rights? For a criticism of the common approach of taking a weighted average of the results reached through different valuation methods see Schaefer, *The Fallacy of Weighing Asset Value and Earnings Value in the Appraisal of Corporate Stock*, 55 S. Cal. L. Rev. 1031 (1982).

C. Freeze-Outs

James Vorenberg, *Exclusiveness of the Dissenting Stockholder's Appraisal Right*, 77 HARV. L. REV. 1189 (1964)*

Statutes giving stockholders who dissent from fundamental corporate transactions the right to force the corporation to buy them out at an appraised value appear in all states but West Virginia. . . . [R]elatively little attention has been directed to the effect of the appraisal remedy on other forms of relief which an aggrieved minority stockholder may wish to pursue. A few states provide in unqualified terms that the appraisal remedy is exclusive, but in most states the appraisal statutes provide little guidance with respect to their effect on other remedies. An examination of the cases leaves one with the impression that generally the results do not turn on close reading of statutory language.

* * *

[I]t is important to inquire whether the availability of appraisal forecloses other relief to such an extent that the majority can use a basic transaction for the purpose of eliminating an unwanted minority stockholder and forcibly acquiring his interest—a sort of private eminent domain proceeding. If the answer should be in the affirmative, it would be a relatively simple matter for the majority to stage an appraisal-triggering transaction—such as a sale of all of the assets and business to themselves in a state where such a sale gives rise to appraisal—and thereby impose an enforced liquidation on the minority. . . .

I. APPRAISAL IN CONNECTION WITH ATTEMPTED FREEZE-OUT

* * *

A. *Judicial Response to Freeze-Outs*

Consideration whether appraisal statutes permit a majority to engage in a merger or sale of assets for the purpose of liquidating the minority must take place against a historical background of judicial hostility to freeze-out attempts in general. Where appraisal was not an issue, courts in a number of cases have enjoined those in control from using dissolution as a method for eliminating the minority. . . .

Is the result different when an appraisal statute applies? . . . . [A] few recent opinions have indicated in broad terms that where appraisal exists the minority may be frozen out. And a number of legal commentators apparently have seen these opinions as indications that freeze-outs have now become permissible.

* * *

B. *Does Appraisal Justify Freeze-Outs?*

It may be appropriate at this point to ask whether an unwillingness to recognize a freeze-out power in the majority where the minority can have appraisal is anything more than a stuffy reluctance to have corporation law reflect the extent to which our society has shifted from "a law centering on ownership to a law centering on claim." It has become fashionable to note the extent to which the "norms" of corporation law have yielded to business needs. . . . Nonetheless, there are still sound reasons to allow a stockholder to retain his status until something more than the majority's desire to be rid of him or to own his shares justifies his elimination.

In the first place, resort to appraisal will, even under the best of the statutory procedures, often give the stockholder less than his stock is worth. Failure to comply with provisions requiring that the dissenter vote against the transaction at the meeting and take other steps required to exercise appraisal rights may deprive him of his appraisal right altogether. Inevitably, the procedure involves delay and uncertainty, with expenses which may cut into his recovery. The valuation process itself may involve a significant financial sacrifice, notwithstanding the attention which courts and writers have recently given to this matter. For our purposes, the nub of the problem is that an absolute freeze-out right would mean that those in control rather than the stockholder himself would decide when he shall sell his stock. It is not simply that they may be able to conceal specific facts, such as a backlog of orders or a grant of a patent, which foretell an improvement in the corporation's earnings, or that they may deliberately depress the market price for the purpose of deceiving the stockholder and the appraiser. Indeed, if the stockholder discovered such concealment or deceit and could establish the facts, he presumably could get relief. Far more difficult is ensuring to departing stockholders the benefit of improved prospects, where, at the time of appraisal, the evidence of improvement is more intuitive than tangible. And it seems unlikely that an appraiser will be able to gauge and give full weight to what a public sale of stock might bring if the company should happen to strike the market's fancy. It is not difficult to imagine instances in which a lawyer serving as appraiser would feel constrained to rely on well-established formulae for valuation, while if he had represented the company or the stockholders in negotiations with an underwriter he would have insisted upon a price per share which would reflect the special appeal which the company or the industry might have in the market at the time. The appraisal process will tend to produce conservative results where the values are speculative, and the majority's power to pick the time at which to trigger appraisal may encourage them to move when full values may be temporarily obscured. Thus the very cases in which the majority may be most tempted to seek a freeze-out are those where it is most difficult to assess the full value of the minority's shares.

Second, particularly with respect to small or relatively closely held corporations, a stockholder may have some other relationship such as employee, patent licensor, or lender. Putting to one side any emotional wrench involved in leaving the corporation, liquidation of his stock interest may undermine in whole or in part the incentive for such other relationship. Of course, in most cases his concern will be the converse—after his other ties have been cut he will not want to maintain that most unenviable role of minority stockholder in a close corporation. And perhaps it is not unreasonable to assume that if the parties proceed on the basis of a link between stockholding and some other connection, it should be protected by a contract or charter provision. Still, it may be worth bearing in mind that in some instances more may be at stake than whether the minority stockholder has a right to continue as such.

Third, in many cases the most serious consequence to a stockholder forced to take cash when the majority chooses to be rid of him will be the impact of the federal capital gains tax payable on any appreciation in value of his stock. If he holds the stock until death, the present tax law gives his beneficiaries a stepped-up basis equal to its value at his death, thus avoiding capital gains tax on the appreciation during his lifetime. Thus, the enforced liquidation of his holding may be a costly disappointment of expectations. It is true that he was always subject to the risk that the majority might dissolve the corporation and thus thrust the capital gains tax on him. But except where 80 per cent or more of the stock is owned by another corporation he has whatever check the majority's own desire to avoid the tax may provide. And the inconvenience of dissolution as a means of transferring a going business, combined with the courts' reluctance to allow dissolutions designed to effect freeze-outs, makes it especially unreasonable to assume that he took and held his investment with an eye to such eventuality.

Identification of the inadequacies of the appraisal remedy could be thought to compel the conclusion that it is wrong to offer appraisal to the minority as the only alternative to a corporate change, even when such change does involve a wholesome business purpose. But recognition of the burden which liquidation at an appraised price may impose does not elevate the minority's interest to an absolute which outweighs all other values. As with eminent domain, a more important goal which may conflict with the minority's interest in maintaining his status has led legislatures and courts to conclude that the minority stockholder may have to settle for cash.

The purpose of this section has been to suggest that only where there is a plausible business purpose of the corporation beyond the majority's desire to enlarge their own stockholdings or to eliminate a minority stockholder should the minority holder be required to choose between what is available to him as a result of the action proposed by the majority and the cash value of his shares. Of course a rule which makes the purpose of a proposed corporate action significant is not self-applying; there will be many cases where courts will have difficulty judging the substantiality and genuineness of what is proposed. . . . But once a determination is made as to what is and is not a recognizable purpose for a corporate change, the task of answering the factual question concerning purpose is one with which courts are familiar. . . .

* * *

J.A.C. Hetherington, *Defining the Scope of Controlling Shareholders' Fiduciary Responsibilities*, 22 WAKE FOREST L. REV. 9 (1987)*

* * *

B. *Elimination of Public Shareholders in Publicly Held Firms*

The state of the law that emerges from the more recent cases on this subject is that the controlling shareholder in a publicly held firm may force the minority to sell its shares at a "fair" price. The requirement that such transactions have a business purpose, apart from the interest of the control group in eliminating the minority, has been explicitly abandoned or severely eroded. Full disclosure of information relevant to the determination of the value of the stock is required, and there may be judicial review of the valuation. This much discussed, and often deplored, state of the law is the converse of the usual problem of minority shareholders in closely held firms whose usual complaint is that their investment is retained in the business while they are excluded from sharing in present and prospective returns generated by the firm. The remedy frequently sought for this situation is a forced buy-out by the majority at a price which fairly reflects the minority's pro rata share of the value of the firm. Forced buy-outs are the solution in the close corporations and the problem in publicly held companies. The behavior of close corporation minorities in seeking this form of relief points to the obvious conclusion that it is better from the investor's standpoint to sell out, provided there is a reasonable assurance of price fairness, than to be locked in while being deprived of earnings generated by one's investment. In both publicly held and close corporations, the sale itself produces costs for which there may not be full compensation, *e.g.*, the seller is subjected to immediate tax liability and may incur search costs in finding a new investment. There may also be a loss of idiosyncratic value if the shareholder values the particular investment for reasons apart from its economic value.

The forced liquidation of a stockholder's investment may be characterized in various ways. It has been called private eminent domain, a label which implies that such a forced sale is or should be improper. The forced taking of one person's property by another, even at a fair price, is a substantial invasion of property ownership rights. As applied to almost any form of property other than an investment security, a forced taking would be unacceptable. But investment securities are a peculiar form of property, as a contractual analysis shows. Majority shareholders have traditionally been able to force changes in the minority's investment and even to force a sale of the investment, through mergers and sales of assets approved by majority vote. The effect of a squeeze-out on the minority is exactly the same. However, the identity of the purchaser is important because of its effect on the majority's incentive. Where the business is being sold to a third party, the majority has an incentive to negotiate the best possible price; where the majority itself is the purchaser, its incentive is the opposite.

In contract terms, the situation of the public shareholder under the present state of the law can be described as follows: the buyer of stock in a publicly held corporation purchases an interest in the company's future income, subject to the possibility that because of circumstances over which she will have no control she may be forced to sell at a price which fairly reflects its then value. One of the circumstances under which such a forced liquidation may occur is the sale of the stock to a person who has assembled a controlling position in the company. Such a controlling shareholder may force such a sale whenever she concludes that her wealth would be enhanced by eliminating public investors in the enterprise. In analyzing this aspect of corporation law, the initial question is not whether such a forced sale of private property should be permitted; it is whether buyers of stock in publicly held companies should be permitted to make contracts containing this provision. The answer to this question ought to turn, at least initially, on whether buyers of stock would wish to make such a contract. If they would, then the question becomes whether there is a reason they should not be permitted to do so, because it appears, judging from the behavior of investors in the market, that they do not regard such contracts as undesirable.

Ex ante, there is no reason for public shareholders to object to this provision, because it enhances the value of their investment by increasing the number of potential bidders for their stock. In view of the fact that repurchase prices in decided cases have always been substantially higher than the then prevailing market prices, there seems to be little reason to think, despite the possibility of undiscovered values being appropriated by insider purchasers, that buyers of stock would object to this rule. The probabilities are that this rule increases the value of their stock and should, therefore, increase the attractiveness of publicly offered equities to rational wealth maximizers.

Rules enabling minority shareholders to challenge buy-outs under a business purpose test or other rules permitting an inquiry into the buyer's motives reduce the value of the investments of all shareholders in publicly held companies by increasing the difficulty (and thereby reducing the frequency) of attempted buy-outs by insiders. Any rule which reduces the aggregate demand for shares held by the public, therefore, reduces their value.

A rule which enables individual shareholders to obstruct such transactions gives rise to the problem that made the old unanimity rule for mergers and sales of assets unworkable, *i.e.*, the last shareholder whose approval was required could capture a disproportionate share of the gain by holding out. The possibility of strategic behavior arises whenever one party stands to lose less from blocking a transaction than another. In such a situation, there is a temptation for the individual with blocking power to coerce a side payment for permitting the transaction to proceed. This suggests that there are serious efficiency costs in permitting minorities to obstruct reorganization transactions and that these risks arise whenever the minority is given rights which enable it to demand more than the "fair" value of its shares as a condition for its consent to a reorganization transaction. . . .

There has been some demand by academic writers that investors should be protected against (that is, should not be permitted to make) investment contracts containing the provisions which have grown up under present law as described above. Of course, the state may restrict or prohibit contracts which, for sufficient reason, are found to be inimical to public or private welfare. However, as long as sellers are permitted to offer investment contracts with differing features and buyers can decline to purchase if the combination of features of the particular investment contract seems disadvantageous as compared with other available opportunities, the fact that some observers disapprove of the term of some of the investment contracts being traded in the market does not make a case for proscribing them. In corporations, as in contract law generally, the substantive content of exchange transactions can in the first instance be left to the participants and intervention reserved for situations in which it appears that the reasonable expectations of the participants are being frustrated.

* * *

Notes and Questions

1. Professors Vorenberg and Hetherington not only have different views of what the law should be, they also express seeming differences as to what the law is. Is this a reflection of changing law in the two decades that separate the two pieces, or is there something else going on here?

One possibility lies in the different methods that a majority shareholder may use to force out the minority. The early cases referred to by Professor Vorenberg typically involved the majority's dissolving the corporation under a plan in which the company transferred its operating assets to a new corporation owned solely by the majority holder, while the minority holders in the original corporation received cash. Courts tended to condemn these transactions, either because the transfer of operating assets to one shareholder and cash to others, rather than auctioning off the assets for cash, was an improper way to liquidate a corporation following dissolution, or, more broadly, because this transaction did not really constitute a dissolution. Thereafter, majorities developed the use of mergers in which the minority received redeemable shares or cash rather than stock in the surviving firm. This technique survived challenges that it did not really constitute a merger within the meaning of the merger statutes. Should the majority's power to freeze out the minority change with the formal technique they use, when the end result of the transaction does not change? For a discussion of the history of freeze-out transactions see Weiss, *The Law of Take Out Mergers: A Historical Perspective*, 56 N.Y.U. L. REV. 624 (1981).

The real difference between Professor Vorenberg's and Professor Hetherington's view however, is not over the existence of a statutory power that might allow the majority to cash out the minority in some cases, but rather over whether this power should be subject to a judicially imposed requirement that the majority have a business purpose for doing so. Here, Professor Hetherington is guilty of oversimplifying the evolution of the law since Professor Vorenberg wrote. What has emerged is a split of authority paralleling the difference between the two writers. While Delaware, after flirting with a contrary rule, requires no business purpose for the majority to meet its fiduciary duty in cashing out a minority, a number of jurisdictions (such as New York and Massachusetts) do. Those jurisdictions in which appraisal is the frozen out minority's sole remedy never get to this issue.

2. Turning to policy, consider Professor Hetherington's argument in favor of allowing freeze-outs without a business purpose limit. Is there any objection to shareholders agreeing to such an arrangement? The Uniform Partnership Act recognizes the power of partners to agree that some members will have the right to expel others from the firm, and partnership agreements often contain expulsion provisions that require no cause to kick out a partner. On the other hand, what is the basis for Professor Hetherington's assertion that this is what shareholders have in fact agreed to? The freeze-out cases typically do not involve shareholder agreements giving the corporation or majority stockholders the option to buy out the minority, nor do they typically entail the redemption of preferred shares pursuant to article provisions giving the corporation this right. Rather, they usually involve the use of statutory merger provisions, often in which the merger is with a shell corporation whose only existence is for purposes of the merger. Under these circumstances, is it clear that shareholders recognized they were buying stock subject to the majority's power to expel them from the company? Does an ordinary reading of statutory merger provisions reveal this scope? Is there a circularity problem here: The expectation exists if the courts interpret the merger provisions to give the majority the power of expulsion without a business purpose and does not exist if the courts interpret the provisions differently?

Professor Hetherington also argues that shareholders will desire this arrangement because a third party may be more willing to make a premium bid to buy the corporation (thereby benefitting most of the shareholders) if he or she is able to remove a non-selling minority. Putting aside the question of why a potential buyer would be unwilling to bid unless he or she could remove a non-selling minority, does this rationale justify the freeze-out power in all situations? What about the situation in which the majority owner is a long-time shareholder, who had the corporation issue shares to the very public owners he or she is now trying to force out, rather than a party attempting a two-step acquisition? For a further development of this point see Green, *Corporate Freeze-out Mergers: A Proposed Analysis*, 28 STAN. L. REV. 487 (1976).

3. Beyond the question of whether to allow the freeze-out, the minority may object to the price they receive. For a discussion of some issues involved in setting a fair price in a freeze-out transaction see Brudney and Chirelstein, *Fair Shares in Corporate Mergers and Takeovers*, 88 HARV. L. REV. 297 (1974). Professor Vorenberg worries that majority owners may have a better feel for a corporation's future prospects than a court can take into account when determining fair value. Does the study excerpted in Chapter IV, which showed insiders achieved abnormal profits when trading in their company's stock, support this argument?

D. Takeover Defenses

Ronald J. Gilson and Reinier Kraakman, *Delaware's Intermediate Standard for Defensive Tactics: Is There Substance to Proportionality Review?*, 44 Bus. Law. 247 (1989)*

* * *

The courts have long struggled with a standard for reviewing management's efforts to deter or defeat hostile takeovers. The usual standards of review in corporate law, the business judgment rule and the intrinsic fairness test, do not seem adequate when courts must evaluate defensive measures that implicate both management's business acumen and its loyalty to shareholder interests. Because evaluating a sale of the company is a complex business decision, management's response to a takeover bid resembles the normal business decisions that the business judgment rule largely insulates from judicial review. At the same time, however, a hostile takeover creates a potential conflict of interest, no matter what response it evokes from management. Target managers who approve an offer may be improperly influenced by post-transaction benefits; target managers who reject an offer may act largely to secure their own positions. From this perspective, responding to a hostile takeover is an interested transaction that calls for judicial review under the intrinsic fairness test. Yet, invoking this rigorous standard would simply condemn most defensive tactics without any justification beyond the standard itself.

In this article, we examine the Delaware courts' most recent response to the tension between the intrinsic fairness standard and the business judgment standard in the takeover context: An intermediate standard of review mandating that management's defensive tactics must be "reasonable in relation to the threat posed" by a hostile offer. . . .

* * *

THE ORIGINS OF THE PROPORTIONALITY TEST

The proportionality test is not the Delaware courts' first effort to wrestle with the difficulty of reviewing defensive tactics. Long before the most recent wave of takeover cases, *Cheff v. Mathes*[5] demonstrated the subtlety with which the Delaware courts could disarm the seeming conflict between the intrinsic fairness and business judgment standards of review in takeover settings. *Cheff* framed a policy conflict/primary purpose test under which management's motives set the standard of review for defensive tactics. If a target's directors could demonstrate disagreement over corporate policy with a would-be acquirer, they were presumed to act from business considerations

5 41 Del. Ch. 494, 199 A.2d 548 (1964).

rather than self-interest. With the specter of a breach of duty of loyalty thus conveniently set aside, the appropriate standard of review became the business judgment rule. . . . Because competent counsel could always document a policy conflict between a would-be acquirer and defending management, the *Cheff* test inevitably reduced to a routine application of the business judgment standard.

Ironically, *Cheff's* resolution of the problem of judicial review survived unchanged only as long as its implication—blanket protection of defensive tactics—remained at least partly submerged. By the early 1980s, this implication was fully visible. Novel financing techniques and a dramatic rise in takeover activity stimulated demand for improved takeover defenses. New defenses, in turn, prompted new litigation and a long string of victories for targets that soon revealed the full scope of management's discretion to block takeovers under *Cheff's* motive analysis. . . .

As *Cheff's* implications became clearly visible, however, they attracted hostile notice from other corners. An outpouring of academic commentary called for constraints on defensive tactics, and it even appeared possible that Congress might act to displace state law—and especially Delaware law—that was considered unduly favorable to target management. . . .

In principle, the Delaware courts had two quite different doctrinal options for reforming the *Cheff* standard. On the one hand, the courts could have restricted defensive tactics by emphasizing the primacy of shareholder choice to accept or reject a hostile offer. This approach recognizes the role of the tender offer with respect to the structure of the corporation. Precisely because target management can unilaterally block a merger or sale of assets, a takeover can occur without management approval only through a tender offer made directly to target shareholders. Thus, management enjoys a monopoly over corporate control unless it is restrained from preventing shareholders from tendering to a hostile offeror. Alternatively, the courts could have moved from the *Cheff* standard to an intermediate standard of judicial review that contemplated a genuine effort to distinguish defensive tactics that might benefit shareholders from suspect tactics designed to entrench management.

In fact, the Delaware Supreme Court opted for the more conservative of the two approaches—the intermediate standard of review—in a trilogy of decisions handed down in 1985 and early 1986: *Unocal v. Mesa Petroleum*,[15] *Moran v. Household International*[16] and *Revlon v. MacAndrews & Forbes Holdings*.[17] These opinions fortify the older *Cheff* standard by adding a second step to the traditional policy conflict/primary purpose analysis. Under the new standard, management can no longer qualify for the protections of the business judgment rule simply by pointing to a "danger to corporate policy" based on a carefully orchestrated record. Now, defensive tactics must also face a proportionality test: They must be shown to be "reasonable in relation to the threat posed."

15 493 A.2d 946 (Del. 1985).

16 500 A.2d 1346 (Del. 1985).

17 506 A.2d 173 (Del. 1986).

The proportionality test brings a novel, objective standard to the review of defensive tactics—a reasonableness test that impliedly allows courts to identify and reject unreasonable tactics, whatever the motives of their authors. . . .

THE MEANING OF PROPORTIONALITY REVIEW

* * *

IS THE NEW STANDARD MORE THAN A THRESHOLD TEST?

One question is whether the proportionality standard is a threshold test or a form of regulatory review. To see this distinction clearly, consider the ambiguous holdings of *Unocal* and *Moran*, which establish that potentially coercive bids justify some forms of defensive action without indicating the range of permissible forms. If the proportionality standard is a threshold test, any hostile offer that is arguably coercive would give management a free hand without further scrutiny by the courts. By contrast, if the standard is a regulatory test, management would be forced to justify its choice of defensive actions by reference to the amount of coercion associated with a particular bid. This difference is significant because any bid, apart from an any-or-all cash bid with a commitment to freeze out non-tendering shareholders at the bid price, may have some coercive effect on target shareholders.[29] Thus, unless the "proportionality" element in the new standard has regulatory import, second-step review will have very little meaning for most offers as they are now framed.

* * *

WHAT CONSTITUTES A THREAT?

Thus far, it appears that, under the proportionality test, the nature of the threat associated with a particular hostile offer limits the range of permissible defensive tactics. It is a short step from this observation to the next question: What constitutes a "threat" under the proportionality test? If "threat" means that a takeover bid must pose a demonstrable risk of injury to target shareholders, might some takeover bids arguably not constitute any threat? . . .

The bids in *Unocal* [and] *Moran* . . . illustrate easy circumstances under the proportionality test for locating threats that might reasonably seem to warrant a defensive response of some kind. In *Unocal* and *Moran*, the structure of the hostile offers threatened to coerce shareholders into tendering on unfavorable terms. . . .

* * *

29 Consider an offer that may seem non-coercive on its face: a 100% cash offer at a significant premium, but without any commitment to buy out non-tendering shareholders at a fixed price. A shareholder who believes that the stock is worth more than the offer, perhaps because he expects a higher offer in the future, would prefer not to tender. However, if he does not tender while other shareholders do tender, he will be left holding minority shares in a controlled corporation with a market value that is likely to be well below the tender offer price. Thus any partial offer, including an any-or-all offer without a freezeout commitment, is potentially coercive. . . .

From the perspective of defensive planners who want to keep a target independent (and "un-restructured"), the critical issue in evaluating Delaware's new two-step proportionality review is . . . what "threats" from hostile bidders, apart from unequal treatment for non-tendering shareholders, are sufficiently grave to justify preclusive defensive tactics without offering any transactional alternative at all? To take an obvious candidate, suppose that management honestly believed that the price of a non-coercive hostile offer was inadequate; in management's view, the securities market undervalued the target company's assets by more than the premium offered by the acquirer. Would a preclusive defense be "reasonably related" to the "threat" that shareholders might accept what management deems to be an inadequate price?

To date, the cases interpreting proportionality review offer little guidance on this single most important issue of what "threats" will support preclusive defenses by target managers. In *Unocal*, where the proportionality test was introduced, the Delaware Supreme Court provided a litany of factors that might bear on the existence of a threat:

> If a defensive measure is to come within the ambit of the business judgment rule, it must be reasonable in relation to the threat posed. This entails an analysis by the directors of the nature of the takeover bid and its effect on the corporate enterprise. Examples of such concerns may include: inadequacy of the price offered, nature and timing of the offer, questions of illegality, the impact on "constituencies" other than shareholders (*i.e.*, creditors, customers, employees, and perhaps even the community generally), the risk of nonconsummation, and the quality of securities being offered in the exchange. . . . While not a controlling factor, it also seems to us that a board may reasonably consider the basic stockholder interests at stake, including those of short term speculators, whose actions may have fueled the coercive aspect of the offer at the expense of the long term investor.

How might these factors rise to the threshold of "threats" able to justify a preclusive defense against a non-coercive takeover bid? Clearly, these factors can be threats only if a target's directors believe that shareholders will mistakenly accept a non-coercive offer.[41] . . .

* * *

MANAGERS' ABILITY TO GENERATE HIGHER PRICE

When managers justify a preclusive defense on the ground that a hostile offer is inadequate, they implicitly claim to be able to obtain greater value for shareholders. Managers might be able to accomplish this in at least three ways: (i) by bargaining for a better price from the bidder at hand; (ii) by locating other bidders who will pay more

---

41 A possible exception concerns the impact of a hostile offer on the target's non-shareholder constituencies. If directors could prefer the interests of these constituencies over those of shareholders, a hostile offer that shareholders would wish to accept in their own interest could pose a threat to non-shareholder interests. . . .

for the company; or (iii) by operating the firm so successfully that share prices will eventually exceed the offer price even without selling the firm. . . .

The least ambitious rationale for defensive tactics is the claim that management needs leverage to negotiate with a hostile bidder. Even in a competitive acquisitions market, disaggregated shareholders may require a bargaining agent to obtain top dollar for target assets. Without a coordinated response from shareholders, any offer can succeed that exceeds the expected value of the firm in the hands of existing management or other competing bidders. By contrast, target managers who have the power to preclude hostile offers by deploying defensive tactics may be able to compel acquirers to pay out the bulk of their transaction gains. Thus, the claim that an offer is too low may simply mean that there is room to dicker: Target managers reasonably believe that the offeror will pay a higher price based on their knowledge of the true value of the target company's assets or of the synergistic gains available to a particular offeror. . . . The claim stands as a distinct justification for poison pills, quite apart from the potential value of the pill defense in insulating shareholders from . . . coercive offers.

Beyond allowing managers to bargain credibly with particular offerors, however, defensive tactics might also benefit target shareholders by providing time for managers to "shop" the firm. In this case, managers who assert that an offer is too low . . . must believe that other potential acquirers can be located who will pay more for the target than the hostile offeror. Because second bidders cannot always be found, this claim is more problematic than management's assertion that it can serve as a local bargaining agent. Nevertheless, "white knights" may emerge over time, particularly when management is willing to share confidential information. The empirical literature indicates that target management often can discover second bidders for target firms.

Finally, the most ambitious rationale for defensive tactics is management's claim that it can better the price offered by a hostile bidder by preserving the target's independence and generating value internally. In effect, management asserts that the value of the target in its hands exceeds not only the target's pre-offer valuation by the securities market, but also the premium price offered by the acquirer. Management may rest an optimistic valuation of the target on confidential information about the company, on beliefs about the future success of the company's strategic plans, or more concretely, on an expert appraisal of the value of the firm's assets. Again, management's claims may well be correct, even when management relies on wholly public information to value the firm; the securities market often appears to "discount" the asset values of target firms. Nevertheless, invoking the target's intrinsic value to justify continued independence in the face of a premium offer is always a delicate argument for the management of a target firm to make. Sooner or later, most shareholders sell their shares on the market, and the market has already assessed managers' efforts. . . .

Even if the securities market undervalues the target firm for reasons other than the company's poor performance, managers can seldom predict when the market will come to accept their own assessment of the value of the company or explain what would cause the market to alter its valuation.

SHAREHOLDER MISTRUST

The mere fact that managers might truthfully claim to be able to improve upon a hostile offer does not itself [justify defensive steps] . . . A second element is also required: Most shareholders must disbelieve managers' claims. Otherwise, shareholders simply would listen to managers' advice and reject underpriced offers out of hand. . . .

. . . [S]hareholders have good reason to mistrust managers' claims of underpricing even if they know that defensive tactics can sometimes improve upon the terms of hostile offers. Both academic analysis and recent experience persuasively demonstrate that managers' efforts to defeat hostile bids often occur or persist despite the best interests of shareholders. Indeed, apart from the bidder itself, no one is less likely to be objective in appraising a hostile offer than the target's incumbent board of directors and its top managers. Knowing this, shareholders must naturally fear that in some cases management's claims of value will be self-serving and, if believed, would impose a significant agency cost, that is, the difference between the offer price and the subsequent lower market price of the company after the offer is defeated. The fact that shareholders—and the securities market—are likely to accept a structurally non-coercive offer, despite management's claims of value, is compelling evidence of the shareholders' belief that the ability of managers to improve on the offer's terms is outweighed by the risk that managers have misrepresented either their abilities or their intentions.

* * *

PROPORTIONALITY AND [INADEQUATE PRICE]. . .

* * *

It follows that a meaningful application of the proportionality test . . . must recognize that management's representations about future value will sometimes be wrong and sometimes be right. For the game to be worth the candle, courts applying the proportionality test must be able to improve on the market's efforts to distinguish when management is right and when it is wrong. Otherwise, the aggregate market data would support a total ban on defensive responses to structurally non-coercive offers.

* * *

Notes and Questions

1. Professors Gilson and Kraakman recognize that judicial review of takeover defenses raises questions both as to the standard of review the court should apply, and how the challenged defense will hold up under that standard. With respect to the standard, what justification do Professors Gilson and Kraakman suggest for Delaware's intermediate level of review. Are directors in a conflict of interest in responding to a takeover? If so, why not a fairness test? Is it true, as Professors Gilson and Kraakman assert, that such a test would condemn most defenses for no reason other than the test itself? Has the test proven that impossibly idealistic when dealing with the normal interested director transaction? On the other hand, is there some difference in the nature of the conflict with a takeover defense as opposed to conventional self-dealing (assuming, of course, that the defense is not itself a transaction between the directors and their corporation as, for example, if they vote themselves a "golden parachute" severance package)? If the conflict is less with a takeover defense than with conventional self-dealing, might this justify a less intrusive level of review than fairness?

2. Professors Gilson and Kraakman also identify two issues with respect to applying the intermediate review to specific cases: What situations (or "threats") may justify a defense, and what defenses will such situations justify? Professors Gilson and Kraakman easily accept the justification that the structure of an offer may render it coercive to shareholders. An example may clarify the concern. Suppose a party announces a tender offer for 51 percent of a target corporation's stock at a price somewhat above market. The offeror also announces his intention to freeze-out the remaining 49 percent of the target's shareholders at a lower price after he gains the 51 percent. If less than 51 percent of the shareholders accept this offer, then it comes to nothing. Each stockholder, however, must worry that his or her fellow stockholders may choose to accept, thereby leaving him or her in the 49 percent getting a worse deal. Moreover, each stockholder must figure that every other stockholder has the same worry. Hence, even if a majority of stockholders felt the price was inadequate, they may nevertheless feel compelled to tender their shares. Notice the interrelationship of this concern with the previous discussion of freeze-outs. Would accepting Professor Vorenberg's view of the law of freeze-outs eliminate the structural coercion problem? Professors Gilson and Kraakman argue there still can be coercion for shareholders who are stuck in the minority after the offeror takes control even if they are not faced with the threat of a low price freeze-out. Why might this be? Consider Professor Elhauge's discussion of the effects of control purchases on non-selling shareholders.

3. Professors Gilson and Kraakman also appear sympathetic with the goal of attempting to get the stockholders more money for their shares. The writers' problem here involves the means. Can the shareholders have any objection to the board's attempting to come up with another buyer willing to pay more for their shares? What might the board need to do, however, to entice a second bidder? Suppose a prospective second bidder demands the board give it a "lock-up"—in other words, an option to buy some of the target corporation's assets at a bargain price if the second bidder does not succeed in acquiring the whole company? Suppose the board agrees to provide such an option in order to entice a first bidder for the company? How can one assess the proportionality of such lock-ups to the goal of producing a high price sale?

Alternately, the board might wish to negotiate with the offeror for a higher price. Is there any objection to the board attempting to persuade the target's stockholders not to tender their shares while the board negotiates a better deal? Given the problems of communicating with a large group of shareholders, is there not something to be said for allowing the board to impose a defense (say, a "poison pill"—some sort of outstanding options triggered by a takeover that make the takeover prohibitively expensive, but which the board can redeem) in order to force the bidder to deal with the board? Do you agree with Professors Gilson and Kraakman's concerns about the proportionality of using any defense beyond communicating with the shareholders in order to achieve the increased price goal?

4. Do you see a difference between the justifications for board action above and the claim often made, as discussed in the excerpt, that the stockholders would be better off holding their shares because of the long-run prospects for the company? The previous rationales for board action all flowed from its ability to take action—avoid coercion, find another buyer, or negotiate—that a multitude of shareholders could not do. Is this true for a simple refusal to sell?

5. Professors Gilson and Kraakman relegate to a footnote the goal of fending off a takeover, regardless of the shareholders' best interests, because it harms employees, lenders or other stakeholders in the corporation. Recall, the other constituencies statutes discussed in Chapter III sought to approve this goal. Professor Elhauge's article raises one other example. Suppose a known corporate looter offers to buy every share in the corporation. Would the duty not to sell to looters still apply? If it does, the benefit runs to the corporation's creditors.

6. For a discussion of further developments in Delaware law since this article see Ragazzo, *Unifying the Law of Hostile Takeovers: The Impact of* QVC *and its Progeny*, 32 HOUSTON L. REV. 945 (1995).

7. Professors Gilson and Kraakman noted that one option open to the Delaware courts would have been to hold the board without the authority to take any defensive steps. Do you see any doctrinal problems with implementing such a passivity rule? For example, suppose, after the board agrees to a merger with one corporation, another company makes an offer contingent upon the board's abandoning the merger. Would a no defense rule require the board to comply with the hostile offeror's demand? Even if not, suppose the board, worried that the shareholders will reject the merger agreement because of the new offer, changes the terms of the merger in a manner that will eliminate the requirement of a shareholder vote; is this a defensive step? What if the board, anticipating the possibility, had structured the merger in such a way as to preclude a shareholder vote to start with? What is a takeover defense anyway?

8. A passivity rule preventing directors from taking any defensive steps may have the effect of encouraging takeovers, even if it means (or perhaps because it may mean) shareholders of a given target corporation get less for their stock than if the board took steps to get a higher price. In some sense, this is simply the mirror image of the notion that the board ought to be able to sacrifice a profit for the shareholders by preventing a takeover in order to protect the interests of other constituencies. These two extreme positions thus raise broader policy questions as to the desirability of hostile takeovers.

Roberta Romano, *A Guide to Takeovers: Theory, Evidence, and Regulation*, 9 YALE J. REG. 119 (1992)*

Introduction

There is a voluminous economic literature seeking to explain takeovers. There is also substantial regulation. This article relates the one to the other, and is a guide to both. It reviews the economic literature in order to facilitate an evaluation of the efficacy of current regulation. The premise is that if some explanations of takeovers are more plausible than others, then certain regulatory regimes make more sense than others. I refer to explanations in the plural because we do not have a comprehensive theory of takeovers. Different theories do well at explaining various subsets of acquisitions, but no theory satisfactorily explains all.

The empirical evidence is most consistent with value-maximizing, efficiency-based explanations of takeovers. Yet the thrust of regulation is to thwart and burden takeovers, as if they were non-value-maximizing wealth transfers. . . .

* * *

I. Theories of Takeovers and Related Transactions

One important, and undisputed, datum about acquisitive transactions should be noted from the outset: acquisitions generate substantial gains to target company shareholders. All studies find that target firms experience statistically significant positive stock price responses to the announcement of takeover attempts or merger agreements. On average, there is a 20% increase over the pre-announcement market price for mergers and a 30% increase for tender offers in the period around the takeover announcement. Abnormal returns in going-private transactions (leveraged buyouts) are of similar magnitude, ranging across studies between 20% and 37%. Without question, the announcement of a bid is good news for target shareholders. The different explanations of acquisitions that will be examined are efforts at explaining the source of these gains.

The data are more ambiguous, however, concerning acquiring firms' returns. Depending on the sample and time period, acquirers experience positive, negative, or zero abnormal returns on a bid's announcement and completion. . . .

* * *

[E]ven when acquirers earn negative returns, when their losses are aggregated with the targets' gains, acquisitions still net a positive abnormal return. . . .

* * *

Studies of the performance of target firms after acquisition also shed light on whether acquisitions are value-maximizing or non-value-maximizing transactions. Here, stock price data are less reliable indicators for, as the interval over which the price is examined increases, changes can no longer be readily attributed to the event in question (the takeover) because it will be confounded with other events. Most of these studies therefore use accounting data to determine long-term changes in performance. As with event studies of the announcement effects on acquirers, the ex-post performance findings are also mixed. While earlier studies find no operating improvements in merged firms, more recent sophisticated studies find that performance improves post-merger.

One difficulty in assessing post-merger performance is in determining the appropriate comparison, which entails constructing a counterfactual benchmark—what the two firms' performances would have been had they not merged. In an important paper, Jarrell compares post-merger performance to analysts' pre-merger forecasts of the firms' performance. She finds that five years post-merger, the merged firms perform significantly better (9%) than the benchmark, although one to two years immediately after the merger the performance was worse than the benchmark. . . .

A. *Value-Maximizing Efficiency Explanations*

* * *

1. *Synergy Gains*

* * *

a. *Operating Efficiencies*

Examples of operating synergistic gains are economies of scale (fixed costs are spread over a larger volume of production), and economies of scope (complementary resources are combined, such as a merger between a firm with a unique product and another with the sales organization to market it).

* * *

. . . There is evidence that supports [this explanation of takeover gains]. . . . [A]cquisitions of firms in related businesses, where gains from economies of scale and scope are most likely, are extremely profitable: acquisitions of unrelated companies in the 1980s produced lower returns than related-firm acquisitions; and a significant portion of the gains from hostile takeovers are due to reallocation of target assets to related acquirers.

b. *Financial Synergy*

* * *

Capital costs are higher when funds are raised externally—flotation and transaction costs are reduced if spread over a larger issue, and eliminated if the merged firm's cash flow is sufficient to produce all necessary cash internally. An acquisition is, correspondingly, a way to redeploy capital efficiently across low and high growth firms. Organizational changes in the 1960s enabled corporate managers to efficiently allocate funds internally to more needy divisions, and this new organizational form's efficient properties were logically extended through acquisitions to create the conglomerate firm. There is an additional, tax-related explanation of cost of capital synergy. Because of the two-tier corporate tax and differential personal tax rates on dividend and capital gain income, firms have an incentive to use retained earnings that are not subject to the dividend taxes to finance projects whose returns are lower than the marginal cost of capital were they to be financed externally. . . .

Some empirical evidence is consistent with this explanation. . . .

2. *Reducing Agency Costs*

* * *

a. *Replacement of Inefficient Management*

The most important agency cost explanation of takeovers is that they reduce managerial slack by replacing inefficient management. Manne put forth this view in a classic article over 20 years ago, and it is one of the central insights in corporate law scholarship. . . .

* * *

A number of studies provide support for this explanation. For example, acquired firms earn low rates of return prior to mergers and acquiring companies are above average in profitability. . . .

* * *

Finally, there is evidence that after mergers, firms' cash flows improve as a result of increased asset productivity. Because the cash flow improvements do not differ across related and unrelated-firm acquisitions, the gains do not appear to come from the realization of operating synergies. This finding suggests that acquirers are better able to manage target assets. . . .

The inefficient management explanation cannot, however, explain all restructuring transactions. It cannot, for example, explain acquisitions in which the acquirer retains incumbent management, a pattern that appears to have been common in large acquisitions by conglomerate firms. In particular, it cannot explain management-led leveraged buyouts (MBOs), because in these transactions top management is part of the acquiring group and stays on the job. . . .

b. *Free Cash Flow*

An alternative explanation that views takeovers as a mechanism for reducing agency costs but does not predict management's replacement is Jensen's "free cash flow" theory. Jensen contends that a cause of takeover activity, especially in the petroleum industry, is the agency cost associated with the conflict between managers and shareholders over the payout of free cash flow. Free cash flow is cash flow in excess of the amount required to fund all of the firm's projects that have a positive net present value. If these funds are paid out to shareholders, managers will have fewer resources under their control, and will thus be unable to waste cash by investing in projects with negative net present values. . . .

* * *

The free cash flow theory of takeovers provides a non-tax explanation for why debt increases upon an acquisition. Issuing debt restricts future free cash flows because, unlike dividends on stock, interest must be paid to avoid the bankruptcy trigger of default. . . .

Lehn and Poulsen educed support for the free cash flow explanation from a study of going-private transactions: they found that the likelihood of firms going private was directly related to the size of their free cash flows and the threat of a hostile takeover (the reason why management is willing to forego free cash flows), and inversely related to growth (that is, firms tended to be taken private when there were no reinvestment opportunities for the cash). . . .

c. *Improved Incentives from Ownership Changes in MBOs*

There is, of course, a simpler agency cost reduction explanation for MBOs than eliminating free cash flows. In an MBO, management's ownership share dramatically increases. By making management a substantial stockowner, the MBO provides powerful incentives to increase productivity. . . .

The explanation of MBO gains as a result of improved incentives from increased ownership is consistent with the substantial evidence, reviewed in Smith, that post-buyout firms experience significant operating efficiencies and productivity improvements. . . .

B. *Value-Maximizing Expropriation Explanations*

* * *

1. *Tax Benefits*

Tax benefits provide another value-maximizing explanation for takeovers. Because interest is deductible, this is a more obvious explanation for leveraged acquisitions than the monitoring story of free cash flows: the increased debt load shelters more income, motivating the transaction. In addition, a firm may have tax attributes, such as favorable deductions, investment tax credits, depreciation allowances, net operating losses, that it cannot use because it has too little income. Since the tax code does not permit the direct sale of tax attributes, the firm may seek to merge with a firm that has income to capture the value of the tax benefit.

* * *

There is . . . little empirical support for the taxpayer expropriation explanation. Auerbach and Reishus collected a comprehensive data set of several hundred mergers from 1968-83 and found that reducing taxes was not a significant reason for the transactions. Only 20% of these mergers could be classified as having obvious potential tax benefits, such as the transfer of losses or credits or a step-up in asset basis, and the estimated value of the tax benefits was only 10% of the target's market value, a figure far below the acquisition premiums. . . .

Auerbach and Reishus' merger sample ends before financing acquisitions by debt became as important a feature of takeovers as it was in the mid-1980s. Studies of the tax effects of leveraged buyouts, where the debt load is substantial, produce different results. For example, in a study of MBOs, Kaplan found that the excess returns to public shareholders are significantly related to tax savings from the new capital structure; in fact, the estimated tax savings explained most of the premium. Schipper and Smith's findings are virtually identical. In both studies, interest deductions are the key tax savings that explain MBO premiums. . . .

Although the Kaplan and Schipper and Smith studies seem to provide strong evidence for an expropriation explanation of MBOs via increased interest deductions, this research presents only one aspect of the tax story. As Jensen, Kaplan, and Stiglan point out, MBOs are also accompanied by increased tax payments by selling target shareholders, by buyout debtholders, and by the long-term increased profitability of the reorganized firm. In their estimation, the net tax payments in these transactions are positive, not negative. . . .

2. *Bondholder Expropriation*

There is a third possible explanation for the use of debt in a takeover. Leveraged acquisitions may simply be mechanisms for expropriating the wealth of bondholders, rather than taxpayers. When a firm increases its leverage, the value of preexisting debt decreases because it is now a riskier investment (the firm's cash flows may not cover the new debt load). As the bondholders are not compensated for this increased risk, the leveraged transaction redistributes wealth to the shareholders. Bondholders can and do, however, protect themselves from losses upon a leveraged acquisition by event-risk indenture provisions.

Several studies have sought to measure the effects of leveraged acquisitions on target debt. Although bond ratings are typically lowered after a leveraged buyout, studies find either no significant bond price effects or a small negative effect which is nowhere near the magnitude of the premium paid to the shareholders. . . .

3. *Expropriation from Labor*

The expropriation explanation of takeovers that attracts the most attention involves labor as the victim. The most sophisticated version of this explanation is Shleifer and Summers' breach of implicit contract explanation of hostile takeovers.

In Shleifer and Summers' scenario, shareholders initially hire trustworthy individuals as managers, in order to make credible long-term contract commitments to workers. The long-term commitments are implicit, rather than explicit contracts. After employees are hired, shareholders will want to breach the implicit contract, in order to increase their returns by lowering labor's share. A trustworthy management prevents them from doing so by honoring the informal agreements. A hostile takeover will, however, permit shareholders to behave opportunistically because, unlike trustworthy incumbents, a raider will not hesitate to break implicit contracts, cutting costs and releasing the pent-up value of the firm to shareholders.

* * *

The labor expropriation explanation, in general or as refined by Shleifer and Summers, has scant empirical support. . . .

Rosett tests Shleifer and Summers' breach of contract explanation more directly by examining union wage contracts before and after takeovers. He finds no support for their thesis: there is, in fact, a positive *gain* in union wealth levels after hostile acquisitions. Although there are losses after friendly acquisitions, even then the losses are insignificant relative to the premiums (when measured over 18 years after the takeover, the union losses in friendly acquisitions equal approximately 5% of the shareholders' gain). Bhagat, Shleifer, and Vishny also find that layoffs occur infrequently, affect high-level white collar workers, are higher when management successfully defeats a bid (either by remaining independent or by finding a white knight) than when a hostile bidder succeeds and, most important, result in losses that are small compared to takeover premiums (10-20%). In sum, while we would need counterfactual data to test the labor expropriation hypothesis fully—we need to know how many workers would have been laid off or what the wage profile would have looked like if the firm had not been acquired—what we do know suggests that expropriation from labor does not motivate takeovers.

4. *Market Power*

A traditional explanation for takeovers that falls in the expropriation category is that takeovers increase market power, thereby allowing the merged firm to obtain a monopoly position and earn monopoly rents. This explanation was popular at the turn of the century, and is less important as a rationale in recent years because such combinations are illegal under the antitrust laws. . . .

* * *

C. *Value-Maximizing Market Inefficiency Explanations*

* * *

1. *Underpricing*

The most general version of the market inefficiency explanation of takeovers is that the capital market simply misprices securities. Acquiring firms identify undervalued securities and profit from the difference between the price they pay and the firm's true value. Given the size of the premiums received in takeovers, this explanation cannot be characterized as an expropriation explanation from current investors in targets to bidders. . . .

There is no evidence supporting the underpricing explanation of takeover gains. In particular, if this explanation was correct, then once a bidder identified a target, its price would rise and remain at the higher true value, regardless of whether the acquisition occurred. Several studies find, however, that the stock price of takeover targets that are not acquired returns to its lower pre-bid price. . . .

2. *Market Myopia*

The market myopia inefficiency explanation is more sophisticated than the underpricing hypothesis. In this explanation, investors are short-sighted and behave myopically to sacrifice long-term benefits for immediate profits. As a consequence, firms that engage in long-term planning and make substantial investments in research and development (R&D) are supposedly undervalued by the market and become takeover targets. . . .

There is, however, no empirical support for a myopia explanation. First, there is no evidence of market myopia regarding long-term investment. The market responds positively to announcements of increases in R&D and other capital investment expenditures. . . .

D. *Non-Value-Maximizing Expropriation Explanations*

* * *

1. *Diversification*

One explanation of takeovers, which focuses on conglomerate mergers, is diversification: merging two income streams to reduce risk. . . .

. . . Modern finance theory indicates that diversification will not increase the market value of the merged entity beyond the sum of the separate values of the two companies, because investors can diversify more cheaply on their own by diversifying their stock portfolios (buying shares in the two companies). . . .

* * *

While most shareholders do not find portfolio diversification costly, and are therefore not benefited by firm-level diversification, there is a special set of individuals who do benefit from such diversification—corporate managers. . . .

* * *

There is some evidence consistent with a non-value-maximizing diversification explanation. Amihud and Lev and Lloyd, Modani, and Hand find that manager-controlled firms are more likely to engage in diversifying mergers than are owner-controlled firms, and the income streams and operations of manager-controlled firms are more diversified than those of owner-controlled firms. . . .

2. *Self-Aggrandizement*

The manager risk reduction diversification explanation is a subset of what can generally be described as a managerialist perspective on the firm. The motivation for an acquisition is the maximization of the manager's utility rather than of the shareholders' wealth, or more simply put, self-aggrandizement. Risk may be a concern, but power or empire-building may be the goal as well, and these are indeed the more traditional managerialist explanations of takeovers.

If the managerialist view of the firm explains mergers, then we would expect a negative correlation between bidder and target returns. Weston, Chung, and Hoag's finding of a significant positive correlation in pure conglomerate and product-extension mergers is inconsistent with managerialism. However, there are studies that provide some support for the thesis. . . . Mitchell and Lehn's finding that bad bidders make good targets is relevant here. While it supports Manne's disciplining story regarding takeovers, it also offers some support for managerialism, for it indicates that at least some acquisitions are profoundly misconceived.

3. *Free Cash Flow on the Acquirers' Side*

While the emphasis in free cash flow theory is on the target, the acquirer may have free cash flow as well. Making an acquisition uses the excess cash. . . .

Several studies provide evidence consistent with this explanation. . . . Finally, a recent study by Lang, Stulz, and Walkling provides further support for this explanation. They find that an increase in free cash flow equal to 1% of a bidder's total assets is associated with a decrease in the bidder's gain from the takeover equal to 1% of its common stock. In addition, free cash flow explains more of the variation in bidder returns than other variables, such as the number of bidders, target management's resistance, and the bidder's size in relation to that of the target. . . .

4. *Hubris and the Winner's Curse*

Roll has expounded another managerialist explanation, which he terms the "hubris" hypothesis. In this view, managers seek to make value-maximizing acquisitions, but they make mistakes and overvalue targets (or their abilities to turn targets around). . . . The transaction thus is a wealth transfer from the acquirer's shareholders to the target's shareholders.

Roll's thesis is related to the winner's curse phenomenon in sealed-bid auctions.[130] When the value to the bidders of the auctioned item is uncertain, the person who has overestimated the value the most will be the winner. This is because a positive evaluation error produces a winning bid, but a negative error does not. . . . The negative returns to bidding firms in the 1980s, when takeover auctions increased, lend support to Roll's hypothesis. . . . However, the finding of several researchers that the net return to acquisitions is positive—target gains are greater than bidder losses, indicates that takeovers involve more than simply a wealth transfer from bidder shareholders to managers and target shareholders: there is either an efficiency gain or a third-party wealth transfer accompanying the transaction.

A winner's curse or hubris hypothesis is, furthermore, not a long-run equilibrium explanation because we expect bidders to learn from their experience and adjust their bids downward (or not bid) to avoid the winner's curse. . . .

* * *

---

130 In some takeover auctions, the competing bidders make sequential public offers. Because these are not sealed bid auctions, they are not subject to the winner's curse (a bidder can learn about the value of the object, and hence the size of its estimation error, from the other bids). However, these sequential public auctions have become relatively rare ever since target boards began to run formal auctions, as they have since the mid-1980s, after the Delaware Supreme Court's decision in Revlon, Inc. v. MacAndrews & Forbes Holdings, Inc., . . .

E. *Summary and Conclusion*

. . . There is a substantial body of research that is consistent with agency cost reduction or synergy gain explanations of takeovers. There is, however, scant support for any of the expropriation explanations, whether the hypothetical victims are bondholders, labor, consumers or the government. There is even less support for market inefficiency explanations.

The data are more ambiguous regarding non-value-maximizing explanations. Manager-controlled firms engage in more diversifying mergers than owner-controlled firms and some acquirers earned negative abnormal returns in the 1980s. . . . Most important, the net gains of acquisitions remain positive when bidder and target returns are matched. This finding undercuts the non-value-maximizing interpretation because it indicates that the gain from acquisitions is more than a simple transfer of wealth from acquirers to targets.

. . . However, different takeover theories each explain best only subsets of acquisitions and, though empirical studies might point in a particular direction, none are conclusive. There may be, then, instances of non-value-maximizing acquisitions as well as acquisitions which transfer wealth from particular groups to target shareholders, but these should be viewed as the exception, rather than the rule.

II. Regulatory Implications

Takeovers are regulated under a dual regime of federal and state laws. The principal federal legislation is the Williams Act, which places disclosure and other substantive requirements on the takeover bidding process. . . . Federal tax and antitrust laws also affect takeovers, and presidential review and approval is required for certain acquisitions by foreigners.

State takeover laws apply to corporations incorporated in the legislating state, although some laws extend to firms with physical operations in the state as well. While the earliest state statutes ("first generation"), which established disclosure and review requirements for bids, were struck down for unconstitutionally burdening interstate commerce in *Edgar v. MITE Corp.*,[137] subsequent statutes ("second generation"), imposing restrictions on acquirers' voting rights, were upheld in *CTS Corp. v. Dynamics Corp. of America*.[138] The primary mechanism of state regulation is, however, judicial, because courts oversee the bidding process, and can thereby immunize management's defensive tactics. Because second generation statutes and judicially-sanctioned defensive tactics go beyond the Williams Act's strictures on bidders, the states have become the more important jurisdiction for takeover regulation.

* * *

A. *Regulation Encouraging Takeover Auctions*

One of the primary effects of takeover regulation is the facilitation of auctions for target firms. Any regulation that delays the consummation of a hostile bid, for example, increases the likelihood of an auction by providing time for another bidder to enter

---

137 457 U.S. 624 (1982).

138 481 U.S. 69 (1987).

the fray, upon the target's solicitation or otherwise. Major federal regulation furthers auctions through the Williams Act's minimum offer period, mandatory withdrawal rights and 5% accumulation disclosure requirements. . . .

Auctions have also been fostered at the state level. First generation state takeover statutes, whose disclosure and hearing requirements had expanded upon the Williams Act's terms, were followed by second generation control share acquisition statutes, which require bidders to wait for a shareholders' meeting before they can either purchase shares or hold shares with full voting rights. These statutes delay the completion of bids. Moreover, the Delaware court's fiduciary duty rules, as expounded in *Revlon, Inc. v. MacAndrews & Forbes Holdings, Inc.*, by commanding managers to maximize the price shareholders receive when their company is put up for sale, may require an auction. Finally, management's principal defensive tactic, the poison pill,[143] also promotes auctions, as it permits the board to negotiate the redemption of the pill with a preferred bidder. . . .

The uniform and persistent adoption of regulations that facilitate takeover auctions raises an obvious question: are auctions desirable? . . .

1. *Should Auctions Be Encouraged At All?*

The practice of encouraging takeover auctions is the subject of a protracted debate in the legal literature. Many commentators maintain that auctions will reduce the number of takeovers because competition raises the winning price, which lowers bidders' returns and consequently makes them less likely to bid in the first place.[145] . . .

Other commentators question the importance of an adverse effect of auctions on the number of takeover bids. In their view, bidders have an alternative means of recouping their investment (selling the shares they accumulate before making an offer into the winning bid) and search costs are low (possibly a result of the role played by financial intermediaries in the bidding process); consequently, auctions will not reduce the number of initial bids, or any decrease will be insignificant.[147] . . . Finally, synergy explanations of takeovers suggest a useful role for auctions: ensuring that the target is acquired by the highest-valuing bidder (the bidder with the highest synergy gain from the acquisition). In this case, an auction may be a cheaper mechanism than a series of resales to move the assets to the highest-valuing user.

---

143 A poison pill is a shareholder rights plan in which the firm issues a warrant on each share of common stock (except those owned by the triggering shareholder) that gives the holder the right to acquire preferred stock for a low price. The right is contingent upon the occurence of either a tender offer for the common or an accumulation of a block of common stock. The preferred stock has superior dividend and liquidation rights and is convertible into shares of the acquirer, at a steep discount, if the common stock is exchanged in a merger. Boards can redeem the rights for a trivial amount in the case of a tender offer, but the rights become nonredeemable upon the block acquisition.

145 *See, e.g.*, Frank H. Easterbrook & Daniel R. Fischel, *The Proper Role of a Target's Management in Responding to a Tender Offer*, 94 HARV. L. REV. 1161 (1981). . . .

147 *See, e.g.*, Lucian A. Bebchuk, *The Case for Facilitating Competing Tender Offers: A Reply and Extension*, 35 STAN. L. REV. 23 (1982); Ronald J. Gibson, *Seeking Competitive Bids Versus Pure Passivity in Tender Offer Defense*, 35 STAN. L. REV. 51 (1982).

* * *

The economic literature cannot readily arbitrate this debate. To do so in a compelling fashion we would need to know the unknowable—how many takeovers there would have been had auctions not been permitted. But there is some suggestive research on the effect of regulations encouraging auctions, and it tends to support auction opponents. Bidder returns tend to be negative after state takeover laws were enacted and poison pill defensive tactics jelled. . . .

* * *

2. *Should Auctions Be Encouraged in Specified Cases?*

While we cannot determine conclusively whether auctions should be banned, we can examine whether, once a bid is made, holding an auction makes more sense in some circumstances than in others. There is an extensive and highly sophisticated economic literature analyzing auctions and identifying procedures which are efficient (i.e., the highest-valuing user obtains the auctioned object) and which maximize returns to sellers. Cramton and Schwartz apply the results of this literature to takeover auctions, and emphasize that the optimal policy is a function of the auction environment. . . .

There are two prototypical auction environments, common value and independent values. In a common value auction, the auctioned object's value is the same to all buyers, whereas in an independent values auction, each buyer values the object differently. . . . If a takeover is undertaken to achieve synergy gains, then the auction setting is one of independent values because the value of the target will vary with the bidder (different bidders can achieve different levels of synergy gains). In this context, an auction is appropriate because it permits the target to identify the highest-valuing bidder. . . .

If a takeover is, however, explained by agency cost reductions (eliminating free cash flow or replacing inefficient management), then the auction environment is likely to be one of common value because many bidders will be able to mitigate the problem and each will obtain the same value from the target. . . .

* * *

. . . I am skeptical whether corporate law should, as Cramton and Schwartz maintain, instruct target boards to pursue social efficiency rather than revenue maximization when presented with a bid. Opting for efficiency rather than revenue maximization stands a commonsense understanding of property rights on its head: our economic system is premised on the consensual transfer of property in private commercial transactions. Yet from a social efficiency standard, the target shareholders ought to be *compelled* to sell to any bidder for a trivial amount above the market price, in order to move the assets to the higher-valuing user. Most of us—except strict utilitarians—would find such a rule unacceptable, but it is the logical implication of implementing such a policy.

A no auctions policy would impose a social cost, a higher price for equity capital, as common stock owners would no longer share in takeover gains. If bidders are public companies, then this would not affect the cost of equity capital because what shareholders lose on the target side they gain on the bidder side. However, in the 1980s many bidders, particularly LBO teams, were privately-held, and therefore the lost premiums would not be offset by gains on other holdings in a diversified portfolio. . . .

Cramton and Schwartz's pursuit of social efficiency can be harmonized within a consensual private property framework as an assertion of which regime shareholders would prefer before a bid is made. Revenue maximization and social efficiency diverge when the analysis is conditioned on the existence of a bid, but the two may coincide when the analysis considers the unconditional effect of auctions on takeovers (whether auctions decrease the number of initial bids). . . .

This recognition highlights the need for a discretionary policy. . . . It recasts the policy question as whether shareholders behind a veil of ignorance (that is, prior to knowing that their firm is the object of a bid) would prefer a lower premium and an increased likelihood of receiving a bid (the "no auctions" policy tradeoff) to a higher premium accompanied by a reduced probability of a takeover and consequent increase in management slack (the "auctions always" tradeoff). Rather than mandate public policy on the basis of speculation concerning shareholder preferences over these tradeoffs, the most appropriate policy is to permit the parties whose wealth is at stake, shareholders, to choose whether or not to hold takeover auctions for their firms. . . .

* * *

B. *Regulation Restricting Two-Tier Takeovers*

Many state takeover laws prevent bidders from making two-tier acquisitions (a tender offer for control followed by a merger to obtain 100% of the shares) that are structurally coercive, that is, front-end loaded. In a front-end loaded, two-tier takeover, the gain is distributed unequally across the two steps to induce target shareholders to tender in the first step, in which the bidder gains control. This type of regulation's explicit concern is horizontal equity, ensuring that all target shareholders receive the same price for their shares. Equal treatment, which is thought to prevent shareholders from being forced to tender, is consistent with the corporate law fiduciary principle that requires shareholder distributions to be pro rata. Examples are fair price, redemption rights, and business combination freeze statutes. The Williams Act's requirement of pro rata acceptance of shares in oversubscribed offers indicates a similar horizontal equity concern.

. . . [I]t is not analytically obvious that two-tier bid restrictions will decrease the number of bids, as they need only redistribute funds among target shareholders rather than increase premiums.

There is very little empirical evidence that statutes restricting two-tier bids deter takeovers. . . . There is also evidence suggesting that the threat of front-end loaded two-tier bids is overstated. Blended premiums in two-tier bids are not significantly different from the premiums in offers for any and all shares.

More important, the voluntary adoption by shareholders of charter amendments with similar effect to these statutes suggests that shareholders may well desire equal treatment. . . .

C. *Regulation Restricting Bidders' Ownership Rights*

Several second and third generation state takeover laws go much further than regulating two-tier offers or encouraging auctions, and, by severely restricting bidders' ownership rights, have the effect of "show-stoppers" (tactics that kill a bid). Control share acquisition statutes deny bidders' shares voting rights (or deny bidders the right to purchase shares) without the approval of all other shareholders. Business combination freeze statutes prohibit bidders from engaging in related transactions with a target after they gain control, for a specified number of years, even if the remaining public shareholders approve of the transaction and a fair price is paid. Disgorgement statutes prevent unsuccessful bidders from selling their target shares at a profit. These statutes raise the cost of some takeovers prohibitively, and thus chill some bids. Shares without voting rights are obviously of no value to acquirers seeking to control to implement their own business plans, highly leveraged buyers need access to target assets to service the debt that makes their bids possible, and firms may not make toehold acquisitions, which may be crucial for a takeover's success, when they face a tax at 100%.

Empirical research shows that these statutes have a far more damaging effect on takeovers than two-tier bid regulation. Hackl and Testani find a steeper decline in successful takeovers in control share acquisition statute states than in other states. . . . Stock price studies also find more significant negative abnormal returns on the enactment of business combination freeze, control share acquisition and disgorgement statutes than fair price and other provisions. Thus, investors assess these statutes' impact more adversely. Moreover, when firms opted out of the Pennsylvania takeover statute, which included the most refined control share acquisition and disgorgement provisions, they experience positive abnormal returns. These data, in conjunction with the evidence that most takeovers are efficiency-enhancing transactions, indicate that statutes whose effect is to thwart bids are poor public policy.

It should be noted, however, that managers are able to thwart bids even without these statutes' assistance, through a number of defensive tactics approved by courts. It appears that poison pills and defensive charter amendments are, in fact, quite potent substitutes for takeover statutes. Karpoff and Malatesta find that the stock price effect of takeover laws is significantly negative for firms without takeover protections, but not for firms with such defenses.

D. *Regulation Introducing Non-Shareholder Interests*

The most recent state takeover statutes introduce non-shareholder interests into decisions about takeovers. "Other constituency" statutes require or permit boards of directors to consider the interests of non-shareholder groups, such as workers and local communities, in their decision-making process. Some statutes also require severance pay for workers who are discharged after a takeover. These statutes make explicit concerns that may motivate legislators when enacting any takeover regulation, that a takeover will adversely affect the local labor market. However, the statutes, ironically, protect managers more effectively than workers. Workers have no right to challenge board decisions for failing to consider their interest, while shareholders' ability to sue managers successfully for opposing a bid is diminished. There is no severance pay for plant closings commenced by incumbent management, but a bidder's ability to reduce costs by layoffs, and hence the value of a takeover, has been reduced.

* * *

The economic literature on takeovers also suggests that these statutes are utterly misguided. As we have seen, the best available data consistently indicate that takeovers are *not* a mechanism for transferring wealth from labor to shareholders. . . . Shareholders, correspondingly, appear to assess these statutes negatively. An event study of one of the earliest versions of another constituency statute, Ohio's 1986 takeover statute instructing managers to consider long-term rather than short-term interests, found the law had a significantly negative impact. . . .

E. *Regulation through the Federal Tax Code*

* * *

2. *Taxing Defensive Tactics*

Two defensive tactics have been singled out for federal tax penalties—golden parachutes and greenmail. Taxing these tactics is ironic because they are likely to benefit shareholders by increasing the probability of a takeover. . . .

Golden parachutes are lucrative severance pay contracts for top management that are triggered by a control change. Although considered a defensive tactic—they raise the price of a bid because the acquirer is burdened with excessive severance payments—golden parachutes benefit shareholders by aligning managers' incentives with the shareholders' interest, as managers are financially rewarded for approving a takeover. Shareholders apparently recognize the beneficial role of golden parachutes: stock prices significantly increase on the announcement of golden parachute plans.

Greenmail refers to a target's repurchase, at a premium, of the shares owned by a hostile bidder. Because the repurchase terminates the takeover, it is viewed as a defensive tactic. But greenmail has a more positive interpretation as well: it facilitates an auction (if the greenmailer is not the highest-valuing user of the target, paying greenmail can result in the target receiving a higher premium from another bidder), serving as compensation for those who supply valuable information to the market by identifying a takeover target and hence aiding in monitoring managers.[226] The idea is that the second, higher-valuing bidder will enter only if it knows that the greenmailer is out of the picture so that there will be no competition to its bid. . . . The difficulty with this story is distinguishing when greenmail is used by faithful managers, who hope that the auction will produce a better bid, as the models hypothesize, and when it is used by self-serving managers who are confident that no subsequent bid will be forthcoming. The possibility that managers will be unfaithful renders the effect of greenmail more ambiguous than that of golden parachutes.

* * *

226 Jonathan R. Macey & Fred S. McChesney, *A Theoretical Analysis of Corporate Greenmail*, 95 YALE L.J. 13 (1985). . . .

Note

The following article develops one other theory of takeover gains.

Lynn A. Stout, *Are Takeover Premiums Really Premiums? Market Price, Fair Value, and Corporate Law*, 99 YALE L.J. 1235 (1990)*

INTRODUCTION

* * *

Curiously, the burgeoning takeover literature largely overlooks the most straightforward explanation for premiums. If the bidder who buys a controlling block of shares in a target firm is "cornering the market" in a unique good with a limited supply, it seems natural that buying larger and larger quantities of stock should inevitably bid up the market price. The idea that large stock transactions exert such "price pressure" has intuitive appeal. Investors, underwriters, and corporate managers have long presumed that selling a large block of stock depresses the market price of that stock, while buying a large block raises the price. Why, then, has the academic literature disregarded that obvious explanation for premiums?

The answer seems to be that most contemporary scholars reject the concept of price pressure because it is inconsistent with modern financial economics. According to orthodox capital asset pricing theory, investors should be able to buy or sell very large amounts of any particular stock without changing its prevailing market price. In economic terms, investor demand for individual stocks should be "perfectly elastic," and the demand function for shares should be horizontal.

* * *

The notion of perfectly elastic demand has gained currency because it enjoys theoretical support from the widely accepted variant of efficient market theory known as the Capital Asset Pricing Model (CAPM). . . .

* * *

I. DEMAND ELASTICITY: THEORIES AND EVIDENCE

A. *The Perfect Elasticity Hypothesis*

Economists use the phrase "demand elasticity" to refer to the degree to which a change in the price of a particular good changes the quantity demanded by consumers. Demand is described as "perfectly elastic" when even a slight rise in price

---

* Reprinted by permission of the Yale Law Journal Company and Fred B. Rothman & Company from The Yale Law School Journal, Vol. 99, pages 1235-1296.

causes consumer demand to fall to zero, while a slight price decline causes demand to expand infinitely. Another way to interpret the notion of perfectly elastic demand is to describe the demand function as horizontal. . . .

* * *

The CAPM incorporates portfolio theory into efficient market theory to predict that, because investors value stocks according to their risk-adjusted returns, stocks with identical estimated levels of market risk should trade at prices that imply an identical estimated rate of return. . . .

The CAPM consequently predicts that in a well developed securities market, potential investors will be able to choose from among a great many stocks bearing identical expected returns for market risk, any one of which serves as a perfect substitute for any other. This notion of perfect substitutability provides the theoretical foundation for a horizontal demand curve. Suppose that IBM is currently trading a price that implies a ten percent return on investment. In an efficient market, substitute stocks with identical market risk—including perhaps ITT, GM, and GE—will also trade at prices implying a ten percent return. If the price of IBM increased so that the implied rate of return from buying IBM fell to nine percent, investor demand for IBM would drop to zero. No rational investor would buy stock promising a nine percent return when the same amount of money could purchase perfect substitutes paying ten percent. Similarly, if the price of IBM were dropped so that buying IBM brought an expected return of eleven percent, *all* investors would want to buy it. What investor would own stocks that pay ten percent when a perfect substitute offers eleven percent?

The notion that any stock should have a large number of perfect substitutes has produced the corporate finance maxim: "seen one stock, seen them all." In other words, in an efficient market a rational investor should be indifferent between purchasing $100 of IBM, or $100 of ITT. . . .

To the layman, however, the idea of perfect substitutability is counter-intuitive. After all, IBM and ITT are very different firms, with different products, management, and prospects. The theoretical consequence of perfect substitutability—perfectly elastic demand—also seems somewhat odd. Consumer demand for goods other than securities usually displays some degree of inelasticity. Price hikes reduce the quantity demanded by consumers but do not eliminate demand entirely; price cuts spark additional purchases, but to a limited degree.

The layman's uneasiness about perfectly elastic demand is mirrored by the refusal of those who participate in securities markets to behave as if large stock transactions do not influence prices. Corporations repurchase their own shares in order to raise prices; underwriters sell stock issues at below-market prices in the belief that this is necessary to sell large amounts of equity successfully. An even more dramatic example of market behavior inconsistent with perfectly elastic demand is the willingness of takeover bidders to pay large premiums over the market price for the stock of target firms. If purchasers can buy any amount of a particular stock without driving price upward, there seems no reason for takeover bidders to pay more than market.

If only because of the large amounts of money involved, it is improbable that market participants' beliefs reflect either a foolish reliance on folklore or an unwillingness to keep abreast of the financial literature. More likely, their opinions are based on their own experience in financial transactions. . . .

The CAPM is far and away the currently dominant stock pricing theory. But at least on the question of demand elasticity, theory directly conflicts with practice. That discrepancy suggests a need to reexamine the theory.

B. *The Heterogeneous Beliefs Hypothesis*

The CAPM was developed by economists during the 1950's and 1960's. . . .

Like all economic models, the CAPM is premised on a number of assumptions concerning investor tastes and behavior. One of those assumptions is that investors share similar opinions of stocks' values. The assumption of homogeneous beliefs provides the foundation for the claim of perfectly elastic demand. Because all investors agree that a stock is worth exactly its market price, at below-market prices all investors view the stock as a bargain and rush to buy it, while at above-market prices all investors see the stock as overpriced and are unwilling to purchase any shares.

The assumption of homogeneous beliefs is at odds with a reality in which investors and analysts differ sharply in their predictions for particular corporations, industries, and the general economy. Individuals have different information, different investment experience, and different psychological perspectives from which they evaluate any stock's prospects. Because valuing stocks requires investors to apply their varying backgrounds and talents to predicting an uncertain future, their estimates of stock value may differ widely. Where one investor predicts that a new line of business will treble a firm's earnings, another believes the venture is doomed to failure; where one shareholder happily tenders her shares in response to a premium offer, another refuses, deeming the price inadequate.

* * *

The CAPM's tenet that investors should regard different stocks as perfect substitutes for each other no longer holds true under a stock pricing model that assumes heterogeneous investor opinions of stock value. Instead, investors should have preferences for buying those stocks they believe are "underpriced" by the market, and aversions to buying stocks they perceive to be "overpriced." Particular securities will tend to be held by those individuals who subjectively value them most highly.

That observation has important implications for the likely elasticity of demand for stocks. When the market price of the stock is low, a large number of investors may believe it to be a "good value" relative to other stocks and choose to buy it for their portfolios. As the price rises, the number of shareholders who subjectively value the stock at market price or above will shrink. But even at very high prices, a small number of "super-optimists" will want to buy shares.

The question naturally arises why, if an investor values a particular stock more highly than its market price, that investor does not buy until she has bid the price up to her own optimistic valuation. If investors were not risk averse, and if they had infinite wealth or unlimited ability to borrow, the entire stock of a particular firm might indeed end up being owned by that single investor whose view of the firm's future was most optimistic.

Investors' resources and credit are limited, however. Few individuals enjoy the wealth needed to own an entire firm. Moreover, the more an individual invests in a single stock, the less she can reduce the riskiness of her investments by diversifying. The risk-averse investor is loath to put all her eggs in even the most attractive basket. Although she may consider a particular stock to be significantly underpriced, at some point the benefits of buying more of it are no longer enough to compensate her for the increased risk of concentrating her portfolio. She will stop buying the stock although she still perceives it to be underpriced. To induce such an investor to purchase more, the price of the stock must be lowered further.

The conclusion of this analysis is that it no longer makes sense to believe that investor demand for a particular stock is nonexistent at prices above the current market price and infinite at prices below. Even at very high prices, a small number of investors may be willing to buy the stock. Lowering price increases demand, both because individuals who do not presently own the stock decide to buy it and because existing shareholders demand additional shares. Investor demand for stocks is not perfectly elastic; incremental changes in price produce incremental changes in quantity demanded.

The concept of less-than-perfectly elastic demand can be depicted as a downward-sloping function. . . . The takeover bidder who wishes to purchase the stock of a target firm from its current shareholders must offer a price that meets or exceeds the shareholders' varying subjective estimates of value. Thus, purchasing larger and larger amounts requires the bidder to offer higher and higher prices.

* * *

C. *Empirical Evidence of Stock Demand Elasticity*

The differing consequences for market behavior of a horizontal demand function and a downward-sloping demand function provide an opportunity to test which model more accurately describes modern securities markets. There is substantial evidence to support the claim that investor demand for stocks is, in fact, significantly downward-sloping.

More than a decade of empirical work has shown that large stock transactions—secondary distributions of blocks held by large shareholders, seasoned issuances of additional stock by corporations, and block purchases and sales by index funds and other institutional investors—are accompanied by significant price changes. . . .

Nevertheless, the extent to which these types of studies support the conclusion that demand is somewhat inelastic is hotly debated. The uncertainty arises from the possibility that the price declines associated with large sales reflect not price pressure, but investors' perceptions of the sale as a negative event which lowers their estimates of stock value. Investors may believe that large shareholders (in the case of secondary distributions) and corporate management (in the case of seasoned issues) have better information concerning the value of the firm's equity than the average shareholder. If so, the market may interpret a secondary distribution or seasoned issuance as a signal that the firm's stock is overpriced and readjust its estimate of stock value accordingly. The resulting price decline would not be attributable to downward-sloping demand, but to an efficient market's rapid incorporation of the information signaled by the fact of the sale.

Because investors may extract information from sales by large shareholders or seasoned issuances by firms, most economists regard the results of large-transaction studies as inconclusive. Other tests of demand elasticity reduce the possibility of an information effect by focusing on the reaction of stock price to a firm's inclusion in the Standard & Poor's 500 Index (S&P 500). The stocks included in the S&P 500 are chosen not for superior performance, but to reflect the market as a whole. Winners and losers are equally represented. The decision to include a new firm in the index consequently is not based on any evaluation of a stock's worth but rather on its "representativeness" of an industry and the market.

S&P 500 listing therefore should not add any information relevant to stock performance beyond that already publicly available. But inclusion in the S&P 500 does trigger large purchase orders on the part of "index funds" which seek to replicate the market's performance by carrying a portfolio of the stocks that make up the index. Those purchases may amount to three percent or more of the firm's outstanding equity. If demand for stock were perfectly elastic, such purchases would have no effect on price. However, index-inclusion studies have found that, on average, index listing is associated with stock price gains of three percent over the earlier market price. That result again suggests average demand elasticity of minus one.

It is possible that investors perceive inclusion in the S&P 500 as a positive signal of firm stability. If so, inclusion alone might affect the market's valuation even in the absence of index fund purchases. While one cannot reject that supposition entirely, it seems (in the words of one commentator) "quite contrived." This is particularly true in light of findings that index inclusion had no discernable effect on prices before index funds became common. Thus, the results of index-inclusion tests support downward-sloping demand over the information hypothesis.

* * *

II. Demand Elasticity and the Regulation of Corporations and Securities Markets

* * *

A. *Corporate Takeovers*

* * *

Once we assume inelastic demand, the behavior of acquisition markets begins to make sense. Bidders offer substantial premiums over market price to induce those holders who value their stock more highly than the market to sell. The "premium" is not really a premium at all. It is simply the price necessary to persuade more-optimistic shareholders with higher reservation prices to sell the shares the bidder must purchase to gain control.

Of course, the scenario described above—in which a bidder obtains ownership of a target through a series of transactions with individual shareholders at varying prices—is unrealistic. A complete acquisition through a series of individually negotiated transactions at different prices poses almost insurmountable practical and regulatory problems for bidders. Although a bidder may begin a takeover attempt by acquiring a modest "toehold" in the target's stock through open-market or private purchases, most corporate acquisitions are completed at a uniform price. Bidders generally buy target firms either in a "one-step" merger or asset sale approved by a majority of the target's shareholders or by acquiring voting control through a tender offer and then, as controlling shareholder, approving a "squeeze-out" merger at the same price.

Acquiring shares at a uniform price costs substantially more than purchasing an equivalent number of shares through private or open-market purchases. A bidder acquiring stock in individually negotiated transactions can price discriminate and offer high prices to more-optimistic shareholders and low prices to relatively pessimistic shareholders, to reflect each group's differing reservation values. In an acquisition at a uniform price, however, the bidder must pay the pessimists as much as the optimists.

At first glance, the consumer surplus[164] enjoyed by the relatively pessimistic shareholders who believe the premium offer exceeds the true value of their shares would seem to imply that mergers at a uniform premium price (or tender offers followed by a merger at the same premium) substantially benefit target shareholders. The flaw in this analysis is that it ignores the fate of the shareholders who do not want to sell their shares. Mergers and asset sales do not require unanimous shareholder approval. In many states, a mere majority is sufficient to approve such transactions. If the deal is approved, shareholders who voted against the transaction are forced to sell their shares along with those who voted in favor of it. Thus, individuals who have more-optimistic estimates of their stock's value become the victims of a less-optimistic majority's rule. Less-than-unanimous shareholder approval of merger and asset sales (whether as an initial one-step acquisition strategy or as a squeeze-out tactic following a tender offer that gives the bidder voting control) forces dissenting shareholders to part with their shares for a price they believe inadequate. From the perspective of dissenting shareholders, such transactions are value-estroying [sic].

The downward-sloping demand hypothesis thus indicates that bidders who acquire target companies at a uniform premium price "overpay" the shareholders who enthusiastically vote to approve the merger and "underpay" the dissenters who are forced to sell if the deal goes through. Approving shareholders enjoy subjective gains while dissenting shareholders suffer subjective losses.

* * *

---

164 Consumer surplus is the difference between the premium price paid and the subjective value of the shares to those shareholders who believe they are worth less than the premium price offered, although more than the earlier prevailing market price. . . .

To some extent, the consumer surplus enjoyed by approving shareholders and the subjective loss suffered by dissenting shareholders in a merger can be expected to "cancel each other out." But because the exact shape and slope of the demand curves for different stocks is unknown, it is difficult to determine whether a bidder who acquires a target firm at a uniform price that overcompensates the approving majority and undercompensates the dissenters has paid a total price that exceeds, or falls short of, the aggregate subjective value that the target's shareholders attached to the property they have given up. Thus, the fact of a premium alone does not tell us whether a target's shareholders, on average, "gain" from selling at a premium.

* * *

The heterogeneous beliefs hypothesis consequently recommends a far greater degree of agnosticism on the subject of the social value of acquisitions than has characterized the takeover debate thus far. Takeover premiums that reflect nothing more than the natural consequence of a downward-sloping demand function tell us little about the efficiency implications of takeovers in general or any individual transaction in particular. . . .

* * *

Notes and Questions

1. For a rebuttal to Professor Stout's thesis see Sedak & Woodward, *Takeover Premiums, Appraisal Rights and the Price Elasticity of a Firm's Publicly Traded Stock*, 25 GA. L. REV. 783 (1991).

2. What are the implications of Professor Stout's thesis on the policy of allowing directors to defend against takeovers? She argues that a premium bid acceptable to the owners of most of the outstanding stock still may produce a net subjective loss for the shareholders overall. An example may help to clarify the point. Suppose a corporation has 100 shares of stock outstanding. The owners of 60 shares value them at $10 per share; the owners of the other 40 value them at $15 per share. A third party makes a bid for the company at $11 per share. The owners of the 60 shares can accept and gain $1 per share more than they thought the stock was worth (for a total subjective gain or "consumer surplus" of $60). The owners of the 40 shares, however, if forced to sell, will receive $4 per share less than they think the stock is worth, for a total subject loss of $160. Would this concern justify the board in attempting to prevent the bid? How often is such a senario likely to occur? Is there any way the board of directors can determine the reservation prices of the numerous shareholders in a publicly held corporation in order to assess whether there will be a net subjective loss?

3. Professor Stout's thesis has implications beyond takeover defenses. For example, the problem of net subjective losses exists because of the power of the majority to sell the company—which is true of friendly acquisitions as well as hostile takeovers. Might this concern justify supermajority voting requirements for corporate mergers and sales of substantially all assets? The problem, however, then is that the optimistic minority can block a deal which produces a net subjective surplus. What does Professor Stout's thesis suggest regarding the debate between Professors Vorenberg and Hetherington regarding freeze-outs? Does it explain why minorities might not wish to sell even at a price a court considers fair? Turning back to insider trading, notice that Professor Stout's thesis supports the notion that insider purchases and sales can move the price of stock in a way to reflect any information they possess. To this extent, it supports the contention of those who defend insider trading as a way to improve market efficiency by impounding in the stock price information which the corporation is not yet willing to disclose.